BURT FRANKLIN RESEARCH AND SOURCE WORKS SERIES #136
(American Classics in History and Social Science Series #21)

THE POLITICAL AND ECONOMIC
DOCTRINES OF JOHN MARSHALL

Frontispiece

The Political and Economic Doctrines of John Marshall

*Who for Thirty-Four Years Was Chief
Justice of the United States. And Also
His Letters, Speeches, and Hitherto
Unpublished and Uncollected Writings*

BY

JOHN EDWARD OSTER, A.M. LL.B

BURT FRANKLIN RESEARCH AND SOURCE WORKS SERIES #136
(American Classics in History and Social Science Series #21)

BURT FRANKLIN
NEW YORK

Published by
BURT   FRANKLIN
235 East 44th St.
New York, N.Y. 10017

First Published
N.Y. 1914
Reprinted 1967

Printed in U.S.A.

This book is respectfully dedicated to

OHIO NORTHERN UNIVERSITY

To the Faculty and President in grateful acknowledgment of the valued encouragement received from them,
who, by their teaching, caused me to become a lover of
learning, and do research work in Political Science.

CONTENTS

PREFACE

By common consent the most notable and one of the most statesmanlike figures in our whole judicial history is that of John Marshall. No other name is comparable with his in fame or honor in this singular field of statesmanlike judicial control,— a field of our own marking out and creation, a statesmanship peculiar to our own annals. Marshall may be said to have created for us the principles of interpretation that have governed our national development. He created them like a great lawyer, master of the fundamental conceptions that have enlightened all great lawyers in the administration of law and have made it seem in their hands a system of life, not a mere body of technical rules; he created them also like a great statesman who sees his way as clearly without precedent as with it to those renderings of charter and statute that will vivify their spirit and enlarge their letter without straining a single tissue of the vital stuff of which they are made.

A thoughtful English judge has distinguished between those extensions of the meaning of law by interpretation that are the product of insight and conceived in the spirit of the law itself and those that are the product of sheer will, of the mere determination that the law shall mean what it is convenient to have it mean. Marshall's interpretations were the products of insight. His learning was the learning of the seer, saturated with the spirit of the law, instinct with its principle of growth. No other method, no other principle, has legitimate place in a system that depends for its very life upon its integrity, upon the candor and good conscience of its processes, upon keeping faith with its standards and its immemorial promises.[1]

Our courts have stood the test, chiefly because John Marshall presided over their processes during the formative period of our national life. He was of the school and temper of Washington. He read constitutions in search of their spirit and purpose and understood them in the light of the conceptions under the influence of which they were framed. He saw in

[1] Woodrow Wilson, "Constitutional Government in U. S.," Columbia Lectures, 1908, p. 158.

7

them not mere negations of power, but grants of power, and he reasoned from out the large political experience of the race as to what those grants meant, what they were intended to accomplish, not as a pedant but as a statesman; and every generation of statesmen since his day have recognized the fact that it was he more than the men in Congress or in the President's chair who gave to our federal government its scope and power. The greatest statesmen are always those who attempt their tasks with imagination, with a large vision of things to come, but with the conscience of the lawyer also, the knowledge that the law must be built, not wrested, to their use and purpose. And so, whether by force of circumstance or by deliberate design, we have married legislation with adjudication and look for statesmanship in our courts.[2] Marshall fulfilled all requirements better perhaps than any other man of his day could have done.

Professor Thayer, of Harvard, in his book on Marshall, says: " No systematic attempt seems ever to have been made to collect Marshall's letters.   It should be done.   Only a few of his family letters have yet found their way into print." Professor Beard in his book, " The Supreme Court and the Constitution," says: " How are we to know what was the intention of the framers of the constitution?   The only method is to make an exhaustive search in the documents of the Convention, and in the writings, speeches, papers, and recorded activities of its members.   New material, printed or in manuscript, may be produced at any moment.   This essay therefore makes no claim to finality.   It is designed to throw light on the subject and to suggest ways in which more light may be obtained." [3]   More light is what is needed.   John Marshall, more than any other man, knew what the intention of the framers of the Constitution was, therefore his point of view is important.   His decisions and his letters and his speeches will show that intention to a greater degree than any other source.   In this volume I have endeavored to give the kernel of his decisions, all the letters that could be obtained, and his most important speeches.

For suggestions from time to time I cheerfully acknowledge

[2] Wilson, " Constitutional Government in U. S.," p. 168.
[3] Pages 15-16.

my obligations to Professor Charles A. Beard, who also first emphasized the importance of Marshall's letters; to Professor Frank Goodnow, of the Columbia Law School; to John Bassett Moore, Professor of Law, Columbia Law School; to William D. Guthrie, Professor of Constitutional Law, Columbia Law School, who also gave me valuable books on Constutional Decisions, and to Professor William Dunning, Columbia University.

I give my thanks to the Librarian of the Congressional Library at Washington, and especially to the Superintendent of Documents in the Manuscript Division for his kindness in giving me free access to the archives and files of manuscript letters; to Professor Mills, Librarian of the Ohio State Historical and Archæological Society Library; to the Librarian of Ohio State Library; to the attendants of the Toledo Public Library; to the Librarian of the New York Public Library; to the Librarian of the Columbia University Library, and especially to Mr. Erb and his efficient and courteous assistants; and to the Librarian of the Columbia Law School.

I have also received valuable aid from Arthur Murnen, Fae John, John A. McGeever,— of the Kentucky and Connecticut bars,— and Mae C. R. Newshafer, who read copy, suggested names of persons who might have or know of letters, and helped in the search for letters written by Chief Justice Marshall.

JOHN EDWARD OSTER.

Columbia University, New York City,
    June, 1914.

CHAPTER I

IN MARSHALL'S DAY NEW PROBLEMS WERE TO BE SOLVED

MARSHALL AN ACKNOWLEDGED LEADER OF THE
FEDERALISTS

NOT only, in the words of Chief Justice Waite, " were the nation, the Constitution, and the laws in their infancy," but a brand-new problem of political science was to be solved,— that is, whether or not it was possible to work successfully a scheme contemplating the contemporaneous supremacy in each of thirteen independent commonwealths of two governments, distinct and separate in their action, yet commanding with equal authority the obedience of the same people, so that each in its allotted sphere should perform its functions without impediment to or collision with the other.[1] Patrick Henry, in the Virginia Convention, denounced " these two coördinate, interfering, unlimited powers of harassing the community " as " unexampled, unprecedented in history, the visionary projects of modern politicians " and " a political solecism." For other gloomy forebodings and disastrous predictions by Patrick Henry see Elliot's Debates pp. 47-51, 58, 156, 325-328, 436, 546, 549.

This problem has been completely solved for us by the experiences of a century. It has been so completely solved that few Americans realize what Professor Bryce calls " that immense complexity which startles and at first bewilders a student of American institutions." The solution depended in a large measure upon the interpretation and enforcement of a written constitution which,— as Mr. Webster said in his argument, and Judge Marshall repeated in his decision, in Gibbons v. Ogden (9 Wheaton, p. 189),— enumerated but did not define the powers that it granted; and thus that scheme assigned to the Supreme Court, as a co-ordinate department of the national government, a part never before undertaken by such a tribunal. Even if the Federal Constitution, when pro-

[1] " Elliot's Debates," Vol. III, 2d ed. 1836, p. 148.

mulgated for adoption, had been accepted by all parties as theoretically perfect, and its provisions as open to but one construction, still a bitter and all but fatal experience gave warning of the dangers to be apprehended from the local and State jealousies, the selfish interests, which were at best conflicting, and which even during the struggle for independence had brought the government of the Confederation into contempt.[2]

At this time of its adoption there was no worship of the Constitution. This worship was of a later growth.[3] Quoting John Quincy Adams, Von Holst says, " The historical fact is that the Constitution had been extorted from the grinding necessity of a reluctant people." Again he says:

" We are compelled to say with Justice Story that we ought to wonder, not at the obstinacy of the struggle of 1787 and 1788, but at the fact that despite everything the Constitution was finally adopted. The simple explanation of this is that it was a struggle for existence, a struggle for the existence of the United States."

The fierce though unsuccessful opposition to the adoption of the Constitution, notably in the Massachusetts, New York, and Virginia Conventions, shows what the frame of mind of the people was at that time. John Marshall,— then thirty-three years old, but already a recognized leader of the Virginia Bar,— was an influential member of the Virginia Convention.

Marshall's speeches in the Virginia Convention in defense of its provisions concerning taxation, the militia, and the judiciary were very strong and able and carried much weight.[4]

With the ratification of the Constitution on June 21, 1788, by New Hampshire, the ninth State, followed by Virginia on June 25, and New York on July 26, the Union under the Constitution became an accomplished fact. It was carried by dangerously narrow majorities,— in the New York Convention by only 30 votes to 27 ; in that of Virginia by only 89 to 79, and in that of Massachusetts by 187 against 168.[5] All evidence points to the fact that if it had been submitted to the vote of the people it would have without a doubt received a deathblow. It would have been rejected by the people if left to

[2] Story's " Comm. I on Const. of U. S." sec. 252-254.
[3] Von Holst's " Constitutional History of the United States," Vol. I, pp. 68-75.
[4] 3 Elliot's " Debates," 2d edition, 1836, pp. 222, 419, 551.
[5] Fiske's " Critical Period of American History," pp. 331, 338, 344.

popular vote, and by the conventions if a few great statesmen had not put forth their best efforts in defending it.[6]

John Marshall never sought public station, but often declined it. His great popularity repeatedly charged him with its duties. Early in 1782 he was elected to the Legislature, in 1783 he was chosen a member of the State Executive Council, and he was again elected to the Legislature in 1784, in 1787, from 1788 to 1792, and without his knowledge and against his will in 1795. To this period, Mr. Justice Story tells us, is to be referred the development of the political opinions and principles that governed his subsequent life.[7] He himself sums this up in a letter found on another page of this volume, in which he says: "The general tendency of State politics convinced me that no safe and permanent remedy could be found but in a more efficient and better organized government," and again: "The questions which were perpetually recurring in the State Legislatures . . . which proved that everything was afloat, and that we had no safe anchorage ground, gave a high value in my estimation to that article in the Constitution which provides restrictions on the States."

In the Virginia Convention Patrick Henry, at the height of his fame, led the attack upon the Constitution, seconded by Grayson and Monroe and others advocating State sovereignty, and opposed by Marshall, Madison, Pendleton, and other noted men. The issue was in doubt during twenty-five days of keen and heated debate.

To Henry's passionate denunciations of the new " consolidated government," as based on principles "extremely pernicious, impolitic, and dangerous," by which "all pretensions to human rights and privileges are rendered insecure, if not lost," and to his strenuous objections to many of its provisions,[8] Marshall replied in three speeches, defending the provisions of the Constitution concerning taxation, the militia, and the judiciary.[9] This drew from Henry the tribute of his "highest veneration and respect" and an acknowledgment of his "candor on all occasions."[10]

[6] Bryce, "The American Commonwealth," Vol. I, p. 223.
[7] "Discourse," etc., Story's "Miscellaneous Writings," pp. 649, 651, 656-8, 662-7.
[8] Elliot's "Debates," Vol. III, p. 44.
[9] Elliot's "Debates," Vol. III, pp. 222, 419, 551.
[10] Elliot's "Debates," Vol. III, p. 578.

In the debate of the Virginia Convention we cannot help but note Marshall's view that under the Constitution, as proposed, a State could not be sued by a citizen of another State. He said: "It is not rational to suppose that the sovereign power shall be dragged before a court. The intent is to enable States to recover claims of individuals residing in other States." [11] In these debates it is also very interesting to notice his emphatic assertions of the right and duty of the Federal courts to declare void a legislative act not warranted by the Constitution.

"If they were to make a law not warranted by any of the powers enumerated, it would be considered by the judges as an infringement of the Constitution which they are to guard. They would not consider such a law as coming under their jurisdiction. They would declare it void." ("Debates," p. 553.)

During the political conflicts that followed the adoption of the Constitution the personal influence, the courage, and the great ability and talents of Marshall became very conspicuous. The Anti-Federalists, under the leadership of Patrick Henry and his friends, though almost defeated in the Convention, had full control of the politics of Virginia; and, notwithstanding the veneration felt for Washington and his unanimous election to the Presidency, in no state in the Union was his administration more harshly criticised than it was in Virginia. He was censured in the Legislature as well as by the Democratic Societies, which, modeled after the fashion of the French Jacobin Clubs, started up all over the country. This was in the year 1783.

Marshall did his best to withdraw from public life. Nevertheless, regardless of his earnest desire, he soon found himself an acknowledged leader of the Federalists, and prominent in the discussion of national affairs. At that time there was an abundance of exciting material on hand. The news of the war between England and France in 1793, promptly responded to by Washington's proclamation of neutrality, was contemporaneous with the arrival of the new French Minister, Genet, whose audacious intrigues quickly bore fruit in all kinds of international complications. The proclamation was strenuously denounced, both as an ungrateful return for

[11] Elliot's "Debates," III, p. 555.

the assistance of France during our own Revolution, and as an unconstitutional exercise of power by the President; and the violence of partisan attacks upon the administration was exceeded only by the virulence of the libels that charged Washington with hatching out a plot by which he could make himself a King.[12]

At that time John Marshall in a bold manner defended the proclamation, though because of his doing so he was denounced as an aristocrat and an arch-enemy of republican principles.

However, at a meeting in Richmond he was successful in carrying resolutions that approved the proclamation. The ratification of Jay's treaty in 1795 added much fuel to the flame. Bitterly denounced by the Republicans everywhere on account of its commercial features as well as its alleged unconstitutionality, it was so odious in Virginia that the friends of Marshall,— who, against his own remonstrance, had again elected him to the Legislature,— urged him for the sake of his own influence, if not for his personal safety, to take no part in the Legislative debates on that subject.[13]

Resolutions had been adopted at a public meeting in Richmond, declaring the treaty "insulting to the dignity, injurious to the interests, dangerous to the security, and repugnant to the Constitution of the United States." John Marshall, with characteristic courage, determined, as he afterward wrote, " to make the experiment, however hazardous it might be." " A meeting was called," he continues, " which was more numerous than I had ever seen at this place, and after a very ardent and zealous discussion which consumed the day, a decided majority declared in favor of a resolution that the welfare and honor of the United States required us to give full effect to the treaty negotiated with Britain." Marshall even compelled his opponents in the Legislature to abandon completely their objections to the constitutionality of this treaty. His argument on this occasion was of great power,— an argument that was admitted on all sides to be conclusive, and " the fame of which spread through the Union, enhancing the estimate of his character even with his political enemies." [14]

12 " McMaster's History," Vol. II, pp. 96-107; 109-112.
13 " McMaster's History," Vol. II, pp. 221-230, and Story's " Discourse," pp. 667, 668.
14 Story's " Discourse," p. 668.

John Quincy Adams once said of his father that, if he had done nothing else to deserve the approbation of his country and posterity, he might proudly claim it for the single act of having made John Marshall Chief Justice of the United States; and, surely, Marshall stands out pre-eminently among the many noble legal minds that have graced the Supreme Court as the greatest of them all. " He was born," said William Pinckney, " to be the Chief Justice of any country into which Providence should have cast him."

Of the work of Marshall upon the bench many volumes might be written; but his decisions need no encomium; they speak for themselves. The Hon. E. T. Phelps, in an address delivered before the American Bar Association, fittingly says of the judgments of John Marshall: " Time has demonstrated their wisdom. They have remained unchanged, unquestioned, unchallenged. All the subsequent labors of that high tribunal on the subject of constitutional law have been founded on, and have at least professed and attempted to follow, them. There they remain. They will stand as long as the Constitution stands; and if that should perish, they would still remain to display to the world the principles upon which it rose, and by the disregard of which it fell."

THE RELATIONSHIP BETWEEN JEFFERSON AND MARSHALL

An article written by the Hon. William A. Maury, formerly Assistant Attorney-General of the United States, shows that Jefferson and Marshall were related. In this article Mr. Maury says:

" John Marshall, who solidified the Union; and Thomas Jefferson, who headed the reactionary movement against the Constitution which set in so soon after its adoption and finally culminated in the Civil War, and Robert E. Lee, who drew his sword to force to their logical result the teachings of Jefferson's pen, were all three descended from Col. William Randolph of Turkey Island, the first of the name who emigrated to Virginia, where he became the progenitor ' of a widespread and numerous race, embracing the most wealthy families and many of the most distinguished names in Virginia history.' Marshall's mother, Mary Keith; Jefferson's mother, Jane Randolph; and Lee's grandmother, Mary Bland,

were all three granddaughters of this William Randolph."
The relationship is clearly illustrated in the following dia-
gram that is given by Mr. Maury:

Col. William Randolph, of Yorkshire, England, and "Turkey Island,"
Virginia, married Mary, daughter of Henry and Catherine Isham, of
Bermuda Hundred, Virginia.

Thomas, 2d son m. Fleming.	Isham, 3d son m. Jane Randolph.	Elizabeth, 9th child m. Richard Bland.
Mary, 3d child m. Wm. Keith.	Jane Randolph, 4th child m. Peter Jefferson.	Mary Bland m. Henry Lee
Mary Randolph Keith m. Col. Thomas Marshall.	Thomas Jefferson.	Henry Lee m. Lucy Grimes
John Marshall.		Henry Lee m. Anne Hill Carter.
		Robert E. Lee.

If John Marshall had lived about fifty years later when
equal suffrage for women was first being discussed, he no
doubt would have been in favor of it, and probably he would
have been one of the champions to fight for the cause. Many
of his writings show that he had great regard for women and
their rights, and if they took part in any public event he was
sure in some way to express his appreciation of whatever they
did.

General Washington, while on his way from Mount Vernon
to New York to take upon himself the charge of the Government as President of the United States, on the 21st of April,
1789, stopped at Trenton, where a reception was given to him.
In describing that entertainment Chief Justice Marshall wrote
as follows:

"At Trenton he was welcomed in a manner as new as it
was pleasing. In addition to the usual demonstrations of respect and attachment, which were given by the discharge of
cannon, by military corps, and by private persons of distinction, the gentler sex prepared, in their own taste, a tribute of
applause indicative of the grateful recollection in which they
held their deliverance twelve years before from a formidable
enemy. On the bridge over the creek, which passes through
the town, was erected a triumphal arch, highly ornamented

with laurels and flowers, and supported by thirteen pillars, each entwined with wreaths of evergreens.   On the front arch was incribed in large gilt letters,

" ' THE DEFENDER OF THE MOTHERS WILL BE THE PROTECTOR
OF THE DAUGHTERS.'

" On the center of the arch above the incription was a dome or cupola of flowers and evergreens, encircling the dates of two memorable events, which were peculiarly interesting to New Jersey.   The first was the battle of Trenton, and the second the bold and judicious stand made by the American troops at the same creek, by which the progress of the British army was arrested on the evening preceding the battle of Princeton.

" At this place he was met by a party of matrons leading their daughters dressed in white, who carried baskets of flowers in their hands, and sang with exquisite sweetness an ode of two stanzas composed for the occasion :

> " ' Welcome, mighty chief, once more
> Welcome to this grateful shore;
> Now no mercenary foe
> Aims again the fatal blow ;
> Aims at THEE the fatal blow.

> " ' Virgins fair and matrons grave,
> Those thy conquering arms did save,
> Build for THEE triumphal bowers.
> Strew, ye fair, his way with flowers,
> Strew your Hero's way with flowers.' "

The following communication was made to the ladies immediately afterward in writing :

" General Washington cannot leave this place without expressing his acknowledgments to the matron and young ladies, who received him in so novel and grateful a manner at the triumphal arch in Trenton, for the exquisite sensations he experienced in that affecting moment.

" The astonishing contrast between his former and actual situation at the same spot, the elegant taste with which it was adorned for the present occasion, and the innocent appearance of the white-robed choir, who met him with the gratulatory song, have made such impressions on his remembrance, as, he assures them, will never be effaced."

The following lines, written but a few months after the death of Chief Justice Marshall, were intended as an inscription for a cenotaph. They were written by Judge Story. This is perhaps the most generous and affecting tribute of that devoted associate, who mourned his loss, not as a friend only, but as a brother,— a tribute less to be valued on account of any poetic beauty than as evidence of that warm affection and that undying and reverential admiration which Story never ceased to entertain for Marshall.

> " To Marshall reared — the great, the good, the wise,
> Born for all ages, honored in all skies;
> His was the fame to mortals rarely given,
> Begun on earth but fixed in aim on Heaven.
> Genius and learning and consummate skill,
> Moulding each thought, obedient to will;
> Affections pure as e'er warmed human breast,
> And love in blessing others doubly blest;
> Virtue unspotted, uncorrupted truth,
> Gentle in age, and beautiful in youth.
> These were his bright possessions. These had power
> To charm through life and cheer his dying hour.
> All these are perished? No! but snatched from time
> To bloom afresh in yonder sphere sublime.
> Kind was the doom (the fruit was ripe) to die —
> Mortal is clothed with immortality."

CHAPTER II

THE place where each of these letters was found, or where it is to be seen in print, is given except in the cases of those that were copied from the originals in the Archives of the Congressional Library. If no reference is given as to the place where the original, or the copy, can be found, then it is in the Congressional Library at Washington.

JOHN MARSHALL, ATTORNEY FOR S. B. CUNNINGHAM.

A document in "The Calendar of Virginia State Papers," Vol. VII, pp. 101-102.

April 8, 1794.

I release two shillings per hundred on the tobacco for which Samuel Baron Cunningham has obtained a judgment against the Commonwealth, if no appeal be prosecuted thereon, but if the appeal be prosecuted, then this release is to be of no effect.

JOHN MARSHALL,
Att'y for S. B. Cunningham.

The judgment obtained by Samuel Baron Cunningham against the Commonwealth is only exceptionable in that part of it which allows eighteen shillings per centum for the Tobacco lost; in every other respect it appears to be founded on the Decree of Court of the Appeals.

JAS. INNES,
pro republica.

LETTER[1] FROM J. MARSHALL TO JAMES WOOD, LIEUTENANT-GOVERNOR

Applies for Arms for Richmond Militia

RICHMOND, April 25, 1794.

SIR: I am requested by several of the militia officers of

[1] "The Calendar of Virginia State Papers," Vol. VII, p. 120.

this city to aid them in an application to the Executive for arms for their several companies.

In support of this application, I beg leave to observe that the possession of arms conduces exceedingly to the improvement of troops in the usual evolutions, and that it is hoped and believed that the public could sustain neither inconvenience or loss from placing muskets in the hands of the militia of this place, as they can with great ease be re-collected should the occasion require it, and as there is every reason to believe that they would be kept safe and in good order.

I have, &c.

J. MARSHALL.

LETTER² OF J. MARSHALL TO THE GOVERNOR
Recommending Shelter for the Artillery

RICHMOND, May 20th, 1794.

It is stated to me by Captain Quarrier that the field pieces in his possession could be kept with great convenience and safety was he permitted to erect a small house on or near the parade ground which might protect them from the injuries they would be exposed to if uncovered. As the ground has been fixed on for the parade some distance out of town for general convenience to the citizens, it will be difficult to remove the pieces on every occasion from town to the place of meeting, and it is hoped that the small expense (for it would not exceed sixty dollars) of a house to cover the pieces might be usefully incurred, the more especially as it might protect all the artillery at this place.

I am, &c.

J. MARSHALL.

LETTER FROM J. MARSHALL TO THE GOVERNOR OF VIRGINIA
Relating to Arrest of the Ship *Unicorn*

SMITHFIELD, July 23d, 1794.

The troop reached this place yesterday morning, between six & seven o'clock. The ship *Unicorn* (the supposed privateer), was in possession of a company of the Isle of Wight Militia, and the revenue cutter lay below her with a detach-

² *Ibid.*, p. 148.

ment of militia from Norfolk, commanded by Capt. Woodside.

Every idea of resisting with violence the execution of the laws, seems to have been abandoned. Immediately on my arrival, the Marshal made a peacable request on Capt. Sinclair to allow his house to be searched for arms supposed to be contained in it, which he did not hesitate to permit.

The search was made, and thirteen pieces of cannon, with some ball, grape shot, and powder was found. There were three pieces lying on the shore. A fatigue party is now employed in getting them on board the *Unicorn,* after which the cutter will conduct her to Bermuda hundred, or to Brodway. I despatched a boat yesterday morning, to stop the vessel which was proceeding down James River with the companies of artillery & Infantry from Richmond, and directed their return. I also ordered Capt. Weisiger to return with the infantry of Prince George, but as the marshal entertains some apprehensions of an attempt to rescue the vessel in the river, I thought it advisable to countermand the orders I had given, & direct Capt. Weisiger to continue his march to this place, with a view to his return in the *Unicorn.*

The situation both of Major Taylor & of the Marshal has been arduous & unpleasant. The Marshal has received personal insult, and seems not to have been free from personal danger. Major Taylor has used great and proper exertions to complete the business he was upon. He at first, experienced great difficulty in procuring aid of any kind, but that difficulty is now removed. Since the arrival of distant militia, those of the country are as prompt as could be wished in rendering any service required from them. Indeed, I am disposed to believe that the original difficulty rested not with the men.

The privates (except those residing in Smithfield) have manifested no disaffection to the Government, or reluctance to support the laws. But of this, & of every circumstance which has occurred, Major Taylor & the Marshal have taken memoranda, & an ample report will be made to you as soon as they shall return to Petersburg.

Captain Sinclair declares that he never designed to violate the laws; that the arms found in the house were not intended for the *Unicorn,* but were purchased for a gentleman to the

Southward; that the ball will not fit the cannon; and that though she was originally designed for a privateer, the intention was changed so soon as the act of Congress prohibiting vessels to be armed in our ports was known; in proof of which he says that a cargo is now engaged for her. These, however, are subjects proper to be discussed in court.

I am sorry to say that the Surveyor of the Port, who is considered here as the informer, seems to entertain great apprehensions from some of those who considered themselves as interested in this business. The vessel will, I trust, be ready to sail tomorrow, and I shall then set out with the troops for Richmond.

With very much respect, I am, &c.

J. MARSHALL.

LETTER [3] FROM J. MARSHALL TO THE
GOVERNOR OF VIRGINIA
Report of Circumstance Attending Arrest of the Ship Unicorn

RICHMOND, July 28th, 1794.
The troop of Cavalry ordered to Smithfield returned yesterday. A longer time than I had counted on was necessary to carry on board the different articles libeled, and to move the *Unicorn,* and this has produced a delay more considerable than was expected. She is now on her way to Bermuda Hundred, guarded by Capt. Weisiger with his company of Light Infantry, and attended by the Revenue Cutter. The additional expense of returning Capt. Weisiger's company in the *Unicorn* is very inconsiderable, and is incurred at the request of the Marshal who did not think her safe unless guarded by armed men. His apprehensions of a rescue seem to have arisen in some measure from reports prevailing in Smithfield, and received in a manner deserving some credit, tho' not so as to be testimony, but principally from the coldness and decision of Capt. Sinclair's character from the high degree of irritation he manifested, and from the well known total inability of the Cutter to afford any effectual aid in case of attack. Captain Sinclair declares his perfect submission to the laws, and avers that he had never meditated resistance to them. There were, however, strong circumstances which might read-

[3] " The Calendar of Virginia State Papers," Vol. VII, pp. 234-235.

ily induce an opinion that violence was contemplated. The night after the *Unicorn* was seized, persons were heard for a considerable time loading firearms in the house of Captain Sinclair. The drawing of iron ramrods, and ramming down the charge were distinctly heard. When the search was applied for, which I mentioned in my former letter, he gave a list of the arms in his possession, and among them were fifteen muskets. These were found all charged. The situation of the house is such as completely to command the Deck of the vessel. I do not think that one hundred men placed in the vessel could have protected her ten minutes from fifteen placed in the house, and at this time, notwithstanding the application to Colonel Wells, and the exertions of Major Taylor and the Marshall in Smithfield, only a guard of six or seven badly armed men had been raised.

Captain Sinclair says that the only resistance he ever contemplated was against an unauthorized attempt, which he understood was to be made to search his house. This may be the fact, but it would scarcely seem to be so, since it was unknown to him that the only search ever designed was under the warrant of a magistrate, which was applied for, but not obtained. This circumstance, added to the evidence that the vessel had been designed for a privateer, did, I own, make such an impression on me, that I should, had the Marshall requested it, increased the guard.

I had, while in Smithfield, frequent conversations with individuals of the Isle of Wight. So far as I can judge of their sentiments from their expressions, I am persuaded that they feel no inconsiderable degree of mortification that a necessity should exist for calling militia from a distance to their neighborhood, to protect from violence the laws of our country, and I am persuaded too that this sentiment will so affect the commanding officers as to secure more activity from them on any future occasion than has been exhibited on this.

They seem not to have been sufficiently impressed with the importance of maintaining the sovereignty of the law; they seem not to have thought it a duty of strong and universal obligation to effect this object, but I do believe that a more proper mode of thinking is beginning to prevail.

The militia on duty have so acted as not to have produced

among the citizens, so far as my information extends, a single murmur.

The cheerfulness with which the troop submitted to labor not usually imposed on Cavalry does them much honor.

It is with great regret I mention an accident which befel one of the Prince George Infantry. The *Unicorn* almost touched the land. The company from Prince George was on board, and was ordered neither to go on shore, or to permit any person from the shore to come on board the vessel. A militia man who had stolen out attempted to return, and on being hailed by the sentinel attempted to rush by him without an answer. It was so extremely dark, that the person could not be distinguished, and the sentinel at the same time pushed with his bayonet and attempted to fire. The rain which had fallen fortunately prevented the discharge of the musket, but a dangerous wound was received from the Bayonet. Dr. Crawford of the Richmond troop, with great humanity dressed his wounds and attended him through the night, but could not procure a probe to ascertain its depth.

I will send to you tomorrow an account of the monies expended by me on the expedition.

With very much respect & esteem, &c.

J. MARSHALL.

OPINION OF JOHN MARSHALL RELATING TO THE PUR-
CHASE AND SALE OF LANDS FOR ARREARS OF TAXES
AND DUTIES

October 15th, 1794.

An agent appointed under the act for the more effectual collecting certain arrears of taxes and duties, has purchased at a sale made in pursuance of that law, a tract of land, which he has since sold for a sum more considerable than he purchased it, and it is inquired whether the surplus is a gain to the Commonwealth, or ought to be credited to the sheriff.

The Act of Assembly is by no means explicit. It will admit of either construction, and there is some weight in the argument in favor of either.

The object of the Commonwealth is not to speculate, but to secure the collection of debts due to itself. The purchase of the agent, therefore, may be considered as a medium of collection. This idea derives aid from the clause directing the agent to sell for specie commutables, or certificates, as the arrears of taxes could or were to be discharged by law. It would seem probable that a discretion would have been left with the agent to have sold for either article as should be most advantageous for the Commonwealth, if the product of the sale was not to be credited to the sheriff.

But on the other hand, if the Sheriff should be credited with the profits of the sale, he ought to be debited with the loss. It is by no means certain that this would be the judgment of the court, for the act speaks of the purchase of the agent as an absolute purchase, and not a mere substitution of himself in the place of the acting sheriff for the sole purpose of selling the property. The act too directs the amount of the sale to be endorsed on the execution. This forms an immediate credit to the sheriff, and the law nowhere authorizes a recharge of the deficiency, should one arise.

I am therefore of opinion, that the agent ought not to credit the Sheriff for the proceeds of the sale made by himself, and I give that opinion with the less reluctance, because should the law be otherwise, the party can immediately bring it before the court, and the Commonwealth will be assured on losing the profit of this sale, that she is secure against loss on a future occasion when the property may sell for less than the sum given by the agent.

J. MARSHALL.

OPINION [4] OF JOHN MARSHALL RELATIVE TO FINES AND PENALTIES UNDER THE MILITIA LAW

Ques. 1st. Are those delinquent who have failed to obey the requisition lately made on the Militia, liable to the fine which is not to exceed one year's pay by the Federal law, & also to ten dollars for not appearing at the place of rendezvous by the State law?

2nd. Are subjects or citizens of foreign powers liable to the penalties from Militia laws?

Ans. 1st. I rather incline to the opinion that the only fine imposed by the Act of Congress ought to be collected.

The words of our Act of Assembly are general, and I have

[4] "The Calendar of Virginia State Papers," Vol. VII, pp. 347-348.

no doubt of the powers of the legislature to give additional penalties for the breach of any law of the Union, but I rather suppose the act of the Virginia Assembly would be construed to apply to cases to which the Congressional Act could not apply.

Ans. 2nd. I do not think the subjects or citizens of foreign powers liable to the penalties of our Militia law. The Act of Congress plainly excludes them from the Militia, and the Act of Assembly is expressed to be enacted for the purpose of carrying into effect the Militia system of the Union.

Oct. 16th, 1794.   J. MARSHALL.

LETTER [5] FROM J. MARSHALL TO THE GOVERNOR OF VIRGINIA

Sept. 13th, 1794.
I enclose you a statement made by the Captain of the Artillery company of this town of the articles required for the preservation or use of the artillery under his care.

I have, &c.
J. MARSHALL.

JOHN MARSHALL'S OPINION [6] THAT THE COMMISSION OF ELISHA WHITE, SHERIFF OF HANOVER, IS FORFEITED FOR FAILURE TO QUALIFY IN TIME

It is stated that Mr. White was commissioned as sheriff on the 13th of August, 1794.

That the preceeding Sheriff continues in office till the 6th of November so that the commission expresses that the power of Mr. White is to commence on the 6th of November.

Several accidents prevented his giving bond and security according to law within two months after the date of his commission, but in the third month he appeared in Court and offered to comply with the law.

It is enquired whether under these circumstances the court ought to have received the bond, or whether the executive ought to proceed to make another appointment.

The case of Mr. White is a hard one, but the law seems to leave no discretion with the Executive to judge of those cir-

[5] *Ibid.*, p. 309.
[6] "The Calendar of Virginia State Papers," Vol. VII, pp. 383-384.

cumstances which shall dispense with a compliance with the law. The law admits of no dispensation, but positively requires the execution of the bond within a limited time, or directs a new commission to issue. The circumstances then do not alter the case, but the sole question seems to me to be whether the date of the commission in effect shall be considered as the appointment. I think the date of the commission must be considered as the appointment because everything to be performed by the Executive is then completed.

J. MARSHALL.

THE OPINION[7] OF JOHN MARSHALL AS TO THE SALE OF CRAIG'S LAND

December 18th, 1794.

The sale made by the sheriff, under the execution which was levied in 1792, seems to me to be void in consequence of the irregular procedure of that officer. He has in nothing obeyed the law. If no provision was made for the case I should have no hesitation in advising the sale of the land under the second execution, even although a verdict of the jury had been rendered against the Commonwealth. But the 22nd section of the 16th chapter of the Acts of 1792, which is copied from the Act of 1787, directs the Auditor, when he shall suspect fraud in the service of an execution, to make report thereof to the Executive, whose duty it shall be to direct the Attorney of the Commonwealth for the district, county, or corporation to file an information thereupon, and if it shall appear that the sale was fraudulent, the property shall not pass thereby.

In this case, the sale is in my opinion not only void through its fraud, but its irregularity likewise. Yet as the irregularity seems mingled with fraud, it may be most proper to pursue the precise mode pointed out by the law.

J. MARSHALL.

The service of the execution vested the property in the Sheriff, so that it became legally his for the purpose of satisfying the execution. In my opinion it passes to his representative, who may and is bound to sell. The question how-

7 "The Calendar of Virginia State Papers," Vol. VII, pp. 403-404.

ever came on before the last General Court, and was not decided.

J. M.

LETTER [8] FROM JOHN MARSHALL TO THE GOVERNOR OF VIRGINIA, RELATING TO THE CONTEST BETWEEN THE COMMONWEALTH AND WILLIAM FAIRFAX

March 2nd, 1795.

The contest between the Commonwealth and Mr. Fairfax, depending in the Court of Appeals, will come on of course for decision at the next term. As I am not certain whether the title of citizen purchasers may be considered as precisely the same with that of Mr. Fairfax, I deem it incumbent on me as the counsel of that gentleman, and hold it a duty to those purchasers not to be dispensed with to assist their title.

I have therefore prepared the enclosed bill, which I am to file in the Court of Chancery. As expedition seems to me to be unquestionably the interest as well of the Commonwealth, as of those who think their plain rights improperly suspended, I take the liberty to enclose the bill to you, Sir, for your perusal, with a hope that the officers of the Commonwealth will be directed not to await the process of subpoenas and attachments, but to bring the question to a fair decision on its merits at the next term. I should not venture, Sir, to make this proposal if I did not suppose it to be the wish as well as interest of the Government to have the Immediate use of the property in contest if its title shall be good.

With, &c.

J. MARSHALL.

LETTER [9] FROM JOHN MARSHALL TO THE GOVERNOR OF VIRGINIA, RELATING TO CERTAIN ARTICLES REQUIRED BY THE CAPTAIN OF ARTILLERY OF RICHMOND

RICHMOND, Sept. 13th, 1794.

I enclose you a statement made by the Captain of the Artillery company of this town of the articles required for the preservation or use of the artillery under his care.

I have, &c.

J. MARSHALL.

[8] "The Calendar of Virginia State Papers," Vol. VII, p. 446.
[9] *Ibid.*, p. 309.

MEMORIAL [10] TO THE GOVERNOR OF VIRGINIA, SIGNED BY
JOHN MARSHALL

The memorial of the inhabitants of Russell county to His Excellency
the Governor, and the Honorable Privy Council of Virginia,
March the 11th, Anno Domini 1795

We beg leave to lay before your Honorable Body, our unhappy situation, to whom alone we have reasons to hope for relief. The season of the year is now approaching in which we have reason to expect our frontiers to be invaded by our avowed enemy, the Indians. Since the first settling of our country we have not escaped their scourge for one year without seeing our country laid waste, and our helpless women and children a prey to their vindictive rage. It would be too tedious for to call your attention to the number of us who has experienced that never ending melancholy sight of returning to our houses from our labours and finding our families lying breathless, and yet bleeding from the scalping knives, until our late Governor and council wisely, and happy for us, covered our frontiers with their troops, known by the volunteer militia, in the spring of 1792, and were continued to December, 1794, during which time peace, in a great measure, blessed our land, for by the vigilance of those troops, the approach of the enemy were generally discovered, or if any of them by any unavoidable accident got into the settlement undiscovered and accomplished their perpetrated murders, never escaped without rendering life for life and restoration of property. Not hearing of the return of those troops, and the season near at hand that we may expect to experience the unhappy misfortunes too recent yet to many of us, tho' prior to the year 1792, we are induced to trouble your Board with this memorial, hoping that, tho' our situation is not personally known by many of your Honorable Body, you will not lend a deaf ear to us, nor put our lives in competition with money. In a very short time the defenceless position of our frontiers will be known to the enemy, on which we have every misfortune to dread. Experience has taught us by the many attempts that has been made to protect the frontiers, that none has proved so effectual in procuring us peace as that of the volunteer militia.

[10] This letter was evidently not written by Mr. Marshall. See "Virginia State Papers," Vol. VII, p. 451.

Hoping that your Excellency and the Honorable the Privy Council will take us under immediate consideration and grant a return of the same kind of troops, conducted by the same officers, under whose protection we can put confidence, and we in duty bound will ever pray.

CALEB FRILEY, JAMES DICKERSON, RICHARD LONG, JOHN MORTON, HENRY DONNIGHE, OLIVER HUGHES, SILAS DELANARY, WM. SMITH, JOHN MARSHALL, JOHN FLANNARY, AND OTHERS.

LETTER[11] FROM JOHN MARSHALL TO THE GOVERNOR OF VIRGINIA, RELATING TO THE PUBLIC GUARD

RICHMOND, Sept. 23d, 1793.

SIR:

Your letter of the 21st was delivered to me. I have written to the officer of the Guard on the subject it relates to. I take the liberty to state to you in that, if the Guard be continued, it will be necessary to adopt some mode for supplying them with rations. This, I believe, may be effected without any other additional expense than the price of the provisions, & I am not certain that the ration will cost more than the allowance to be made for it. It will also be necessary to erect a sentry box to protect the Sentinel from inclement weather.

With very much Respect,
I am, Sir,
Your Ob't Serv't.
J. MARSHALL.

LETTER[12] FROM JOHN MARSHALL TO THE GOVERNOR OF VIRGINIA, ENCLOSING LETTER FROM J. MITCHELL EXPRESSING FEARS OF NEGRO INSURRECTION

RICHMOND, September 24th, 1793.

SIR:

I take the liberty to enclose you a letter I have just re-

[11] "Virginia State Papers (Calendar)," Vol. VI, p. 546.
[12] Ibid., p. 547.

ceived from Mr. Mitchell, & beg leave to suggest the propriety of furnishing the Guard with cartridges.
With very much Respect,
I am, Sir, your Ob't Serv't.
J. MARSHALL.

LETTER [13] FROM JOHN MARSHALL TO THE GOVERNOR OF VIRGINIA, RELATING TO THE PUBLIC GUARD

RICHMOND, October 5th, 1793.
SIR:
I believe the officer of the Guard might contract with a butcher for the rations necessary for the militia on duty. If this be approved of, enquiry may immediately be made to ascertain the price at which the ration is to be procured.
I am, sir, with very much Respect,
Your Ob't Serv't.
J. MARSHALL.

SIR:
I enclose a pay-roll of the Company of Guards. The Rations are not estimated. I will with pleasure give every aid in my power to ascertain their value. I transmit also an account of the officer of the Guard, which he prays the Hon'ble Executive to direct the payment of.
I am, with very much Respect,
Your Ob't Serv't.
J. MARSHALL.

LETTER [14] FROM JOHN MARSHALL TO THE GOVERNOR OF VIRGINIA, RELATING TO THE PHOENIX

October 15th, 1793.
SIR:
You have received the examination of the Captain of the Phœnix, of a passenger, & of a boy belonging to her. Altho' every person on board seems healthy, she still appears to come under the description of those vessels which ought to perform quarantine, & I have some reasons for thinking so in addition

[13] " The Calendar of Virginia State Papers," Vol. VI, p. 581.
[14] " The Calendar of Virginia State Papers," Vol. VI, pp. 600-601.

to those afforded by the examination as transmitted to you. The Captain swore that his vessel had not been in the Delaware for ten weeks before she sailed from Milford to Wilmington, in order to clear out from Virginia. The boy swore she was at Wilmington about a fortnight before she sailed from Milford, at which place he left her, & came on board her again at Milford. The Capt. swore she received her cargo at Milford, & there is reason to believe this may be untrue, as the boy came on board very soon after, and found her laden at that time. The Captain too appeared very uneasy at the examination of the boy, & seemed apprehensive that something might escape him which would be unfavorable. He said after the affidavit of the boy that when he said the vessel had not been in the Delaware for ten weeks, he misunderstood the question, & had supposed it related to his being at or near Philadelphia. One of the crew was examined (not on oath) by a gentleman of the city (Mr. Brown) from whom it appeared that the vessel had gone to Philadelphia after the boy had left her at Wilmington. But admitting the statement of the Captain to be perfectly true, it does not appear at what time the young woman who is dead was last in Philadelphia, & therefore she may have had the infection & have communicated it to others on board, who have not yet broke out with it. I am imformed too by a Mr. Denny, to whom I believe the vessel was consigned, that he received a letter by her from one of the owners, dated Philadelphia, the 26th of September, but one of the owners reside in Philadelphia & the other in Wilmington.

I am very Respectfully,
Y'r Ob't Servant,
J. MARSHALL.

GENERAL MARSHALL DECLINES TO ACT FOR COMMONWEALTH AGAINST MARTIN'S HEIRS

Letter [15] from Robert Brooke to the Governor of Virginia

I am informed by Mr. Thurston, Escheator for the County of Frederic, that some time early in the last winter, it was advised by the Executive that Gen. Marshall, Mr. Randolph, and myself should advise him with respect to the claims of the Commonwealth to the real estate of the late Bryan Martin, which

[15] "The Calendar of Virginia State Papers," Vol. IX, p. 12.

was by him devised for the benefit of aliens, and was supposed upon that ground to be escheatable. I have upon the information of Mr. Thurston given him my opinion on the subject, but Gen. Marshall considers himself engaged for Martin's family, and I believe Mr. Randolph waits to hear from the Executive, as he informed me he had no official communications on the subject.

Mr. Thurston presses me very much to attend his inquest, which is to be taken on the 16th of the next month at Winchester, but this I presume cannot be considered as making a part of my ex-officio duty, nor could I comply with the request without incurring much expense and occasioning no inconsiderable inconvenience.

I have the honor, &c.

LETTER[16] FROM JOHN MARSHALL TO THE GOVERNOR OF VIRGINIA, INFORMING HIM OF HIS APPOINTMENT AS SECRETARY OF STATE OF THE UNITED STATES

ALEXANDRIA, June 7th, 1800.

Having been appointed by the President of the United States to the office of Secretary of State, I am no longer a representative in Congress of the District for which I was elected.

I should have sooner notified this vacancy to you had I been certain that it would have existed.

With very much respect, I have, &c.

J. MARSHALL.

LETTER[17] FROM J. MARSHALL, CHIEF JUSTICE OF THE UNITED STATES, TO THE GOVERNOR OF VIRGINIA, CONCERNING A REPORTED INTENTION TO RESCUE LOGWOOD, CONVICTED OF FELONY IN COURT OF UNITED STATES

RICHMOND, May 31, 1804.

The intelligence you gave me respecting an intention to rescue Logwood who is convicted of felony in the Court of the United States would certainly have induced me to order a guard for his security, if the laws had entrusted the Judge with that power.

[16] "The Calendar of Virginia State Papers," Vol. IX, pp. 115-116.
[17] Ibid., p. 399.

But I find no act of Congress to that effect, and am therefore not satisfied that I ought to exercise it. I think it most advisable that an application should be made to the Executive of the United States on this subject, where alone the requisite authority exists.

I am, &c.
J. MARSHALL.

LETTER [18] FROM JOHN MARSHALL TO GOVERNOR ST. CLAIR

DEPARTMENT OF STATE, WASHINGTON,
February 10, 1801.

SIR: —

The President of the United States being desirous to avail the public of a continuance of your services as Governor of the Territory of the United States northwest of the Ohio River, I have the pleasure of inclosing your commission, and of expressing the sentiment of esteem with which

I am, sir, etc.
J. MARSHALL.

LETTER [19] FROM GOVERNOR ST. CLAIR TO
JOHN MARSHALL [20]

CINCINNATI, August 5, 1800.

SIR: —

I have been honored with your letter of the 9th of June, relating to the Connecticut Reserve, and also that of the 12th of the same month, covering the act for dividing this Territory. In pursuance of the first, a county has been erected, called Trumbull, comprehending all the land contained within the boundaries by which the reservation was made, when the cession of the claim of Connecticut to western lands generally was accepted by Congress.

In that country an unfortunate accident has happened already, the killing of two Indian men and the wounding of two children, of which I received the account this Morning in a letter from Colonel Hamyramck. The inclosed is a copy of it. I shall send another to the Secretary of War. There has been

[18] "The St. Clair Papers," by Wm. Henry Smith, p. 530.
[19] Ibid., p. 497.
[20] Secretary of State.

for a considerable time past a great restlessness amongst the Indian tribes, and some of them have been committing depredations upon other tribes, and much appearances that war between them should be enkindled, while others have been stealing many horses from the white people, which is a common prelude to hostilities. I am persuaded that if they do not quarrel amongst themselves it will not be long that they will be at peace with us; to obviate, however, as much as possible the ill effects of this present affair, I shall go to the county of Trumbull immediately, and if the circumstances will justify it, appoint a special court of oyer and terminer for the trial of the person who is taken.

LETTER [21] FROM CHIEF JUSTICE MARSHALL TO
JOSIAH QUINCY

RICHMOND, April 23, 1810.

DEAR SIR:

Permit me to request that you will be so good as to charge yourself with the enclosed letter to Rev. Mr. Eliot.

The Federalists of the South participate with their brethren of the North in the gloomy anticipations which your late elections must inspire.[22]   The proceedings of the House of Representatives already demonstrate the influence of those elections on the affairs of the Union.

I had supposed that the late letter to Mr. Armstrong, and the late seizure of an American vessel, simply because she was an American, added to previous burnings, ransoms, and confiscations, would have exhausted to the dregs our cup of servility and degradation; but these measures appear to make no impression on those to whom the United States confide their destinies. To what point are we verging?

With very much respect and esteem, I am, Dear sir, your obedient

J. MARSHALL.

[21] "Life of Josiah Quincy," by Edmund Quincy, p. 204.

[22] At the March elections Elbridge Gerry, the Democratic candidate, had been chosen Governor of Massachusetts, and in New Hampshire John Langdon had defeated Gov. Jeremiah Smith.

Edmund Quincy says: "The above letter from Chief Justice Marshall shows how fully that eminent man shared in the anxieties and the forebodings of the Federal Party."

LETTER [23] FROM CHIEF JUSTICE MARSHALL TO JOSIAH QUINCY

About the time Josiah Quincy became the President of Harvard College, Nathan Dane,— illustrious for having drawn up the Northwestern Ordinance, by which slavery was excluded from the regions northwest of the Ohio River,— founded the professorship of law which bears his name, and Judge Story was appointed the first professor. The next year Mr. Dane advanced a sum of money sufficient to authorize the Harvard Corporation to erect the building known as the Dane Law College. On the dedication of this building, in October, 1831, Mr. Quincy delivered an address, which was published and widely distributed. The following letter from Chief Justice Marshall contains his testimony to the value of such a school as one of the departments of a university.

RICHMOND, December 10, 1832.

DEAR SIR:

I am much indebted to you for the renewed proof of your recollection given by sending me a copy of your address at the dedication of Dane Law College. You have added to my respect for that estimable gentleman, who has bestowed a large portion of the acquisition of a valuable life on an institution which promises to be so advantageous to the profession he had adopted. I had not supposed that law was so negligently studied in your country, whatever it may be in the South, as you represented. But, however this may be, you satisfy me entirely that it may be read with greatly increased benefit in an institution connected with your University. I can very readily believe that 'to disincorporate this particular science from general knowledge is one great impediment to its advancement.' The vast influence which the members of the profession exercise in all popular governments, especially in ours, is perceived by all; and whatever tends to their improvement benefits the nation.

I am, with great respect and esteem, your servant,

J. MARSHALL.

[23] " Life of Josiah Quincy," by Edward Quincy, p. 443.

LETTER [24] FROM JOHN MARSHALL TO ALBERT GALLATIN

RICHMOND, January 3, 1790.

DEAR SIR:

I have received yours of the 23d of December, and wish it was in my power to answer satisfactorily your question concerning our judiciary system, but I was myself in the army during that period concerning the transactions of which you enquire, and have not since informed myself of the reasons which governed in making those changes which took place before the establishment of that system which I found on my coming to the bar. Under the colonial establishment the judges of common law were also judges of chancery; at the Revolution these powers were placed in different persons. I have not understood that there was any considerable opposition to this division of jurisdiction. Some of the reasons leading to it, I presume, were that the same person could not appropriate a sufficiency of time to each court to perform the public business with requisite despatch; that the principles of adjudication being different in the two courts, it was scarcely to be expected that the eminence in each could be attained by the same man; that there was an apparent absurdity in seeing the same men revise in the characters of chancellors the judgments they had themselves rendered as common-law judges. There are, however, many who think that the chancery and common-law jurisdiction ought to be united in the same persons. They are actually united in our inferior courts; and I have never heard it suggested that this union is otherwise inconvenient than as it produces delay to the chancery docket. I never heard it proposed to give the judges of the general court chancery jurisdiction. When the district system was introduced in '82, it was designed to give the district judges the powers of chancellors, but the act did not then pass, though the part concerning the court of chancery formed no objection to the bill. When again introduced it assumed a different form, nor has the idea ever been revived.

The first act constituting a high court of chancery annexed a jury for the trial of all important facts in the cause. To this, I presume, we were led by that strong partiality which the citizens

[24] "Life of Albert Gallatin," by Henry Adams, pp. 81-83.

of America have for that mode of trial. It was soon parted with, and the facts submitted to the judge, with a power to direct an issue wherever the fact was doubtful. In most chancery cases the law and fact are so blended together that if a jury was impanelled of course the whole must be submitted to them, or every case must assume the form of a special verdict, which would produce inconvenience and delay.

The delays of the court of chancery have been immense, and those delays are inseparable from the court if the practice of England be observed. But that practice is not necessary. 'Tis greatly abridged in Virginia by an Act passed in 1787, and great advantages result from the reform. There have been instances of suits depending for twenty years, but under our present regulations a decision would be had in that court as soon as any other in which there were an equal number of weighty causes. The parties may almost immediately set about collecting their proofs, and so soon as they have collected them they may set the cause on the court docket for a hearing.

It has never been proposed to blend the principles of common law and chancery so as for each to operate at the same time in the same cause; and I own it would seem to me to be very difficult to effect such a scheme, but at the same time it must be admitted that could it be effected it would save considerable sums of money to the litigant parties.

I enclose you a copy of the act you request. I most sincerely condole with you on your heavy loss. Time only, aided by the efforts of philosophy, can restore you to yourself.

I am, dear sir, with much esteem, your obedient servant,

J. MARSHALL.[25]

[25] The above letter appears in the Chapter on "The Legislature, 1789-1801," in the "Life of Albert Gallatin," who was one of those persons who thought the new Constitution went much too far. Henry Adams says: "He would, doubtless, have preferred that all the great departments,— executive, legislative, and judicial,— should have been more closely restricted in their exercise of power, and that the President should be reduced to a cypher."

"Gallatin seems to have been interested in an attempt to lessen the difficulties growing from the separation of law and equity. On this subject he wrote early to John Marshall for advice, and although the reply has no very wide popular interest, yet, in the absence of any collection of Marshall's writings, this letter may claim a place here, illustrating, as it does, not only the views of the future chief justice, but the interests and situation of Mr. Gallatin." (P. 81, "Life of Gallatin," by Adams.)

LETTER [26] FROM JUDGE MARSHALL TO ARTHUR LEE

RICHMOND, March 5, 1787.

DEAR SIR:

Your favour of the 10th of January is now before me. I have not sent the letter you enclosed me in search of Mr. Imlay, because I am told by my brother, who is much better acquainted with him than I am, that he either now is, or will very soon be in New-York.

I have in my possession the notes you enquire for. I very much fear that the conduct of some unthinking men in the western country will embroil us with Spain, unless there be some more vigorous interposition of government than we seem disposed to make. A memorial signed by some of the most respectable persons of Kentucky has lately been presented to the governor on this subject, in which the conduct of Gen. Clark, I am told, is a good deal criminated. Whether the cession for a time of the navigation of the Mississippi would conduce to the interest of the western country or not must depend on facts of which I have but little information, and therefore have never formed a decided opinion on the subject; but the people of this as well as of the Kentucky country, who seem to form no adequate ideas of the magnitude of danger while at a distance, have pronounced upon it without hesitation. Mr. Henry, whose opinions have their usual influence, has been heard to say that he would rather part with the Confederation than relinquish the navigation of the Mississippi; but, as we have been ' fortiter in modo,' I dare say we shall be ' suaviter in re.'

I congratulate you on the prospects of re-establishing order and good government in Massachusetts. I think their government will now stand more firmly than before the insurrection, provided some examples are made, in order to impress on the minds of the people a conviction that punishment will surely follow an attempt to subvert the laws and government of the commonwealth. Our attention is now turned entirely towards the next elections. The debtors as usual are endeavouring to come into the assembly, and as usual I fear they will succeed.

I am, dear sir, with the highest esteem, your obedient servant,   J. MARSHALL.

Hon. Arthur Lee, Esq.

[26] "Life of Arthur Lee," by R. H. Lee, Vol. II, pp. 321-322.

LETTER [27] FROM CHIEF JUSTICE MARSHALL TO HENRY CLAY

RICHMOND, April 4, 1825.
DEAR SIR:

I have received your address to your former constituents; and, as it was franked by you, I presume I am indebted to you for it. I have read it with great pleasure as well as attention, and am gratified at the full and complete view you have given of some matters which the busy world has been employing itself upon. I required no evidence respecting the charge made by Mr. Kremer, nor should I have required any had I been unacquainted with you or with the transaction, because I have long since ceased to credit charges destitute of proof, and to consider them as mere aspersions. The minuteness of detail, however, will enable your friends to encounter any insinuations on that subject which may be thrown out in their hearing. More of this may be looked for than any hostility to you would produce. There is unquestionably a party determined to oppose Mr. Adams at the next election, and this party will attack him through you. It is an old, and has been a successful stratagem. No part of your letter was more necessary than that which respects your former relations with that gentleman.

LETTER [28] FROM CHIEF JUSTICE MARSHALL TO HENRY CLAY

RICHMOND, January 5, 1828.
DEAR SIR:

I thank you for the copy of your address on the charges made against you respecting the election of President, which I have read with the more pleasure because it combines a body of testimony much stronger than I had supposed possible, which must I think silence even those who wish the charge to be believed.

With sincere wishes for the improvement of your health, and with real esteem, I am,
      Dear sir,

            Yours, etc.,

                  J. MARSHALL.

[27] " The Private Correspondence of Henry Clay," Colton, p. 121.
[28] *Ibid.*, p. 189.

LETTER [29] FROM CHIEF JUSTICE MARSHALL TO HENRY CLAY

RICHMOND, November 28, 1828.

MY DEAR SIR:

In consequence of my inattention to the post-office, I did not re. ive your letter of the 23d till yesterday afternoon. I need not say how deeply I regret the loss of Judge Trimble. He was distinguished for sound sense, uprightness of intention, and legal knowledge. His superior can not be found. I wish we may find his equal. You are certainly correct in supposing that I feel a deep interest in the character of the person who may succeed him. His successor will, of course, be designated by Mr. Adams, because he will be required to perform the most important duties of his office, before a change of administration can take place.

Mr. Crittenden is not personally known to me, but I am well acquainted with his general character. It stands very high. Were I myself to designate the successor of Mr. Trimble, I do not know the man I could prefer to him. Report, in which those in whom I confide concur, declares him to be sensible, honorable, and a sound lawyer. I shall be happy to meet him at the Supreme Court as an associate. The objection I have to a direct communication of this opinion to the President arises from the delicacy of the case. I can not venture, unasked, to recommend an associate justice to the President, especially a gentleman who is not personally known to me. It has the appearance of assuming more than I am willing to assume. I must, then, notwithstanding my deep interest in the appointment, and my conviction of the fitness of Mr. Crittenden — a conviction as strong as I could well feel in favor of a gentleman of whom I judge only from a general character — decline writing to the President on the subject.

LETTER [30] FROM CHIEF JUSTICE MARSHALL TO HENRY CLAY

RICHMOND, May 7, 1832.

DEAR SIR:

On my return to this place, from a visit to my friends in our

[29] " The Private Correspondence of Henry Clay," by Colton, p. 212.
[30] Ibid., p. 339.

upper country, I had the pleasure of receiving your report on the public lands, which I have read with attention. The subject is of immense interest, and has long produced and is still producing great excitement.

My sentiments concur entirely with those contained in the report, which are so clearly and so well expressed that it must, I think, be approved by a great majority of Congress. Unanimity is not to be expected in anything.

I thank you for this mark of attention, and am with great and respectful esteem your obedient servant,

J. MARSHALL.

LETTER [31] FROM CHIEF JUSTICE MARSHALL TO HENRY CLAY

WASHINGTON, March 13, 1833.

DEAR SIR:

My nephew, Marshall Jones purposes to remove to New Orleans with a view to the practice of the law, and is, I believe, now in that place. The circumstances under which he left Virginia increase my solicitude for his success. A personal rencounter with a young gentleman who had abused him wantonly and grossly terminated very unfortunately in the death of his adversary. This compelled him to fly from Virginia and from very flattering professional prospects. After visiting Canada and Texas, he has at length, I am told, determined on trying his fortune in New Orleans. I am extremely desirous of promoting his object, but with the exception of Mr. Johnston, am not acquainted with a single individual in that place. May I ask the favor of you to mention him to some of your friends, not as a person known to yourself, but as my friend and relation whom I strongly recommend. I have the most entire confidence in his honor, integrity, and amiable qualities; and shall feel myself greatly obliged by your bestowing on him so much of your countenance as may favor his introduction into society and his professional exertions. For the rest, he must depend upon himself. With great respect and esteem, I am, dear sir, your obedient servant,

J. MARSHALL.

[31] *Ibid.*, pp. 352-353.

LETTER [32] FROM JOHN MARSHALL, SUBSEQUENTLY CHIEF
JUSTICE OF THE UNITED STATES, TO JAMES IREDELL

RICHMOND, Dec. 15th, '96.

DEAR SIR:

I had not the pleasure of receiving till yesterday your favor
of the 3d instant. Since then, I have seen the votes of North
Carolina, and you, I presume, those of Virginia. Mr. Adams
would have received one other vote had Mr. Eyre really been
elected, but he was left out by accident. There was supposed to
be no opposition to him, and in consequence of that opinion the
people in one county, on the eastern shore, did not vote at all,
and in the other a very few assembled. On the day of election
the people of Princess Ann, whose Court day it happened to be,
assembled in numbers, and elected Mr. ——, who voted for
Mr. Jefferson. From that gentleman you will have heard there
were twenty votes for Mr. Samuel Adams, fifteen for Mr.
Clinton, three for Burr, Gen. Washington one, Mr. Pinckney
one, and Mr. John Adams one. I received a letter from Philadelphia, stating that five votes south of the Potomac would be
necessary to secure the election of Mr. Adams. It is then
certain that he cannot be elected. Our assembly, which you
know is in session, displays its former hostility to federalism.
They have once more denied wisdom to the administration of
the President, and have gone so far as to say in argument, that
we ought not by any declarations to commit ourselves, so as to
be bound to support his measures as they respect France. To
what has America fallen! Is it to be hoped that North Carolina will, in this particular, rather adopt such measures as have
been pursued by other States, than tread the crooked paths of
Virginia?

I have received a letter from Mr. Dallas, and will furnish him
with my argument in the case of the British debts. I expect to
be under the necessity of getting the opinions of the Judges,
except yours, from Mr. Dallas, whose report of the case will
be published before mine.

With very much respect and esteem,

I am, dear sir,

Your Obed't   J. MARSHALL.

[32] "Life and Correspondence of James Iredell, One of the Associate
Justices of the Supreme Court of the United States," by Griffith J. Mc-
Ree, Vol. II, pp. 482-483.

LETTER[33] FROM CHIEF JUSTICE MARSHALL ADDRESSED
TO THE REV. R. R. CURLEY, SECRETARY OF THE AMER-
ICAN COLONIZATION SOCIETY

RICHMOND, Dec. 14, 1831.

DEAR SIR:

I received your letter of the 7th, in the course of the mail, but
it was not accompanied by the documents you mention.

I undoubtedly feel a deep interest in the success of the
Society, but, if I had not long since formed a resolution against
appearing in print on any occasion, I should now be unable to
comply with your request. In addition to various occupations
which press on me very seriously, the present state of my family
is such as to prevent my attempting to prepare anything for
publication.

The great object of the Society, I presume, is to obtain
pecuniary aid. Application will undoubtedly be made, I hope
successfully, to the several State Legislatures by the societies
formed within them respectively. It is extremely desirable
that they should pass permanent laws on the subject, and the
excitement produced by the late insurrection makes this a favorable moment for the friends of the Colony to press for such
acts. It would be also desirable, if such a direction could be
given to State Legislation as might have some tendency to
incline the people of color to migrate. This, however, is a
subject of much delicacy. Whatever may be the success of
our endeavors to obtain acts for permanent aids, I have no
doubt that our applications for immediate contributions will
receive attention. It is possible, though not probable, that more
people of color may be disposed to migrate than can be provided
for with the funds the Society may be enabled to command.
Under this impression I suggested, some years past, to one or
two of the Board of Managers, to allow a small additional
bounty in lands to those who would pay their own passage in
whole or in part. The suggestion, however, was not approved.

It is undoubtedly of great importance to retain the countenance and protection of the General Government. Some of
our cruisers stationed on the coast of Africa would, at the same

[33] At the Fifteenth Annual Meeting of the American Colonization Society, January 16, 1832, in the Hall of the House of Representatives of
the United States, to a packed house the above letter was read with others from Lafayette, Ex-President James Madison, and others. Many
great men were unable to gain admittance on account of the large crowd.

time, interrupt the slave trade — a horrid traffic detested by all good men, and would protect the vessels and commerce of the Colony from pirates who infest those seas. The power of the government to afford this aid is not, I believe, contested. I regret that its power to grant pecuniary aid is not equally free from question. On this subject, I have always thought, and still think, that the proposition made by Mr. King, in the Senate, is the most unexceptionable, and the most effective that can be devised.

The fund would probably operate as rapidly as would be desirable, when we take into view the other resources which might come in aid of it, and its application would be, perhaps, less exposed to those constitutional objections which are made in the South than the application of money drawn from the Treasury and raised by taxes. The lands are the property of the United States, and have heretofore been disposed of by the government under the idea of absolute ownership. The cessions of the several States convey them to the General Government for the common benefit without prescribing any limits to the judgment of Congress, or any rule by which that judgment shall be exercised. The cession of Virginia indeed seems to look to an apportionment of the fund among the States, " according to their several respective proportions in the general charge and expenditure." But this cession was made at a time when the lands were believed to be the only available fund for paying the debts of the United States and supporting their Government. This condition has probably been supposed to be controlled by the existing constitution, which gives Congress " power to dispose of, and make all needful rules and regulations respecting the territories or the property belonging to the U. States. It is certain that the donations made for roads and colleges are not in proportion to the part borne by each State of the general expenditure. The removal of our colored population is, I think, a common object, by no means confined to the slave States, although they are more immediately interested in it. The whole Union would be strengthened by it, and relieved from a danger, whose extent can scarcely be estimated. It lessens very much in my estimation the objection in a political view to the application of this ample fund that our lands are becoming an object for which the States are to scramble, and which threatens to sow the seeds of discord among us instead of being what they might be — a source of national wealth.

I am, dear sir, with great and respectful esteem,
Your obedient servant,
J. MARSHALL.

TO CHARLES CARTER

RICHMOND, May 8th, 1833.

MY DEAR SIR:

Your letter of the 27th of April reached me two or three days past. Let me congratulate you on the equanimity with which you contemplate your [the next few words are illegible] rocks and mountains. They can be rendered pleasant by one step and by one only. That your own feelings will readily suggest, and will urge upon you with irrestible force.

Mr. Pendleton died on the 23d of October 1803. I do not know his age exactly. He was about eighty. I am uncertain whether he had completed his 8oth year or was to it. I do not know whether he wrote the political article suggested to him by Mr. Jefferson in his letter of Jan. 29 & Feb. 24. So many essays appear on that subject that my memory does not retain them. I have however no recollection that any one of them was ascribed to Mr. Pendleton.

The long home letter was a subject of much conversation at the time. I know of no person who is intimately acquainted with all its inner [the next few words are illegible] but Col. John Nichols. It is possible that he may have retained a copy of it. If he has not a copy it might be found in the papers published by Augustine Davis but I know not where that paper is to be found.

Mr. Sujt has received a letter from your brother making enquiries respecting this letter, and I have referred him to Col. Nichols. It was generally ascribed at the time to Mr. Carr.

I suspect the intention of attacking your brother's observations on the writings of Mr. Jefferson is abandoned. I am inclined to believe that the friends of the gentleman are willing to permit the subject to sink into oblivion if possible.

I believe that the reference of Mr. Ritchie to a paper published by Mr. Pendleton was to one written by him after the election of Mr. Jefferson which was headed " The danger not over." Its particular object was to keep up jealousy and suspicion against the federalists. I do not recollect that it was directed particularly against the X Y & Z dispatch.

I am my dear Sir with great regard
and esteem
Your obed't
J. MARSHALL.

WASHINGTON, Jany 29, 1832.
DEAR SIR:
I received two or three days past your letter of the 26th of Nov. through Major Lewis. That written about three weeks earlier to which you refer has never reached me.

I have heard of the work to which you allude, and it has been well spoken of. The pen from which it proceeds authorizes high expectations, and I am sure, although it may attract much abuse, it will be read with great avidity. For any defense of myself I shall of course be grateful; and have certainly no wish that it should (ever act) or encroach on your paper. Were my own wishes to be consulted I certainly would not make a principal figure in the piece, and shall think my place fully as conspicuous as it ought to be if I am classed with those you mention, and am proportionately, I have so much vanity as to say equally noticed. I am sure I shall not think your researches indifferent much less injurious.

I have never allowed myself to be excited (or intimidated) by Mr. Jefferson's unprovable and unjustifiable aspersions on my conduct and principles, nor have I ever noticed them except on one occasion when I thought myself called on to do so, and when I thought that declining to enter upon my justification might have the appearance of crouching under the lash, and admitting the justice of its infliction.

I believe no copy of the dispatches of the Envoys of whom I was one is now to be found except in the volumes of state papers published by the governments of foreign communications to the French Directory. I never saw a copy nor do I believe that one having the appearance of authority was ever published. If any supposititious paper was uttered in any federal gazette I do not recollect to have seen it, nor do I recollect that federalists ever charged the party led by Mr. Jefferson with having applied for military aid. We suspected, and the scanty communications we received confirmed the suspicion, that the logic of Logan's Mission was to answer the Directory that they had gone too far and that their party in this country would be ruined, should they persist in the course of outrage and hostility which had been commenced with so much violence.

I do not believe that Logan's transactions in France have ever been published. Certainly I have no account of them, nor have I the possession of any documents which can throw light on that affair. I recollect that something was published by Logan himself respecting it long after his return but I do not remember the substance of his publication and have no copy of it.

Our dispatches, which were laid before Congress and published contain all the information it would be in my power to give relative to our communications with the directory or its agents. I did indeed keep a journal in which was inserted our various conversations with the agents of Mr. Tallyrand. The most interesting communication which I recollect was the assurance which the most confidential of them gave us that if we supposed we should be supported by our countrymen we were mistaken; that the influence of France in the United States was such that we should find our countrymen ready to take part against us. I do not recollect the words but this was the substance.

Your book will be looked for with impatience generally certainly by myself.

I am, dear Sir, with the best wishes for your happiness, very respectfully your obedt servant,

J. MARSHALL.

TO BUSHROD WASHINGTON

RICHMOND, Oct. 31, 1819.

DEAR SIR:

I received this morning yours of the 26th. The cases which will come before you in Philadelphia, if the indictments are drawn on the last act of Congress must depend, if the accused are guilty, on the very point I have adjourned to the supreme court, because that question whether, in any case whatever, a communication can take place under that act. In the trial at Richmond the evidence was perfectly clear & the case was unequivocally a case of piracy according to the laws of every civilized nation. The doubt I entertain is whether there is any such thing as Piracy as " defined by the laws of nations."

All nations punish robbery committed on the high seas by vessels not commissioned to make captures, yet I doubt seriously whether any nation punishes otherwise than by force of its own particular statute.

This account given by the editor of the union is not correct. The subscription was four dollars per annum instead of five unless the subscriber was in arrears & I was in advance. I had paid to Col. [the name is not clear], the authorized agent of Mr. Bronson, when the Gazzette of the United States became the Union it was advertised that in future the paper would be five dollars, but that this charge would not affect those who were in advance for the paper until the time for which they had paid should elapse. I was then in advance to last June, consequently I only owe for that time. I am not however disposed to quibble about it. Mr. Bronson I presume has sold out his accounts with his paper and has credited me only from the time his agent has settled with him, in consequence of which he has charged me five instead of four dollars. I request you therefore to pay the amount.

I am dear Sir yours [torn off]

J. MARSHALL.

WASHINGTON; Jany 18th, '34.

DEAR SIR:

I received some time past your letter informing me that you had presented your " Life of Washington " to a literary friend and requesting another copy. Not having an opportunity of forwarding to you this record copy, I deferred the business till my arrival in Washington when I might commit it to the care of your friend Major Lewis in the hope that it would reach you safely. The letter you have received from Mr. Madison removes the evil which the misspelling of a name had cast over the letter published in Mr. Jefferson's Correspondence to which you allude.

You are right in supposing that I was on very intimate terms with your Father about the time to which you refer in your letter of the 17th of September last, and afterward to the close of his life. We served together in the legislature of the state and generally acted together in the assembly of Virginia as well as in Congress. He was during the whole of that time the personal as well as political friend both of General Washington and Colonel Hamilton, and supported the administration of General Washington during his first Presidency as well as for the second term, in every measure but one. He was seriously and warmly opposed to the assumption of the state debts, and took an active part in the House of Delegates against the administration and some resolutions which were offered condemnatory of that part of Hamilton's system of finance. I know however that this course neither estranged him from General Washington nor Col. Hamilton. The friendship between them I have reason to believe was never interrupted. I am inclined to believe, but of this I am not certain, that General Lee also disapproved that part of the system which gave to holders of certificates the full value expressed on their face. My recollection on this point is uncertain, but on the assumption it is positive because I well remember his eloquence and earnest speeches on the subject.

I suspect however that the confidence and friendship of the parties was not impaired by this opposition of sentiment on this question. Of this you have I doubt not, abundant proof in the correspondence of your Father.

We have a stormy session abounding with subjects of great excitement. The old federalists see much to deplore and not much to approve.

We fear that the fabric created for us by our predecessors is about to tumble into ruin. But I mix so little with politicians that it would be presumptuous in me to hazard conjecture on the future. The papers will give you some idea of the state of public feeling. Providence has saved us more than once, and I hope will save us again.

I am dear Sir with great respect and regard
Your obedt
J. MARSHALL.

On the outside of the following letter was the address: Mr. Hon'ble Bushrod Washington, Alexandria, June 10, '16.

I expected these numbers would have concluded my answer to Hampden but I must write two others which will follow in a few days. If the publication has not commenced I would rather wish the signature to be changed to " A Constitutionalist."

A friend of the Constitution is so much like a friend of the Union that it may lead to some suspicion of identity. It is however of no great consequence. I hope the publication has commenced unless the editor should be unwilling to devote so much of his paper to this discussion. The letters of Amphyction & of Hampden have made no great impression in Richmond, but they were designed for the country & have had considerable influence there. I wish the refutation to be in the hand of some respectable members of the legislature and may prevent some act of the assembly (equally) silly & wicked. If the publication be made, I should like to have two or three sets of the papers to be used if necessary.

I will settle with the printer.

The above five or six letters, all in a fair state of preservation, are in the manuscript department of the Library of Congress. They were nearly all sent to Bushrod Washington. There are words, names, and addresses written on the backs of some of the letters, which, by the way, have never been published before.

UNPUBLISHED LETTER

From Chief Justice Marshall to George Washington, of Georgetown, on the occasion of the death of Judge Bushrod Washington. Contributed by Mr. William Alexander Smith, of New York City

RICHMOND, VA., Nov. 29th, 1829.

To Hon. George Washington,
                    Georgetown.

MY DEAR SIR:

I am much obliged by the kind attention manifested by your letter of the 26th inst. The intelligence it communicates is indeed most afflicting. I had few friends whom I valued so highly as your Uncle, or whose loss I should regret more sincerely.

I had flattered myself when we parted last spring that I should leave him on the bench when retiring from it myself; but Heaven has willed otherwise. We have been most intimate friends for more than forty years, and never has our friendship sustained the slightest interruption.   I sympathise most truly with Mrs. Washington.

With great respectful esteem,
I am, dear sir,
your obedt.
J. MARSHALL.[34]

RICHMOND, July 27th, 1812.

DEAR SIR:

I had this morning the pleasure of receiving your letter of the 24th— The paper you mention reached me a few days past & was read with attention and approbation.   Your wish respecting its republication will not be forgotten.

The view you take of the edict purporting to bear date on the 28th of April, 1811, appears to me to be perfectly correct.   I am astonished, if in these times anything ought to astonish, that the same impression is not made on all.

Although I have for several years forborn to intermingle with those questions which agitate & excite the feelings of party, it is impossible that I could be inattentive to passing events, or an unconcerned observer of them.   As they have increased in their importance, the interest, which as an American I must take in them, has also increased; and the declaration of war has appeared to me, as it has to you, to be one of those portentous acts which ought to concentrate on itself the efforts of all those who can take an active part in rescuing their country from the ruin it threatens.   All minor considerations should be waived; the lines of subdivision of parties, if not absolutely effaced, should at least be covered for a time; and the great division between the friends of peace & the advocates of war ought alone to remain.   It is an object of such magnitude as to give to almost every other, comparative insignificance; and all who wish peace ought to unite in the means which may facilitate its attainment, whatever may have been their differences of opinion on other points.

On reading the decree of the 28th of April I could not avoid asking myself questions such as these.

This decree having been obviously fabricated since the official declaration of the Prince Regent that the orders in council

[34] The above letter is printed in *The Magazine of American History*, Vol. XII, p. 278.

would stand repealed so soon as the decrees of Berlin & Milan should be proved by an authentic document to be revoked, why was it not dated on the 1st of November 1810 instead of the 28th of April 1811? Since the one date might have been affixed to it as readily as the other, why was not that date affixed which would have saved the feelings of the American government by supporting the assertion it has uniformly made in its diplomatic intercourse with foreign governments, in its domestic official communications, & in its legislative acts? — assertions on the truth of which our whole system stands? Had France felt for the United States any portion of that respect to which our real importance entitles us, would she have failed to give this proof of it? But regardless of the assertion made by the President in his Proclamation of the 2d of Novr 1810. regardless of the communications made by the Executive to the Legislature, regardless of the acts of Congress, and regardless of the propositions which we have invariably maintained in our diplomatic intercourse with Great Britain, the Emperor has given a date to his decree, & has assigned a motive for its enactment, which in express terms contradict every assertion made by the American nation throughout all the departments of its government, & removed the foundation on which its whole system has been erected. The motive for this offensive & contemptuous proceeding cannot be to rescue himself from the imputation of continuing to enforce his decree after their formal repeal, because this imputation is precisely as applicable to a repeal dated the 28th of April 1811 as to one dated the 1st of November 1810, since the execution of those decrees has continued after the one date as well as after the other. Why then is this obvious fabrication such as we find it? Why has Mr Barlow been unable to obtain a paper which might consult the honor & spare the feelings of the government? The answer is not to be disguised. Bonaparte does not sufficiently respect us to exhibit for our sake, to France, to America, to Britain, or to the world, any evidence of his having receded one step from the position he had taken. He could not be prevailed on, even after we had done all he required, to soften any one of his acts so far as to give it the appearance of his having advanced one step to meet us. That this step or rather the appearance of having taken it, might save our reputation was regarded as dust in the balance. Even now, after our solemn & repeated assertions that our discrimination between the beligerants is founded altogether on a first advance of France,— on a decisive & unequivocal repeal of all her obnoxious decrees; after we had engaged in a war of the most calamitous character, avowedly, because France had repealed those decrees, the Emperor scorns to countenance the assertion or to leave it uncontradicted. He avers to ourselves, to our selected enemy, & to the world, whatever pretexts we may assign for our conduct, he has in fact ceded nothing, he has made no advance, he stands on his original ground & we have marched up to it. We have submitted, completely submitted; & he will not leave us the poor consolation of concealing that submission from ourselves. But not even our submission has obtained relief. His cruizers still continue to capture, sink, burn, & destroy.

I cannot contemplate this subject without excessive mortification as well at the contempt with which we are treated as at the infatuation of my countrymen. It is not however for me to indulge these feelings though I cannot so entirely suppress them as not sometimes though rarely to allow them a place in a private letter.

With respectful esteem
I am Sir your obedt servt
J Marshall.[35]

Richmond Novr 7th 1834.

My dear Grandson:

I had yesterday the pleasure of receiving your letter of the 29th of November, and am quite pleased with the course of study you are pursuing. Proficiency in Greek and Latin is indispensable to an accomplished scholar, and may be of great real advantage in our progress through human life. Cicero deserves to be studied still more for his talents than for the improvement in language to be derived from reading him. He was unquestionably, with the single exception of Demosthenes, the greatest orator among the ancients. He was too a profound Philosopher. His " de officiis " is among the

---

[35] The above letter is printed in *The Pennsylvania Magazine*, Vol. 25, pp. 263-265. The letter was sent to R. Smith. No further address was given. The original is in the Dreer Collection of the Historical Society of Pennsylvania.

most valuable treatises I have ever seen in the latin language.

History is among the most essential departments of knowledge; and, to an American, the histories of England and of the United States are most instructive. Every man ought to be intimately acquainted with the history of his own country. Those of England and of the United States are so closely connected that the former seems to be introductory to the latter. They form one whole. Hume, as far as he goes, to the revolution of 1688, is generally thought the best Historian of England. Others have continued his narative (sic) to a late period, and it will be necessary to read them also.

There is no exercise of the mind from which more valuable improvement is to be drawn than from composition. In every situation of life the result of early practice will be valuable. Both in speaking and writing, the early habit of arranging our thoughts with regularity, so as to point them to the object to be proved, will be of great advantage. In both, clearness and precision are most essential qualities. The man who by seeking embellishment hazards confusion, is greatly mistaken in what constitutes good writing. The meaning ought never to be mistaken. Indeed the readers should never be obliged to search for it. The writer should always express himself so clearly as to make it impossible to misunderstand him. He should be comprehended without an effort.

The first step towards writing and speaking clearly is to think clearly. Let the subject be perfectly understood, and a man will soon find words to convey his meaning to others. Blair, whose lectures are greatly and justly admired, advises a practice well worthy of being observed. It is to take a page of some approved writer and read it over repeatedly until the matter, not the words, be fully impressed on the mind. Then write, in your own language, the same matter. A comparison of the one with the other will enable you to remark and correct your own defects. This course may be pursued after having made some progress in composition. In the commencement, the student ought carefully to reperuse what he has written, correct, in the first instance, every error of orthography and grammar. A mistake in either is unpardonable. Afterwards revise and improve the language.

I am pleased with both your pieces of composition. The subjects are well chosen and of the deepest interest. Happiness is pursued by all, though too many mistake the road by which the greatest good is to be successfully followed. Its abode is not always in the pallace or the cottage. Its residence is the human heart, and its inseparable companion is a quiet conscience. Of this, Religion is the surest and safest foundation. The individual who turns his thoughts frequently to an omnipotent omniscient and all perfect being, who feels his dependence on, and his infinite obligations to that being will avoid that course of life which must harrow up the conscience.

My love to your mother & the family
Your affectionate Grandfather,
J. Marshall.

This letter was sent to the editor of *The Nation,* by Mr. William F. Abbot, of Worcester, Massachusetts, on February 2, 1901. At that time he wrote as follows:

Sir:

I enclose to you for publication a letter of John Marshall's, the original of which is in my possession, and, so far as I know, has never been printed before. It is addressed to:

" Mr. John Marshall Jr.
" of Mont blanc
" near Oak hill
" Fauquier."

It is postmarked " Richmond, Va., Dec. 8." This, with the allusion to his grandson's letter of November 29, shows that its date should be December 7 instead of November 7. It is of great interest as showing the great jurist's ideas on education.

LETTER [36] OF JOHN MARSHALL TO JOHN ADAMS

4 February 1801.

Sir:

I pray you to accept my grateful acknowledgement for the honor conferred on me in appointing me Chief Justice of the United States. This additional and flattering mark of your

[36] The above letter is printed in the "Life and Works of John Adams," Vol. IX, p. 96.

good opinion has made an impression on my mind which time will not efface.

I shall enter immediately on the duties of the office and hope never to give you occasion to regret having made the appointment.

With the most respectful attachment &c

J. MARSHALL.

JOHN MARSHALL [37] TO JAMES MONROE

RICHMOND, 2 December 1784.

DEAR SIR:

Yours of the fourteenth of November I have just received. I congratulate you sincerely on your safe return to the Atlantic part of the world. I wish with you that our assembly had never passed those resolutions respecting the British debts which have been so much the subject of reprehension throughout the states. I wish it, because it affords a pretext to the British to retain possession of the forts on the lakes, but much more because I ever considered it as a measure tending to weaken the federal bands, which in my conception are too weak already. We are about, though reluctantly, to correct the error. Some resolutions have passed a committee of the whole house, on which a bill is to be brought in removing all impediments in the way of the treaty, and directing the payment of debts by installments. The resolutions were introduced by your uncle. As the bill at present stands, there are to be seven annual payments, the first to commence in April, 1786. We have as yet done nothing finally. Not a bill of public importance, in which an individual was not particularly interested, has passed. The exclusive privilege given to Rumsey and his assigns to build and navigate his new invented boats is of as much, perhaps more, consequence than any other bill we have passed. We have rejected some which in my conception would have been advantageous to this country. Among these I rank the bill for encouraging intermarriages with the Indians. Our prejudices, however, oppose themselves to our interests, and operate too powerfully for them. The two subjects which now most engross the attention of the legislature are the general assessment and circuit court bills.

[37] The above letter is printed in Bancroft's "History of the Constitution of the United States," Vol. II.

I am apprehensive they will both be thrown out. When supported by all the oratory and influence of Mr. Henry, the former could scarcely gain admission into the house; and now, when he is about moving in a sphere of less real importance and power, his favorite measure must miscarry. I am sorry the members of council were appointed before your letter recommending Colonel Mercer had reached me. Had I known that that gentleman wished an appointment in the executive, I should certainly not have been unmindful of the debt I contracted with him on a former similar occasion. Mr. Jones supplies the vacancy made by the resignation of Mr. Short, and Mr. Roane and Mr. Selden take the places of our old friend Smith, and of Colonel Christian. I exerted myself, though ineffectually, for Carrington. He was excessively mortified at his disappointment, and the more as he was within one vote of Selden, and as that vote was lost by the carelessness of Colonel Jack Nicholas, who walked out just as we were about to ballot the last time, and did not return till it was too late to admit his ticket. I endeavored, too, to promote the interests of your friend Wilson Nicholas, who is just about to form a matrimonial connection with Miss Smith, of Baltimore; but he was distanced. I showed my father that part of your letter which respects the western country. He says he will render you every service of the kind you mention which is within his power with a great deal of pleasure. He says, though, that Mr. Humphrey Marshall, a cousin and brother of mine, is better acquainted with the lands, and would be better enabled to choose for your advantage than he would. If, however, you wish rather to depend on my father, I presume he may avail himself of the knowledge of his son-in-law. I do not know what to say to your scheme of selling out. If you can execute it, you will have made a very capital sum; if you retain your lands, you will be poor during life, unless you remove to the western country, but you will have secured for posterity an immense fortune. I should prefer the selling business, and, if you adopt it, I think you have fixed on a very proper price.

Adieu.

May you be very happy is the wish of your

J. MARSHALL.

RICHMOND, March 29, 1832.

DEAR SIR:
Your letter of the 25th reached me last night. The transaction concerning which you enquire passed in the following manner. As the stage passed through Philadelphia some passenger mentioned to a friend he saw in the street the death of General Washington. The report flew to the hall of Congress and I was asked to move an adjournment. I did so. General Lee was not at the time in the House. On receiving the intelligence, which he did on the first arrival of the stage, he retired to his room and prepared the resolutions which were adopted, with the intention of offering them himself. But the house of Representatives had risen on my motion, and it was expected by all that I would on the next day announce the lamented event and propose resolutions adapted to the occasion. General Lee immediately called on me and shewed me his resolutions. He said it had now become improper for him to offer them, and wished me to take them. As I had not written anything myself and was pleased with his resolutions, which I entirely approved, I told him I would offer them the next day, when I should state to the House of Representatives the confirmation of the melancholy intelligence received the preceding day. I did so. You will see the fact stated in a note to the preface to the Life of Washington, p. v, and again in a note to the 5th vol, p 765.

J. MARSHALL. [38]

LETTER OF JOHN MARSHALL TO HIS SON,
EDWARD C. MARSHALL

WASHINGTON, Feb. 15, 1832.

MY DEAR SON:
Your letter of the 10th gave me great pleasure, because it assured me of the health of your family and the health of the other families in which I take so deep an interest. My own has improved. I strengthen considerably, and am able, without fatigue, to walk to court, a distance of two miles, and return to dinner. At first this exercise was attended with some difficulty, but I feel no inconvenience from it now. The sym-

[38] The above letter is printed in " The Writings of George Washington," Vol. XIV, p. 262, footnote. This letter was written by Judge Marshall to Charles W. Hansen.

pathetic feeling to which you allude sustains no diminution; I fear it never will. I perceive no symptoms, and I trust I never shall, of returning disease. The question of Mr. Van Buren's nomination (minister to England) was not exempt from difficulty. Those who opposed him, I believe, thought conscientiously that his appointment ought not to be confirmed. They felt a great hostility to that gentleman from other causes than his letters to Mr. McLane. They believe him to have been at the bottom of a system which they condemn. Whether this conviction be well or ill founded, it is their conviction; at least I believe it is. In such a case it is extremely difficult, almost impossible, for any man to separate himself from his party.

This session of Congress is indeed peculiarly interesting. The discussion of the tariff and on the bank, especially, will, I believe, call forth an unusual display of talents. I have no hope that any accommodation can take place on the first question. The bitterness of party spirit on that subject threatens to continue unabated. There seems to be no prospect of allaying it. The two great objects in Virginia are internal improvements and our coloured population. On the first, I despair. On the second, we might do much if our unfortunate political prejudices did not restrain us from asking the aid of the Federal Government. As far as I can judge, that aid, if asked, would be freely and liberally given. The association you speak of, if it could be made extensive, might be of great utility, and I would suggest the addition of a resolution not to bring any slave into the country.

I am, my dear son,
Your affectionate father,
J. MARSHALL.

LETTER FROM JOHN MARSHALL TO HIS GRANDSON

WASHINGTON, March 11, 1835.

MY DEAR GRANDSON:

I have received your letter of the 25th of February, and am not a little gratified at the account you give of your standing in your class. It does you great honor as a student to remain so long at the head of it.

Cicero was an elegant scholar, and the greatest orator of

his day. Besides his orations he has written several essays which have attracted much admiration.

I am very glad to hear of your progress in arithmetic, and to see that you improve in your handwriting. It is a fault which, I am glad to believe, you will not commit. You have had a very severe winter, but that is unfavorable to study. If you have been unable to go to school, the time, I am sure, has not been lost. Nothing is more precious than time, especially to the young, and yet nothing slips from us less regarded or less valued.   I am, my dear grandson,

Your affectionate grandfather,

J. MARSHALL.

LETTER FROM JOHN MARSHALL TO HIS SON, JAMES KEITH MARSHALL, OF FAUQUIER COUNTY, VIRGINIA

RICHMOND, December 14, 1828.

MY DEAR SON:

You hogs arrived on Wednesday evening. I had twelve of them killed on Friday morning. They weighed 1891. The remaining thirteen will be killed as soon as the weather will permit, perhaps to-morrow, but the weather I fear is too hot. I fear you will be disappointed in the price. It is four dollars only. An immense quantity has come in from the West. I shall give you four and a quarter, and take myself what I cannot sell at that price. As I know nothing about the title to the land in question, I presume your object is to make some inquiries respecting the characters of Mr. M. and Mr. A. Of Mr. A., I know nothing. Mr. M. is a lawyer of eminence, who was formerly a judge. He unfortunately engaged in some purchases in the mad times that have gone by, which wasted his fortune, in consequence of which he resigned his seat on the bench and returned to the bar. He is a sensible man, and I should place confidence in what he says. Were it my business I should procure the information he asks and give him a moiety of the land if he will prosecute the claim at his own expense. I should have feared that the act of limitations was already a bar, but Mr. M.'s judgment may be relied on. You mother's love to the family.

I am, my dear son,

Your affectionate father,

J. MARSHALL.

When absent from his wife, Chief Justice Marshall, a most dutiful husband, wrote to her quite frequently, cheering her weary hours of pain with graphic and lively sayings and doings at the nation's capital. He usually called his wife Polly.

The following is a part of a letter to Mrs. Mary W. Marshall, Richmond, Virginia:

WASHINGTON, Feb., 1829.

Our sick judges have at length arrived and we are as busy as men can well be.

. I do not walk so far as I formerly did, but I still keep up the pastime of walking in the morning. We dined on Friday last with the President, and I sat between Mrs. Adams and the lady of a member of Congress whom I found quite agreeable as well as handsome. Mrs. Adams was as cheerful as if she was to continue in the great house for the ensuing four years. The President also is in good health and spirits. I perceive no difference in consequence of the turn the late election has taken. General Jackson is expected in the city within a fortnight and is to put up in this house. I shall, of course, wait on him. It is said he feels the loss of Mrs. Jackson very seriously. It would be strange if he did not. A man who at his age loses a good wife loses a friend whose place cannot be supplied. I dine to-morrow with the British Minister and the next day again with the President. I have never before dined with the President twice during the same session of the Court. That on Friday was an official dinner. The invitation for Tuesday is not for all the other judges, and I consider it a personal civility. Tell Mr. Call all the Secretaries are sick, and Mr. Clay among them. He took cold by attending the Colonization Society and has been indisposed ever since. The town, it is said, was never so full as at present. The expectation is that it will overflow on the 3d of March. The whole world, it is said, will be here. This, however, will present no temptation to you to come. I wish I could leave it all and come to you. How much more delightful would it be to sit by you than to witness all the pomp and parade of the inauguration.[39]

[39] The above, a part of a letter, was contributed to the *Green Bag* by Sallie E. Marshall, a great-granddaughter of the Chief Justice. It is printed in the December number, 1896.

From 1788 to 1797 Marshall practiced law with the earnest desire, as he said, to accumulate sufficient fortune to insure the comfort and happiness of his wife and children. About this time he wrote the following letter.

LETTER FROM JOHN MARSHALL TO
JUDGE ARCHIBALD STUART

I cannot appear for Donaghoe. I do not decline his business from any objection to his bank. To that I should like very well to have free access, and would certainly discount from it as largely as he would permit; but I am already fixed by Rankin, and as those who are once in the bank do not, I am told, readily get out again, I despair of being ever able to touch the guineas of Donaghoe.

Shall we never see you again in Richmond? I was very much rejoiced when I heard that you were happily married, but if that amounts to a ne exeat, which is to confine you entirely to your side of the mountain, I shall be selfish enough to regret your good fortune, and almost to wish you had found some little crooked rib among the fish and oysters which would once a year drag you into this part of our terraqueous globe.

You have forgotten, I believe, the solemn compact we made to take a journey to Philadelphia this winter, and superintend for a while the proceedings of Congress. I wish very much to see you. I want to observe how much honester men you and I are (than) half one's acquaintance. Seriously, there appears to me every day to be more folly, envy, malice, and damned rascality in the world than there was the day before; and I do verily begin to think that plain, downright honesty and unintriguing integrity will be kicked out of doors.

We fear, and not without reason, a war. The man does not live who wishes for peace more than I do, but the outrages committed upon us are beyond human bearing.

Farewell.

Pray heaven we may weather the storm.

Yours,

J. MARSHALL.[40]

[40] The fashion of Marshall's wit and a glimpse of his friendly geniality are shown in the above letter. This letter is published in the *Green Bag*, Vol. 10.

EXTRACT OF A LETTER

From John Marshall, Esq., Secretary of State, to Rufus King, Minister Plenipotentiary of the United States at London

DEPARTMENT OF STATE, September 20, 1800.

The impressment of our seamen is an injury of very serious magnitude, which deeply affects the feelings and the honour of the nation.

This valuable class of men is composed of natives and foreigners who engage voluntarily in our service.

No right has been asserted to impress the natives of America. Yet they are impressed, they are dragged on board British ships of war, with the evidence of citizenship in their hands, and forced by violence there to serve, until conclusive testimonials of their birth can be obtained. These must most generally be sought for on this side of the Atlantick. In the mean time acknowledged violence is practised on a free citizen of the United States, by compelling him to engage, and to continue in foreign service. Although the lords of the admiralty uniformly direct their discharge on the production of this testimony, yet many must perish unrelieved, and all are detained a considerable time in lawless and injurious confinement.

It is the duty as well as the right of a friendly nation, to require that measures be taken by the British government to prevent the continued repetition of such violence by its agents. This can only be done by punishing and frowning on those who perpetrate it. The mere release of the injured, after a long course of service and of suffering is no compensation for the past, and no security for the future. It is impossible not to believe, that the decisive interference of the government in this respect, would prevent a practice, the continuance of which must inevitably produce discord between two nations which ought to be the friends of each other.

Those seamen, who, born in a foreign country, have been adopted by this, were either the subjects of Britain or some other power.

The right to impress those who were British subjects has been asserted, and the right to impress those of every other nation has not been disclaimed.

Neither the one practice nor the other can be justified.

With the naturalization of foreigners, no other nation can

interfere further than the rights of that other are affected. The rights of Britain are certainly not affected by the naturalization of other than British subjects. Consequently those persons who, according to our laws, are citizens, must be so considered by Britain, and by every other power not háving a conflicting claim to the person.

The United States therefore require positively, that their seamen who are not British subjects, whether born in America or elsewhere, shall be exempt from impressments.

The case of British subjects, whether naturalized or not, is more questionable; but the right even to impress them is denied. The practice of the British government itself, may certainly in a controversy, with that government, be relied on. The privileges it claims and exercises ought to be ceded to others. To deny this would be to deny the equality of nations, and to make it a question of power and not of right.

If the practice of the British government may be quoted, that practice is to maintain and defend in their sea service all those, of any nation, who have voluntarily engaged in it, or who, according to their laws, have become British subjects.

Alien seamen, not British subjects, engaged in our merchant service, ought to be equally exempt with citizens from impressments: we have a right to engage them, and have a right too and an interest in their persons to the extent of the service contracted to be performed. Britain has no pretext of right to their persons or to their service. To tear them, then, from our possession, is at the same time an insult and an injury. It is an act of violence for which there exists no palliative.

We know well that the difficulty of distinguishing between native Americans and British subjects has been used, with respect to natives, as an apology for the injuries complained of. It is not pretended that this apology can be extended to the case of foreigners, and even with respect to natives we doubt the existence of the difficulty alleged. We know well that among that class of people who are seamen, we can readily distinguish between a native American and a person raised to manhood in Great Britain or Ireland; and we do not perceive any reason why the capacity of making this distinction should not be possessed in the same degree by one nation as by the other.

If, therefore, no regulation can be formed which shall effectually secure all seamen on board American merchantmen, we have a right to expect from the justice of the British government, from its regard for the friendship of the United States and its own honour, that it will manifest the sincerity of its wishes to repress this offense, by punishing those who commit it.

We hope, however, that an agreement may be entered into satisfactory and beneficial to both parties. The article which appears to have been transmitted by my predecessor, while it satisfies this country, will probably restore to the naval service of Britain a greater number of seamen than will be lost by it. Should we even be mistaken in this calculation, yet the difference cannot be put in competition with the mischief which may result from the irritation justly excited, by this practice, throughout the United States. The extent and the justice of the resentments it produces, may be estimated, in Britain, by inquiring what impressions would be made on them by similar conduct on the part of this government.

Should we impress from the merchant service of Britain, not only Americans but foreigners, and even British subjects, how long would such a course of injury unredressed be permitted to pass unrevenged? How long would the government be content with unsuccessful remonstrance and unavailing memorials?

I believe, sir, that only the most prompt correction of, compensation for, the abuse, would be admitted as satisfaction in such a case.

If the principles of this government forbid it to retaliate by impressions, there is yet another mode which might be resorted to. We might authorize our ships of war, though not to impress, yet to recruit sailors on board British merchantmen. Such are the inducements to enter into our naval service that we believe even this practice would very seriously affect the navigation of Britain. How, sir, would it be received by the British nation?

Is it not more advisable to desist from, and to take effectual measures to prevent, an acknowledged wrong, than by perseverance in that wrong to excite against themselves the well founded resentments of America, and force our government into measures which may very possibly terminate in an open rupture.

J. Marshall.[41]

EXTRACT FROM A LETTER [42]
From Mr. Marshall, Secretary of State, to Mr. King

September 20, 1800.

The right to confiscate vessels bound to a blockaded port has been unreasonably extended to cases not coming within the rule as heretofore adopted.

On principle, it might be well questioned, whether this rule can be applied to a place not completely invested by land as well as by sea. If we examine the reasoning on which is founded the right to intercept and confiscate supplies designed for a blockaded town, it will be difficult to resist the conviction that its extension to towns invested by sea only is an unjustifiable encroachment on the rights of neutrals. But it is not of this departure from principle (a departure which has received some sanction from practice) that we mean to complain. It is, that ports, not effectually blockaded by a force capable of completely investing them, have yet been declared in a state of blockade, and vessels attempting to enter therein have been seized, and, on that account, confiscated.

This is a vexation proceeding directly from the Government, and which may be carried, if not resisted, to a very injurious extent. Our merchants have greatly complained of it with respect to Cadiz and the ports of Holland.

If the effectiveness of the blockade be dispensed with, then every port of all the belligerent Powers may, at all times, be declared in that state, and the commerce of neutrals be thereby subjected to universal capture. But if this principle be strictly adhered to, the capacity of blockade will be limited by the naval force of the belligerent, and, of consequence, the mischief to neutral commerce cannot be very extensive. It is,

[41] The above letter is printed in "State Papers and Publick Documents" of the United States, from the accession of George Washington to the Presidency, exhibiting a complete view of our foreign relations since that time. Second edition, Vol. IX. Boston, printed and published by T. B. Wait and Son, 1817, pp. 23-26.

[42] The above letter is printed in the "American State Papers," Class I, Vol. III, pp. 370-371.

therefore, of the last importance to neutrals, that this principle be maintained unimpaired.

I observe that you have passed this reasoning on to the British minister, who replies, that an occasional absence of a fleet from a blockaded port ought not to change the state of the place.

Whatever force this observation may be entitled to where that occasional absence has been produced by accident, as a storm, which for a moment blows off the fleet and forces it from its station, which station it immediately resumes, I am persuaded that where a part of the fleet is applied, though only for a time, to other objects, or comes into port, the very principle requiring an effective blockade, which is, that the mischief can then only be co-extensive with the naval force of the beliggerent, requires that during such temporary absence the commerce of neutrals to the place should be free.

LETTER [43] FROM JOHN MARSHALL TO THE PRESIDENT OF
THE UNITED STATES

Communicated to the House of Representatives, February 27, 1801

DEPARTMENT OF STATE, February 27, 1801.
SIR:

The order of the House of Representatives of the 24th of this month, requesting an account of the depredations committed on the commerce of the United States by vessels of Great Britain, of which complaint has been made to the Government, having been referred to this department, I have the honor to transmit herewith an abstract of such cases as have been complained of since the commencement of the year 1800.

The order of the House having fixed no period at which the account it requests is to commence, I have, from a consideration of the short space for which the present session can continue, thought it compatible with their view to limit the abstract to the time above mentioned.

From various reasons, it is to be presumed that many captures have been made, of which no complaint has been forwarded to the Government. Under this impression, and for the purpose of giving a comprehensive view of the subject,

[43] The above letter is printed in the "American State Papers," Class I, Vol. II, "Foreign Relations," p. 345.

I have thought it not improper to annex to the abstract several extracts of letters from our consuls, and also an extract of a letter from the President of the Chamber of Commerce at Philadelphia to the Secretary of the Navy.

I will also take the liberty to observe, that neither the communications from our minister at London, nor my conversations with the charge d'affaires of his Britannic Majesty in the United States, would lead to an opinion that any additional orders have been lately given by the British Government, authorizing the system of depredation alluded to in the letter from Mr. Fitzsimmons.

I am, sir, &c.
J. Marshall.

The President of the United States.

Department of State, February 27, 1801.

Sir:

In my report of this day to the President, on the subject of British captures, which he will have transmitted to Congress, it was accidentally omitted to insert the case of the brigantine Ruby, Captain Wrigley, belonging to Mr. Ambrose Vasse, of Philadelphia. This vessel, proceeding for Port-au-Prince, with a cargo consisting of American produce and some German goods, was lately captured by the British ship of war Tisiphone, and carried to Jamaica, where, the owner informs me, both vessel and cargo were condemned as enemy's property.

I therefore request that the House will consider this letter as an appendage to my report above alluded to.

I have the honor to be, &c.
J. Marshall.[44]

The Honorable the Speaker of the House of Representatives.

THE SECRETARY OF STATE TO MR. KING

Department of State, August 23, 1800.

Sir:

Your letters, stating your negotiations with Lord Grenville respecting the differences which have arisen in execut-

[44] The above letter is printed in the "American State Papers," Vol. II, Class I, p. 345.

ing the sixth article of our treaty of amity, commerce, and navigation with Great Britain, have been laid before, and considered by, the President.

He still retains the opinion that an amicable explanation of that article is greatly to be desired; and, therefore, receives with much regret the information, that the British Cabinet is indisposed to enter on the discussion of this interesting subject.

He perceives with a concern, not entirely unmixed with other sensations, that the secession of two commissioners from the Board lately sitting in Philadelphia, has been attributed, not to its real cause, but to motives which in no instance have ever influenced the American Government.

That Government is, as it has ever been, sincerely desirous of executing, with perfect and scrupulous good faith, all its engagements with foreign nations. This desire has contributed, not inconsiderably, to the solicitude it now manifests for the explanatory articles you have been instructed to propose. The efforts of the American commissioners to proceed and decide on particular cases, instead of laying down abstract principles, believed to be untrue in themselves, ought to have rescued their Government from suspicions, so very unworthy, and so little merited by the general tenor of its conduct. The resolutions, maintained by a majority of the late Board of Commissioners, are such as the Government of the United States can never submit to. They are considered, not as constructive of an existing treaty, but as imposing new and injurious burthens, unwarranted by compact, and to which, if in the first instance plainly and intelligibly stated, this Government never could and never would have assented.

This opinion is not lightly taken up; it is a deep and solemn conviction, produced by the most mature and temperate consideration we are capable of bestowing on the subject.

This being the fixed judgment of the United States, it is impossible not seriously to apprehend, unless we could forget the past, that no attempt by arbitration to adjust the claims of individuals under the sixth article of the treaty, previous to an explanation of it by the two Governments, can be successful. A second effort at this adjustment, by the proposed modification of the Board, while the principles heretofore contended for receive the countenance of the British Government, would most probably, unless, indeed, the Board should again be dissolved, subject us to the painful alternative of paying money, which, in our best judgment, the commissioners had no power to award, or of submitting the public faith to imputations from which it could only be freed by a correct and laborious investigation of the subject. In such a situation, presenting to us only such an alternative, we are extremely unwilling to be placed.

It is, then, very seriously desired that the explanations required by this Government should be made. They are believed to be so reasonable in themselves, and to be so unquestionably in the spirit, and to the full extent of the existing treaty, that it is hoped the difficulties, on the part of the British cabinet, may yet be removed.

The President, therefore, requests that you will take any proper occasion, should one in your judgment present itself, to renew your application to Lord Grenville on this subject. Perhaps a change of temper may be produced by a change of circumstances; and there may be a state of things in which you may perceive a disposition favorable to the accomplishment of an object which ought to be desired by both nations, because it is just in itself, and because it will remove a subject of controversy, which may, in the course of events have a very unhappy influence on that good understanding and friendly intercourse, which it is the interest of both to preserve.

The note of the 18th of April, addressed to you by Lord Grenvelle, stating the determination of the British cabinet, not to modify, but to reject, without discussion, the explanatory articles proposed by you on the part of the United States, assumes, as the base of its decision, a principle not only so different from those admitted by this Government, but so different from those recognized by both nations in the treaty of amity negotiated between them, and which ought, therefore, to be adhered to in all explanations of that treaty, as to warrant a hope that the determination announced in that note may not be unalterable.

His Lordship assumes as a fact that " the fourth article of the treaty of peace not having been duly executed on the part of the United States, the British Government withheld the delivery of the forts on the frontier of Canada, in order that these might serve as a pledge for the interests and rights secured to the British creditors under that article."

But this is a fact which the American Government has ever controverted, and which has never yet been established.

Without entering into the always unavailing and now improper discussion of the question, which nation committed the first fault, it ought never to be forgotten that the treaty in which the claim of the British creditors, on the United States originated, was avowedly entered into for the purpose of terminating the difference between the two nations " in such a manner as, without reference to the merits of their respective complaints and pretentions, may be the best calculated to produce mutual satisfaction and good understanding."

In questions growing out of such a treaty, neither nation can be permitted to refer to and decide the merits of those respective complaints and pretensions, by asserting that the other, and not itself, has committed the first fault.

Lord Grenville, then, proceeds on the idea that the commissioners appointed by the American Government have withdrawn from the Board, merely because awards were rendered against their opinion, and on claims which they believed to be unjust.

But this idea is neither warranted by the conduct or declaration of the American Commissioners, nor of the Government which appointed them. It has been, and still is, expressly disavowed. The commissioners and their Government acquiesced under opinions which they conscientiously believed to be formed on erroneous principles, but on principles submitted by the treaty to their decision. Awards conforming to such opinions, unless by mutual consent the subject shall assume some other form, will be paid by the United States. It was not until a majority of the Board had proceeded to establish a system of rules for the Government of their future decisions, which, in the opinion of this Government, clearly comprehended a vast mass of cases never submitted to their consideration, that it was deemed necessary to terminate proceedings believed to be totally unauthorized, and which were conducted in terms and in a spirit only calculated to destroy all harmony between the two nations.

We understand the treaty differently from what Lord Grenville would seem to understand it, when he says the decision of the Board, constituted according to the provisions of that instrument, " was expressly declared to be in all cases final and conclusive."

These terms have never been understood by us as authorizing the arbiters to go out of the special cases described in the instrument creating and limiting their powers. The words " all cases " can only mean those cases which the two nations have submitted to reference. These are described in the preceding part of the article, and this description is relied on, by the United States, as constituting a boundary, within which alone the powers of the commissioners can be exercised. This boundary has, in our judgment, been so totally prostrated, that scarcely a trace of it remains. The reasoning on which we have formed this judgment it would be unnecessary to detail to you, because you are in perfect possession of it.

Believing the British cabinet disposed to act justly and honorably in a case in which we conceive their reputation, as well as ours, to be concerned, we have been confident in the opinion, that to obtain their serious attention to the subjects of difference between the two nations, was to secure the establishment of that reasonable and liberal construction of the article for which America has contended. We shall abandon this opinion with reluctance and regret.

Although the President decidedly prefers the amicable explanations which have been suggested to any other mode of adjusting the differences which have arisen in executing the sixth article of our treaty with Great Britain, yet it is by no means the only mode to which he is willing to resort. He does not even require that you shall press this proposition in a manner which, in your judgment, may lessen the probability of settling existing differences, or further than may comport with the interests of the United States. Your situation, your full and near view of all the circumstances which can influence the negotiation, enable you to decide more certainly than can be done on this side of the Atlantic, on the precise course which it may be most advantageous to pursue. To your discretion, therefore, the President entirely submits this part of the subject.

If the explanatory articles so much desired by the United States be unattainable, the substitution of a gross sum, in full compensation of all claims, made or to be made on this Government, under the sixth article of our treaty of amity, commerce, and navigation with His Britannic Majesty, is deemed the most eligible remaining mode of accommodating those differences which have impeded the execution of that article.

It is apparent that much difficulty will arise in agreeing on the sum which shall be received as compensation. The ideas of the two Governments, on this subject, appear so different, that, without reciprocal sacrifices of opinion, it is probable they will be as far from agreeing on the sum which ought to be received, as on the merits of the claims for which it will be paid. This difficulty is, perhaps, increased by the extravagant claims which the British creditors have been induced to file. Among them are cases believed to be so notoriously unfounded, that no commissioners retaining the slightest degree of self-respect, can establish them. There are many others where the debtors are as competent to pay as any inhabitants of the United States; and there are others where the debt has been fairly and voluntarily compromised by agreement between the creditor and debtor. There are even cases where the money has been paid in specie, and receipts in full given. I do not mention these distinct classes as comprehending all the cases of claims filed, which can never be allowed; but as examples of the materials which compose that enormous mass of imagined debt, which may, by its unexamined bulk, obstruct a just and equitable settlement of the well-founded claims which really exist.

The creditors are now proceeding, and, had they not been seduced into the opinion that the trouble and expense inseparable from the pursuit of old debts might be avoided by one general resort to the United States, it is believed they would have been still more rapidly proceeding in the collection of the very claims, so far as they are just, which have been filed with the commissioners. They meet with no obstructions, either of law or fact, which are not common to every description of creditors, in every country, unless the difficulty, with respect to interest during the war, may be so denominated. Our judges are even liberal in their construction of the fourth article of the treaty of peace, and are believed, in questions growing out of that treaty, to have manifested no sort of partiality for the debtors. Indeed, it is believed that, with the exception of the contested article of war, interest, and possibly, of claims barred by the act of limitations during the war, the United States are justly chargeable with the debts of only such of their citizens as have become insolvent subsequent to the peace, and previous to the establishment of the federal courts. This opinion is founded on a conviction that our judges give to the fourth article of the treaty of peace a construction as extensive as ought to be given to it by commissioners appointed under the sixth article of the treaty of amity, commerce, and navigation.

Those who have attended most to this subject are of opinion that the sum which might properly be awarded against the United States would fall far short of any estimate which has probably been made of it in England, or by the British creditors or agents in this country. We are, however, sensible that commissioners, acting within their powers, may extend the sum further than justice or a fair construction of the article would extend it; and we have been taught to apprehend a construction, of which, at the ratification of the treaty, no fear was entertained. From this persuasion, and from a solicitude to perform what even rigid and unfavorable judges may suppose to be enjoined by good faith, the interests of the United States may require, and the President is, therefore, willing, that the agreement should not be strictly limited by the sum for which, in our opinion, we ought to be liable. He will be satisfied with four millions of dollars. He will not consent to exceed one million sterling.

If a gross sum, in satisfaction of all other claims, be accepted, you will of course stipulate for the lowest possible sum, and for the most favorable installments which may be attainable.

Should it be found impossible to negotiate reasonable explanatory articles, or to agree on a sum to be received as compensation for the claims of the creditors, much doubt is entertained concerning the proposition for new modelling the Board, as proposed by the British minister. While the Government itself professes to approve the conduct of its late commissioners, much fear is entertained that their successors may bring with them those extravagant and totally inadmissible opinions which have dissolved the past, and will most probably dissolve any future Board. Before the United States proceed to take a new step in a case where experience has done so much to teach them caution, some assurances of the temper in which the commissioners to be appointed will meet ought to be received. And yet we are not satisfied that good faith does not require that, notwithstanding the past, we should consent to make a second effort for the execution of the sixth article of the treaty, in the forms it has prescribed.

On this part of the subject, however, the President has come to no determination; so soon as his decision shall have been made it shall be communicated to you.

With very much respect, &c.,

J. MARSHALL.[45]

J. MARSHALL, SECRETARY OF STATE, TO SAMUEL SITGREAVES, ESQUIRE, LONDON

DEPARTMENT OF STATE, December 2, 1800.

DEAR SIR:

I have had the pleasure of receiving your letters to the 29th of September, and among them that of the 23d, enclosing a copy of your letter of the 22d of April, the original of which had unfortunately miscarried.

It is probable that, before this can reach you, the negotiation respecting the sixth article of our treaty of amity, commerce, and navigation with Great Britain will have terminated, and that Mr. King will have come to some agreement with Lord Grenville, or will be able to state precisely the ultimata of the British cabinet on this subject. Should it, contrary to our expectation, remain open, the President is of opinion that informal explanations may be received in lieu of the articles required, provided sufficient assurances acompany them that the commissioners, on the part of His Britannic Majesty will, in the true spirit of conciliation, conform to those explanations.

The idea suggested to Lord Grenville by Mr. King, of sending over confidential characters to the United States, with power to make arrangements for facilitating the just and impartial execution of the treaty, and with an eventual appointment as commissioners, is a valuable one. If no positive agreement can be made which will enable us to enter again on the execution of the sixth article without submitting to injurious and disgraceful imposition, this idea may perhaps be so im-

---

[45] This letter is printed in the "American State Papers," Vol. II, Class I, Foreign Relations, pp. 386-387.

proved as to become the foundation of a reasonable accommodation. It is certainly recommended by the probabilities you have suggested.

If the system of informal explanation should be adopted, and the new Board be constituted, in the mode intimated by Lord Grenville, there will undoubtedly be considerable difficulty in agreeing on rules which shall guide its proceedings, and in obtaining security that these rules will not be departed from. The explanatory articles which before your departure were digested by this Government, and committed to you, are believed to be a liberal as well as just construction, and would be, therefore, with reluctance receded from: indeed, there are among them some from which we never ought to recede. Such, for example, as that, to charge the United States, the British creditor must bring his case completely within the treaty, and not require that the United States should furnish evidence to discharge themselves from every claim which may be at present, or, on the signature of the treaty of amity, may have been unpaid. Such a construction appears to us so totally unreasonable, that we should never have deemed it necessary to guard against it, had not the principle been already asserted, and it is of course a construction to which we never can and never ought to submit. Other principles were insisted on which seem to us not less objectionable. But if it shall be found that a new Board is to be resorted to, it will become necessary to revise the instructions which have been given, and to modify them so far as a proper respect for justice and our own character will permit.

The President allows you to return to the United States as soon as the negotiation shall have taken a turn which in your opinion may render your longer continuance in England unnecessary, or so soon as you shall have communicated fully to Mr. King all the ideas on the interesting subject of your mission, which your intimate acquaintance with it has enabled you to acquire.

With vry much respect and esteem, I am, sir, &c.,

J. Marshall.[46]

Samuel Sitgreaves, Esq., London.

[46] The above letter is printed in the "American State Papers," Vol. II, pp. 388, 389. Class 1, "Foreign Relations."

J. MARSHALL, SECRETARY OF STATE, TO RUFUS KING, ESQUIRE

DEPARTMENT OF STATE, December 4, 1800.

DEAR SIR:

Your letters to No. 85, inclusive, have been received.

In my No. 2 I stated to you the opinion of the President that an adjustment, by explanatory articles of the differences which arose on executing the treaty with Great Britain, was preferred to the stipulation of a sum in gross, to be paid in lieu of the compensation to creditors demandable from the United States.

This opinion is still retained. But it has been suggested that, however unreasonable the principles asserted by the British commissioners may be, it will be difficult, perhaps impossible, to induce the British cabinet formally to abandon them. That the same thing may probably be obtained in an informal way, which would be withheld if required in the shape of a solemn public stipulation.

Under the impression that this may be the fact, the President directs me to inform you that an informal agreement, provided it be perfectly understood, will be satisfactory to this Government.

If, however, on any such agreement, a new Board should be constituted it is of the last importance that the persons appointed to act as commissioners should possess dispositions inclined to conciliation, and characters which impress you with a favorable opinion of the impartiality to be expected in their decisions. These are requisites, the materiality of which we have been taught by experience, and on them must greatly depend our assent to another Board.

If you have brought the negotiations to a conclusion respecting the sum in gross mentioned in a former letter, or if it is in such a train that no change can without embarrassment, be made, it is not intended to derange or unsettle the business. But if no agreement has been concluded, or has progressed so far as to pledge the United States, it is decidedly the judgment of the President that it will be most advisable to execute the treaty in the manner originally agreed on, provided satisfactory informal assurances can be obtained, that we shall not be subjected, by a majority of the Board, to an enormous burthen not imposed by the original contract.

If persons could be deputed to make arrangements here, for facilitating the execution of the treaty, with an eventual appointment as commissioners, some difficulties might perhaps be surmounted which, at present, appear very considerable, and the business might be greatly expedited.

As we cannot know the precise state of the negotiation, it is impossible to do more than to communicate, in general terms, the course which the President most wishes it to take. Having done this, to your judgment it must be submitted.

The most desirable plan of accommodation is by public explanatory articles, placing the treaty on its true principles, in terms not easily to be misunderstood.

Second to this is the system of informal explanation, by which we may be enabled, without great injustice, to execute the treaty in the mode originally designed. If, in neither the one way nor the other, a new Board can be so constituted as to comply with the engagements we have made according to their real import, without exposing the United States to the immense losses threatened by that which has been dissolved, then the stipulation for a sum in gross will be deemed more eligible than to permit things to remain in their present unsettled situation.

We are surprised that, at the date of your No. 85, no letter on this subject had been received from this Department.

With the most respectful esteem, &c.,

J. MARSHALL.[47]

RUFUS KING, ESQ.

LETTER [48] FROM JOHN MARSHALL TO THE HON.
DUDLEY CHASE

WASHINGTON, February 7, 1817.

SIR:

Your letter, enclosing a copy of the bill " to provide for reports of the decisions of the Supreme Court," in which you do

[47] The above letter is printed in the "American State Papers," Vol. II, p. 339, Class I.

[48] The above letter is printed in the "American State Papers," Class X, Miscellaneous, Vol. II, pp. 419-420, Documents Legislative and Executive, published by Gales and Seaton, Washington, 1834.

me the honor to request, for the committee, " my views relative to the object and utility of the proposed act," was yesterday received, and communicated to the judges.

We all concur in the opinion that the object of the bill is in a high degree desirable.

That the cases determined in the Supreme Court should be reported with accuracy and promptness, is essential to correctness and uniformity of decision in all the courts of the United States. It is also to be recollected that from the same tribunal the public receive that exposition of the constitution, laws, and treaties of the United States as applicable to the cases of individuals which must ultimately prevail. It is obviously important that a knowledge of this exposition should be attainable by all.

It is a minor consideration, but not perhaps to be entirely overlooked, that, even in cases where the decisions of the Supreme Court are not to be considered as authority except in the courts of the United States, some advantage may be derived from their being known. It is certainly to be wished that independent tribunals having concurrent jurisdiction over the same subject should concur in the principles on which they determine the causes coming before them. This concurrence can be obtained only by communicating to each the judgments of the other, and by that mutual respect which will probably be inspired by a knowledge of the grounds on which their judgments respectively stand. On great commercial questions, especially, it is desirable that the judicial opinions of all parts of the Union should be the same.

From experience, the judges think there is much reason to apprehend that the publication of the decisions of the Supreme Court will remain on a very precarious footing if the reporter is to depend solely on the sales of his work for a reimbursement of the expenses which must be incurred in preparing it, and for his own compensation. The patronage of the Government is believed to be necessary to the secure and certain attainment of the object.

Law reports can have but a limited circulation. They rarely gain admission into the libraries of other than professional gentlemen. The circulation of the decisions of the Supreme Court will probably be still more limited than those of the courts of the States, because they are useful to a smaller number of the

profession.   Only a few of those who practice in the courts of
the United States, or in great commercial cities, will often
require them.   There is, therefore, much reason to believe that
no reporter will continue to employ his time and talents in preparing those decisions for the press after he shall be assured
that the Government will not countenance his undertaking.

With very great respect, I am, sir, your obedient servant,

J. MARSHALL.

THE HON. DUDLEY CHASE.

LETTER [49] TO RICHARD SODERSTROM, ESQ.

WASHINGTON, November 26, 1800.

SIR:

I have received your letters of the 24th and 25th instant,
accompanying one from the Governor General of the Danish
West India islands, bearing date of the 6th of August last.

Be assured, sir, that the Government of the United States
respects, as it ought to do, the friendship and flag of His Danish
Majesty, and will not intentionally commit an act which may
insult the one, or diminish the other.   If, in any instance, our
cruisers have violated a really neutral flag, they have, in doing
so, departed from the instructions under which they sail.

It is not, however, to be disguised, that means have been
devised by which the Danish flag has been used in the West
Indies for purposes which we believe His Danish Majesty
would not countenance.

I have communicated the letters from yourself and the Governor General of the Danish West India islands, to the Secretary of the Navy.   He informs me that Lieutenant Maley has
been dismissed the service principally on account of the improper manner in which he has conducted himself toward
neutrals.

With respect to the particular case of the Mercator, it is certainly advisable to prosecute an appeal.   If she was really a
neutral bottom, she will not, it is presumed, be condemned.
Without deciding absolutely that the United States will or will
not consent, when the case shall be ultimately decided, to pay

[49] The above letter is printed in the "American State Papers," Class I,
Vol. III, "Foreign Relations," p. 344.

for the vessel and cargo if confiscated, we are certainly not sufficiently informed at present to take any responsibility on ourselves, in the event of an unfavorable issue of that affair.

J. MARSHALL.

LETTER [50] FROM JOHN MARSHALL TO R. KING

RICHMOND, April 25, 1796.

DEAR SIR:

I take the liberty to avail myself of your aid for forwarding to Mr. Hamilton the inclosed letter.[51]

The ruling party of Virginia are extremely irritated at the vote of today and will spare no exertion to obtain a majority in other counties. Even here they will affect to have the greater number of freeholders and have set about counter Resolutions to which they have the signatures of many respectable persons, but of still a greater number of mere boys; and altho' some caution has been used by us in excluding those who might not be considered authorized to vote, they will not fail to charge us with having collected a number of names belonging to foreigners and to persons having no property in the place. The charge is as far untrue as has perhaps ever happened on any occasion of the sort. We could, by resorting to that measure, have doubled our list of petitioners.

I have endeavored to take means to procure similar applications from various parts of the State. Exitus in dubio est.

With very much respect & esteem, &c.

J. MARSHALL.

[50] The letter to Hamilton here mentioned is of the same date as the above, and may be found in "Works of Hamilton," Vol. VI, p. 108. It relates to the feeling in Virginia relative to the question of the adoption of Jay's Treaty, and of the temper of the House of Representatives, especially of the Virginia members, who bitterly opposed its ratification; it also speaks of the meeting called that day in Richmond by those who desired the ratification of the treaty, saying that a resolution had been passed by a decided majority, after long discussion, "that the welfare and honor of the nation required us to give full effect to the treaty negotiated with Britain." He says further: "I think it would be very difficult, perhaps impossible, to engage Mr. H. (probably Mr. Hamilton) on the right side of this question."

[51] "Life and Correspondence of Rufus King," Vol. II, pp. 45-46.

LETTER [52] FROM J. MARSHALL TO R. KING

RICHMOND, May 24, 1796.

DEAR SIR:

Mr. Henry has at length been sounded on the subject you committed to my charge.   Genl. Lee and myself have each conversed with him on it, tho' without informing him particularly of the persons who authorized the communication.   He is unwilling to embark in the business.   His unwillingness, I think, proceeds from an apprehension of the difficulties to be encountered by those who shall fill high Executive offices.

With very much respect and esteem &c.

J. MARSHALL.

Endorsed by R. King:

Ansd.   1 June.—regretting &c and observing that it wd. be requisite to fix on another person without delay.

LETTER [53] FROM J. MARSHALL TO RUFUS KING

RICHMOND, May 5, 1802.

DEAR SIR:

This unfortunate accomplishment of the long & difficult negotiation with which you were charged, is peculiarly gratifying to those who unite a knowledge of the embarassing circumstances attending it, to a real wish that your embassy may be as honorable to yourself as it has been useful to our country.

You have effected what, in America, has been heretofore deemed impracticable.   You have made a treaty with one of the great rival Nations of Europe, which is not only acceptable to all, but the merit of which is claimed by both parties. The advocates of the present administration ascribe to it great praise, for having, with so much dexterity & so little loss, extricated our country from a debt of twenty-four million of dollars in which a former administration had involved it; while the friends of the ancient state of things, are not slow in adding the present happy accomodation to the long list of their Merits.

Yet amidst this universal approbation so correctly given to an adjustment of differences which unquestionably deserve it,

[52] Letter in " Life and Correspondence of R. King," Vol. II, p. 48.
[53] *Ibid.*, Vol. IV, pp. 116-118.

the mortifying reflection obtrudes itself, that the reputation of the most wise and skillful conduct depends, in this our capricious world, so much on accident.   Had Mr. Adams been re-elected President of the United States, or had his successor been a gentleman whose political opinions accorded with those held by the preceding executive, a very different reception, I still believe, would have been given to the same measure.   The payment of a specific sum would then have been pronounced, by those who now take merit to themselves for it, a humiliating national degradation, an abandonment of national interest, a free will offering of millions to Britain for her grace & favor, by those who sought to engage in war with France, rather than repay, in part, by a small loan to that republic, the immense debt of gratitude we owe her.

Such is, & such I fear will ever be human justice!

When I recollect the advantage actually gained by Great Britain, on having obtained the fifth commissioner, I am truly surprised at the sum agreed on.   I believe it is as much, & not more than, in strict justice, ought to be paid, but, after the impressions made by the late board of commissioners I really apprehended strict justice to be unattainable; & I think, not only, that great credit is due to the American Negotiator for having reduced this enormous claim to a reasonable amount, but that, all circumstances considered, some sentiment of respect should be felt for the moderation & equity of the English Minister.

The national tribunals, I hope will continue to manifest, in the exposition of the treaty of peace, "that share of prudence," which is required by justice, & which can alone preserve the reputation of the nation.

Public opinion in this quarter of the union has sustained no essential change.   That disposition to coalesce with what is, now, the majority in America as well as in this state, which was strongly display'd by the minority twelve months past, exists no longer.   It has expired.   But the minority is only recovering its strength & firmness.   It acquires nothing.

Our political tempests will long, very long, exist after those who are now toss'd about by them shall be at rest.

Your obedt. Servt.

J. MARSHALL.

A LETTER OF MARSHALL TO JEFFERSON,
DECEMBER 12, 1783

In the centennial period of the Lewis and Clark expedition much interest was shown in one of the manuscripts in the Draper Manuscript Collection in the Wisconsin Historical Library,— a note from Thomas Jefferson, dated Annapolis, December 4, 1783, to General George Rogers Clark, suggesting to the latter an exploration toward the Pacific Ocean, similar in character to that which Jefferson twenty years later succeeded in inducing Meriwether Lewis and William Clark (younger brother of George) to undertake.   This letter is printed in the " American Historical Review," Vol. III, p. 673, and has been printed in several other magazines.   Some time ago Prof. R. E. N. Dodge, of the University of Wisconsin, presented the Wisconsin Historical Library with an autograph letter of Chief Justice John Marshall, that throws additional light on this famous letter of Jefferson to George Rogers Clark.   This letter, one of the few that were written to Jefferson by Marshall, was written at Williamsburg, Va., and was addressed to Thomas Jefferson.   In it Marshall, who was at that time a member of the state executive council, acknowledges the receipt of a letter written by Jefferson on the fifth instant, inclosing " letters to General Clark and Mr. Banks " which " I yesterday delivered."   General Clark was at that time in Williamsburg, trying to push his claims for reimbursement for money spent in his celebrated campaign against Vincennes.   This letter of Marshall to Jefferson is noteworthy because of its connection with the latter's early project of an exploration through the Spanish Domain beyond the Mississippi, and for its characteristic allusions to Patrick Henry, Col. R. H. Lee, Colonel Nicholas, and others famous in that day.
The letter is as follows: —

WILLIAMSBURG, VA., Dec. 12th, 1783.

DEAR SIR:

The letters to Genl Clark and Mr. Banks enclosed in yours of the 5th. inst. I yesterday deliver'd.   Should a letter to Majr. Crittenden arrive by the next post I can give it a certain and immediate conveyance.   I gave you in my last some account of the proceedings of the Assembly.   The Commutable bill has at length pass'd and with it a suspension of the collections of taxes till the first of January next. I told you the principal speakers for and against the measure. Col. R. H. Lee has not attended this Session. This is not all. His services in the Assembly are lost forever. 'Tis conjectur'd that Col. Harry Lee of the Legionary corps, will take his place. You know the character of that Gentleman better than I do and can best determine whether the public will be injur'd by the change. The idea of rendering Members of Congress eligible to the Genl. Assembly has not been taken up. Indeed the attention of the house since the passage of the Commutable bill has been so fix'd on the Citizen bill that they have scarcely thought on any other subject. Since the rejection of the bill introduc'd by Taylor, Col. Nicholas (politician not fam'd for hitting a medium) introduced one admitting into this Country every species of Men except Natives who had borne arms against the state. When the house went into Committee on this bill Mr. Jones introduc'd by way of amendment, one totally new and totally opposite to that which was the subject of deliberation. He spoke with his usual sound sense and solid reason. Mr. Henry opposed him. The Speaker replied with some degree of acrimony and Henry retorted with a good deal of tartness but with much temper; 'tis his peculiar excellence when he altercates to appear to be drawn unwillingly into the contest and to throw in the eyes of others the whole blame on his adversary. His influence is immense. The house rose for the day without coming to any determination and the bill is yet in suspense. The principal point on which they split is the exclusion of the Statute Staple Men. I really am uncertain what will be the determination on this subject.

The Officers will soon begin to survey their lands on the Cumberland. Has Crittenden your Millitary warrant? The report from Congress with respect to the cession has not yet reached us; of course the assembly can have determined nothing about it. My Father set out for the western Country about the 5th, of Novr. I have not heard a syllable from Crittenden since his departure.

As ever I am with the greatest esteem yours

J. MARSHALL.

Banks has applied to me for a considerable sum, on your

account but I presume Your letter to him was on that subject. I parry every applicant as well as possible.

Yours   J. M.

LETTER OF JOHN MARSHALL TO JAMES WILKINSON

This letter is printed in the " American Historical Review," Vol. XII, pp. 347-348.   The publishers acknowledge their indebtedness to Col. Reuben T. Durrett, LL.D., of Louisville, Kentucky, for the letter.   At that time Colonel Durrett writes:

" This letter was written to Gen. James Wilkinson, at that time a resident of Kentucky, although his name does not appear in the address.   His name and address were on the envelope, which has since been destroyed."

This letter, as Colonel Durrett intimates, shows a kindly feeling between writer and recipient that Humphrey Marshall, the historian (John Marshall's cousin), would hardly have been willing to admit.   He also calls attention to the efforts that Col. Thomas Marshall (father of John) made in 1791 toward securing Wilkinson's reappointment to the army of the United States.   Colonel Marshall, however, it should be said, gives as a reason for this that Wilkinson was a dangerous man while not engaged, but that the danger might be removed by giving him employment.   Colonel Durrett suggests that possibly John Marshall may have been moved by similar considerations in trying to obtain for him a passport out of the United States.   The first paragraph in regard to the Governor, Edmund Randolph, is not exactly clear.

RICHMOND, Jan. 5th, 1787.

DEAR SIR:

It is with a great deal of mortification I tell you that I have failed in obtaining the passport I applied for.   On my mentioning the subject to the Governor he said he was acquainted with you and would with great pleasure do anything which was proper to serve you.   He took time to consider the subject and after several applications, told me today that to grant the passport as an official act was entirely improper because it could only extend to the limits of Virginia to which you had a right to go without his permit and that he could not write a private letter of recommendation to the Governor without having some acquaintance with him.   On these reasons sir, my application in your favor was rejected.   I am much chagrined at my disappointment.

I am much indebted to you for the clear and succinct account you have given me of the two expeditions against the Indians.   I fear with you that so long as you remain connected with Virginia it will be absolutely impossible to act on any great occasion with reputation or success.   Just information from such a distance will never be obtained by government without a solicitude about intelligence which seldom exists in a proper degree on the eve of a separation.   You are considered as being certainly about to part with us, and therefore less attention will be given to any regulations respecting your country than if the disunion was not expected.

All is gloom in the eastern states.   Massachusetts is rent into two equal factions and an appeal I fear has by this time been made to the God of battles.   Three of the leaders of the opponents to Government have been taken and imprisoned in Boston.   The whole force of the party is collected for their relief.   The last intelligence gives us reason to fear that before this time the attempt to relieve them has been made with the whole power of one party and opposed by the whole power of the other.   But of this I suppose you receive better information than I can give you.   We have contradictory accounts of the motives and views of the insurgents.   We are sometimes informed that they are a British faction supported secretly from Canada, whose immediate object is to overthrow the present and restore the former government, at other times we are told that it is a mere contest for power between Bowdoin and Hancock and that the Hancock faction are aiming at the destruction of all public securities and the subversion of all public faith.   Whatever may be the cause of these dissentions or however they may terminate, in their present operation they deeply affect the happiness and reputation of the United States. They will, however, I presume tend to people the western world if you can govrn yourselves so wisely as to present a safe retreat to the weaker party.   These violent, I fear bloody dissensions in a state I had thought inferior in wisdom and virtue to no one in the union, added to the strong tendency which the politics of many eminent characters among ourselves have to promote private and public dishonesty cast a deep shade over that bright prospect which the revolution in America and the establishment of our free governments had opened to the votaries of liberty throughout the globe. I fear, and there is no opinion no more degrading to the dignity of man, that these have truth on their side who say that man is incapable of governing himself. I fear we may live to see another revolution.

I am dear sir, with high esteem and respect,

Your obed't serv't.

J. MARSHALL.

The correspondence of Alexander Hamilton proves that he decided the question of the Presidency. Hamilton wrote a great many letters about the last of 1800 and the first part of 1801. He made his decision under circumstances and from motives that show that he was governed solely by the highest and largest considerations of the public welfare. It was at that time clearly ascertained that either Burr or Jefferson would be President. Hamilton seemed to see that it would never do to have Burr President; he said, " As to Burr, there is nothing in his favor." He also said, " Jefferson is not so dangerous a man by far."

Hamilton wrote to Morris:

" I trust the Federalists will not finally be so mad as to vote for Burr. I speak with an intimate and accurate knowledge of character. His elevation can only promote the purposes of the desperate and profligate. If there be a man in the world I ought to hate, it is Jefferson. With Burr I have always been personally well. But the public good must be paramount to every private consideration. My opinion may be freely used with such reserves as you shall think discreet."

Hamilton also addressed a letter to Marshall, of which no copy is preserved, but there is no doubt but that it was very similar to the one quoted above. Marshall replied to this letter at once as follows:

January 1st, 1801.

DEAR SIR: —

I received this morning your letter of the 26th of December. It is, I believe, certain that Jefferson and Burr will come to the House of Representatives with equal votes. The returns have been all received, and this is the general opinion.

Being no longer in the House of Representatives, and consequently compelled by no duty to decide between them, my own mind had scarcely determined to which of these gentlemen the preference was due. To Mr. Jefferson, whose political character is better known than that of Mr. Burr, I have felt almost insuperable objections. His foreign prejudices seem to me totally to unfit him for the chief magistracy of a nation which cannot indulge those prejudices without sustaining deep and permanent injury. In addition to this solid and immovable objection, Mr. Jefferson appears to me to be a man who will embody himself with the House of Representatives. By weakening the office of President he will increase his personal power. He will diminish his responsibility, sap the fundamental principles of the government, and become the leader of that party which is about to constitute the majority of the legislature. The morals of the author of the letter to Mazzei cannot be pure.

With these impressions concerning Mr. Jefferson, I was in some degree disposed to view with less apprehension any other characters, and to consider the alternative now offered as a circumstance not to be entirely neglected.

Your representation of Mr. Burr, with whom I am totally unacquainted, shows that from him still greater danger than even from Mr. Jefferson may be apprehended. Such a man as you describe is more to be feared, and may do more immediate, if not greater, mischief. Believing that you know him well, and are impartial, my preference would certainly not be for him; but I can take no part in this business. I cannot bring myself to aid Mr. Jefferson. Perhaps respect for myself should, in my present situation, deter me from using any influence (if, indeed, I possessed any) in support of either gentleman. Although no consideration could induce me to be the Secretary of State while there was a President whose political system I believed to be at variance with my own, yet this cannot be so well known to others, and it might be suspected that a desire to be well with the successful candidate had, in some degree, governed my conduct.

With you I am in favor of ratifying our treaty with France, though I am far, very far, from approving it. There is, however, one principle which I think it right to explain.

Our envoys were undoubtedly of opinion that our prior treaty with Britain would retain its stipulated advantages, and

I think that opinion correct. Were our convention with any other nation than France, I should feel no solicitude on this subject. But France, the most encroaching nation on earth, will claim a literal interpretation, and our people will decide in her favor. Those who could contend that a promise not to permit privateers of the enemy of France, to be fitted out in our ports, amounted to a grant of that privilege to France, would not hesitate to contend that a stipulation giving to France, on the subject of privateers and prizes, the privileges of the most favored nation, placed her on equal ground with any other nation whatever. In consequence of this temper in our country, I think the ratification of the treaty ought to be accompanied with a declaration of the sense in which it is agreed to. This, however, is only my own opinion.

With very much respect and esteem,

I am, dear Sir, yours obediently,

J. MARSHALL.

MARSHALL TO HAMILTON

WASHINGTON, August 23d, 1800.

DEAR SIR:

I received today your letter of the 19th inst, accompanying a memorial from the Governor-General of the Danish West India Islands, respecting the conduct of some of our ships of war.

This paper shall be immediately communicated to the Secretary of the Navy. Our dispatches from Paris come no later than the 17th of May. There is nothing in them on which a positive opinion respecting the result of that negotiation can be formed.

Connecting the then state of things with the European events which have since happened, and with intelligence from America which has since reached them, I shall not be surprised if the paragraph from St. Sebastian should be true.

With very much respect and esteem, &c.

J. MARSHALL.[54]

---

[54] The above letter is printed in "Hamilton's Works," by John C. Hamilton, Vol. VI, p. 460.

MARSHALL TO HAMILTON

RICHMOND, April 25th, 1796.

DEAR SIR:

Yours of the 14th only reached me by the mail this evening. I had been informed of the temper of the House of Representatives, and we had promptly taken such measures as appeared to us fitted to the occasion. We could not venture an expression of the public mind under the violent prejudices with which it has been impressed, so long as a hope remained, that the House of Representatives might ultimately consult the interest or honor of the nation. But now, when all hope of this has vanished, it was deemed advisable to make the experiment, however hazardous it might be. A meeting was called, which was more numerous than I have ever seen at this place; and after a very ardent and zealous discussion which consumed the day, a decided majority declared in favor of a resolution that the welfare and honor of the nation required us to give full effect to the treaty negotiated with Britain. This resolution, with a petition drawn by an original opponent of the treaty, will be forwarded by the next post to Congress. The subject will probably be taken up in every county in the State, or at any rate in very many of them. It is probable that a majority of the counties will avow sentiments opposed to ours, but the division of the State will appear to be much more considerable than has been stated. In some of the districts there will certainly be a majority who will concur with us, and that perhaps may have some effect. As man is a gregarious animal, we shall certainly derive much aid from declarations in support of the constitution and of appropriations, if such can be obtained from our sister States. The ground we take here is very much that of Mr. Hillhouse. We admit the discretionary constitutional power of the representatives on the subject of appropriations, but contend that the treaty is as completely a valid and obligatory contract when negotiated by the President and ratified by him, with the assent and advice of the Senate, as if sanctioned by the House of Representatives also under a constitution requiring such sanction. I think it would be very difficult, perhaps impossible, to engage Mr. H. on the right side of this question. If you have any communications which might promote a concurrence of action, we shall be proud to receive them.

With much respect and esteem,

From, dear Sir, your obedient servant,

JOHN MARSHALL.[55]

At a meeting of the Massachusetts Historical Society held in November, 1900, Mr. Charles C. Smith communicated some unpublished letters of Chief Justice Marshall, and said:

" In examining the Pickering Papers, to revive my recollection of the correspondence between Chief Justice Marshall and Colonel Pickering, my eye fell on two letters from the former which it seems worth while to print in full in the proceedings. The first is an answer to two letters from Colonel Pickering, respectively dated January 17 and January 24, 1826, the rough draughts of which are in the Pickering Papers. In them Pickering, among other things, expressed his gloomy forebodings at the extension of slavery, his estimate of the talents and party services of William B. Giles, and his detestation and contempt for the acts and sentiments of Governor Troup, of Georgia."

Judge Marshall's reply is as follows:

Col. Timothy Pickering,
    Salem, Massachusetts.

Mr. Story.

WASHINGTON, March 20th, '26.

DEAR SIR:— I had the pleasure of receiving your letters of the 17th & 23d of Jany by Mr. Story & congratulate you very sincerely on the vigorous health which your letters manifest. It is consoling to think that we may look forward to very advanced life with the hope of preserving with health & temperance so large a share of mental & bodily strength as to make life still desirable & agreeable.

I concur with you in thinking that nothing portends more calamity & mischief to the Southern States than their slave population. Yet they seem to cherish the evil and to view with immovable prejudice & dislike everything which may tend to diminish it. I do not wonder that they should resist any attempt, should one be made, to interfere with the rights of

[55] The above letter is printed in " Hamilton's Works," Vol. VI, pp. 108-109.

property, but they have a feverish jealousy of measures which may do good without the hazard of harm that is, I think, very unwise.

All America, I believe, will join you in opinion respecting the late intemperate course of the Governor of Georgia. I very much fear that the embarassment into which the purchase from the Creeks has thrown us will be prolonged by a rejection of the last treaty.

You are undoubtedly right in supposing Mr. Giles to be a disconted man. He was unquestionably a very poweful debater on the floor of either branch of the legislature, & has seen men placed before him by the party which he has served very effectually to whom he gave precedence very reluctantly. He fell out with Virginia too, but seems now determined to write himself again into favour. His health has been for some years very bad, but he is now getting rather better and would be very glad to come forwards once more in political life. He is undoubtedly desirous of recommencing his career as a public man. He may probably be successful as he undoubtedly possesses & is believed to possess, considerable talents and avows opinions which are very popular in Virginia.

Your recollection of events which took place for the last twenty years is very accurate, and you replace in my memory many things which I had almost forgotten. There are not many who retain them as fresh as you do, and I am persuaded that they will soon be entirely lost. Those who follow us will know very little of the real transactions of our day, and will have very untrue impressions respecting men & things. Such is the lot of humanity.

Farewell. With warm wishes for your health & happiness, and with great and respectful esteem,

I am, dear Sir, your obedt.

J. MARSHALL.

The second letter is in answer to a very long and elaborate letter from Colonel Pickering, describing General Washington's military character and capacity as being " strikingly deficient in quick discernment and instant decision." This letter, which fills nearly thirty quarto pages, is not mentioned in Mr. Upham's " Life of Pickering "; but it seems to have been carefully copied by Pickering for publication, and prefixed to his

copy are a title page and an " Advertisement," at the close of
which he writes, referring to Judge Marshall: " I thought
that candour towards so excellent a man and my friend, as
well as a regard to my own reputation, required me to state
explicitly to Judge Marshall some principal facts on which my
opinion of Washington's military character was formed; and
also to glance at some incidents tending to show that he was
not endowed with the talents of a statesman, as I knew that
he did not possess those of a general."

Judge Marshall's letter acknowledging the receipt of this
letter is a fine model of courteous and cautious restatement of
opinion for anyone who is determined not to be drawn into
a useless controversy. Of this Pickering was fully aware,
and in a letter to Marshall written nearly a year later
he says: " The amicable tenor of your letter of the 14th
(15th) of March was highly gratifying to me," and again,
" I was happy that you took in good part my frank statement
of facts representing General Washington."

Judge Marshall writes:

Col. Timothy Pickering,   Mr. Justice Story.
    Salem,
        Massachusetts.

WASHINGTON, March 15th, 1827.

MY DEAR SIR:

I was much obliged by your favor of the 14th of Feby,
through our friend Mr. Mercer. I am always gratified at being recollected by my old friends, for I find myself incapable
of making new ones.

I have seen in the papers the discussions between my brother
Johnson and yourself respecting Count Pulaski and the battle of Germantown. It is not a little gratifying to us who are
treading close upon your heels to observe how firmly you
step & how perfectly you retain your recollection. You are a
little before me, and I find myself almost alone in the world.
With the exception of Judge Peters, yourself, and Mr. Wol-
cot, I can scarcely find any person who was conspicuous on
the great theatre of our country when I first began to mix in
public affairs. Things are very much changed as well as men.

Is it probable that you will ever travel as far south as Washington? Few things would give me so much pleasure as to

see you, but that is a pleasure which I scarcely dare promise myself. It is probable that the line which circumscribes your movements to the south will never intersect that which bounds me on the north.

You give a great many interesting anecdotes of General Washington which serve to develope his character. Your opportunities of personal observation enable you to take a near view of the man. I have seen him only at a distance. I have looked at him through those actions which were the result of mature deliberation and consultation with those to whom he gave his confidence. The conclusion to which this view of him has conducted me is extremely favourable to his judgment, his wisdom, and his virtue. If he did not possess that rapidity of decision which distinguishes many men of genius, there seems to have been a solidity in his mind which fitted him in a peculiar manner for occupying the high place he filled in the United States in the critical times in which he filled it. No feature in his character was more conspicuous than his firmness. Though prizing popular favour as highly as it ought to be prized, he never yielded principle to obtain it, or sacrificed judgment on its altar. This firmness of character added to his acknowledged virtue enabled him to stem a torrent which would have overwhelmed almost any other man, and did, I believe, save his country.

Such is my impression of Washington, an impression certainly not formed on a near view of him, but on a very attentive consideration of his character, his conduct, and his papers. You could take a closer view of him, especially as a military man, than was in my power, and have consequently better means of judging correctly than I possess.

With the best wishes for your health and happiness and with sincere and respectful esteem,

I am, dear Sir, your obedt

J. MARSHALL.

OPINIONS OF THE LATE CHIEF JUSTICE OF THE UNITED STATES, JOHN MARSHALL, CONCERNING FREE MASONRY

A gentleman in Norfolk County, Mass., supplied the following letter from the late Chief Justice of the United States to the Hon. Edward Everett on the subject of Freemasonry:

RICHMOND, July 22d, 1833.

My Dear Sir:

I have received your favor of the 16th, enclosing a printed copy of your letter respecting Masonry to Mr. Atwell, accompanied by printed copies of letters from Gen. Washington and Mr. Madison on the same subject.

Soon after entering the army I was made a Mason. In addition to the motives, which usually actuate young men, I was induced to become a candidate for admission into the society, by the assurance that the brotherly love which pervaded it and the duties imposed on its members, might be of great to me in the vicissitudes of fortune to which a soldier was exposed. After the army was disbanded, I found the order in high estimation, and every gentleman I saw in this part of Virginia was a member. I followed the crowd for a time without attaching any importance to its object, or giving myself the trouble to inquire why others did. It soon lost its attraction, and though there are several Lodges in the city of Richmond, I have not been in one of them for more than forty years, except once, on an invitation to accompany General La Fayette, nor have I been a member of one of them for more than thirty. It was impossible not to perceive the useless pageantry of the whole exhibition. My friend, Mr. Story, has communicated my opinions to you truly. I thought it, however, a harmless plaything, which would live its hour and pass away, until the murder or abstraction of Morgan was brought before the public; — that atrocious crime, and I had almost said, the still more atrocious suppression of the testimony concerning it, demonstrated the abuse, of which the oaths prescribed by the order were susceptible, and convinced me that the institution ought to be abandoned, as one capable of producing much evil, and incapable of producing any good, which might not be effected by safe and open means. I give you my sentiments without reserve, but in confidence. I have attained an age when repose becomes a primary wish. I am unwilling to embark on any tempestuous sea or to engage as a volunteer in any controversy, which may tend to excite the angry passions. I am unwilling to appear in the papers on any question, especially if it may produce excitement.

The Antimasonic controversy has not crossed the Potomac. With you it has become a party question, which a public man cannot escape, and on which a decent, manly opinion must be firmly and frankly expressed. But I am not a public man; and if I were, many and extravagant are the tests by which we try the fitness of agents for the service of our country. This has not as yet become one of them. Several of my personal friends are Masons; some few of them more zealous than myself. You will therefore pardon the unwillingness I express that any allusion to this letter should be made in the papers. Receive the assurances of the great and respectful esteem, with which I remain,

Your obedient,
J. MARSHALL.[56]

The following statement connecting Marshall with the Masonic society appears in the " Vindication of General Washington from the stigma of adherence to secret societies by Joseph Ritner, Governor of the Commonwealth of Pennsylvania, communicated by request of the House of Representatives to that body on the 8th of March, 1837, with the proceedings which took place on its reception " (Boston, printed by Ezra Lincoln) :

" The annexed pamphlet by Ex-Governor Ritner of Pennsylvania is, strange as the fact may appear, a vindication of the character of the father of his country against the charge of Freemasonry! That Washington was an initiate we do not doubt, as many other respectable individuals have been, among whom may be numbered a Marshall, a Rush, a Wirt, and others; for it has been the policy of the detestable, murderous society to seduce into their ranks the most respectable members of society, and then to bind them to the most shocking, anti-christian oaths, and under the still more shocking penalties of death, in various horrid forms, to keep the secrets of the institution, which chiefly consists, like a band of pirates and robbers, of the signs by which they may be known to each other! It is hardly necessary to add that of 100 initiates 99, though bound by their oaths to silence, have little more to do with the institution, although claimed as a member and ' brother.' Such were ' brother Washington,' ' brother Judge Marshall,' and a great number of others who have been hypo-

[56] The above letter and explanatory matter is printed in the " Freemasonry Pamphlets," Vol. III, Smithsonian Institution.

critically brought within the pale of Freemasonry. But Washington did not die without leaving to his country his warning voice against all obstructions to the execution of the laws, all combinations and associations under whatever plausible character. He might, we repeat, have been an initiate, but no freemason, as the reader of the annexed pamphlet will see. That Freemasonry 'obstructed the execution of the laws' in the trial of Masonic culprits in the western counties of New York state by false oaths and every other possible way, there is the most unequivocal evidence. 'In a word,' says the late Myron Holley, speaking of Freemasonry, 'more detestable principles cannot be imagined; they excite to crime and were intended for shelter and protection of practical iniquity!' This was literally a truth; they truly afforded shelter and protection to the murderers of William Morgan! But if, as the memorable wretches tell you, that Freemasonry is a virtuous society it is asked why females or ladies are excluded,— why insulted? Who can read the following oath of a Master Mason, having a mother, wife, or sisters, without the height of indignation. 'Furthermore [that is in addition to fifteen other oaths] do I promise and swear that I will not be at the initiating, passing, or raising of an old man in dotage, a young man in non-age, an atheist, irreligious libertine, madman, hermaphrodite, woman, or a fool.' And again, 'Furthermore do I promise and swear that I will not violate the chastity of a Master Mason's wife, mother, sister, or daughter, nor suffer it to be done by others, if in my power to prevent it, I knowing them to be such,' thus giving a Master Mason free access to every other woman in society. Such is freemasonry, and but a small part of that diabolical institution. Washington saw not only the folly but the wickedness of such oaths and consequences that might follow from an institution of such a character. And now (1841), would it be believed, an effort is making by despicable or thoughtless individuals to revive it! Let us then, one and all, frown on the base attempt; let the warning voice of the father of his country be listened to and obeyed; let not a vestige remain of the accursed institution. In a special manner, let that degrading and disgraceful silver plate, which now lies under the corner stone of the Bunker Hill Monument, be removed and the place supplied by some Patriotic Inscription."

At the fourth Antimasonic Republican Convention of Massachusetts Held at Boston, Sept. 11, 12, and 13, 1833, for the nomination of candidates for Governor and Lieutenant Governor of the Commonwealth, and " for the purpose of consulting upon the common good, by seeking redress of wrongs and grievances suffered from the secret societies," on motion of Mr. Odiorne, the Officers of the Convention were appointed to communicate to the venerable Chief Justice Marshall, of the United States Supreme Court, the fact that he is publicly held up by Freemasons and by Masonic presses as an ardent advocate of that Institution, which he is represented here as having recently declared to be " a jewel of inestimable value " ; and respectfully to inquire of him whether, as the biographer of Washington, he knows of the existence of any authentic originals or copies of letters addressed by Washington to Masonic bodies. See Freemasonry Pamphlets, Smithsonian Institution, Vol. III, p. 43.

If corroboration were required, it is furnished by the following letter from Chief Justice Marshall, in reply to one from citizens of Massachusetts inquiring of him whether or not, as biographer of Washington, he knew of the existence of any authentic originals or copies of letters addressed by Washington to Masonic bodies. The same persons also inquired whether or not the Chief Justice had declared the institution of Masonry to be " a jewel of the utmost value."

The letter follows. See Freemasonry Pamphlets, Vol. III, p. 18.

RICHMOND, October 18, 1833.

SIR,—

Your letter of the 11th, transmitting a resolution of the Antimasonic Convention of the State of Massachusetts, passed the 13th of last September, has just reached me. The flattering terms in which that resolution is expressed claim and receive my grateful acknowledgments.

The circumstances represented as attending the case of Morgan were heard with universal detestation, but produced no other excitement in this part of the United States, than is created by crimes of uncommon atrocity. Their operation on masonry, whatever it might be, was silent, rather arresting its progress and directing attention from the society, than inducing any open, direct attack upon it. The agitations which convulse the North, did not pass the Potomac. Consequently, an individual so much withdrawn from the world as myself, entering so little into the party conflicts of the day, could feel no motive, certainly I felt no inclination, to volunteer in a distant conflict, in which the wounds that might be received, would not be soothed by the consoling reflection that he suffered in the performance of a necessary duty. I never did utter the words ascribed to me, nor any other words importing the sentiment they convey. I never did say "Freemasonry is a jewel of the utmost value, that the pure in heart and life can only appreciate it fully, and that in a free government it must, it will be sustained and protected." The fact mentioned in the resolution, that I have been in a Lodge but once, so far as I can recollect, for nearly forty years, is evidence that I have no disposition to volunteer in this controversy, as the zealous partisan, which this language would indicate. In fact I have sought to abstain from it. Although I attach no importance to their opinions I may entertain respecting masonry, yet I ought not to refuse on application, to disavow any expressions which may be ascribed to me, that I never used. I have said that I always understood the oaths taken by a mason, as being subordinate to his obligations as a citizen to the laws, but have never affirmed that there was any positive good or ill in the institution itself.

The resolution also inquires "whether, as a friend and biographer of Washington, I have in my possession or recollection, any knowledge of any acts of General Washington, or any documents written by him to masonic bodies, approving of masonry."

The papers of General Washington were returned many years past to my lamented friend, his nephew, and are now, I believe, in the possession of Mr. Sparks. I do not recollect ever to have heard him utter a syllable on the subject. Such a document, however, not being of a character to make any impression at the time, may have passed my memory.   With great respect,

I am, Sir,

Your ob't servant,

To JOHN BAILEY, ESQ.   J. MARSHALL.

TO HON. JUDGE STORY

RICHMOND, November 26th, 1826.

My Dear Sir:

I have deferred thanking you for the copy of your Discourse before the Society of Phi Beta Kappa, until there was some probability that my letter might find you at Salem.

But it is time to return to your discourse. I have read it with real pleasure, and am particularly gratified with your eulogy on the ladies. It is a matter of great satisfaction to me to find another Judge, who though not as old as myself, thinks justly of the fair sex, and commits his sentiments to print. I was a little mortified, however, to find that you had not admitted the name of Miss Austen into your list of favorites. I had just finished reading her novels when I received your discourse, and was so much pleased with them that I looked in it for her name, and was rather disappointed at not finding it. Her flights are not lofty, she does not soar on eagle's wings, but she is pleasing, interesting, equable, and yet amusing. I count on your making some apology for this omission. . . .

Farewell.

With esteem and affection,

I am yours,

J. MARSHALL.[57]

TO HON. JOSEPH STORY

RICHMOND, July 31st, 1833.

My Dear Sir:

I have finished reading your great work, and wish it could be read by every statesman, and every would-be statesman in the United States. It is a comprehensive and an accurate commentary in our Constitution, formed in the spirit of the original text. In the South, we are so far gone in political metaphysics that I fear no demonstration can restore us to common sense. The word " State Rights," as expounded by the resolutions of '98 and the report of '99, construed by our legislature, has a charm against which all reasoning is vain. Those resolutions and that report constitute the creed of every

[57] The above letter is printed in the " Life and Letters of Judge Story," Vol. I, pp. 505-506.

politician, who hopes to rise in Virginia; and to question them, or even to adopt the construction given by their author, is deemed political sacrilege. The solemn and interesting admonitions of your concluding remarks will not, I fear, avail as they ought to avail against this popular frenzy.

I am grateful for the very flattering terms in which you speak of your friend in many parts of this valuable work, as well as in the dedication. In despite of my vanity, I cannot suppress the fear, that you will be supposed by others, as well as myself, to have consulted a partial friendship farther than your deliberate judgment will approve. Others may not contemplate this partiality with as much gratification as its object.

Your affectionate friend,
J. MARSHALL.[57a]

TO HON. JOSEPH STORY

RICHMOND, July 31st, 1833.

MY DEAR SIR:

I have received the third number of the " National Portrait Gallery," and know not in what terms to express my obligations to you for the more than justice you have done the character of your brother Judge. In this instance, too, all must perceive the partiality of a friend. Be assured that he, on whom that partiality is bestowed, will carry with him to the grave a deep sense of it. I am particularly gratified by the terms in which you speak of my father. If any contemporary, who knew him in the prime of manhood, survived, he would confirm all you say of him.

I have received the paper containing your opinion in the very important case of Allen V. McKean. It is impossible a subject could have been brought before you on which you are more completely au fait. It would seem as if the State legislatures (many of them, at least) have an invincible hostility to the sacredness of charters. From the paper, I should conjecture that this case will proceed no further.

Your affectionate friend,
J. MARSHALL.[58]

[57a] Story's " Life and Letters," Vol. II, pp. 135-136.
[58] The above letter is printed in Story's " Life and Letters," Vol. II, p. 150.

RICHMOND, October 6th, 1834.

MY DEAR SIR:

On my return a day or two past from an annual visit to our mountains, I had the real gratification of receiving a number of the New England Magazine for August last, containing an essay, entitled " Statesmen: their rareness and importance," forwarded to me by yourself, and thank you truly for the real pleasure afforded by its perusal.

The justness and solidity of its sentiments, the distinguished individual who is selected as an example of the real statesman, and the kind notice taken of an old friend who is under so many obligations to you, designate the author as certainly as if his name had been affixed to the work.

It is in vain to lament, that the portrait which the author has drawn of our political and party men, is, in the general, true. Lament it as we may, much as it may wound our vanity or our pride, it is still, in the main, true; and will I fear, so remain.

In the South, political prejudice is too strong to yield to any degree of merit; and the great body of the nation contains, at least appears to me to contain, too much of the same ingredient. To men who think as you and I do, the present is gloomy enough; and the future presents no cheering prospect. The struggle now maintained in every State in the Union seems to me to be of doubtful issue; but should it terminate contrary to the wishes of those who support the enormous pretensions of the Executive, should victory crown the exertions of the champions of constitutional law, what serious and lasting advantage is to be expected from his result? In the South (things may be less gloomy with you) those who support the Executive do not support the Government. They sustain the personal power of the President, but labor incessantly to impair the legitimate powers of the Government. Those who oppose the violent and rash measures of the Executive (many of them nullifiers, many of them seceders,) are generally the bitter enemies of a constitutional government. Many of them are the avowed advocates of a league; and those who do not go the whole length, go great part of the way. What can we hope for in such circumstances? As far as I can judge, the Government is weakened, whatever party may prevail.   Such is the impression I receive from the language of those around me.

Before leaving Richmond I had finished your treatise on " The Conflict of Laws," and am much pleased with it.   I was a good deal surprised at the diversity of opinion among writers on the general law of Continental Europe.   I was surprised to find that there were still more doubtful questions growing out of the civil than out of the common law.   I wonder, too, how you ever have performed so laborious a task.   You certainly love work for its own sake.

With us the natural atmosphere has been as stormy, as tempestuous, and in all respects as extraordinary as the political.   Yet, I remain in good health, and as usual,

Your faithful friend,
J. MARSHALL.[58a]

The following twenty-six letters, dealing mainly with the political and legal questions of that period, were written by Marshall to Story between the dates 1819 and 1834.   They were first published by the Massachusetts Historical Society.

THE HON'BLE JOSEPH STORY,

Salem, Massachusetts.

RICHMOND, March 24th, 1819.

DEAR SIR:

Since my return to Washington I mentioned to a very near friend who owns an extensive nail factory that I had understood that some machinery was in use in & about Boston which greatly facilitated the making of nails.   He was anxious to have some account of the machine which I was totally unable to give.

I have some idea that the subject was mentioned by you,— at any rate it was mentioned in your presence.   I understood that there were two machines, one very expensive, the other almost equally valuable & costing only about one hundred dollars.   If you have leisure will you have the goodness to mention in a letter to me what these machines are called, what is their operation, & what they cost?   You can probably say something about their advantages.

[58a] Story's "Life and Letters," Vol. II, p. 172.

Our opinion in the Bank case has roused the sleeping spirit of Virginia, if indeed it ever sleeps. It will, I understand, be attacked in the papers with some asperity, and as those who favor it never write for the publick it will remain undefended & of course be considered as damnably heretical.

Yours truly,
J. Marshall.

The Bank case mentioned is the case of McCulloch v. the State of Maryland (4 Wheaton Reports), denying the right of a state to tax the Bank of the United States.

At the foot of this letter is the following memorandum in the handwriting of Daniel Webster:

" Mr. Baldwin & Mr. May referred me to Mr. Geo. Odiorne. I have seen him; he says he will send one, all fitted for use, for 200 Dlls., altho that is below his usual price, & he would not engage to sell another at that rate. The machine can be shipped here for Richmond, on request. I believe this to be the least expensive, & is the machine which is in successful operation in various places. D. W."

The Hon'ble Joseph Story,

    Salem,
        Massachusetts.

Richmond, May 27th, 1819.

My Dear Sir:

I had the pleasure of receiving a few days past your favour of the 15th, & thank you very sincerely for the information you have given respecting the nail machines in use in your country. The information will be valuable to my friend.

I am much obliged by the alterations you have made in the opinion in the Dartmouth College case, & am highly gratified by what you say respecting it. The opinion in the Bank case continues to be denounced by the democracy in Virginia. An effort is certainly making to induce the legislature which will meet in December to take up the subject & to pass resolutions not very unlike those which were called forth by the alien and sedition laws in 1799. Whether the effort will be successful or not may perhaps depend in some measure on the sentiments of our sister states.   To excite this ferment the opinion has been grossly misrepresented; and where its argument has been truly stated it has been met by principles one would think too palpably absurd for intelligent men.   But prejudice will swallow anything.   If the principles which have been advanced on this occasion were to prevail the constitution would be converted into the old confederation.   The piece to which you allude was not published in Virginia.   Our patriotic papers admit no such political heresies.   It contained, I think, a complete demonstration of the fallacies & errors contained in those attacks on the opinion of the Court which have most credit here & are supposed to proceed from a high source, but was so mangled in the publication that those only who had bestowed close attention to the subject could understand it.   There were two numbers & the editor of the Union in Philadelphia, the paper in which it was published, had mixed the different numbers together so as in several instances to place the reasoning intended to demonstrate one proposition under another.   The points & arguments were so separated from each other, & so strangely mixed as to constitute a labyrinth to which those only who understood the whole subject perfectly could find a clue.

I wish to consult you on a case which to me who am not versed in admiralty proceedings has some difficulty.   The Little Charles was libelled for a violation of the first embargo act in 1808.   She was acquitted in the District, but condemned in the Circuit Court.   After a thousand delays a question is now before the Circuit Court as a Court of Admiralty for judgement on the bond given on the property being restored.   Several objections are made, two of which deserve consideration.

The first is that the order for restoration was made, not in court, but by the Judge out of court, not at a called court (and) second that the bond was taken by the marshal to himself & not to the U. S.   Upon this order the vessel was delivered, & this bond has been returned to court, but has not been acted on.   Nor is there any act of the Court approving the proceeding.   It is contended to be a mere act in pais not sanctioned by the court.   That it is the unauthorized act of the marshal who might release the bond or sue upon it, and that the court cannot consider it as in the place of the vessel and so act upon it.

With great regard and esteem, I am, dear Sir,

your obedt

J. MARSHALL.

THE HON'BLE JOSEPH STORY,
  Salem,
    Massachusetts.

RICHMOND, July 13th, 1819.

MY DEAR SIR:

I had the pleasure, this morning of receiving your letter of the 7th, by which I am greatly obliged. I shall at the next term decide the case of the Little Charles in conformity with your reasoning. It is, I think, perfectly sound; & were this even questionable the practice of the courts ought to be uniform.

Another admiralty question of great consequence has occurred at the last term which I would bring before the Supreme Court, if I could, but as I have not the privilege of dividing the Court when alone, & as the sum is only about 1500$, it must abide by my decision. It is, however, one of general importance, & I must ask the favor of you to give me your views of it.

A vessel belonging to the port of Richmond in Virginia was hypothecated for necessary repairs in New York & has been libelled in the District Court of this State. The District Judge condemned her, & the case is before me on an appeal. It has been agreed that New York is as much foreign to Virginia as Ireland or Guernsey to England. It has also been agreed that the power of hypothecation on simple interest is not so strictly guarded as the power of pledging the ship on bottomry for usurious interest.

From a consideration of this case I have been led to doubt what rule ought to be adopted in the United States, & to question the propriety of applying the rule in England to our situation. The foundation of the rule is that in a foreign port this exercise of ownership on the part of the master may be necessary whereas in a domestic port it cannot be presumed to be so. Now let the ports of one state be considered as foreign or domestic with respect to the vessels of another & cases may arise in which the literal application of the rule would violate its principle.   It would be absurd that a vessel belonging to Amboy should be hypothecated in New York. But the same vessel at New Orleans or in the mouth of Columbia would be completely out of the reach of the owner. The necessity for exercising this power by the master would be much stronger than in the case of a vessel belonging to one side of the bay of Passimiquoddy hypothecated in a port on the other.

I do not think a republication of the piece you mention in the Boston papers to be desired, as the antifederalism of Virginia will not, I trust, find its way to New England.   I should also be sorry to see it in Mr. Wheaton's appendix because that circumstance might lead to suspicions respecting the author & because I should regret to see it republished in its present deranged form with the two centres transposed.

I am highly gratified by the sentiments you express, & shall always feel a grateful recollection of them.   The esteem of those we esteem is among the most delightful sensations of the human heart.

I had never thought of preparing an opinion in the militia case.   That is committed to you, & cannot be in better hands. I shall just sketch my ideas for the purpose of examining them more closely, but shall not prepare a regular opinion.   As at present disposed I do not think we shall differ.

With very much esteem and regard,

I am, dear Sir, your obed

J. MARSHALL.

The Lottery case mentioned in the following letter is that of Cohens v. Virginia (6 Wheaton's Reports), in which the Court maintained its jurisdiction, even in a criminal case, to review the judgments of the State Courts on Federal questions.

Spencer Roane, a judge of the Virginia Court of Errors and a warm friend of Jefferson, attacked the Supreme Court in the *Richmond Enquirer,* under the pseudonym of Algernon Sydney,— a name that has often been adopted by writers of the press.

Mr. Justice Story,
   Salem,
      Massachusetts.

                 Richmond, June 15th, 1821.

Dear Sir:

A question has occurred in the course of this term which I have taken under advisement for the purpose of enquiring whether it has been decided by my brethren. It is this: A & B trading under the firm of A, B & Co. were indebted to the U. S. on bonds for duties. They made an assignment of all their social effects to secure certain creditors of the firm. A had private property to a considerable amount, which he afterwards conveyed to secure his individual creditors. The question is, whether the first conveyance was an act of insolvency within the act of Congress so that the priority of the U. S. attached on the social effects, or whether the act of insolvency was not committed until the execution of the second deed. The question arises on a contest between the creditors secured by the two deeds, each contending that the claim of the U. S. should be satisfied by the other. Had the second deed never been executed, would the first have amounted to an act of insolvency on the part of the firm? If the case has ever occurred in your circuit, I shall be glad to know how it has been decided. If it has never occurred, you will oblige me by stating your opinion on it if you have one.

The opinion of the Supreme Court in the Lottery case has been assaulted with a degree of virulence transcending what has appeared on any former occasion. Algernon Sidney is written by the gentleman who is so much distinguished for his feelings towards the Supreme Court, & if you have not an opportunity of seeing the Enquirer I will send it to you. There are other minor gentry who seek to curry favor & get into office by adding their mite of abuse, but I think for coarseness & malignity of invention Algernon Sidney surpasses all party writers who have ever made pretensions to any decency of character. There is on this subject no such thing as a free press in Virginia, and of consequence the calumnies and misrepresentations of this gentleman will remain uncontradicted & will by many be believed to be true. He will be supposed to be the champion of state rights, instead of being what he really is, the champion of dismemberment. With great regard and esteem,

I am, dear Sir, yours, &c.,

J. MARSHALL.

I am anxious to know whether that amendment of the constitution on which Mr. Webster & yourself were so distinguished has been approved or rejected by your sapient people.

The last part of the above letter is in reference to the part taken by Mr. Webster and Judge Story in the debates on the apportionment of the Senate and the House of Representatives. The people rejected the amendment when it was submitted to them.

The letter commented on by Judge Marshall in the following letter is very likely the one to William C. Jarvis, printed in Washington's edition of the " Writings of Thomas Jefferson," Vol. VII, pp. 177–179, in which Jefferson denies the right of the judges to issue a mandamus to any " executive or legislative officer to enforce the fulfillment of their official duties," and asserts that it is a " very dangerous doctrine " " to consider the judges as the ultimate arbiters of all constitutional questions."

At the end of the next to the last paragraph there is this sentence, " The case of the mandamus may be the cloak, but the batture is recollected with still more resentment." The first part of this sentence refers to the opinion of the Chief Justice in the case of Marbury v. Madison, 1 Cranch, 153. The second part refers to the protracted litigation which involved the title to what was known as the batture, near New Orleans, in which Mr. Jefferson took a strong personal interest. The copy of the debates he asks for are the Debates in the Massachusetts Convention, which were published in 1821, from the reports of the " *Boston Daily Advertiser,*" and which were reprinted in 1853.

THE HON'BLE MR. JUSTICE STORY,
    Salem,
            Massachusetts.   RICHMOND, July 13th, 1821.
MY DEAR SIR:
    I had yesterday the pleasure of receiving your letter of the

27th of June, by which I am greatly obliged. I shall decide the case concerning which I enquired in conformity with your opinion. The law of the case I have thought very doubtful; the equity of it is, I think, pretty clear.

Your kind expression respecting myself gratify me very much. Entertaining the truest affection & esteem for my brethren generally, & for yourself particularly, it is extremely grateful to believe that it is reciprocated. The harmony of the bench will, I hope & pray, never be disturbed. We have external and political enemies enough to preserve internal peace.

What you say of Mr. Jefferson's letter rather grieves than surprises me. It grieves me because his influence is still so great that many, very many, will adopt his opinions, however unsound they may be, & however contradictory to their own reason. I cannot describe the surprize & mortification I have felt at hearing that Mr. Madison has embraced them with respect to the judicial department.

For Mr. Jefferson's opinion as respects this department it is not difficult to assign the cause. He is among the most ambitious, & I suspect among the most forgiving of men. His great power is over the mass of the people, & this power is chiefly acquired by professions of democracy. Every check on the wild impulse of the moment is a check on his own power, & he is unfriendly to the source from which it flows. He looks of course with ill-will at an independent judiciary.

That in a free country with a written constitution any intelligent man should wish a dependent judiciary, or should think that the constitution is not a law for the court as well as the legislature would astonish me, if I had not learnt from observation that with many men the judgement is completely controlled by the passions. The case of the mandamus may be the cloak, but the batture is recollected with still more resentment.

I send you the papers containing the essays of Algernon Sydney. Their coarseness & malignity would designate the author if he was not avowed. The argument, if it may be called one, is, I think, as weak as its language is violent and prolix. Two other gentlemen have appeared in the papers on this subject; one of them is deeply concerned in pillaging the purchasers of the Fairfax estate, in which goodly work he fears no other obstruction than what arises from the appelate power of the Supreme Court, & the other is a hunter after office who hopes by his violent hostility to the Union, which in Virginia assumes the name of regard for state rights, & by his devotion to Algernon Sydney, to obtain one. In support of the sound principles of the constitution & of the Union of the States, not a pen is drawn. In Virginia the tendency of things verges rapidly to the destruction of the government & the re-establishment of a league of sovereign states. I look elsewhere for safety.

> With very much esteem & affection,
>> I am, dear Sir, your
>>> J. MARSHALL.

I will thank you for the copy of the debates.

The Mr. Hall mentioned in the following letter was Mr. John E. Hall, editor of a law journal published in the city of Philadelphia. From 1808 to 1817 he published " The American Law Journal." In 1821 he published one volume of " The Journal of Jurisprudence," which was intended to be a continuation of the former periodical, but no more volumes were published. The article referred to in this letter, against the Supreme Court, is not printed in this journal. The address which Mr. Story made to the Suffolk Bar was not printed until 1829, when it was printed in the " American Jurist."

You will notice the reference Judge Marshall makes in this letter to his greatest enemy, Thomas Jefferson. Judge Marshall was almost certain that Mr. Jefferson was back of the whole movement. What they really meant to do was to oust Judge Marshall; all the evidence available at present seems to substantiate this.

THE HON'BLE MR. JUSTICE STORY,
    Salem,
        Massachusetts.

> RICHMOND, Septr 18th, 1821.

MY DEAR SIR:

I had yesterday the pleasure of receiving your favor of the 9th. I thank you for your quintal of fish, & shall try my possibles to observe your instructions in the cooking department.

I hope to succeed, but be this as it may I promise to feed on the fish with an appetite which would not disgrace a genuine descendent of one of the Pilgrims.

I am a little surprized at the request which you say has been made to Mr. Hall, although there is no reason for my being so.   The settled hostility of the gentleman who has made that request to the judicial department will show itself in that & in every other form which he believes will conduce to its object.   For this he has several motives, & it is not among the weakest that the department would never lend itself as a tool to work for his political power.   The Batture will never be forgotten.   Indeed there is some reason to believe that the essays written against the Supreme Court were, in a degree at least, stimulated by this gentleman, and that although the coarseness of the language belongs exclusively to the author, its acerbity has been increased by his communications with the great Lama of the mountains.   He may therefore feel himself in some measure required to obtain its republication in some place of distinction.   But what does Mr. Hall purpose to do?   I do not suppose you would willingly interfere so as to prevent his making the publication, although I really think it is in form & substance totally unfit to be placed in his law journal.   I really think a proper reply to the request would be to say that no objection existed to the publications of any law argument against the opinion of the Supreme Court, but that the coarseness of its language, its personal & official abuse, & its tedious prolixity constituted objections to the insertion of Algernon Sydney which were insuperable.   If, however, Mr. Hall determines to comply with this request, I think he ought, unless he means to make himself a party militant, to say that he published that piece by particular request, & ought to subjoin the masterly answer of Mr. Wheaton.   I shall wish to know what course Mr. Hall will pursue.

I have not yet received the debates in your convention.   Mr. Caldwell I presume has not met with an opportunity to send the volume.   I shall read it with much pleasure.

I have seen a sketch of your address to the Suffolk bar, & shall be very glad to have it at large.   I have no doubt of being much gratified by the manner in which the subjects you mention are treated.

A deep sign to convert our government into a mere league

of states has taken a strong hold of a powerful & violent party in Virginia. The attack upon the judiciary is in fact an attack upon the union. The judicial department is well understood to be that through which the government may be attacked most successfully, because it is without patronage, & of course without power. And it is equally well understood that every subtraction from its jurisdiction is a vital wound to the government itself. The attack upon it, therefore, is a masked battery aimed at the government itself. The whole attack, if not originating with Mr. Jefferson, is obviously approved & guided by him. It is, therefore, formidable in other states as well as in this, & it behooves the friends of the union to be more on the alert than they have been. An effort will certainly be made to repeal the 25th sec. of the judicial.

I have a case before me which cannot be carried up to the Supreme Court & which presents difficulties which appear to me to be considerable. It is an action of debt brought by the U. S. for a forfeiture incurred by rescuing some distilled spirits which had not been proceeded on by the distiller according to law.

The declaration charges in the alternative that the defendants, or one of them, rescued or caused to be rescued, &c.

It is clear enough that this would be ill in an indictment or information, but I am inclined to think it is cured by our statute of jeofails. The defendants insist that this statute does not apply to suits brought by the U. S., but I think it does.

Another difficulty has puzzled me so much that I have taken the case under advisement with the intention of consulting some of my more experienced brethren.

The difficulty is this. At the trial the rescue was proved only by two depositions. Each contains the following expressions, " On Novr 17th, 1815, agreeable to written & verbal instructions from Mr. William McKinley, collector," &c.

The defendants demurred to the testimony & the District Court gave judgement for the plaintiffs.

It is contended, 1st, That there is no sufficient evidence that McKinley is collecter. His commission ought to be produced & its absence cannot be supplied, but there is not even a direct averment that he is collector. 2d, The written instructions of the collector ought to be produced to show that the seizure was made under his authority.

You are accustomed to these cases. Will you aid me with your advice?

Yours truely & sincerely,

J. MARSHALL.

THE HON'BLE MR. JUSTICE STORY,
   Salem,
      Massachusetts.

RICHMOND, July 2d, 1823.

MY DEAR SIR:

I had the pleasure a few days past of receiving your letter of the 22d of June & am greatly obliged by your friendly attention to my son. I am sorry that he misunderstood me so far as to request an advance of money from you when you could not have funds of mine in your hands. I gave him what I hoped would be sufficient for all his purposes until he should enter college, but told him, should I be mistaken respecting the amount of his expenditures, to apply to you. I did not suspect that his application would be made till the month of August.

The case concerning the securities of the cashier of the Bank goes to the Supreme Court & will probably be reversed. I suppose so, because I conjecture that the practice of banks has not conformed to my construction of the law. The Judge, however, who draws the opinion must have more ingenuity than I have, if he draws a good one.

The main question respects the validity of the bond on which the suit was instituted. It was signed at different times and left in possession of the cashier, certainly, I suppose, in the expectation that he would forward it to the proper place. The plea of non est factum was put in among other pleas & the plaintiff proved the signature of the obligors & relied on the possession of the bond & the suit on it as evidence to be left to the jury of its delivery & acceptance.

The cause was argued with very great ability, and it was contended that this would not be sufficient in any case, but if in general, not in this case.

I held very clearly that in the case of an individual obligee the evidence would authorize the jury to infer delivery, but not in the case of the Bank of the United States.

The incorporating act requires that befo:e the cashier shall be permitted to enter on the duties of his office he shall give bond with security to be approved by the board of Directors for the faithful performance of its duties. I had no doubt that the suit upon the bond was evidence of its acceptance & consequently of its being approved, if that fact could be established by parol evidence, but I was of opinion that it could not be so established. The board of Directors, I thought, could only speak by their record. They cannot speak or act as individuals speak or act. They speak & act by their minutes. Their approbation & acceptance of the bond could not be expressed otherwise than officially on their minutes, & no other evidence than the minutes could establish the fact. I therefore did not permit the bond to go to the jury.

The question was entirely new, & I was at first rather in favor of the plaintiffs. But in so lax a manner was this business conducted as to show very clearly that the cashier was in the full performance of his duty before the bond was executed, & to leave it very doubtful whether the breaches assigned were not committed before the bond passed out of the possession of the cashier. There was reason to believe that it had never been seen by the Board of Directors till he was removed from office, if then. It was impossible not to foresee that if the bond went to the jury questions would immediately arise on the time of its commencing obligation. The date could not be the guide, because it was not executed at its date. If the time when it was signed by the last obligor should be insisted on, it was obvious that it had not then been seen or approved by the Directors, nor was it accepted by them. The delivery, therefore, could not be complete. If the time when it came to the possession of the Directors were to be taken, it probably never came to their possession. These difficulties produced a close examination of the point, the result of which was a perfect conviction that the minutes of the Board could alone prove the acceptance of the bond. I did not doubt that the board of Philadelphia might have authorized the board of Richmond to accept the bond, but such authority ought to appear by the minutes of the board at Philadelphia.

I shall bow with respect to the judgement of reversal, but till it is given I shall retain the opinion I have expressed.
With great & affectionate esteem, I am your

J. MARSHALL.

You alarm me respecting the successor of our much lamented friend. I too had heard a rumour which I hoped was impossible. Our Presidents, I fear, will never again seek to make our department respectable.

The case mentioned at the end of the above letter is that of the Bank of the United States v. Dandridge (12 Wheaton's Reports). As he anticipated in the letter, the opinion of Judge Marshall was reversed. He gave this opinion when he was sitting as Circuit Judge. The opinion of the majority of the Court was given by Judge Story, while Chief Justice Marshall gave a much longer dissenting opinion.

The much lamented friend mentioned was Brockholst Livingstone, one of the Associate Justices of the Supreme Court. He died March 11, 1823, and was succeeded by Smith Thompson.

The correspondence mentioned in the following letter, the publication of which was so extremely regretted, was the " Correspondence between the Hon. John Adams, late President of the United States, and the late Wm. Cunningham, Esq., beginning in 1803 and ending in 1812," published in 1823 by E. M. Cunningham, Esq.

THE HON'BLE MR. JUSTICE STORY,
    Salem, Massachusetts.

RICHMOND, Decr 9th, 1823.

MY DEAR SIR:

I had the pleasure yesterday of receiving your letter of the 24th ultimo & congratulate you on passing through your circuit in such good health & spirits. Our brother Washington was so unwell as to be under the necessity of adjourning the court at Philadelphia without going through the docket. I am still engaged at this place in a sort of dilatory way, doing very little, and still having something to do. A case was argued yesterday which I would send to the Supreme Court if I could, but I cannot. The Pilot, an American vessel, was captured by pirates & converted into a piratical cruiser. She was then recaptured by one of our squadron under Commodore Porter after a sharp action. She was brought into Norfolk, libelled as prize, & claimed by the original owner. The attorney for the captors abandoned the claim as prize, and asked salvage. This claim was resisted on the ground that the capture was not within the act of 1800, because that applies only to recaptures from an enemy of the United States, not to recaptures from a pirate. It was insisted too that the act of 1819 does not give salvage for a recapture made by a national ship, because although an American vessel recaptured by a merchantman or private vessel is to be brought in, yet such vessel recaptured by a national ship is not to be brought in. As there is no salvage given by statute, the claim, it was said, must rest upon general law. It was admitted that according to that law salvage is due for a vessel recaptured by a private ship, but not for a vessel recaptured by a national ship, because the nation owes protection to all its people, and it is a part of the duty of the national force to afford this protection. In the present case it was one of the objects of the expedition. It was said that the general dicta that salvage is due for recaptures made from pirates must be limited to such as are made by private ships or by the public ships of some other nation than that of the recaptured vessel.

The counsel for the recaptors relied chiefly on the general principle that by the law of nations, or by the general maritime law, salvage is due for all vessels recaptured from pirates.

The District Judge gave salvage, & the owners have appealed. I do not know that the question has ever arisen in any of the courts of the United States. Perhaps your information may be more extensive, and I will thank you to give it to me. If the case has not been decided you will greatly oblige me by your sentiments on it, as I know that you are more au fait on these questions than I am. The sooner I hear from you, provided you are satisfied in the case, the better.

I have read the correspondence to which you refer and regret its publication extremely. I feel great respect for Mr. Adams, and shall always feel it whatever he may do. The extreme bitterness with which he speaks of honourable men who were once his friends is calculated to mortify and pain those who remain attached to him.   A comparison of the language he applies to gentlemen of high character in Massachusetts with that which in the early part of the correspondence he applied to those who were always his enemies and gross calumniators, who cannot even now treat him with decency, inspires serious reflections.   We can only say, non est qualis erat.

I think I can guess, although not born north of the Hudson, what you hint at respecting the Presidential election; but I shall be as careful not to commit my guess as you are respecting your scheme.

Farewell.   Providence, I hope, will continue to take care of us.   With affectionate esteem,

I am, dear Sir, your obedt
J. MARSHALL.

The portrait mentioned at the beginning of the following letter is now hanging in Memorial Hall in the dining-room of Harvard College, at Cambridge, Mass.   This portrait was given by Judge Story's will to the President and Fellows of Harvard College.

Appleton's "Cyclopaedia of American Biography" states (Vol. II, p. 757) that Horatio Greenough made a marble bust of Judge Marshall; and in a letter to his brother Henry, dated February 28, 1828, he writes: "I had this morning the first sitting from Chief Justice Marshall.   Judge Story says that anyone would recognize my sketch; that it is capital." See "Letters of Horatio Greenough to his brother Henry Greenough," p. 31.

THE HON'BLE MR. JUSTICE STORY,
    Salem, Massachusetts.

RICHMOND, March 26, 1828.

MY DEAR SIR:

I beg you to accept my portrait for which I sat in Washington to Mr. Harding, to be preserved when I shall sleep with my fathers, as a testimonial of sincere and affectionate friendship. The remaining hundred dollars you will be so good as to pay to Mr. Harding for the head and shoulders I have bespoke for myself.   I shall not wish the portrait designed for myself to be sent to Richmond till I give directions for it to be accompanied by the head Mr. Greenough means to cast for me. You will very much oblige me by letting me know when those castings are accomplished what is the price at which he sells them, because if they should be held higher than I think my head worth I may probably order more than of them.   I hope Mrs. Story & yourself have had a pleasant journey & have found your little family in perfect health.   I congratulate you both on this anticipated happiness.   I had a pleasant sail through a smooth sea to Norfolk & thence to Richmond.   I have seen scarcely any person out of my own family since my return, but, if I may credit appearances, there is rather a more stormy and disturbed atmosphere on land than I encountered in the Bay.   The spirit of party is understood to be more bitter than I could have supposed possible.   I am, however, on the wing for my friends in the upper country, where I shall find near and dear friends occupied more with their farms than with party politics.

I had one of your fish dressed yesterday, and found it excellent.

I am, dear Sir, with real regard and esteem,
Your obedt
J. Marshall.

I had nearly forgotten to say that I received to-day under cover from Mr. Webster Mr. McGruder's letter announcing the loss of my surtout.   I thank you for the trouble you have taken as much as if it had terminated more successfully.

Once more farewell.
Your

J. M.

The Hon'ble Mr. Justice Story,
     Salem, Massachusetts.

Richmond, May 1st, 1828.

My dear Sir:

Yesterday on my return from a visit to my sons in our upper country I had the pleasure of receiving your very friendly letter of the 10th of April.   The kind partiality you have always manifested towards me has been ever most grateful to my heart.   No gratification is more pure or more exalted than the regard of those we esteem.   I received at the same time a letter from Mr Harding dated the 6th of April informing that he should leave Washington within a fortnight from that day, and requesting me to direct the disposition he should make of the portrait I had requested him to draw for my use. As he had left Washington ten days before his letter reached me I could give no directions on the subject and have not written to him. I presume he is in Boston. Will you have the goodnes to let him know that his letter was not answered because it was not received, & that I will thank him if he has left the portrait in Washington to let me know with whom it remains, and if it is with him to deliver it to you? I shall rely on you to give it house room till the representation of the Court in costume is prepared when I must make arrangements to have both, together with the head in plaister, conveyed to this place. I believe I said something to you on this subject in my last letter.

I was a good deal provoked at the publication in the Marylander, not because I have any objection to its being known that my private judgement is in favor of the re-election of Mr Adams, but because I have great objections to being represented in the character of a furious partisan. Intemperate language does not become my age or office, and is foreign from my disposition and habits. I was therefore not a little vexed at a publication which represented me as using language which could be uttered only by an angry party man. As I knew I had never conversed on the subject except confidentially with friends I was persuaded that the communication to the printer could not have been direct, and that it had been a good deal metamorphosed in its journey to him. On my late visit to the upper country I was informed that this was the fact. One of my nephews for whom I feel great regard and who was on the Adams convention was asked in Baltimore by a gentleman of that place if he knew my opinion respecting the candidates for the Presidency. On his answering that I seldom mentioned the subject, but that he had heard me say that though I had not voted for upwards of twenty years I should probably vote at the ensuing election, the gentleman observed that he supposed I should consider the election of Jackson as a virtual dissolution of the government. The observation was received with a smile & some light expression of its extravagance, and upon the strength of this circumstance a communication was made which produced the publication in the Mary-lander. On seeing it my nephew wrote to a friend in Balti-more requesting him to enquire whether it was made on the strength of his communication, and if it was, enclosing a pub-lication denying that he had ever authorized it or had ever heard me use such language as had been ascribed to me. The editor of the Marylander was in a situation when the letter was received to prevent the enquiry which was directed, and his death has put an end to that part of the business. My nephew stated the affair to me while in the mountain country, and was too much chagrined for me to add to his mortification by blaming him. I must bear that newspaper scurrility which I had hoped to escape, and which is generally reserved for more important personages than myself. It is some consolation that it does not wound me very deeply.

I am glad to hear that Mrs Story and yourself had a pros-perous journey homeward. The epidemic you mention has prevailed extensively in Richmond, and has in some instances been fatal. I am happy to hear that it has not been so in your family.

You will soon be on your spring circuit, if (not) already engaged on it. I wish you a pleasant [torn], and am, with affection and esteem,

Your
J. Marshall.

The Hon'ble Mr. Justice Story,
    Salem, Massachusetts.

Richmond, Oct. 29th, 1828.

My dear Sir:

I have just finished the perusal of your centennial discourse on the first settlement of Salem, and while fresh under its influence take up my pen to thank you for the pleasure it has given me. You have drawn a vivid picture, and, I believe, a faithful likeness of those extraordinary men who first peopled New England, and my feelings as well as my judgement have accompanied you in your rapid sketch of the character and conduct of their descendants. I wish the admonitory part may have its full effect on others as well as on those to whom it was particularly addressed. Some of our southern friends might benefit from the lesson it inculcates.

But I have been still more touched with your notice of the red man than of the white.   The conduct of our forefathers in expelling the original occupants of the soil grew out of so many mixed motives that any censure which philanthropy may bestow upon it ought to be qualified.   The Indians were a fierce and dangerous enemy whose love of war made them sometimes the aggressors, whose numbers and habits made them formidable, and whose cruel system of warfare seemed to justify every endeavour to remove them to a distance from civilized settlements.   It was not until after the adoption of our present government that respect for our own safety permitted us to give full indulgence to those principles of humanity and justice which ought always to govern our conduct towards the aborigines when this course can be pursued without exposing ourselves to the most afflicting calamities.   That time, however, is unquestionably arrived, and every oppression now exercised on a helpless people depending on our magnanimity and justice for the preservation of their existence impresses a deep stain on the American character.   I often think with indignation on our disreputable conduct (as I think) in the affair of the Creeks of Georgia; and I look with some alarm on the course now pursuing in the Northwest.   Your observations on this subject are eloquent and in perfect accordance with my feelings.   But I turn with most pleasure to that fine passage respecting the Lady Arabella Johnson.   I almost envy the occasion her sufferings and premature death have furnished for bestowing that well merited eulogy on a sex which so far surpasses ours in all the amiable and attractive virtues of the heart,— in all those qualities which make up the sum of human happiness and transform the domestic fireside into an elysium.   I read the passage to my wife, who expressed such animated approbation of it as almost to excite fears for that exclusive admiration which husbands claim as their peculiar privilege.   Present my compliments to Mrs Story and say for me that a lady receives the highest compliment her husband can pay her when he expresses an exalted opinion of the sex, because the world will believe that it is formed on the model he sees at home.

I have read with much interest the character you have drawn of our deceased friend and brother, the lamented Judge Trimble.   Most richly did he merit all you have said of him.

His place, I fear, cannot be completely supplied. I was desirous of having the character republished in our papers, but was restrained by the flattering introduction of my name. My modesty was alarmed by the apprehension that the request for its publication might be ascribed as much to vanity as to my deep feeling for departed worth.

Most cordially do I congratulate you on the appointment of our friend Hopkinson.

With affectionate esteem, I am, dear Sir,

Your

J. MARSHALL.

Robert Trimble, of Kentucky, who is mentioned at the end of the above letter, was appointed one of the Justices of the Supreme Court May 9, 1826, and died August 25, 1828. Judge Story's sketch of his character was printed in the *Columbian Sentinel* of September 17. See Story's "Life and Letters of Joseph Story," Vol. I, pp. 541-543.

Joseph Hopkinson, also mentioned at the end of the letter, was appointed in 1828 by President J. Q. Adams, Judge of the District Court for the Eastern District of Pennsylvania, and held the office until his death in January, 1842.

THE HON'BLE MR. JUSTICE STORY,
Salem, Massachusetts.

RICHMOND, June 11th, 1829.

MY DEAR SIR:

I had the pleasure some time past of receiving your letter inclosing a copy of that which transmitted a copy of his commission to our friend Judge Hopkinson. I am the more gratified by the flattering terms of the letter when I recollect by whom the copy was taken. I am sure you told her in my name by anticipation how much I was delighted by such a letter copied by such a hand.

I am almost ashamed of my weakness and irresolution when I tell you that I am a member of our convention. I was in earnest when I told you that I would not come into that body, and really believed that I should adhere to that determination; but I have acted like a girl addressed by a gentleman she does not positively dislike, but is unwilling to marry. She is sure to yield to the advice and persuasion of her friends.

I wrote from Washington signifying my wish not to be brought forward, and desiring that the attention of the district might be directed to some other person, but the letter was mentioned to a very few, and those few advised that it should not be communicated, but that I should remain free to act on my return as my judgement might direct.

The committee appointed at this place to nominate had written to me at Washington, but the letter reached that place the day of my departure or the day afterwards, and of course was not received. A duplicate was transmitted to me a few days after my arrival in Richmond, which I answered immediately, acknowledging my grateful sense of the favorable opinion which had led to my nomination, but declaring my unwillingness to become a member of the convention, and declining the honour intended me. The committee would not act upon this letter; but in the meantime it was rumoured in the town that I declined being voted for, in consequence of which I was pressed so earnestly on the subject by friends whose opinions I greatly value that my resolution began to stagger. It was said that whether I took any part in the debate or not, my services were counted on as of real importance. The committee addressed a second letter to me containing assurances of their anxious desire that I would reconsider the resolution I had formed, and assent to what they were certain was the general wish of the district. As is usual I yielded and gave a reluctant consent to serve if I should be elected. Such is the history of the business. I assure you I regret being a member, and could I have obeyed the dictates of my own judgement I should not have been one. I am conscious that I cannot perform a part I should wish to take in a popular assembly; but I am like Molière's Medecin malgré lui.

The body will contain a great deal of eloquence as well as talent, and yet will do, I fear, much harm with some good. Our freehold suffrage is, I believe, gone past redemption. It is impossible to resist the influence, I had almost said contagion of universal example.

With great esteem and affection,

I am, my dear Sir, your obedt

J. MARSHALL.

The convention referred to in this letter was the convention for revising the Constitution of Virginia.

THE HON'BLE MR. JUSTICE STORY,
        Salem, Massachusetts.
                        RICHMOND, July 3d, 1829.

MY DEAR SIR:

Your favor of the 23d of June accompanying Mr. Brazer's discourse at the interment of Doctor Holyoke, and your very interesting address to the bar of Suffolk at their anniversary on the 4th of Septr, 1821, reached me a few days past. It is impossible to read the first without strong impressions of the worth both of Doctor Holyoke and Mr. Brazer.

Your address was of course read with pleasure and attention. It takes, as is your custom, a very comprehensive view of the subject, of the law and of the distinguished persons who have adorned it. It presents strong incentives to exertion.

Directly after writing my last letter I saw your appointment to the Dane Professorship, and anticipated your acceptance of it. The situation imposes duties which I am sure you will discharge in a manner useful to others and conducive to your own fame. I did not, however, anticipate that the labour would immediately press so heavily on you as your letter indicates. Four octavo volumes in five years is a heavy requisition on a gentleman whose time is occupied by duties which cannot be neglected. I am confident that no person is more equal to the task than yourself, but I cannot help thinking that the publication may be postponed to advantage. I presume the work will be in the form of lectures, and I suspect you will find it advisable to postpone the publication of them till they have been revised for a second course. Precipitation ought carefully to be avoided. This is a subject on which I am not without experience.

I hope your attention has been turned to the two great cases we have under advisement. I wish you would place your thoughts upon paper. I am the more anxious about this as I have myself not considered them, and fear that I shall be prevented from bestowing on them the attention they ought to receive. Mr. Thompson, I presume, will look thoroughly into that from New York and be prepared in it, but if the majority of the Court should not concur with him it will be necessary that preparation should be made for such an event.

We shall have a good deal of division and a good deal of

heat, I fear, in our convention. The freehold principle will, I believe, be lost. It will, however be supported with zeal. If that zeal could be successful I should not regret it. If we find that a decided majority is against retaining it I should prefer making a compromise by which a substantial property qualification may be preserved in exchange for it. I fear the excessive [torn] cident to victory after a hard fought battle continued to the last extremity may lead to universal suffrage or something very near it. What is the prop[erty] qualification for your Senate? How are your Senators apportioned on the State? And how does your system work?

The question whether white population alone, or white population compounded with taxation, shall form the basis of representation will excite perhaps more interest than even the freehold suffrage. I wish we were well through the difficulty.

Farewell. I am, my dear Sir, affectionately & truely

Your

J. MARSHALL.

THE HON'BLE MR. JUSTICE STORY,
Cambridge, Massachusetts.

RICHMOND, Septr 30th, 1829.

MY DEAR SIR:

I have read with great pleasure your discourse pronounced as Dane Professor of Law in Harvard University. It is in your best style of composition.

You have marked out for yourself a course of labour which is sufficiently arduous; but I believe you love to struggle with difficulty, and you have generally the good fortune or merit to overcome it. At seventy-four you will find indolence creeping over you. But we will not anticipate the evil.

You have not spared the students of law more than the Professor. You have prescribed for them a most appalling course. Our southern youths would stumble at the threshold, and think such a task too formidable for even a commencement. You Yankees have more perseverance, or think more justly on the proposition that he who attempts much may accomplish something valuable, should his success not be complete.

I hope I shall live to read your lectures. They will form an exception to the plan of life I had formed for myself to be adopted after my retirement from office, that is to read nothing but novels and poetry.

Our convention approaches. I still feel vain regrets at being a member. The chief though not the only cause of these regrets is that non sum qualis eram. I can no longer debate. Yet I cannot apply my mind to any thing else.

Farewell,— with affectionate esteem I remain your

J. MARSHALL.

THE HON'BLE MR. JUSTICE STORY,
    Cambridge, Massachusetts.

RICHMOND, October 15th, 1830.

MY DEAR SIR:

Ascribe my delay in thanking you for the sermon drawing the character of your late Chief Justice, and for the excellent addendum you have made to it, to the indolence and negligence of age, or to any cause rather than to indifference to any mark of your kind recollection. I have read both with attention and with real gratification. I had formed a high opinion of the late Chief Justice Parker from what I had heard of him, especially from yourself, but that opinion was certainly raised by the more minute detail of his qualities and by the abridged biography contained in the work for which I am thanking you. My regret for the loss of this estimable gentleman was much enhanced by the fear that Massachusetts might be able to supply his place by seducing from the Federal bench a gentleman whose loss would be irreparable. I felicitate myself and my country on the disappointment of this apprehension.

While I am acknowledging favors I thank you also for a box of fish received the other day. I have not yet tasted them, but have no doubt of their excellence, and shall not be long in putting it to the test.

I find our brother McClean could not acquiesce in the decision of the Court in the Missouri case. I am sorry for this, and am sorry too to observe his sentiments on the 25th sec. of the judicial act. I have read in the last volume of Mr Peters the three dissenting opinions delivered in that case, and think it requires no prophet to predict that the 25th section is to be repealed, or to use a more fashionable phrase, to be nullified by the Supreme Court of the United States. I hope the case in which this is to be accomplished will not occur during my time, but accomplished it will be at no very distant period.

I am mortified at the number of causes left undecided at the last term. I am still more mortified at the circumstance that I am unable to prepare opinions in them. The cases of Soulard and of Smith I suppose must wait for additional information or for the certainty that none is to be obtained, but I had hoped to prepare something in the lottery case. I am chagrined at discovering that I have left the statement of the case behind me. It is also cause of real surprise as well as chagrin to find that the case of Cathcart and Robertson was not decided. I really thought the Court had made up an opinion on it.

I have read with peculiar pleasure the letter of Mr. Madison to the editor of the North American Review. He is himself again. He avows the opinions of his best days, and must be pardoned for his oblique insinuations that some of the opinions of our Court are not approved. Contrast this delicate hint with the language Mr. Jefferson has applied to us. He is attacked with some bitterness by our Enquirer, who has arrayed his report of 1799 against his letter. I never thought that report could be completely defended; but Mr. Madison has placed it upon its best ground, that the language is incautious, but is intended to be confined to a mere declaration of opinion, or is intended to refer to that ultimate right which all admit, to resist despotism, a right not exercised under a constitution, but in opposition to it.

Farewell,— with the best wishes for your happiness,
I am yours affectionately.

J. MARSHALL.

The sermon mentioned in the above letter is a sermon on the decease of Chief Justice Isaac Parker by John Gorman Palfrey. Appended to it is "a sketch of Judge Parker's character as an advocate and lawyer," "by an eminent Judge of the Supreme Court of the United States."

The "brother McLean" mentioned was John McLean who became an Associate Justice of the Supreme Court in January, 1830. The case here referred to was Craig v. Missouri (4 Peters, 410), in which for the first time the Court considered what was meant by the prohibition on the States to emit bills of credit. The subject was closely connected with the validity of the issues of the State banks.   The views of Judge McLean finally prevailed.

The letter written by Mr. Madison to the Editor of the *North American Review*, is printed in the *North American Review* for October, 1830, at the end of Mr. Everett's article on the debate in the Senate of the United States on Mr. Foot's resolution.

In the following letter mention is made of "boarding the Judges." During this period the Justices of the Supreme Court were not accompanied by their families when they went to Washington, but had rooms together in some private boarding-house, presumably for the greater convenience it afforded for consultation and discussion of their problems.

The "copy of Algernon Sydney" refers most likely to "The Letters of Algernon Sydney, in defense of Civil Liberty and against the Encroachments of Military Despotism," which were written by Benjamin Watkins Leigh, and were first printed in the *Richmond Enquirer* in 1818-1819. Afterward they were published in 1830, in an octavo pamphlet.

THE HON'BLE MR. JUSTICE STORY,
    Cambridge near Boston.
                    RICHMOND, May 3d, 1831.

MY DEAR SIR:

By the schooner King I send you a barrel containing a few hams which are to be deposited for you with Fisher and Power of Boston.   As the address is marked on the cask I hope they will reach you in safety, and will be found reasonably well flavoured.

What do the wise men in the East say to the tabula rosa which is made in the cabinet?   Our quid nuncs were astonished at first, but soon discovered that the really voluntary resignations were proofs of unparallelled magnanimity and patriotism, and that those which were compulsory were quite comme il faut. This is not only as it should be, but as it always will be.

I am apprehensive that the revolutionary spirit which displayed itself in our circle will, like most other revolutions, work inconvenience and mischief in its progress.   I believe Mr Brown does not count on boarding the Judges next winter; and if any other arrangement is made 'tis entirely unknown to me.

We have like most other unquiet men, disconted with the things that are, discarded accommodations which are reasonably convenient without providing a substitute.   We pull down without enquiring how we are to build up.   The matter rests I understand with our younger brother, and he has probably committed it to some other person.   If he had made an arrangement we should I presume, have heard something about it.   I think this is a matter of some importance, for if the Judges scatter ad libitum the docket, I fear, will remain quite compact, losing very few of its causes; and the few it may lose will probably be carried off by seriatim opinions.   Old men, however, are timid, and I hope my fears may be unfounded.

I sent you some time past a copy of Algernon Sydney.   It is rather antediluvian, but you expressed a wish to see it.   The writer is among our ablest men.   Most of his friends have been classed among the Jacksonians, but I think their hostility to Mr. Adams rather than their affection for General Jackson has arranged them under his banners.

The world has been so convulsed by peace that I suspect it must have war in order to be made quiet.   Materials in abundance have been prepared for a general conflagration, and unless the mass of debts operates as an extinguisher I perceive nothing which can prevent the spread of the flame.   I am quite in amaze at the reform in Great Britain, and can come to only one conclusion, which is that I know nothing about it, and can form no opinion at all satisfactory even to myself.   The great teacher, experience, can alone inform us what is best for ourselves and for the world.

I presume you are engaged on your new circuit.   I set out the last of this week.

Farewell, with every wish for your happiness, I am yours truely.

J. MARSHALL.

The Hon'ble Mr. Justice Story,
    Cambridge, Massachusetts.

RICHMOND, June 26th, 1831.

My dear Sir:

I have received your two letters of the 25th & 31st of May and have adopted your opinion respecting the admiralty jurisdiction, though in doing so I have reversed the decree of my

brother Barbour.   I felt some doubt whether General Smith
was not shaken by the case of Ramsay v. Allyne, in which the
court supposed that the note certainly ousted the admiralty of
its jurisdiction, without deciding whether independent of the
note jurisdiction would have existed.   I think there is a good
deal of force in the argument of Wirt and Meredith that the
original cause of action did not merge in the note.   However, I have maintained the jurisdiction.

I am greatly perplexed about our board for next winter.
You know what passed while you were with us, and how much
discontent was expressed at all previous arrangements.   I was
unwilling to say any thing for two reasons.   Being at any rate
a bird of passage, whose continuance with you cannot be long,
I did not chuse to permit my convenience or my wishes to
weigh a feather in the permanent arrangements of my brethren.
But in addition, I felt serious doubts, although I did not mention them, whether I should be with you at the next term.
What I am about to say is, of course, in perfect confidence
which I would not breathe to any other person whatever.   I
had unaccountably calculated on the election of P—t taking
place next fall, and had determined to make my continuance
in office another year dependent on that event.   You know
how much importance I attach to the character of the person
who is to succeed me, and calculate the influence which probabilities on that subject would have on my continuance in office.
This, however, is a matter of great delicacy on which I cannot
and do not speak.   My erroneous calculation of the time of
election was corrected as soon as the pressure of official duty
was removed from my mind, and I had nearly decided on my
course, but recent events produce such real uncertainty respecting the future as to create doubts whether I ought not to await
the same chances in the fall of 32 which I had intended to await
in the fall of 31.   This obliges me to look forward to our quar-
ters for the next winter.   This uncertainty as to my being with
you which had prevented my taking any part in our previous
consultations on this subject, if consultations they may be
called, prevented my saying anything on the last day.   It
seemed then to be conclusively determined that we did not
remain with Brown, and I understood that Judge Baldwin
would provide lodgings.   He said something of relying on his
sister to select them, to which I was perfectly agreed.   He was

of course to communicate anything which might be done. Not having heard a syllable from him I conclude nothing has been done. We cannot, however, do anything for ourselves till we know that he does nothing for us. In this state of uncertainty I have thought of writing to him when he comes to Philadelphia in the fall, and if he has made no arrangement to provide for ourselves. You, Judge Thompson, Judge Duval, and myself may, I hope, continue to mess together. Brother Duval must be with us or he will be unable to attend consultations. I have supposed you may mention this subject to our brother Thompson, and if he concurs in it write to brother Duval to engage the old rooms for us at Brown's or to locate us at some other place in the neighborhood. This, however, must depend on the intelligence to be obtained from Judge Baldwin.

I hear with feelings of deepest sympathy the family affliction you have sustained, and participate sincerely in the grief which both Mrs. Story and yourself must feel. There are wounds into which time, and time alone, can pour its healing balm. Consolation is vain. I thank you for the verses which the melancholy occasion has produced. They are replete with the deep parental feeling it was calculated to call forth.

You ask me if Mrs. Marshall and myself have ever lost a child. We have lost four, three of them bidding fairer for health and life than any that have survived them. One, a daughter about six or seven, was brought fresh to our minds by what you say of yours. She was one of the most fascinating children I ever saw. She was followed within a fortnight by a brother whose death was attended by a circumstance we can never forget. When the child was supposed to be dying I tore the distracted mother from the bedside. We soon afterwards heard a voice in the room which we considered as indicating the death of the infant. We believed him to be dead. [I went] into the room and found him still breathing. I returned [and] as the pang of his death had been felt by his mother and [I] was confident he must die, I concealed his being alive and prevailed on her to take refuge with her mother who lived the next door across an open square from her. The child lived two days, during which I was agonized with its condition and with the occasional hope, though the case was desperate, that I might enrapture his mother with the intelligence of his restoration to us. After the event had taken place his mother could not bear to return to the house she had left and remained with her mother a fortnight.   I then addressed to her a letter in verse in which our mutual loss was deplored, our lost children spoken of with the parental feeling which belonged to the occasion, her affection for those who survived was appealed to, and her religious confidence in the wisdom and goodness of Providence excited.   The letter closed with a pressing invitation to return to me and her children.   This letter has been delayed for the purpose of sending you a copy of what I wrote.   But 't is lost.

Your affectionate
J. MARSHALL.

The child mentioned in the above letter was Judge Story's youngest child, which died in May, 1831.   The verses referred to are printed in Story's "Life and Letters of Joseph Story," Vol. II, pp. 57-9.

The Doctor Physic mentioned in the letter below was Dr. Philip S. Physic, who was at that time the most eminent surgeon in Philadelphia, if not in the whole country.   In a memoir of Doctor Physic by Doctor Randolph of Philadelphia there is an interesting account of the operation on Chief Justice Marshall.[59]

THE HON'BLE MR. JUSTICE STORY,
    Cambridge, Massachusetts.

PHILADELPHIA, Oct. 12th, 1831.

MY DEAR SIR

I had the pleasure of receiving in the course of the mail your very friendly letter of the 6th.

I have been under the doctor ever since my return in May from North Carolina and have been regularly growing worse. My disease, for which I have to blame myself, was mistaken. My physician suspected it, but I was so confident against him that he never made the experiments necessary to establish the fact.   At length I suffered so much pain and became so alarmed as to determine on a visit to this place.   I have been here a fortnight.   Doctor Physic, whom I consulted immediately, proceeded very circumspectly.   He made some examinations which led to the belief that I had probably stone in the bladder, and on applying the sound at different intervals has decided that I

[59] *Medical Examiner*, Vol. II, pp. 280-281.

have one. The usual operation was to have been performed a day or two past but the rainy weather has confined the doctor, whose health is extremely delicate, and I must wait till we see the return of the sun. We have now the promise of a fair day, and should our anticipations be realized I count on going through the operation tomorrow.

I place the most entire confidence in Doctor Physic. never was man better calculated to inspire confidence in a patient than he is. His profound attention to the case and his patient in investigation of the symtoms, added to his very high reputation for skill as a surgeon, produce a firm conviction that nothing will be omitted which can contribute to my recovery. I look with impatience for the operation.

Our brother Baldwin is here. He seems to have resumed the dispositions which impressed us both so favorably at the first term. This is as it should be. He spoke of you in terms not indicating unfriendliness. He mentioned our next winter's accommodations in such A manner as to show his decided preference for Mrs. Peyton's, but he has not engaged the apartments. We must make some positive engagement before the meeting of Congress or we shall separate, and each be under the necessity of providing for himself. I should have urged an immediate decision had I not been restrained by some communications which have passed between Mr. Peters And Mr. Ringold. When Mr. Peters mentioned that subject to me I expressed my decided approbation to the proposal of our friend to receive us in his house provided it was agreeable to our brothers. On reflection I suspect the situation of the house, between the palace and Georgetown, will not be to your mind nor to the mind of the other Judges. I shall suggest this to Peters. Should this conjecture be well founded, I think we shall do well to engage immediately with Mrs. Peyton.

On the most interesting part of your letter I have felt and still feel, great difficulty. You understand my general sentiments on that subject as well as I do myself. I am most earnestly attached to the character of the department, and to the wishes and convenience of those with whom it has been my pride and my happiness to be associated for so many years. I cannot be insensible to the gloom which lours over us. I have a repugnance to abandoning you under such circumstances which is almost invincible. But the solemn convictions of my judgment sustained by some pride of character admonish me not to hazard the disgrace of continuing in office a mere inefficient pageant.

In the course of the summer I resorted to different courses of medicine none of which were of any service to me, but which had a sensible influence on my general health. My nerves, my digestion, and my head were seriously affected. I had found myself unequal to the effective consideration of any subject, and had determined to resign at the close of the year. This determination, however, I kept to myself, being determined to remain master of my own conduct. I at length resolved to take no more medicine, after which I was slowly restored to my former self. This occurred about the time of my leaving Richmond for this place, and notwithstanding the pain I feel, I recover strength daily. I have therefore determined to meet you at the next term, and to postpone anything definitive till then.

Present my most respectful good wishes to Mrs. Story. I indulge the hope that both of you have recovered firmness enough to receive the dispensations of Providence, however severe, with a mindfulness of the great duties which still remain to be performed.

With esteem and affection yours truely,

J. MARSHALL.

THE HON'BLE MR. JUSTICE STORY,
    Cambridge, Massachusetts.

PHILADELPHIA, Novr 10th, 1831.

MY DEAR SIR:

I learn with much regret from our friend Mr. Peters that you have been seriously indisposed. I fear your various duties confine you too closely. You must, my dear Sir, be careful of your health. Without your vigorous and powerful cooperation I should be in despair, and think the " ship must be given up."

I have had a most tedious confinement. At length, however, I leave my bed and walk across my room. This I do with a tottering feeble step. It is, however, hourly improving, and I hope next week to take the boat for Richmond in time to open my court on the 22d. Doctor Physic has added to consumate skill the most kind and feeling attention. I shall never forget him.

There has been some difficulty about our next winter's arrangement. You perceive I speak confidently of meeting you. At length it seems fixed that we are to quarter with Ringold. Mr. Peters has written you all about it. I was a little apprehensive that you would be unwilling to locate yourself so far out of the centre of the city, but your other friends seem to think you will be greatly pleased. I am told that our accommodations as to rooms will be convenient, and as to everything else you know they will be excellent. Mr. Johnson, I am told, will quarter by himself, and our brother McLean will of course preserve his former position. The remaining five will, I hope, be united.

The Circuit Court is in session in Philadelphia. Our brother Baldwin has called on me frequently. He is in good health and spirits, and I, always sanguine, hope that the next term will exhibit dispositions more resembling those displayed in the first than the last.

I am at present and have been all the summer very unfit for serious business. I was not one moment free from pain from the time I parted with you till the operation was performed which extracted about 1000 calculi. You may judge how much I suffered. The pain increased daily and disqualified me for serious thought. Thank Heaven, I have reason to hope that I am relieved. I am, however, under the very disagreeable necessity of taking medicine continually to prevent new formations. I must submit too to a severe and most unsociable regimen. Such are the privations of age. You have before you, I trust, many, very many years unclouded by such dreary prospects.

Farewell. You have the best wishes of him who is with affectionate esteem

Your   J. MARSHALL.

The volume referred to in the following letter as " The American Library of Useful Knowledge " was published in 1831, and contained among other essays a discourse by Judge Story on " Developments of Science and Mechanic Art," delivered before the Boston Mechanics' Institute, and reprinted in Story's " Miscellaneous Writings."

Hon. Charles F. Mercer and Hon. John S. Barbour, who are referred to in the following letter, were members of the House of Representatives, from Virginia.

THE HON'BLE MR. JUSTICE STORY,
   Cambridge, Massachusetts.

                    RICHMOND, August 2d, 1832
MY DEAR SIR:

I am greatly in your debt, more especially for the first volume of the American Library of Useful Knowledge, and have so long neglected to acknowledge my obligations that I am not sure I should not, according to the practice of insolvents, have put it off altogether had I not been placed in a situation to ask further assistance from you.

Congress has passed an act to increase and improve its law library, a copy of which has just been transmitted to me by the librarian. It appropriates 500$ for the present year, to be expended in the purchase of law books by the librarian, in pursuance of such catalogue as shall be furnished him by the Chief Justice of the United States. I wish it had been "as shall be furnished him by Mr. Justice Story." However, we must correct this erratum as well as we can.

As I know your appetite for labor, I feel the less compunction in offering you a very large share like this. Indeed, if you can take the whole I can readily spare it. Will you then transmit me a list of such law books as you would wish (or rather, as ought in your judgement) to be added to the law library. You probably recollect enough of them without seeing a catalogue to supply a list of those which are wanting. Say if you think there ought to be duplicates of particular books.

The librarian informs me that he has already ordered a continuation of those British reports which are in progress of which he has the beginning volumes, and of the American reporters.

I ascribe the honor now done me to our friend Peters, and therefore think I may ask him also for aid in my difficulty. I shall probably write to him.

We are up to the chin in politics. Virginia was always insane enough to be opposed to the bank of the United States, and therefore hurras for the veto. But we are little doubtful how it may work in Pennsylvania.   It is not difficult to account for the part New York may take.   She has sagacity enough to see her interests in putting down the present bank. Her mercantile position gives her a control, a commanding control, over the currency and the exchanges of the country, if there be no bank of the United States.   Going for herself she may approve this policy; but Virginia ought not to drudge for her benefit.

We show our wisdom most strikingly in approving the veto on the harbor bill also.   That bill contained an appropriation intended to make Richmond a seaport, which she is not at present, for large vessels fit to cross the Atlantic. The appropriation was whittled down in the House of Representatives to almost nothing, in consequence of the total misunderstanding of the case by Mercer.   Yet we wished the appropriation because we were confident that Congress when correctly informed, would add the necessary sum.   This too is vetoed; and for this too our sagacious politicians are thankful.   We seem to think it the summit of human wisdom, or rather of American patriotism, to preserve our poverty.

Our great political and party guide, The Enquirer, has not been able to make Mr. Barbour pull in the traces.   He has broke loose and is fairly in the field.   I do not precisely know how this will work.   He is supported by the most violent of the state right party, who are also strong for the existing President.   There might be some difficulty in managing this tangled business were not the Jackson majority so overwhelming as to leave his friends nothing to fear from a division. Some of the friends of Barbour are secretly for Calhoun; but though attached to nullification in principle they dare not favor the name.   Besides the basement story is so firm that those who are supported on it dare not totter.

Things to the South wear a very serious aspect.   If we can trust appearances the leaders are determined to risk all the consequences of dismemberment.   I cannot entirely dissmiss the hope that they may be deserted by their followers,— at least to such an extent as to produce a cause at the Rubicon.   They undoubtedly believe that Virginia will support them.   I think they are mistaken both with respect to Virginia and North Carolina.   I do not think either State will embrace this mad and wicked measure.   New Hampshire and Maine seem to belong to the tropics. It is time for New Hampshire to part with Webster and Mason. She has no longer any use for such men.

I am just preparing for my usual excursion to the mountains. Would that I could meet you there. It would secure you from the cholera. Our whole seaboard will, I fear, be overrun with it. In New York it has, I perceive, been carried to the western frontier. It is too visiting our lakes. You are surrounded by it. That Providence may protect us, especially Boston and Richmond, is the earnest prayer of your truely affectionate

J. MARSHALL.

THE HON'BLE MR. JUSTICE STORY,
    Cambridge, Massachusetts.

RICHMOND, September 22d, 1832.

MY DEAR SIR:

I am greatly indebted to you for your favor of the 14th. Without your assistance I should have found it impossible, or at least very difficult, to comply with the duty assigned me by Congress. I have given you a great deal of trouble, which I regret,— the less because you love law and love labor. Forty years hence your passion for the one and the other may be somewhat diminished.

I have curtailed your list of books very much for two reasons. One, that by far the greater number of those you have mentioned are already in the library, and I am unwilling to exhaust the fund by procuring duplicates; the other, that we may supply what is required by a better selection of duplicates when we meet this winter, if we should meet, and shall have the advantage of knowing precisely how much money remains to be employed. I have said nothing about the American reports, because I understand from the librarian that he has already directed them all to be purchased. In my letter inclosing the list I have said that I so understand his communication and have requested, if I have misunderstood him, that he will correct the error by purchasing all the American reports not in the library. This is a fund of information on which the Supreme Court must be always at liberty to draw ad libitum.

I am very much gratified at hearing that you are so near

completing your course on constitutional law, and enriching the political and legal literature of your country with it.   The task was arduous, but not above your strength, and you have engaged in it with hearty good will.   I anticipate much pleasure as well as information from perusing the work, and can assure you in anticipation that I shall not be among the growlers you may expect to hear.   I shall not be among those who bring on you the charge of " apostacy " and ultraism.   I shall like to see how in your quotations from the sage you mention you imitate the bee in extracting honey from poison.   I have no doubt, however dexterous the operation, that you will be well stung in requital for your skill and industry.

If the prospects of our country inspire you with gloom how do you think a man must be affected who partakes of all your opinions and whose geographical position enables him to see a great deal that is concealed from you.   I yield slowly and reluctantly to the conviction that our constitution cannot last.   I had supposed that north of the Potowmack a firm and solid government competent to the security of rational liberty might be preserved.   Even that now seems doubtful. The case of the south seems to me to be desperate.   Our opinions are incompatible with a united government even among ourselves.   The union has been prolonged thus far by miracles.   I fear they cannot continue.

Yours affectionately,
J. MARSHALL.

THE HON'BLE MR. JUSTICE STORY,
   Cambridge, Massachusetts.

RICHMOND, Decr 25th, 1832.

MY DEAR SIR:

I had yesterday the pleasure of receiving your letter of the 19th, inclosing a proof sheet of the title page of your great work.   I anticipate the pleasure its perusal will give me.

Truely sensible as I am that the commendation bestowed on the Chief Justice, both in the dedication and the preface, greatly transcends his merit, and confident as I am that the judgement of the public will confirm this opinion, I am yet deeply penetrated by the evidence it affords of the continuance of that partial esteem and friendship which I have cherished for so many years, and still cherish as one of the choicest treasures of my life. The only return I can make is locked up in my own bosom, or communicated in occasional conversation with my friends.

I congratulate you on the accomplishment of your purpose and on finishing the Herculean task you had undertaken. I know no person but yourself who could have sustained properly this vast additional labor. I cannot doubt either the ability or correctness with which it is executed, and am certain in advance that I shall read every sentence with entire approbation. It is a subject on which we concur exactly. Our opinions on it are, I believe, identical. Not so with Virginia or the South generally.

Our legislature is now in session, and the dominant party receives the message of the President to Congress with enthusiastic applause. Quite different was the effect of his proclamation. That paper astonished, confounded, and for a moment silenced them. In a short time however, the power of speech was recovered, and was employed in bestowing on its author the only epithet which could possibly weigh in the scales against the name of " Andrew jackson," and countervail its popularity. Imitating the Quaker who said the dog he wished to destroy was mad, they said Andrew Jackson had become a Federalist, even an ultra Federalist. To have said he was ready to break down and trample on every other department of the government would not have injured him, but to say that he was a Federalist,— a convert to the opinions of Washington, was a mortal blow under which he is yet staggering.

The party seems to be divided. Those who are still true to their President pass by his denunciation of all their former theories; and though they will not approve the sound opinions avowed in his proclamation are ready to denounce nullification and to support him in maintaining the union. This is going a great way for them,— much farther than their former declarations would justify the expectation of, and much farther than mere love of union would carry them.

You have undoubtedly seen the message of our Governor and the resolutions reported by the committee to whom it was referred,— a message and resolutions which you will think skillfully framed had the object been a civil war. They undoubtedly hold out to South Carolina the expectation of support from Virginia; and that hope must be the foundation on which they have constructed their plan for a southern confederacy or league. A want of confidence in the present support of the people will prevent any direct avowal in favor of this scheme by those whose theories and whose secret wishes may lead to it; but the people may be entangled by the insane dogmas which have become axioms in the political creed of Virginia, and involved so inextricably in the labyrinth into which those dogmas conduct them, as to do what their sober judgement disapproves.

On Thursday these resolutions are to be taken up, and the debate will, I doubt not, be ardent and tempestuous enough. I pretend not to anticipate the result. Should it countenance the obvious design of South Carolina to a form of southern confederacy, it may conduce to a southern league,— never to a southern government. Our theories are incompatible with a government for more than a single State. We can form no union which shall be closer than an alliance between sovereigns. In this event there is some reason to apprehend internal convlusion. The northern and western section of our State, should a union be maintained north of the Potowmack, will not readily connect itself with the South. At least such is the present belief of their most intelligent men. Any effort on their part to separate from Southern Virginia and unite with a northern confederacy may probably be punished as treason. " We have fallen on evil times."

I thank you for Mr. Webster's speech. Entertaining the opinion he has expressed respecting the general course of the administration, his patriotism is entitled to the more credit for the determination he expressed in Faneuil Hall to support it in the great effort it promises to make for the preservation of the union. No member of the then opposition avowed a similar determination during the Western Insurrection, which would have been equally fatal had it not been quelled by the well timed vigor of General Washington. We are now gathering the bitter fruits of the tree even before that time planted by Mr. Jefferson, and so industriously and perseveringly cultivated by Virginia.

You have doubtless heard from Mr. Peters the affliction

with which our brother Baldwin has been visited. It cannot, I trust, be of long continuance.
We shall meet once more at Washington, Till then adieu.
Your faithful and affectionate friend.

J. Marshall.

The speech mentioned in the above letter was delivered by Daniel Webster at a crowded meeting held in Faneuil Hall, in the forenoon of December 17, 1832. It is preserved only in the contemporary newspaper reports, which are said to be somewhat abridged. Referring to President Jackson's Proclamation, Mr. Webster said: "Mr. Chairman, the general principles of the Proclamation are such as I entirely approve. I esteem them to be the true principles of the Constitution. It must now be apparent to every man, that this doctrine of nullification means resistance to the laws by force. It is but another name for civil war. . . . The President has declared that in meeting the exigencies of this crisis, it is his determination to execute the laws, to preserve the Union by all constitutional means; to arrest, if possible, by moderate, but fair measures, the necessity of a recourse to force; and so to conduct, that the curse impending on the shedding of fraternal blood shall not be called down by any offensive act on the part of the United States. In all this I most cordially concur. . . . I think I can say nothing more satisfactory at this meeting, or to the people of this Commonwealth than that in this way of meeting this crisis I shall give the President my entire and cordial support. . . . Mr. Chairman, in this alternative my choice is made. I am for the Union as it is. I am content with no Government less than that which embraces the whole Four and Twenty States. I am for the Constitution as it is; a Constitution under which those Four and Twenty States have risen to a height of prosperity, unexampled, in the history of mankind. I shall support the President in maintaining this Union and this Constitution; and the cause shall not fail for want of any aid, any effort, or any zealous co-operation of mine."

The "affliction with which our brother Baldwin has been visited," mentioned above, is best explained in a letter from Philadelphia, dated December 27, in which Mr. Webster writes to Judge Story: "I learn that Judge Baldwin has recently manifested an alienation of mind. He is now under the hands of medical men & confined to his own house. It is said to be a decided case." Henry Baldwin was born in New Haven, Connecticut, January 14, 1780, and was appointed by President Jackson an Associate Justice of the Supreme Court in January, 1830, which office he held until his death, in Philadelphia, April 21, 1844. In 1837 he published a voluminous pamphlet entitled " A general View of the Origin and Nature of the Constitution and Government of the United States," in opposition to the constitutional doctrines of Judge Marshall and Judge Story.

The " totally forgotten letter " mentioned in the following letter was written at the time Judge Marshall was chosen a Corresponding Member of the Massachusetts Historical Society, August 29, 1809. In his letter of acceptance, dated Richmond, September 20, 1809, Judge Marshall wrote to the Corresponding Secretary of the Society as follows:

" On my return from a tour to our mountains I had the pleasure of finding your letter of the 1st inst., which I hasten to acknowledge. Permit me, Sir, through you to assure the Massachusetts Historical Society that I receive with just sensibility the honor they have been pleased to confer on me in placing me among their corresponding members. Should I be less useful than many of those with whom I am associated, that circumstance, I entreat them to believe, will not be imputable to an improper estimate of the value of the institution, or to a want of respect for those who compose it. For the flattering terms in which you have been pleased to communicate the vote of the Society I pray you to accept my thanks. I shall not be in Washington till February. Perhaps some member of Congress may without inconvenience find room in his baggage for the volume you mention."

In a second letter to Dr. Eliot, dated April 23, 1810, Judge Marshall writes: " I had the pleasure of receiving from Mr. Quincy your letter of the 3d of Novr, together with the two volumes which accompanied it. Permit me to offer my thanks for this attention, & to rely upon it as a pledge that the additional trouble I am about to give you will not be irksome. I could wish to place in my library as many of the volumes of the Collections of the Society as are attainable without inconvenience, but while I solicit your aid in the accomplishment of this wish I must accompany it with a request that you will procure those volumes only, which either by having gone through a second edition or from the numbers of the first are now attainable with entire facility. I would by no means impose on your goodness so far as to render any research necessary. As I neither know the number of volumes which come within the scope of this request nor the price of them, I cannot remit the precise sum which may be necessary, but assure that on the first intimation from yourself this unavoidable omission shall be supplied."

The " compliment paid by your Athenæum " refers to the request of the Trustees of the Boston Athenæum, made several years before, that Chief Justice Marshall would sit for his portrait. At a meeting of the Trustees, December 8, 1829, it was " Voted, That the sum of two hundred dollars be appropriated for a portrait of Chief Justice Marshall by Mr. Harding, and that the Vice-President of this institution be a committee to request Judge Marshall to sit for the same." In his letter to Mr. Harding, the Vice-President, the Hon. Francis C. Gray, writes: " We expect a first-rate picture and hope you will not stint the size nor neglect the execution of any account." The portrait was completed in season to be exhibited for the first time in the Athenæum's exhibition of Paintings in the summer of 1830. It is the full-length portrait which now hangs in the entrance hall of the Athenæum. A copy of this portrait was given to the Law School at Harvard, in 1847, by Professor Greenleaf and others.

THE HON'BLE MR. JUSTICE STORY,
    Cambridge, Massachusetts.

RICHMOND, April 24th, 1833.

MY DEAR SIR:

I had the pleasure some days past of receiving your favor of the 10th, but deferred my answer till I could also acknowledge your very valuable present which it announced. The Lucy & Abigail is now arrived, and has delivered the package containing your Commentaries and Allison's Sermons, for both of which I thank the donors.

As favors generally beget a disposition to make farther demands on the kindness which confers them, I have ventured to impose on you the trouble of distributing some books among your friends and neighbors to whom I wish to be civil, and have sent a few copies of the Life of Washington for that purpose. One you will perceive is for Mr. Webster and one for Mr. Adams.

In looking over some old papers the other day to determine how many of them were worthy of being committed to the flames, I found a totally forgotten letter (you need not communicate this) from the Historical Society of Massachusetts (or Boston), announcing that I had been elected an honorary member. To show my gratitude for this distinction, I ask them to accept my book,— a poor return indeed, but the only one I can make.

You know what a compliment has been paid me by your Athenæum. I have been truly flattered by it, and hope the society will receive my book,— not surely as anything like an equivalent, but as a testimonial of my grateful sense of the favorable sentiment that society has manifested for me. The widow's mite, you know, proved the heart more than the rich gifts of the wealthy.

I wish you to present the copy intended for Mrs. Ledyard in your very best manner. Tell her how infinitely I feel the obligation she has conferred on me. I was extremely anxious to obtain Allison's Sermons for the reasons I mentioned to you, and you may assure Mrs. Ledyard that their value is enhanced greatly by the hand which gives them.

In the receipt which I took for the freight Captain Newcomb promised to deliver the box to his owners — I think he calls them George Thresher & Co. or George Thorcher & Co., Long Wharf. Though you New England men, all or most of you, beat copperplate in your writing this captain rather poses me. If I mistake his letters, you, however, probably know his owners.

I am truly delighted that your Commentaries are published. I shall read them eagerly myself, and wish most ardently that they may be read by others to whom they would be still more useful. The copy intended for the schools will do much good where the teachers introduce it. I greatly fear that south of the Potomack, where it is most wanted, it will be least used. It is a Mahomedan rule, I understand, " never to dispute with the ignorant," and we of the truth faith in the

South abjure the contamination of infidel political works. It would give our orthodox nullifyer a fever to read the heresies of your Comentaries. A whole school might be infected by the atmosphere if a single copy should be placed on one of the shelves of a bookcase.

By the way, since I have breathed the air of James River I think favorably of Clay's bill. I hope, if it can be maintained that our manufactures will still be protected by it. Have you ever seen anything to equal the exhibition in Charleston and in the far South generally? Those people pursue a southern league steadily or they are insane. They have caught at Clay's bill, if their conduct is at all intelligible, not as a real accommodation, a real adjustment, a real relief from actual or supposed oppression, but as an apology for avoiding the crisis and deferring the decisive moment till the other States of the South will unite with them.

With affectionate esteem I am
Your
J. MARSHALL.

THE HON'BLE MR. JUSTICE STORY,
    Cambridge, Massachusetts.

RICHMOND, June 3d, 1833.

MY DEAR SIR:

I am greatly obliged by your letter of the 24th of May. Your conjecture that my enquiry related to Randolph's case was well founded. My letter did not present the difficulty because I did not then comprehend it myself. I wrote it on the bench, just after seeing a paper which stated that a warrant to apprehend him would be demanded. No copy of the laws of Congress was in the courtroom, and the hour for closing the mail was arrived. I wrote without looking at the act. As I anticipated, the application was made on my return, and I felt the difficulty of the case. The reason and policy of apprehending in the States for trial in the District or in a territory are obvious. The fact too that Mr. Watkins had been arrested in Pensylvania for trial in Washington seemed to be a decision, perhaps by a Judge of the United States, in favor of issuing the warrant. Yet the language of the 33d Sec. appeared to me to limit the power of arrest to cases where the person was arrested for trial before a court which by the Judicial Act has cognizance of the offence. This restraint upon the power is absurd, and could not, I believe, have been imposed, had the Congress perceived its effect, but it cannot be disregarded.

I was truely embarrassed, but at length determined not to grant the warrant.

The application was accompanied with an able opinion of the Attorney General in support of it. He found himself in some measures on proceedings which have taken place in some previous cases, in some measures on the fact that several courts have been constituted since the passage of the act of 1789, and in some measures on the circumstance that all the courts are now in the exercise of jurisdiction under the act of 1802, not under the act of 1789.

These are serious difficulties, but Congress ought to remove them. In the meantime they deserve the consideration of all the Judges.

I rejoice to hear that the abridgement of your Commentaries is coming before the public, and should be still more rejoiced to learn that it was used in all our colleges and universities. The first impressions made on the youthful mind are of vast importance; and most unfortunately, they are in the South all erroneous. Our young men generally speaking, grow up in the firm belief that liberty depends on construing our constitution into a league instead of a government; that it has nothing to fear from breaking these United States into numerous petty republics. Nothing in their view is to be feared but that bugbear, consolidation; and every exercise of legitimate power is construed into a breach of the constitution. Your book, if read, will tend to remove these prejudices.

Your affectionate friend.

J. Marshall.

The Hon'ble Mr. Justice Story,
    Cambridge, near Boston.

Richmond, Novr 16th, 1833.

My Dear Sir:

I thank you for your last letter. Though my thanks are postponed they are not the less sincere. The difficulty suggested is somewhat changed in its aspect, but is not removed.

The attachment was served in my absence, and an application is made to a State Judge for a writ of habeas corpus. It is now under consideration, and will probably be awarded. Whether the motion be granted or rejected, I expect the question to be brought before me, and shall if possible bring it before the Supreme Court or suspend it till the Judges can be consulted.

I have just received a letter from Mr. Ringold informing me that he has moved his family out of the city and consequently cannot accomodate us next winter. What is to become of us? What arrangement can be made? Shall we go to the place selected by our brother Johnson near the capitol, or what other location shall we make? If you have held any communication with our brother Thompson since his last and greatest affliction, or can hold any with him, will you consult him and if possible determine on something? I will hold myself in readiness to join you anywhere. If you fix on any place, let me know it. If you do not then say where we shall meet.

The political world, at least our part of it, is surely moved topsy-turvy. What is to become of us and of our constitution? Can the wise men of the East answer the question? Those of the South perceive no difficulty. Allow a full rage to state rights and state sovereignty, and, in their opinion, all will go well.

What think you of the late decision of our brother McClain in Tennessee? Does it accord exactly with his last opinion in the Cherokee case?

Farewell.

With affectionate esteem, I am still & shall ever be

Yours truly.

J. MARSHALL.

THE HON'BLE MR. JUSTICE STORY,
   Cambridge, Massachusetts.

RICHMOND, Decr 3d, 1834.

MY DEAR SIR:

I am so accustomed to rely on you for aid when I need it that you must not be surprised at the present application. I trust however that it will not give you much trouble.

You will perceive in the 2 v of the Life of Washington, 2d ed., p. 307-8, an account of the defeat of Harden. It is stated that the battle was fought on the St. Joseph. I have received a letter from a gentleman in Chilicothe which gives probability to the opinion that it was really fought on Paint Creek, a stream which empties into the Scioto not far from Chilicothe. Will you have the goodness at your leisure to make some enquiries of Mr. Sparks, and learn whether the letter to General Washington giving an account of this battle states it to have been fought on the St. Joseph or on Paint Creek. You need not hurry yourself on this subject. The information will be in full time when I meet you in Washington, where I purpose to be as usual in January.

I perceive you have been much employed in dispatching a batch of pirates. I trust I may congratulate you on having finished it to your own satisfaction. My circuit duties are not arduous, and will terminate this week.

You will perceive that our House of Delegates has re-elected their Jackson Speaker. This, however, is not absolutely a test of the strength of parties. The decisive battle will be fought on the election of a Senator. Both parties appear to be sanguine. The administration has undoubtedly a majority in the Senate,— the opposition in the House of Delegates. We are insane on the subject of the Bank. Its friends, who are not numerous, dare not, a few excepted, to avow themselves. You will perceive by the message of our Governor that he is a complete nullifier in the Georgia sense of the term.

I conjecture from symptoms in the papers that Mr. Van Buren gains strength in Virginia. This opinion is founded on the fact that the papers in his interest did not for a long time allude to him as their candidate. They emptied their cup of malignant calumny on every other person who was named as a candidate, hoping by the destruction of others to sustain him. They now begin to bring him forward. This shows that in their opinion he is stronger than he was.

I anticipate with much pleasure our meeting at Washington. It is among the most painful of the emotions excited by the prospect of leaving public life, an event which though not intended to be immediate cannot be very distant, that I shall part forever from friends most dear to me.

I am, my dear Sir, with true and affectionate esteem,

Your,

J. MARSHALL.

The following three letters were written by John Marshall to General Washington during the time when Marshall was in Europe upon the " X Y Z " Mission. It is interesting to observe the impression that the Europe of 1797 and 1798 made upon such a mind as that of Marshall. The text of these letters, derived first from the transcripts among the Sparks papers in the Library of Harvard University, has been carefully compared with that of the original letters among Washington papers in the Library of the Department of State by Mr. S. M. Hamilton of that library. In " Washington's Writings," Ford Edition, XIII, pp. 432-436, will be found, under date of December 4, 1797, a letter from General Washington in reply to the first of the three following communications.

THE HAGUE, 15th Sept. 1797.

DEAR SIR

The flattering evidences I have receiv'd of your favorable opinion, which have made on my mind an impression only to wear out with my being, added to a conviction that you must yet feel a deep interest in all that concerns a country to whose service you have devoted so large a portion of your life, induce me to offer you such occasional communications as, while in Europe I may be enabled to make, and induce a hope too that the offer will not be deemed an unacceptable or unwelcome intrusion.

Until our arrival in Holland we saw only British and neutral vessels. This added to the blockade of the Dutch fleet the Texel, of the French fleet in Brest and of the spanish fleet in Cadiz manifests the entire dominion which one nation at present possesses over the seas. By the ships of war which met us we were three times visited and the conduct of those who came on board was such as would proceed from general orders to pursue a system calculated to conciliate America. Whether this be occasion'd by a sense of justice and the obligation of good faith, or solely by the hope that the perfect contrast which it exhibits to the conduct of France may excite keener sensations at that conduct, its effects on our commerce are the same.

The situation of Holland is truly interesting. Tho the face of the country still exhibits a degree of wealth and population perhaps unequalled in any other part of Europe, its decline is visible. The great city of Amsterdam is in a state of blockade. More than two thirds of its shipping lie unemployed in port. Other seaports suffer tho not in so great a degree. In the meantime the requisitions made upon them are enormous. They have just completed the payment of 100,-000,000 of florins (equal to 40,000,000 of dollars) stipulated by treaty, they have sunk, on the first entrance of the French a very considerable sum in assignats; they made large contributions in specifics; and they pay feed and cloath an army estimated, as I am informed, at near three times its real number. It is supposed that France has by various means drawn from Holland about 60,000,000 of dollars. This has been paid, in addition to the national expenditures, by a population of less than 2,000,000. Nor, shou'd the war continue, can the contributions of Holland stop here. The increasing exigencies of France must inevitably increase her demands on those within her reach.— Not even peace can place Holland in her former situation. Antwerp will draw from Amsterdam a large portion of that commerce which is the great source of its wealth; for Antwerp possesses, in the existing state of things, advantages which not even weight of capital can entirely surmount. The political divisions of this country and its uncertainty concerning its future destiny must also have their operation. Independent of the grand division between those for and against the Stadtholder, between those who favor an indivisible and those who favor a federal republic, there is much contrariety of opinion concerning the essential principles of that indivisible consolidated republic which the influence of France imposes on the nation. A constitution which I have not read, but which is stated to me to have contain'd all the great fundamentals of a representative government, and which has been prepared with infinite labor, and has experienc'd an uncommon length of discussion was rejected in the primary assemblies by a majority of nearly five to one of those who voted.   The objections do not accompany the decision, but they are said to be to the duration of the constitution which was to remain five years unaltered, to the division of the legislature into two chambers, and to its power of definitive legislation, the substitute wish'd for, by its opponents, is a legislature with a single branch having power only to initiate laws which are to derive their force from the sanction of the primary assemblies.   I do not know how they would organize their executive, nor is it material how they would organize it.   A constitution with such a legislature would live too short a time to make it worth the while to examine the structure of its other parts.   It is remarkable that the very men who have rejected the form of government propos'd to them have reelected a greater majority of the persons who prepared it and who will probably make from it no essential departure.   Those elected are now assembled in convention at this place, but we know not in what manner they are proceeding.   It is also worthy of notice that more than two thirds of those entitled to suffrage including perhaps more than four fifths of the property of the nation, and who wish'd, as I am told the adoption of the constitution withheld their votes on this very interesting question.   Many were restrained by an unwillingness to take the oath required before a vote cou'd be receiv'd; Many, disgusted with the present state of things, have come to the unwise determination of revenging themselves on those whom they charge with having occasion'd it by taking no part whatever in the politics of their country, and many seem to be indifferent to every consideration not immediately connected with their particular employments.

The political opinions which have produc'd the rejection of the constitution, and which, as it wou'd seem, can only be entertain'd by intemperate and ill inform'd minds, unaccustom'd to a union of the theory and practice of liberty, must be associated with a general system which if brought into action will produce the same excesses here which have been so justly deplor'd in France.   The same material exists tho not in so great a degree.   They have their clubs, they have a numerous poor and they have enormous wealth in the hands of a minority of the nation.   On my remarking this to a very rich and intelligent merchant of Amsterdam and observing that if one class of men withdrew itself from public duties and offices it would immediately be succeeded by another which wou'd acquire a degree of power and influence that might be exercis'd to the destruction of those who had retired from society, he replied that the remark was just, but that they relied on France for a protection from those evils which she herself had experienced. That france would continue to require great supplies from Holland and knew its situation too well to permit it to become the prey of anarchy. That Holland was an artificial country acquir'd by preserving industry and which cou'd only be preserved by wealth and order. That confusion and anarchy wou'd banish a large portion of that wealth, wou'd dry up its sources and wou'd entirely disable them from giving France that pecuniary aid she so much needed. That under this impression very many who, tho friends to the revolution saw with infinite mortification french troops garrison the towns of Holland, wou'd now see this departure with equal regret. Thus they willingly relinquished national independence for individual safety. What a lesson to those who wou'd admit foreign influence into the United States!

You have observ'd the storm which has been long gathering in Paris. The thunderbolt has at length been launch'd at the heads of the leading members of the legislature, and has, it is greatly to be fear'd, involved in one common ruin with them, the constitution and liberties of their country.

The inclos'd papers will furnish some idea of a transaction which may be very interesting to America as well as to France. Complete and impartial details concerning it will not be easily obtain'd, as the press is no longer free. The journalists who had ventur'd to censure the proceedings of a majority of the directory are seiz'd, and against about forty of them a sentence of transportation is pronounced. The press is plac'd under the superintendence of a police appointed by and dependent on the executive. It is suppos'd that all private letters have been seiz'd for inspection.

From some Paris papers it appears, that on the first alarm several members of the legislature attempted to assemble in their proper halls which they found clos'd and guarded by an armed force. Sixty or seventy assembled at another place and began to remonstrate against the violence offer'd against their body but fear soon dispersed them. To destroy the possibility of a rallying point the municipal administrations of Paris and the central administration of the Seine were immediately suspended and forbidden by an arrêté of the directoire to assemble themselves together.   Many of the administrators of the departments through France elected by the people, had been previously removed and their places filled by persons chosen by the directory.   Moreau who commanded the army of the Sambre and the Meuse by which he was deservedly loved and who was consider'd as attach'd to the fallen party was, as is reported, invited from his army to Paris under the pretext of a personal consultation.   We have not heard of his arrival or of his fate.   The command of his army during his absence did not, we learn, devolve on the oldest officer but was given to Genl Hoche who also commands the army of the in [mutilated] Carnot is at one time said to have been kill'd in defending himself from some soldiers who pursued and attempted to take him, at another time he is said to have affected his escape.   The fragment of the legislature convok'd by the directory at L'Odeon and L'ecole de sañte, hasten'd to repeal the law for organizing the national guards, and authoriz'd the directory to introduce into Paris as many troops as should be judged necessary.   The same day the liberty of the press was abolish'd by a line, property taken away by another and personal security destroy'd by a sentence of transportation against men unheard and untried.   All this is stiled the triumph of liberty and of the constitution.

To give a satisfactory statement of the origin and progress of the contest between the executive and legislative departments would require more time than could devoted to the subject, did I even possess the requisite information, and to you, Sir, it would be unnecessary because I have no doubt of your having receiv'd it through other channels.   I shall briefly observe that the controversy has embrac'd a variety of interesting subjects.   Since the election of the new third, there were found in both branches of the legislature a majority in favor of moderate measures, and, apparently, wishing sincerely for peace.   They have manifested a disposition which threaten'd a condemnation of the conduct of the directory towards America, a scrutiny into the transactions of Italy, particularly those respecting Venice and Genoa, an inquiry into the disposition of public money and such a regular arrangement of the finances as would prevent in future those dilapidations which are suspected to have grown out of their disorder.

They have sought too by their laws to ameliorate the situation of those whom terror had driven out of France, and of those priests who had committed no offense. Carnot and Bethelemy two of the directory were with the legislature.

The cry of conspiracy to reestablish royalism was immediately rais'd against them. An envoy was despatched to the army of Italy to sound its disposition. It was represented that the legislature was hostile to the armies, that it witheld their pay and subsistence, that by its opposition to the directory it encouraged Austria and Britain to reject the terms of peace which were offer'd by France, and which but for that opposition would have been accepted, and finally that it had engag'd in a conspiracy for the destruction of the constitution and the republic and for the restoration of royalty. At a feast given to the armies of Italy to commemorate their fellow soldiers who had fallen in that country the generals address'd to them their complaints plainly spoke of marching to Paris to support the directory against the Council and receiv'd from them addresses manifesting the willingness of the soldiers to follow them. The armies also addressed the directory and each other, and addresses were dispatched to different departments. The directory answered them by the strongest criminations of the legislature. Similar proceedings were had in the army of the interior commanded by Genl Hoche. Detachments were mov'd within the limits prohibited by the constitution, some of which declared they were marching to Paris to bring the legislature to reason. Alarmed by those movements the council of five hundred call'd on the directory for an account of them. The movement of the troops within the constitutional circle was attributed to accident and the discontents of the army to the falts committed by the legislature who were plainly criminated as conspirators against the army and the republic. The message was taken up by Troncon in the council of ancients and by Thibideau in the council of five hundred. I hope you have seen their speeches. They are able, and seem to me to have entirely exculpated the legislature. In the meantime the directory employ'd itself in the removal of the administrators of many of the departments and cantons and replacing those whom the people had elected by others in whom it could confide, and in the removal generally of such officers both civil and military as could be trusted to make room for others on whom it could rely. The legislature on its part, passed several laws to enforce the constitutional restrictions on the armies and endeavor'd to organize the national guards. On this latter subject especially Pichegru great and virtuous I believe in the cabinet as in the field, was indefatigable. We understand that the day before the law for their organization would have been carried into execution the decisive blow was struck.

To support the general charge of a conspiracy in favor of royalty I know of no particular facts alleg'd against the arrested members except Pichegru and two or three others. An abridgment of the paper constituting the whole charge against Pichegru will be found in the inclos'd supplement. I have seen the paper at full length. The story at large is still more improbable than its abridgment because Pichegru is made in the first moment of conversation to unbosom himself entirely to a perfect stranger who had only told him that he came from the Prince of Conde and could not exhibit a single line or testimonial of any sort to prove that he had ever seen the Prince or that he was not a spy employ'd by some of the enemies of the General.

This story is repelled by Pichegru's character which has never been defiled. Great as were the means he possess'd of personal aggrandizement he returned clean handed from the army without adding a shilling to his private fortune. It is repel'd by his resigning the supreme command, by his numerous victories subsequent to the alleged treason, by its own extreme absurdity and by the fear which his accusers show of bringing him to trial according to the constitution even before a tribunal they can influence and overawe, or of even permitting him before that prostrate body which is still term'd the legislature and which in defiance of the constitution has pronounc'd judgment on him. Yet this improbable and unsupported tale seems to be received as an establish'd truth by those who, the day before his fall bow'd to him as an idol. I am mortified as a man to learn that even his old army which conquered under him, which adored him, which partook of his fame and had heretofore not join'd their brethren in accusing the legislature, now unite in bestowing on him the heaviest execrations and do not hesitate to pronounce him a traitor of the deepest dye.

Whether this conspiracy be real or not, the wounds inflicted on the constitution by the three directors seem to me to be mortal.   In opposition to the express regulations of the constitution the armies have deliberated, the results of their deliberations addressed to the directory has been favorably received, and the legislature since the revolution has superadded its thanks.   Troops have been march'd within those limits which by the constitution they are forbidden to enter but on the request of the legislature.

The directory is forbidden to arrest a member of the legislature unless in the very commission of a criminal act and then he can only be tried by the high court, on which occasion forms calculated to protect his person from violence or the prejudice of the moment are carefully prescribed.   Yet it has seiz'd by a military force about fifty leading members not taken in a criminal act and has not pursued a single step mark'd out by the Constitution.

The councils can inflict no penalty on their own members other than reprimand, arrest for eight and imprisonment for three days.   Yet they have banished to such place as the directory shall choose a large portion of their body without the poor formality of hearing a defence.

The legislature shall not exercise any judiciary power or pass any retrospective law.   Yet it has pronounc'd this heavy judgment on others as well as its own members and has taken from individuals property which the law had vested in them.

The members of the directory are personally secur'd by the same rules with those of the legislature.   Yet three directors have deprived two of their places, the legislature has thus banished [them] without a hearing and has proceeded to fill up the alleg'd vacancies.   Merelin late minister of justice and Francois de Neufchatel have been elected.

The constitution forbids the house of any man to be enter'd in the night.   The orders of the constituted authorities can only be executed in the day.   Yet many of the members were seized in their beds.

Indeed Sir the constitution has been violated in so many instances that it would require a pamphlet to detail them.   The detail would be unnecessary for the great principle seems to be introduc'd that the government is to be administer'd according to the will of the armies and not according to the will of the nation.

Necessity, the never to be worn out apology for violence, is alleged — but could that necessity go further than to secure the persons of the conspirators? Did it extend to the banishment of the printers to the slavery of the press? If such a necessity did exist it was created by the disposition of the people at large, and it is a truth which requires no demonstration that if a republican form of government cannot be administered by the general will, it cannot be administered against that will by an army.

After all, the result may not be what is apprehended. France possesses such enormous power, such a vast population that she may possibly spare another million and preserve or reacquire her liberty. Or, the form of the Government being preserv'd, the independence of the legislature may be gradually recovered.

With their form of government or revolutions we have certainly no right to intermeddle, but my regrets at the present state of things are increased by an apprehension that the rights of our country will not be deemed so sacred under the existing system, as they would have been had the legislature preserved its legitimate authority.

Genl Pickney (with whom I cannot but be very well pleased) [and I] have waited impatiently for Mr Gerry and shall wait until Monday the 18th inst. On that day we set sail for Paris.

The negotiations with Austria and Britain are still pending and are of very uncertain issue.

This letter has extended itself to an unexpected length. I have fatigued you, Sir and will only add that I remain
with sincere and respectful attachment
Your Obedt Servt
J. MARSHALL.

I just now learn that fifteen hundred persons have been arrested at Lyons. That resistance is made at Avignon and that Massina is marching to quell it.

PARIS, October 24th, 1797.

DEAR SIR

I did myself the honor of addressing to you from the Hague by Capt Izzard, a very long letter which I hope you have receiv'd. The offer therein made of occasionally communicating to my observations of the great and interesting events of europe was not even entitled to the small value which in my own mind I had bestowed upon it. Causes which I am persuaded you have anticipated, forbid me to allow myself that free range of thought and expression which could alone apologize for the intrusive character my letters bear. Having however offer'd what I cannot furnish, I go on to substitute something else perhaps not worth receiving.

You have heard it said in the United States that the agriculture of France has in the course of the present war been considerably improv'd. On this subject I am persuaded there has been no exaggeration. In that part of the country through which I have passed the evidences of plenty abound. The whole earth appears to be in cultivation and the harvests of the present year appear to be as productive as the fields which yield them are extensive. I am inform'd that every part of the country exhibits the same aspect. If this be a fact, there will probably remain, notwithstanding the demands of the armies, a surplus of provisions. Manufactures have declined in the same ratio that the cultivation of the soil has increas'd. War has been made upon the great manufacturing towns and they are in a considerable degree destroy'd. With manufactures France does not supply herself fully from her internal resources. Those of Britain flow in upon her notwithstanding the most severe prohibitory laws. The port of Rotterdam is purposely left open by the English and their goods are imported by the Dutch under Prussian and other neutral colors. They are smuggl'd in great quantities into France. Peace then will find this nation entirely competent to the full supply of her colonies with provisions and needing manufactures to be imported for her own consumption. This state of things will probably change; but it is unquestionably the state of things which will exist at, and for some time after, the termination of the present war. France can take from America tobacco and raw cotton, she can supply us with wines, brandies, and silks.

The papers which I transmitted to you contain'd the evidence on which were founded the transactions of the 18th fructidor or 4th of September.   Since then a letter has been published bearing the signature of Gen Moreau and produced as an unequivocal testimonial of the treason alleg'd to have existed.   You will have seen the letter and have made upon it your own comments, but you will be astonished to hear that perhaps a majority of the people do not believe that Moreau ever wrote it.

The existing political state of France is connected with certain internal and powerfully operating causes by which it has been and will continued to be greatly influenc'd.   Not the least of these is the tenure by which property is held.

In the course of the revolution it is believ'd that more than half of the land of France has become national.   Of this a very considerable proportion has been sold at a low rate.   It is true that much of this property formerly belong'd to the church, but it is also true that much of it belong'd to those who have fallen under the Guillotine or have been termed emigrants.   Among the emigrants are many whose attachment to their country has never been shaken; and what is remarkable, among them are many who were never out of France.   The law upon this subject is worthy of attention.   Any two persons no matter what their reputation, may, to some authority, I believed the municipality of the district, write and subscribe against any person whatever a charge, that such person is an emigrant, on receipt of which the person so charged is without further investigation inscribed on the list of emigrants.   If the person so inscribed be afterwards apprehended while his name remains on the list; the trial, as I understand, is, not of the fact of emigration, but of the identity of the person, and if this identity be established, he is instantly fusilleered.   This law is either rigidly executed or permitted to be relax'd, as the occasion or the temper of the times may direct.

During intervals of humanity some disposition has been manifested to permit the return of those who have never offended, who have been banished by a terror which the government itself has reprobated, and to permit in cases of arrestation, an investigation of the fact of emigration as well as of the identity of the person accused.

There is too a great deal of property which has been sold as national but which in truth was never so, and which may be reclaimed by the original proprietors.

In this state of things the acquirers of national property are of course extremely suspicious.   They form a vast proportion of the population of France.   They are not only important in consequence of their numbers, but in consequence of their vigor, their activity and that unity of interest which produces a unity of effort among them.   The armies too have been promis'd a milliard.   This promise rests upon the national property for its performance.   The effect of these circumstances cannot escape your observation.   Classes of citizens are to be disfranchis'd against the next elections.

Our ministers have not yet, nor do they seem to think it certain that they will be, receiv'd.   Indeed they make arrangements which denote an expectation of returning to America immediately.   The captures of our vessels seem to be only limited by the ability to capture.   That ability is increasing, as the government has let out to hardy adventurers the national frigates.   Among those who plunder us, who are most active in this infamous business, and most loud in vociferating criminations equally absurd and untrue, are some unprincipled apostates who were born in America.   These sea rovers by a variety of means seem to have acquir'd great influence in the government.   This influence will be exerted to prevent an accommodation between the United States and France, and to prevent any regulations which may intercept the passage of the spoils they have made on our commerce, to their pockets. The government I believe is but too well disposed to promote their views.   At present it seems to me to be radically hostile to our country.   I coud wish to form a contrary opinion but to do so I must shut my eyes on every object which presente itself to them, and fabricate in my own mind non existing things, to be substituted for realities, and to form the basis of my creed.   Might I be permitted to hazard an opinion it would be that the Atlantic only can save us, and that no consideration will be sufficiently powerful to check the extremities to which the temper of this government will carry it, but an apprehension that we may be thrown into the arms of Britain.

The negotiations with the Emperor are said not to have been absolutely broken off.   Yesterday it was said that peace with him was certain.   Several couriers have arriv'd lately from Bonaparte and the national debt rose yesterday from seven to ten livres in the hundred.   Whether this is founded on a real expectation of peace with Austria or is the mere work of stock jobbers is not for me to decide.   We are told that Mantua is no longer the obstacle of peace that it is surrendered by the Emperor and that the contest now is for Istria and Dalmatia.

October 27th.—

The definitive peace is made with the Emperor.   You will have seen the conditions.   Venice has experienced the fate of Poland England is threatened with an invasion.

PARIS, march 8th 1798

DEAR SIR

Before this reaches you it will be known universally in America, that scarcely a hope remains of accommodating on principles consistent with justice, or even with the independence of our country, the differences subsisting between France and the United States.   Our ministers are not yet, and it is known to all that they will not be recogniz'd without a previous stipulation on their part, that they will accede to the demands of France.   It is as well known that those demands are for money — to be used in the prosecution of the present war.   It was, some little time past expected, that, convinc'd of the impracticability of effecting the objects of their mission, our ministers were about to demand their passports and to return to the United States,— but this determination if ever made is, I am persuaded, suspended if not entirely relinquish'd. The report has been that so soon as it shall be known that they will not add a loan to the mass of American property already in the hands of this government they will be order'd out of France and a nominal as well as actual war will be commenc'd against the United States.   My opinion has always been that this depends on the state of the war with England. To that object the public attention is very much turn'd, and it is perhaps justly believed that on its issue is staked the independence of Europe and America.   The preparations for an invasion are immense.   A numerous and veteran army lines the coast, and it is said confidently that if the landing of 50,000 men can be effected, no force in England will be able to resist them.   The often repeated tale that the war is made not against the people but the government, maintains, in spite of experience some portion of its credit, and it is believ'd here that a formidable and organiz'd party exists in Britain ready, so soon as a landing shall be effected, to rise and demand a reform. It is supposed that England revolutioniz'd under the protection of a french army will be precisely in the situation of the batavian and Cisalpine Republics and that its wealth, its commerce, and its fleets will be at the disposition of this government. In the meantime this expedition is not without its hazards. An army which arriving safe would sink England may itself be encountered and sunk in the channel. The effect of such a disaster on a nation already tir'd of the war and groaning under the pressure of an enormous taxation, which might discern in it the seeds of another coalition, and which perhaps may not be universally attach'd to existing arrangements, might be extremely serious to those who hold the reins of government.

It is therefore believed by many who do not want intelligence that these formidable military preparations cover and favor secret negotiations for peace. It is rumored (but this is mere rumor) that propositions have been made to England to cede to her the possessions of Portugal in America, in consideration of her restoring the conquests she has made on France Spain and Holland and of her consent that Portugal in Europe shall be annexed to the spanish monarchy. This report is derived from no source in any degree to be relied on, and is supported by no circumstance rendering it in any degree probable other than the existing disposition for partitioning and disposing of empires. I am however persuaded that some secret negotiation with England is now on the tapis. I know almost certainly that a person high in the confidence of this government, who is frequently employed in unofficial negotiation has passed over into that island. We can only conjecture his objects.

You probably know that the affairs of Rastadt are substantially decided. The Emperor and the King of Prussia have declared themselves in favor of ceding to France the whole territory on the left of the rhine on the principle of compensation in the interior of Germany. This would seem to me to take from England the hope of once more arming Austria and Prussia in her favor, for certainly had those powers contemplated such an event they would not have effected

the pacification of the empire.   This circumstance will probably
influence the secret negotiations with England.   It will probably
too very much influence the affairs of Swisserland.   The determination of France to revolutionize the helvetic body has
been long known.   In the pais de vaud belonging to the Can-
ton of Berne this revolution has commenced and is completely
effected under the protection and guidance of a french army
for which that little country has already paid about 800,000
livres Swiss.   France has insisted on extending the revolution throughout Swisserland.   The existing governments in
some of the cantons and especially in Bern declare their willingness to reorganize their constitution on the base of an equality
of rights and a free representation, but they protest against
foreign interposition and against a revolutionary intermediate
government.   In support of this resolution they have collected
all their force and most of the cantons which have already
changed their form of government have furnished their con-
tingents.   The mass of the people in Bern are firmly united
and seem to join the government in saying that they will to the
last man bury themselves under the ruins of the country rather
than submit to the intermeddling of the foreigners in the formation of their constitutions.   Such is the present truly interesting state of Swisserland.   A powerful military force is
advancing upon them and at the same time it is said that the
negotiations are to be opened.   The terms offered however are
supposed to be such as if accepted will place that country in
the same situation as if conqured.   A revolutionary government is insisted on.

The Swiss have observed an exact neutrality throughout the
late war on the continent and have ever since the peace sought
to preserve the forbearance of France by concessions not perfectly compatible with the rights of an independent nation.

On the side of Italy it is believ'd that materials are preparing to revolutionize Sardinia and Naples.

Some jealosies exist with respect to Spain.   Augereau has
been ordered some time since to Perpignan a position from
which he may with advantage overawe that monarchy, invade
Portugal or preserve order in the south during the ensuing
elections.   It is the common opinion that shoud the elections in
any respect disappoint the wishes of the directory it will be on
the side of Jacobinism.   The existing government appears to

me to need only money to enable it to effect all its objects. A numerous brave and well disciplined army seems to be devoted to it. The most military and the most powerful nation on earth is entirely at its disposal. Spain Italy and Holland with the Hanseatic towns obey its mandates. Yet there is a difficulty in procuring funds to work this vast machine. Credit being annihilated the actual impositions of the year must equal the disbursements. The consequence is that notwithstanding the enormous contributions made by foreign nations France is overwhelmed with taxes. The proprietor complains that his estate yields him nothing. Real property pays in taxes nearly a third of its produce and is greatly reduc'd in its price. The patriotic gifts for the invasion of England to which men have been stimulated by all possible means have not exceeded by the highest calculation 100,000 livres. This is the amount stated by a person who charges the officers of the treasury with peculation. The treasury admits 65,000 livres. It is supposed that recourse will be had to a forc'd loan and that the neighbors of the republic will be required to contribute still further to its wants. A very heavy beginning has been made with Rome.

March 10th.—

The papers announce that the troops of France and Swisserland have had some severe encounters in which those of the latter have been worsted and the French entered Fribourg and Soluere. Report (which as yet wants confirmation and indeed is disbelieved) also says that Berne has submitted.

LETTER TO GEORGE WASHINGTON

RICHMOND, July 11th. 1796.

SIR:

I will not attempt to express those sensations, which your letter of the 8th instant has increased. Was it possible for me in the present crisis of my affairs to leave the United States, such is my conviction of the importance of that duty, which you would confide to me, and (pardon me if I add) of the fidelity with which I should attempt to perform it, that I would certainly forego any consideration not decisive with respect to future fortunes, and would surmount that just diffidence I have ever entertained of myself, to make an effort to convey

truly and faithfully to the government of France those sentiments, which I have ever believed to be entertained by that of
the United States.

I have forwarded your letter to Mr. Pinckney. The recall
of our minister at Paris has been conjectured, while its probable necessity has been regretted by those, who love more than
all others our own country. I will certainly do myself the
honor of waiting on you at Mount Vernon.

>With every sentiment of respect and attachment,
>>I am, &c.
>>>J. MARSHALL.

The above letter is in reply to the following letter from
Washington, which is labelled " Private," and which is printed
in " Washington's Writings," by Jared Sparks, Vol. XI,
p. 143 :

>MOUNT VERNON, 8 July, 1796.

DEAR SIR,

In confidence I inform you, that it has become indispensably
necessary to recall our minister at Paris, and to send one in his
place, who will explain faithfully the views of this government, and ascertain those of France.

Nothing would be more pleasing to me, than that you should
be this organ, if it were only for a temporary absence of a few
months; but, it being feared, that even this could not be made
to comport with your present pursuits, I have, in order that as
little delay as possible may be incurred, put the enclosed letter
under cover, to be forwarded to its address, if you decline the
present offer, or to be returned to me if you accept it. Your
own correct knowledge of circumstances renders details unnecessary. I shall only add, therefore, that I am, dear Sir, &c.

>>GEORGE WASHINGTON.

>PHILADELPHIA, Jany 16th, 1800.

SIR

Accept my sincere thanks for a copy of the oration delivered
at New Rochelle on the 1st of Jany. which has reached me
today.

I have read it with that melancholy pleasure which is inspired by well merited & well executed eulogies on those whose

deaths we greatly lament, & whose memory is most dear to us.

To the friends of the departed patriot whose talents & virtues you have valiantly & so justly celebrated, & to the friends of the American character, the deep & universal grief which has been every where manifested, & the impressive orations which have flowed from that grief, constitute some consolation for the irreparable loss our country has sustained.

With very much respect
I am Sir your obedt. Servt.
J. MARSHALL.[59a]

Marshall's conception of the judicial character placed the office where it should be, on the highest plane of morals, and served in tempestuous times to maintain the dignity and power of his court in the estimation of all fair-minded lawyers.

Mr. Jay, the first Chief Justice of the United States, on his first circuit had declined the numerous invitations of his friends to reside with them, saying, in delicate terms to one of his friends: " As a man, and your friend, I should be happy in accepting it, but as a judge I have my doubts — they will occur to you without details."

In 1834 Marshall received an invitation to attend a public dinner given at Petersburg, Virginia, in honor of Mr. Leigh, which he declined in the following letter, addressed to the committee:

RICHMOND, October 6, 1834.

GENTLEMEN —

I have received your polite and flattering invitation to the dinner to be given to Mr. Leigh by his friends in Petersburg, on the 15th of this month. United, as I have long been with that gentleman, by ties of personal friendship, and feeling as I do the highest respect for his talents and character, I should make a point of manifesting these sentiments by accepting your kind invitation, were I not restrained by considerations which have uniformly influenced my conduct; and which I do not think

[59a] The above letter was found in " Homes of American Statesmen, with Anecdotal, Personal, and Descriptive Sketches by Various Authors. Illustrated with engravings on wood, from drawings by Döpler and Daguerreotypes: and Fac-similes of Autograph Letters." New York, Alfred W. Upham, 1860, pp. 274-276. No information to show to whom this letter was sent can be found.

myself at liberty to disregard.   I have always believed, and acted on the opinion, that the delicacy belonging to my peculiar official situation, ought to prevent my engaging in the political conflicts of the day.   I could not yield to the inclination I feel to show my grateful sense of the partial kindness expressed in your letter of invitation, without affording at least the appearance of departing from a rule which has been prescribed by a conviction of its propriety.   I am therefore compelled to deny myself the pleasure of participating in the festivities of the occasion; wishing you, gentlemen, and those you represent, all the happiness you expect,

I remain your obliged and obedient servant,

J. MARSHALL.[60]

TO MESSRS. GEORGE W. HARRIS AND OTHERS.

LETTER [61] FROM JOHN MARSHALL TO GEORGE WASHINGTON

RICHMOND, May 1st, 99

DEAR SIR

You may possibly have seen a paragraph in a late publication, stating that several important offices in the gift of the executive, & among others that of secretary of state, had been attainable by me.   Few of the unpleasant occurrences produced by my declaration as a candidate for congress (& they have been very abundant) have given me more real chagrin than this.   To make a parade of proffered offices is a vanity which I trust I do not possess, but to boast of the never in my power would argue a littleness of mind at which I ought to blush.

I know not how the author may have acquired his information, but I beg leave to assure you that he never received it directly nor indirectly from me.   I had no previous knowledge that such a publication was designed, or I would certainly have suppressed so much of it as relates to this subject.

The writer was unquestionably actuated by a wish to serve me & by resentment at the various malignant calumnies that have meen so profusely bestowed on me.   One of these was that I only wished a seat in Congress for the purpose of ob-

[60] The above letter is printed in the "Niles Register," 1834, and in the *American Law Review*, Vol. XXII, p. 711.

[61] On the other side of this letter is written in Washington's handwriting, "From General Marshall, 1st May, 1799."

taining some office which my devotion to the administration might procure. To repel this was obviously the motive of the indiscreet publication I so much regret.

A wish to rescue myself in your opinion from the imputation of an idle vanity which forms if I know myself, no part of my character, will I trust apologize for the trouble this explanation may give you.

Messrs Goode & Gray who are the successors of Messrs Clarborne & Harrison are both Federalists. Mr. Hancock who opposed Mr. Tris will, to our general disappointment not succeed. At least such is our present information. Should Haywood or Preston be elected the Virginia delegation will stand ten in opposition to the government's nine in support of it.

Parties, I hear will not be so nearly balanced in our state legislature. With the most respectful attachment
I remain Sir, your Obedt Servt
J. MARSHALL.

LETTER FROM JOHN MARSHALL TO GEORGE WASHINGTON

RICHMOND, May 16th 1799.

DEAR SIR

Neither Col. Carrington nor Col. Heth are now in town. So soon as they arrive your letter of the 12th inst. with its inclosures, will be communicated to them. I wish it may be in our power to furnish any useful information on the subjects inquired into.

Returns of all the elections have been received. The failure of Col. Hancock & of Major Haywood was unexpected & has [not clear] us to sight in the legislature of the Union.

In the State elections very considerable changes have been made. There are from fifty to sixty new members. Unfortunately, the strength of parties is not materially varied. The opposition maintains its majority in the house of Delegates. The consequence must be an antifederalist Senator & Governor. In addition to this the baneful influence of a legislature hostile perhaps to the Union — or if not so,— to all its measures will yet be kept up.

If it be true that France has declared war against Austria, it will be now apparent that it would have been wise to have attempted the relief of Ehrenbreitstein & the preservation of Naples & Sardinia. Even this instructive lesson will probably make no impression on the nations of Europe or the people of America.

With the utmost respect & attachment,
I am Sir, your Obed't Serv't,
J. MARSHALL.

LETTER FROM JOHN MARSHALL TO GEORGE WASHINGTON

RICHMOND, June 12th 99.

DEAR SIR

Your letter of the 6th inst. which came by the last mail was communicated to Col. Carrington & would have been shown also to Col. Heth had he been within our immediate reach.

Col. Croppin is a man of fair character correct politics & unquestionable courage. No doubt can be entertained of his fitness for the command of a regiment nor should I have hesitated to transmit him immediately your letter, but for one consideration produced by his former military station. He was in our late army a Lieut. Col. & he performed the duties of that office with reputation. It is probable that he may feel wounded at being offered the same grade under others whom he thus commanded & who are perhaps in nothing his superiors. It is presumed that officers in the actual army will command those of the same grade in the eventual army. If you are correct in this then Colonels Bentley & Parker who were bothe subalterns when Col. Croppin was a field officer, & who are not supposed to have manifested any superiority over him, will now take rank of him. The former relative rank of officers ought certainly not to be the rule which should positively decide their present rank. But among gentlemen in other respects equal it is difficult entirely to lose sight of it. It is suggested by Col. Carrington that if the eventful army shall be called into actual service Brigadiers General will necessarily be appointed from Virginia & he has supposed that Genl. Clarke & Col. Croppin, to whom I will take the liberty of adding Genl Posey, would be proper persons to contemplate for the station.

For this single reason Col. Carrington & myself deemed it advisable to detain your letter to Col. Croppin until your further directions can be reviewed. Should you still incline to transmit it to him, we trust the delay will produce no inconvenience.

Col. [name not clear] who resides in the county of Bedford, was in the late war brigade Major to Genl Muhlenberg.   He is a man of considerable energy of character.   His activity & courage recommend him as a military man, but those who know him best suppose him better fitted for the command of a battalion than of a regiment.   It is probable that he would accept a majority under a man he could respect, sufficiently respect to serve under without mortification.   Col. James Breckenbridge of [not clear] although never heretofore in service is believed to possess many excellent qualities as a soldier, to which he adds a weight of character which would I think induce Col. Munnis to be content with a majority of his regiment.   To the appointment of Col. Breckenbridge there would be this objection.   It would take him out of the State Legislature where he is a valuable & influential member.

Genl Porterfield of Augusta is in every respect proper for the command of a regiment.

Genl. Blackwell of Fauquier was a Captain in the late army & in my opinion, one of our most valuable officers.   He is a cool steady sensible & brave man whose conduct is always correct & who would in my opinion command a regiment with reputation to himself & advantage to his country.

Col Swearingen of Berkley was also a captain in the late army & maintains a very high reputation.   I am not personally acquainted with him but Cols Carrington & Heth are & they speak highly of him.

I do not immediately recollect any others among the old officers whom I could name for so high an office as the command of a regiment.   I am aware that those I have mentioned cannot should you on further enquiry approve of them, be all appointed, but I have named them because it is possible that those first applied to may be disinclined to enter into the Army.

Virginia has sustained a very serious loss which all good men will long lament, in the death of Mr. Henry.   He is said to have expired on Thursday last.   The intelligence is not absolutely certain but scarcely a hope is entertained of its untruth.

With the most respectful attachment

I remain Sir, your obt Servt.

J. MARSHALL.

LETTER FROM JOHN MARSHALL TO GEORGE WASHINGTON

RICHMOND, June 21st 99.

DEAR SIR

An accidental absence from town prevented my returning by the last mail the inclosed letter.

I am extremely happy that the liberty we have taken to suspend its transmission to Col Cropper has not displeased you.

Your second letter to that gentleman is just received & will be immediately put in the post office with a proper direction.

With the most perfect respect & attachment

I remain Sir your obedt Servt

J. MARSHALL.

LETTER FROM JOHN MARSHALL TO JAMES MONROE

RICHMOND July 13th 1825.

DEAR SIR.

I am greatly flattered by your letters of the 29th of June accompanying the documents stating your claims on the United States.

There was undoubtedly great reason for your requesting such a final settlement of all your accounts as would relieve you from future disquiet; and in making that settlement you have I think a right to expect that the justice of your country will not be stinted by any implied concession made under circumstances when it could not be with held.   I can perceive no reason why you should not receive as much as has ever been allowed to others for similar services; and I trust this reasonable expectation will not be disappointed.

With the sincerest wishes for your health and happiness and with high and respectful esteem

I am dear Sir,

Your obedt

J. MARSHALL.

LETTER FROM JOHN MARSHALL TO GEORGE WASHINGTON

PHILADELPHIA July 7th. 97.

SIR.

I have had the pleasure of receiving from Mr. Pickering your letter to me inclosing others for France intrusted to my care, to the delivery of which I shall be particularly attentive.

Receive Sir my warm & grateful acknowledgments for the polite &, allow me to add, friendly wishes which you express concerning myself as well as for the honor of being mentioned in your letter.

I expect to embark in the course of the next week in the Grace for Amsterdam there to join Genl Pinckney, & thence to proceed if we be permitted to proceed to Paris. Mr. Gerry, if he accepts the appointment, which is not yet certain, he having requested some short time for deliberation, will follow. Claypole's paper by the mail of today exhibits the case of M. Blount. Opinions here are as various on this subject as on every other — not with respect M. Blount — all concur in giving him up, but with respect to the object of the scheme, the means of execution & the degree of crime or indiscretion attached to different foreign ministers. It is by some conjectured that M Blount himself gave to the Spanish minister the intelligence on which was founded his application to the government of the United States.

I remain Sir with the most respectful attachment
Your Obedt Servt.   J. MARSHALL.

LETTER FROM JOHN MARSHALL TO GEORGE WASHINGTON

PHILADELPHIA, June 22d 98.

DEAR SIR

Your letter to Genl Dumas was delivered by me to his lady from whom in consequence of it I received during my stay in Paris the most polite and flattering attention. She delivered me the enclosed answer which was written in Copenhagen & forwarded to her.

Having heard that Mrs Marshall is in Westchester I hope immediately to set out for that place.

Permit me to acknowledge the receipt of your very polite & obliging letter in answer to that which I did myself the honor to address to you from the Hague. I had not Sir expected to draw you into a correspondence which might intrude on your leisure but merely to do myself the pleasure of communicating to you occasionally such facts as it might be agreeable to you to receive.

With the most sincere respect & attachment
I remain Sir your Obedt Servt.
J. MARSHALL.

LETTER FROM JOHN MARSHALL TO JAMES MADISON

RICHMOND November 29. 1790

DEAR SIR:

My friend Mr. Giles will present you this— He is particularly desirous of being known to you. I should not presume so far on the degree of your acquaintance with which I have been honored as to introduce any gentleman to your attention if I did not persuade myself that you will never regret or change any favorable opinion you may form of him.

With much respect & esteem
I am dear Sir
Your obedt Servt
J. MARSHALL.

LETTER FROM JOHN MARSHALL TO JAMES MONROE

RICHMOND, June 25th 1812.

DEAR SIR.

On my return today from my farm where I pass a considerable portion of my time in laborious relaxation, I found a copy of the message of the President of 1st inst. accompanied by the report of the committe of foreign relations & the declaration of war against Britain [not clear].

Permit me to subjoin to my thanks for this mark of your attention my fervent wish that this momentous measure may, in its operation on this interest of honor of our country, disappoint only its enemies.

Whether my prayer be heard or not I shall remain with respectful esteem

Your obedt Servt.
J. MARSHALL.

LETTER FROM JOHN MARSHALL TO JAMES MONROE

WASHINGTON March 7th 1825.

DEAR SIR.

Permit me to ask your acceptance of our colonia history which is offered as a mark of the affectionate revolutions excited in the bosom of the author when he looks back to times long since gone by.

In the momentous and then unlooked for events which have since taken place, you have filled a large space in the public mind, and have been conspicuously instrumental in effecting objects of great interest to our common country. Believe me when I congratulate you on the circumstances under which your political course terminates, and that I feel sincere pleasure in the persuasion that your administration may be reviewed with real approbation by our wisest statesmen.

With great respect & esteem
I am dear Sir
Your obedt
J. MARSHALL.

LETTER FROM JOHN MARSHALL TO JAMES MONROE

RICHMOND June 13. 1822.

SIR.

I have received the copy of your message to Congress on the subject of internal improvements which you did me the honor to transmit me and thank you for it. I have read it with great attention and interest.

This is a question which very much divides the opinions of intelligent men; and it is not to be expected that there will be an entire concurrence in that you have expressed. All however will I think admit that your views are profound and that you have thought deeply on the subject. To me they appear to be most generally just.

A general power over internal improvements, if to be exercised by the Union would certainly be cumbersome to the government, & of no utility to the people. But to the extent you recommend, it would be productive of no mischief, and of great good.

I despair however of the adoption of such a measure.

With great respect and esteem
I am Sir, your Obedt Servt
J. MARSHALL.

LETTER FROM JOHN MARSHALL TO JAMES MONROE

RICHMOND December 9. 1823.

DEAR SIR.

I received yesterday the message of the President to Congress, franked by yourself. Allow me to express the grateful sentiment with which I acknowledge this mark of polite attention, and this wide use of your recollection of times which are long passed away.   I shall not forget it.

I have read with interest and attention the comprehensive views which you have taken of our affairs, and think with you that we cannot look on the present state of the world with indifference.

With great respect and esteem
I remain your obedt
J. Marshall.

LETTER FROM JOHN MARSHALL TO JAMES MONROE

Richmond Dec. 13th 1824.

Sir

I am indebted to your polite attention for a copy of your message to Congress and am much gratified by this mark of your recollection.

While I take the liberty to express my personal regrets that your retirement approaches so nearly, and that circumstances are supposed to forbid your continuing to afford your services to your country.   I may be permitted to congratulate you on the auspicious circumstances which have attended your course as Chief Magistrate of the United States, and which crown its termination.   You may look back with pleasure to several very interesting events which have taken place during your administration, and have the rare felicity not to find the retrospect darkened by a single spot the reviewer of which ought to pain yourself or your fellow citizen.

With great & respectful esteem
I remain your obedt
J. Marshall.

LETTER FROM JOHN MARSHALL TO JAMES MONROE

Richmond July 30. 1826.

Dear Sir.

I have had the pleasure of receiving your letter recommending Mr. Randall to the vacant office in the clerkship of the Supreme Court.   I trust I need not say that there is no person whose recommendation contains more influence with me than yours.   I feel the utmost confidence in the merit of this gentleman, and that this office, should he receive the appointment will be well bestowed. To myself personally, though I am not acquainted with him, it will be far from [not clear].

I have never in my life been required to perform a more painful duty than making this appointment. In addition to the numbers & great respectability of the applicants, a circumstance which of itself would create sufficient difficulty in making a selection, the list exhibits many of my highly valued personal friends, and the sons of others with whom I have been connected by ties of close affection & esteem. I cannot point to one without looking at others, who must be excluded, with extreme regret. Among those too who have supported individual and of course opposing candidates, are the most valued friends I have in the world. In this to me new as well as a distressing situation. I have made no positive determination, but have uniformly said that a clerk must be appointed, and that some sacrifice of individual preference must be made to effect this necessary object. That under this conviction, I shall go into the election prepared to support that one of the many I could wish to appoint Who can unite a sufficient number of votes to secure an appointment. I shall feel much more chagrined at being compelled to pass by 10 manly deserving men to whom I feel the best disposition. Than of pleasure at giving my voice in favor of the successful candidate. I hope you are not in danger of famine from the drought as many of us are. With great respectful esteem

I am dear Sir, your Obedt

J. MARSHALL.

Letter from John Marshall and Andrew Ronold to Thomas Jefferson. Their opinion that Farrell and Jones have a legal claim against Randolph and Wayler. This letter is in Manuscript Division of Library of Congress, Series 6, Vol. 3, No. 86.

April 1, 1791.

We are decidedly of opinion that if any engagement relative to the consignment of a Gumeaman to Randolph & Wayler was entered into subsequent to the receipt of Mr. Wayler's letter of the 14th of May 1772, That Messrs Farrel & Jones have a good claim on the writer of that letter for indemnity.

1st April 1791.

ANDREW RONOLD

J. MARSHALL.

Letter from John Marshall to Thomas Jefferson.   This letter is plainly dated " March 4th, 1781."   But 1781 must be wrong, for on the other side of the letter is written in Jefferson's hand: " March 4th, 1801.   Marshall John."

March 4th 1781.
[corrected 1801]

SIR.

I have received your letter requesting me to perform the duties of Secretary of State until a successor be appointed.   I shall with great pleasure obey this request & beg leave to assure you that I am with high & respectful consideration

Your obedt Humble Servt.

J. MARSHALL.

Letter from John Marshall to Thomas Jefferson.   This letter is in Series 6, Vol. 6, No. 8, Manuscript Division of Library of Congress.   It is labeled as having been dated probably 1797.

J. Marshall begs leave to accompany his respectful compliments to Mr. Jefferson with assurance of the regret he feels at being absent when Mr. Jefferson did him the honor to call on him.

J. Marshall is extremely sensible to the obliging expression contained in Mr. Jefferson's polite billet of yesterday.

He sets out tomorrow for Winchester & would with pleasure charge himself with any commands from Mr. Jefferson to that part of Virginia.

(On the back is written " Marshall John.")

LETTER FROM JOHN MARSHALL TO THOMAS JEFFERSON

WASHINGTON March 2. 1801.

SIR.

I am this instant honored with yours of today.   Not being the Secretary of State, & only performing the duties of that office at the request of the President, the request becomes indispensably necessary to give validity to any act which purports to be done on the 4th of March.

In the confidence that it will be viewed I shall immediately proceed to sign the sea letters.   No form is prescribed.   Any letter desiring me to do the duties of the office generally on the 4th of March will be sufficient.

I shall with much pleasure attend to administer the oath of office on the 4th & shall make a point of being punctual. The records of the office of the department of state furnish no information respecting the oaths which have been heretofore taken. That prescribed in the constitution seems to me to be the only one which is to be administered. I will however enquire what has been the practice.

The chief clerk of this department will attend you at the time requested

I have the honor to be with great respect Sir
Your most obedt hble servt
J. MARSHALL.

LETTER FROM JOHN MARSHALL TO JOHN AMBLER, ESQ., OF NEAR WILLIAMSBURG, VA.

PHILADELPHIA Dec. 29th 99.

DEAR SIR.

Receive our sincere congratulations on your marriage & our wishes for the happiness of Mrs. Ambler and yourself. We have at this place no news but what is contained in the public papers. They will show you the manner in which we have manifested our deep affection for the loss of Genl Washington. Never was mourning more universal or so generally sincere.

Nothing of very serious importance has yet come before Congress. The material business of the session is preparing in the committees. I hope a mutual spirit of toleration and forbearance will succeed to the violence which seemed in too great a degree to govern last year. As far as I can judge from present appearances this will be a temperate session & I wish most devoutly that the prevalence of moderation here may diffuse the same spirit among our fellow citizens at large.

In the State of Pennsylvania there appears to be a considerable degree of exasperation among parties. The new Governor has, it is said, greatly increased it by turning or threatening to turn out of office every man however respectable & well qualified, who voted against him. I am told that every clerk in the state is removed. The clerks here, who are [not clear], hold their offices during the pleasure of the Governor.

This is a very irritating measure & will koop up in a considerable degree that party use for which this state has been long so remarkable.

Molly joins me in compliments to Mr. Ambler.

I am dear Sir with much regard

Your Obedt

J. MARSHALL.

LETTER [62] FROM J. MARSHALL TO DANIEL WEBSTER

RICHMOND, June 6, 1832.

MY DEAR SIR:

I thank you very sincerely for the copy with which you have favored me of your speeches on the bill for renewing the charter of the Bank of the United States. I need not say that I consider an accommodation of the tariff question itself as scarcely more interesting to our country than the passage of that bill. Your argument presents the subject in its strongest point of view, and to me seems unanswerable. Mr. Ritchie, in his Inquirer, informs the people of Virginia that Mr. Tazewell has refuted you completely. This he may have done in opinion of Mr. Ritchie. I have not seen Mr. Tazewell's speech, and do not understand from The Inquirer whether his refutation applies to your speech in favor of the bill or to that against the amendment offered by Mr. Moor. By the way, your argument against that amendment is founded in an idea which to me is quite novel. I had often heard it advanced that the States have no constitutional power to establish banks of circulation, but never that Congress might not introduce into the charter a restraining principle, which might prohibit branches altogether, or require the assent of a State to their introduction, or a principle which might subject them to State taxation. This may be considered nòt as granting power of taxation to a State, for a State possesses that power; but as withdrawing a bar which the constitution opposes to the exercise of this power over a franchise created by Congress for national purposes, unless the constitution of the franchise in its creation has this quality engrafted on it. I however am far from undertaking to dissent from your proposition; I only say it is new, and I ponder on it.

[62] "Private Correspondence of Daniel Webster," Vol. I, pp. 518-519.

With great and respectful esteem, I am your obedient servant,

J. MARSHALL.

P. S. I only meant to express my obligation for your attention, and I have betrayed myself into the politics of the day.

LETTER [63] FROM CHIEF JUSTICE MARSHALL TO DANIEL WEBSTER

RICHMOND, April 3, 1826.

DEAR SIR:

I had the pleasure of receiving a few days past, under cover from you, the documents accompanying the late message of the President to the House of Representatives on the Panama mission. We anticipate a tolerably animated discussion of this subject. I thank you very sincerely for this mark of polite recollection, and beg you to believe that I remain with sincere regard,

Yours,
J. MARSHALL.

LETTER [64] FROM CHIEF JUSTICE MARSHALL TO DANIEL WEBSTER

RICHMOND, May 20, 1826.

DEAR SIR,— I returned yesterday from North Carolina, and had the pleasure of finding your speech on the mission to Panama, under cover from yourself. I had previously read it with deep interest, but was not on that account the less gratified at this polite mark of your attention. I can preserve it more certainly in a pamphlet form, than in that of a newspaper.

Whatever doubts may very fairly be entertained respecting the policy of the mission, as an original measure, I think it was not involved in much difficulty when considered as it came before the House of Representatives.

I congratulate you on closing a most laborious session, and am with great and respectful esteem,

Your obedient servant,
J. MARSHALL.

[63] " Private Correspondence of Daniel Webster," Vol. I, p. 405.
[64] " *Ibid.*, pp. 406-407.

LETTER [65] FROM CHIEF JUSTICE MARSHALL TO
DANIEL WEBSTER

January 23, 1831.

DEAR SIR:

I have just received the copy of you " Speeches and Forensic Arguments," and am much flattered by this mark of your attention.   I beg you to present my compliments to Mrs. Webster; and to say that I think myself, in part, indebted to her for it.   At all events, she has, I perceive, had some agency in conferring the favor.

I shall read the volume with pleasure, and preserve it with care.

Will you allow me to say that, on looking over the contents, I felt at the first moment some disappointment at not seeing two speeches delivered by you in the first Congress, I believe, of which you were a member.

With great and respectful esteem,

I am, your obedient,

J. MARSHALL.

One of the first acts of Mr. Webster on entering Congress was to introduce certain resolutions calling upon the Executive for information respecting the time and mode in which the repeal of the French Decrees had been communicated to our Government.   As this whole matter stood before the public at the time of the declaration of war, it appeared that our Government had been deceived by the French Ministry, or that they were in possession of a repealing decree when the war was declared, and had withheld it; for no such degree had made its appearance until after the declaration had passed through Congress.   Mr. Webster considered that the reputation of this country was at stake in this affair, because the French foreign secretary had declared to the American Minister at Paris, on the 1st of May, 1812, that a copy of the repealing decree had been furnished to his predecessor, and that another had been transmitted to the French Minister at Washington at the time of its date, which was April 28, 1811. Mr. Webster, therefore, for the purpose of eliciting all the facts, and in order to have them placed in their true light before the country, so framed his resolutions that, if they were

[65] " Life of Daniel Webster," Curtis, Vol. I, p. 110.

answered at all, the whole matter must be disclosed. The resolutions were introduced by him on the 10th of June, 1813, accompanied by some temperate remarks concerning the doubt in which this matter was then enveloped. What Mr. Webster said on this occasion strongly attracted the attention of Chief Justice Marshall.

Nearly twenty years afterward, when Mr. Webster's collected speeches were first published, we see by the above letter that the Chief Justice was greatly disappointed at not finding the speech, here alluded to, in the volume.

On the same day that the above letter was written to Webster by Marshall Judge Story wrote one to Webster also, which further explains the above letter, and also verifies it in an excellent manner, and shows the aged Chief Justice, now seventy-five years old, to have a freshness of memory very unusual. The letter from Judge Story to Daniel Webster was as follows:

WASHINGTON, January 23, 1831.

MY DEAR SIR:—

After the Chief Justice (Marshall) had received the volume of your speeches this morning, he came into my chamber, and told me he had been looking over the index, and noticed two omissions of speeches which he remembered you had made in Congress at an early period of your public life, and which he had then read. One was on some resolutions, calling upon President Madison for the proof of the repeal of the Berlin and Milan Decrees; the other on the subject of the Previous Question. He observed: "I read these speeches with very great pleasure and satisfaction at the time. At the time when the first was delivered, I did not know Mr. Webster; but I was so much struck with it, that I did not hesitate then to state that Mr. Webster was a very able man, and would become one of the very first statesmen in America, and perhaps the very first."

Such praise from such a source ought to be very gratifying. Consider that he is now seventy-five years old, and that he speaks of his recollections of you some eighteen years ago with a freshness which shows you how deeply your reasoning impressed itself on his mind. Keep this in memoriam rei.

Yours very truly,

THE HON. DANIEL WEBSTER.   JOSEPH STORY.

LETTER [66] FROM JOHN MARSHALL ON THE MODE OF
SELECTING A PRESIDENT

James Wilson of Pennsylvania, one of the ablest and wisest men of the country, in the Convention that framed the Constitution (as appears in the "Debates" of that body, reported by Madison,) on the 24th of July, 1787, said the great difficulty seems to spring from the Mode of election. He suggested a mode, that the Executive be elected for six years, by not more than fifteen members of the national legislature, to be drawn from it by lot, and to make the election without separating, thus avoiding intrigue in the first instance, and also diminishing dependence.

James Hillhouse was one of the strong men of the first age of the Republic. On the 12th of April, 1808, he introduced in the Senate of the United States certain articles of amendment of the Constitution, which included a reduction of the term of office of the President to one year, of Senators to three years, Congressmen to one year, and also the abolition of the office of Vice-President.

Nothing came at the time from the proposals of either Mr. Wilson or Mr. Hillhouse. The plans of these two distinguished statesmen, like other truths, cannot be made acceptable, by any force of reason or persuasion, but only by experience. Upham in his Life of Pickering says: "Experience long ago wrought a conviction in the best minds known in our history, that such a mode of selecting a President as Mr. Hillhouse, following Mr. Wilson, had urged, ought to be adopted." After the former had retired from public life, and more than twenty years had intervened, he opened a correspondence on the very same subject with some of the most eminent of his former associates and acquaintances. Chief Justice Marshall, writing in 1830, says his "views of this subject had changed a good deal since 1808." He also says: "Your plan comes in conflict with so many opposing interests and deep-rooted prejudices, that I would despair of its success, were its ability still more apparent than it is." Again, "We must proceed with our present system, till its evils become still more obvious." His views are fully presented in the following passage:

[66] "Life of Pickering," Vol. III, pp. 108, 109.

" My own private mind has been slowly and reluctantly advancing to the belief that the present mode of choosing the Chief Magistrate threatens the most serious danger to the public happiness. The passions of men are inflamed to so fearful an extent, large masses are so embittered against each other, that I dread the consequences. The election agitates every section of the United States, and the ferment is never to subside. Scarcely is a President elected, before the machinations, respecting a successor, commence. Every political question is affected by it. All those who are in office, all those who want office, are put in motion. The angriest, I might say the worst, passions are roused, and put into full activity. Vast masses united closely, move in opposite directions, animated with the most hostile feelings towards each other. What is to be the effect of all this? Age is, perhaps, unreasonably timid. Certain it is, that I now dread consequences that I once thought imaginary. I feel disposed to take refuge under some less turbulent and less dangerous mode of choosing the Chief Magistrate; and my mind suggests none less objectionable than that you have proposed. We shall no longer be enlisted under the banners of particular men. Strife will no longer be excited, when it can no longer effect its object. Neither the people at large, nor the councils of the nation, will be agitated by the all-disturbing question, Who shall be President? Yet he will, in truth, be chosen substantially by the people. The Senators must always be among the most able men of the States. Though not appointed for the particular purpose, they must always be appointed for important purposes, and must possess a large share of the public confidence.

If the people of the United States were to elect as many persons as compose one Senatorial class, and the President was to be chosen among them by lot, in the manner you propose, he would be substantially elected by the people; and yet, such a mode of election would be recommended by no advantages which your plan does not possess. In many respects, it would be less eligible.

" Reasoning a priori, I should undoubtedly pronounce the system adopted by the Convention the best that could be devised. Judging from experience, I am driven to a different conclusion."

Chancellor Kent wrote as follows: " The popular election of the President (which, by the way, was not intended by the framers of the Constitution) is that part of the machine of our government that I am afraid, is doomed to destroy us." " Our plan of election of a President, I apprehend, has failed of its purpose, as it was presumed and foretold that it would fail, by some of the profoundest statesmen of 1787 . . . has already disturbed and corrupted the administration of the government, and cherishes intrigue, duplicity, abuse of power," etc.

LETTER [67] FROM CHIEF JUSTICE MARSHALL TO JAMES K. PAULDING

RICHMOND, April 4th 1835.

SIR:

Your favor of the 22d of March was received in the course of the mail, but I have been confined to my room, and am only now resuming my pen.

The single difficulty I feel in complying with your request arises from my repugnance to anything which may be construed into an evidence of that paltry vanity which, if I know myself forms no part of my character. To detail any conversation which might seem to insinuate that General Washington considered my engaging in the political transactions of the United States an object of sufficient consequence to induce him to take an interest in effecting it, may look like boasting that I held a more favorable place in the opinion of that great man than the fact would justify. I do not, however, think that this, perhaps, fastidious feeling would justify a refusal to answer an enquiry made in terms entitled to my sincere acknowledgments.

All who were then old enough to notice the public affairs of the United States, recollect the arduous struggle of 1798 and 1799. General Washington, it is well known, took a deep interest in it. He believed that the real independence, the practical self government of our country, depended greatly on its issue — on our resisting the encroachments of France.

I had devoted myself to my profession, and, though actively and zealously engaged in support of the measures of his ad-

[67] *Lippincott's Magazine,* Vol. II, pp. 624-625.

ministration in the legislature of Virginia, had uniformly declined any situation which might withdraw me from the bar. In 1798 I was very strongly pressed by the Federalists to become a candidate for Congress, and the gentleman of the party who had offered himself to the district, proposed to resign his pretensions in my favor. I had however positively refused to accede to the proposition and believed that I could not be induced to change my determination. In this state of things, in August or September 1798 as well as I recollect, I received an invitation from General Washington to accompany his nephew, the late Judge Washington on a visit to Mount Vernon. I accepted the invitation, and remained at Mount Vernon four or five days. During this time the walk and conversation in the Piazza mentioned by Mr. Lewis took place.

General Washington urged the importance of the crisis, expressed his decided conviction that every man who could contribute to the success of sound opinions was required by the most sacred duty to offer his services to the public, and pressed me to come into the Congress of the ensuing year.

After the very natural declaration of distrust in my ability to do any good, I told him that I had made large pecuniary engagements which required close attention to my profession, and which would distress me should the emoluments derived from it be abandoned. I also mentioned the assurance I had given to the gentleman then a candidate, which I could not honorably violate.

He thought that gentleman would still willingly withdraw in my favor, and that my becoming a member of Congress for the present, would not sacrifice my practice as a lawyer. At any rate the sacrifice might be temporary.

After continuing this conversation for some time, he directed my attention to his own conduct. He had withdrawn from office with a declaration of his determination never again, under any circumstances, to enter public life. No man could be more sincere in making that declaration, nor could any man feel stronger motives for adhering to it. No man could make a stronger sacrifice than he did in breaking a resolution thus publicly made, and which he had believed to be unalterable. Yet, I saw him, in opposition to his public declaration, in opposition to his private feelings, consenting, under a sense of duty, to surrender the sweets of retirement, and again to enter the most arduous and perilous station which an individual could fill.

My resolution yielded to this presentation. After remarking that the obligation which had controuled his course was essentially different from that which bound me — that no other man could fill the place to which his country had called him, whereas my services could weigh but little in the political balance, I consented to become a candidate, and have continued, ever since my election, in public life.

This letter is intended to be private, and you will readily perceive the unfitness of making it public. It is written because it has been requested in polite and obliging terms, and because I am willing, should your own views induce you to mention the fact derived from Mr. Lewis, to give you the assurance of its truth.

With very great respect,
I am, Sir,
Your Obed't Serv't,
J. Marshall.

Mr. James K. Paulding was gathering material for a life of Washington when he heard of a story concerning Marshall's candidacy for Congress. He wrote to Marshall about it, and this letter was then written,— a short while before Chief Justice Marshall died.

CHAPTER III

President Washington's letter offering to John Marshall the office of Attorney General, which he declined, because he preferred professional life to public,— was as follows:

PHILADELPHIA, August 26, 1795.

DEAR SIR:

The office of Attorney-General of the United States has become vacant by the death of Mr. Bradford. I take the earliest opportunity of asking if you will accept the appointment? The salary annexed thereto and the prospect of a lucrative practice in this city, the present seat of the government, must be as well known to you as, better perhaps, than they are to me and therefore I shall say nothing concerning them. If your answer is in the affirmative, it will readily occur to you, that no unnecessary time should be lost in repairing to this place. If on the contrary it should be in the negative, which I should be very sorry for, it might be as well to say nothing of this offer. But in either case I pray you give me an answer as promptly as you can.

With esteem and regard, I am, etc.,

GEORGE WASHINGTON.

A short time after Justice Story completed his three volumes of " Commentaries on the Constitution " he wrote an Abridgment of it, which was prepared as a text-book for the Law School and College. This work was dedicated to Chief Justice Marshall in the letter that follows.

To THE HONORABLE JOHN MARSHALL, LL.D., CHIEF JUSTICE OF THE UNITED STATES OF AMERICA

CAMBRIDGE, January, 1833.

SIR:

I ask the favor of dedicating this work to you. I know

not to whom it could with so much propriety be dedicated, as
to one whose youth was engaged in the arduous enterprises
of the Revolution; whose manhood assisted in framing and
supporting the national Constitution; and whose maturer years
have been devoted to the task of unfolding its powers and illustrating its principles.   When, indeed, I look back upon your
judicial labors, during a period of thirty-two years, it is difficult to suppress astonishment at their extent and variety, and
at the exact learning, the profound reasoning, and the solid
principles which they everywhere display.   Other judges have
attained an elevated reputation by similar labors, in a single
department of jurisprudence.   But in one department, (it
need scarcely be said that I allude to that of constitutional
law,) the common consent of your countrymen has admitted
you to stand without a rival.   Posterity will assuredly confirm, by its deliberate award, what the present age has approved, as an act of undisputed justice.   Your expositions of
constitutional law enjoy a rare and extraordinary authority.
They constitute a monument of fame far beyond the ordinary
memorials of political and military glory.   They are destined
to enlighten, instruct, and convince future generations; and
can scarcely perish but with the memory of the Constitution
itself.   They are the victories of a mind accustomed to grapple
with difficulties, capable of unfolding the most comprehensive
truths with masculine simplicity and severe logic, and prompt
to dissipate the illusions of ingenious doubt, and subtle argument, and impassioned eloquence.   They remind us of some
mighty river of our own country, which, gathering in its
course the contributions of many tributary streams, pours at
last its own current into the ocean, deep, clear, and irresistible.

But I confess that I dwell with even more pleasure upon
the entirety of a life adorned by consistent principles, and
filled up in the discharge of virtuous duty; where there is nothing to regret, and nothing to conceal; no friendships broken;
no confidence betrayed; no timid surrenders to popular clamor;
no eager reaches for popular favor.   Who does not listen with
conscious pride to the truth, that the disciple, the friend, the
biographer of Washington, still lives, the uncompromising advocate of his principles?

I am but too sensible that, to some minds, the time may not
seem yet to have arrived, when language like this, however

true, should meet the eyes of the public. May the period be yet far distant, when praise shall speak out with that fullness of utterance which belongs to the sanctity of the grave.

But I know not that, in the course of Providence, the privilege will be allowed me hereafter to declare, in any suitable form, my deep sense of the obligations which the jurisprudence of my country owes to your labors, of which I have been for twenty-one years a witness, and in some humble measure a companion. And if any apology should be required for my present freedom, may I not say that, at your age, all reserve may well be spared, since all your labors must soon belong exclusively to history?

Allow me to add, that I have a desire (will it be deemed presumptuous?) to record upon these pages the memory of a friendship, which has for so many years been to me a source of inexpressable satisfaction; and which, I indulge the hope, may continue to accompany and cheer me to the close of life.

I am, with the highest respect,

Affectionately your servant,

JOSEPH STORY.

LETTER FROM THOMAS JEFFERSON TO JOHN MARSHALL

Chief Justice Marshall went to France as one of the Envoys, with Pinckney and Gerry. Upon his return from France the following note was received from Thomas Jefferson, who was at the time secretly trying to ruin him. In after years the Chief Justice frequently laughed over it, saying, " Mr. Jefferson came very near writing the truth; the added *un* to lucky policy alone demanded." The note, now the property of one of his granddaughters, is as follows:

Thos. Jefferson presents his compliments to General Marshall. He had the honor of calling at his lodgings twice this morning, but was so *un*lucky as to find that he was out on both occasions. He wished to have expressed in person his regret that a pre-engagement for today, which could not be dispenced with, would prevent him the satisfaction of dining in company with Genl. Marshall, and therefore begs leave to place here the expressions of that respect which in company with his fellow citizens he bears him.

GENL. MARSHALL

at Oeller's Hotel, June 23d, 1798.

JOHN MARSHALL SWORN IN AS COUNCILOR

In the " Calendar of Virginia State Papers and Other Manuscripts, from January, 1782, to December 31, 1784," in the Capitol at Richmond, is to be found the following anouncement:

November 30th,
Richmond.
John Marshall
sworn as
Counsellor.

City of Richmond, ss:

This day personally appeared before me, one of the Aldermen of the said City, John Marshall, Esq'r, and took the Oaths of fidelity and a Privy Counsellor as prescribed by law.

Certified under my Hand this thirtieth day of November, 1782.

J. AMBLER.

CHAPTER IV

AUTOBIOGRAPHY OF JOHN MARSHALL

" I was born on the 24th of September, 1755, in the county of Fauquier in Virginia. My father, Thomas Marshall, was the eldest son of John Marshall, who intermarried with a Miss Markham, and whose parents migrated from Wales, and settled in the county of Westmoreland in Virginia, where my father was born. My mother was named Mary Keith; she was the daughter of a clergyman of the name of Keith who migrated from Scotland, and intermarried with a Miss Randolph on James River.

" I was educated at home, under the direction of my father, who was a planter, but was often called from home as a surveyor. From my infancy I was destined for the bar; but the contest between the mother country and her colonies drew me from my studies and my father from the superintendence of them; and in September 1775, I entered into the service as a subaltern. I continued in the army until the year 1781, when, being without a command, I resigned my commission, in the interval between the invasions of Virginia by Arnold and Phillips.

" In the year 1782, I was elected into the legislature of Virginia; and in the fall session of the same year was chosen a member of the executive council of that State.

" In January, 1783, I intermarried with Mary Willis Ambler, the second daughter of Mr. Jacquelin Ambler, then treasurer of Virginia, who was the third son of Mr. Richard Ambler, a gentleman who had migrated from England, and settled at Yorktown in Virginia.

" In April, 1784, I resigned my seat in the executive council, and came to the bar, at which I continued, declining any other public office than a seat in the legislature, until the year 1797, when I was associated with General Pinckney and Mr. Gerry in a mission to France. In 1798, I returned to the United States; and in the spring of 1799 was elected a mem-

ber of Congress, a candidate for which, much against my inclination, I was induced to become by the request of General
Washington.

"At the close of the first session, I was nominated, first to
the Department of War, and afterwards to that of state, which
last office I accepted, and in which I continued until the beginning of the year 1801, when Mr. Ellsworth having resigned,
and Mr. Jay having declined his appointment, I was nominated
to the office of Chief Justice, which I still hold.

"I am the oldest of fifteen children, all of whom lived to
be married, and of whom nine are now living. My father
died when about seventy-four years of age; and my mother,
who survived him about seven years, died about the same age.
I do not recollect all the societies to which I belong, though
they are very numerous. I have written no book, except the
Life of Washington, which was executed with so much precipitation as to require much correction."

A pamphlet entitled "An Address on the Life, Character
and Influence of Chief Justice Marshall, delivered at Richmond on the fourth day of February, 1901, at the request of
the State Bar Association of Virginia and the Bar Association of the City of Richmond, by Horace Gray," contains the
above autobiography. Justice Gray says that his earliest
knowledge of the existence of such an autobiography was obtained from a thin pamphlet, published at Columbus, Ohio, in
1848, which was found in an old bookstore in Boston. It
contained,— besides Marshall's famous speech in Congress on
the case of Jonathan Robbins,— only a letter, entitled "Autobiography of John Marshall." The internal evidence of its
genuineness is very strong; and its authenticity is put almost
beyond a doubt by a facsimile,— at present in the Virginia
State Library,— of a folio sheet in Marshall's handwriting,
which, although it contains neither the whole of the letter
nor its address, bears the same date, and contains the principal paragraph of the letter, word for word, with the correc-
tions of the original manuscript, immediately followed by his
signature. Justice Gray says that in his researches, incited
by the invitation to speak on the life of Marshall, he found a
letter from Chief Justice Marshall, dated Richmond, March
22, 1818, and addressed to Joseph Delaplaine, Esq., Phila-

delphia. Delaplaine was then publishing, in numbers, his
" Repository of the Lives and Portraits of Distinguished American Characters," which was discontinued soon afterward, without ever including Marshall. The letter purports to have been
written in answer to one " requesting some account of my
birth, parentage, and so on," and the autobiography was the
result. It reads as if it was meant for publication, and no
doubt would have been published if the " Repository " had ever
been completed.

THE WILL OF CHIEF JUSTICE MARSHALL

The will of John Marshall is on file in Richmond, Virginia.
It is in many respects a singular will. The estate consists
chiefly of land, part of which is known as the famous " Gren-
way Court," which was the forest home of Lord Fairfax. George Washington surveyed this land, and was quite
often a guest at the place. Sallie E. Marshall Hardy says
that the Chief Justice bought part of this property; the rest
he received as a fee for arranging the dispute between the
State of Virginia and Lord Fairfax's heir,— Dr. Fairfax, of
England,— who, it was claimed, was an " alien enemy during
the Revolutionary War, and therefore had forfeited his in-
heritance."

The will is dated April 9, 1832, and has five codicils, of
which the last was written but a short time before his death.
The codicils are dated as follows: August 13, 1832; March
29, 1834; July 3, 1834; November 6, 1834; July 3, 1835; and
at the end of each the following sentence appears: " This
codicil was wholly written by myself.— J. Marshall." The
will,— which was probated in Richmond, in July, 1835,— is in
his own characteristic handwriting.

" I, John Marshall, do make this my last will and testament,
entirely in my own handwriting, this ninth day of April, 1832.
I owe nothing on my own account," and so on.

Then he arranged for the disposal of an estate he held in
trust and for the settlement of a suit for some property which
he purchased and for the note of a friend which he had endorsed. The settlement of the suit did not take place until
about forty years after the death of Marshall, so great was the

law's delay, and when it was settled the multiplicity of heirs
was so great that each one received but eleven dollars as a
share of several thousands.

The estate was equally divided between his five sons and an
only daughter. He leaves the share of his daughter in trust,
and says:

" I have long thought that the provision intended by a
parent for a daughter ought, in common prudence, to be secured to herself and children, so as to protect her and them
from distress, whatever casualties may happen. Under this
impression, without derogating from the esteem and affection I feel for my son-in-law, I give to my nephew, Thomas M.
Anbler, in trust, to apply the annual profits to the maintenance
of my daughter and her family and for the education of her
children, for her and their separate use, not to be subject to
the control of her husband or to the payment of his debts."
He then recommends that the son-in-law be employed as agent
to manage the daughter's estate, and in the event that he
should survive her, there was to be paid to him one-half of
the annual profits for his own use, out of the profits of the
property bequeathed to the daughter and her offspring.

John Marshall had a very deep love and lasting reverence
for his wife, who died several years before he did. Part of
the will shows that he remembered her slightest wish, for at
her request he gives to one of her friends the dividends on ten
bank shares during life, " as a token of my wife's gratitude for
long and valuable attentions." That part of the will is as follows:

" My beloved wife requested me while living to hold in
trust for our daughter one hundred bank-shares, to pay the
dividends to her during my life and to secure the same to her
and her children when Providence should call me, also, from
this world. In compliance with the wish of her whose sainted
spirit has fled from the sufferings inflicted on her in this life, I
give," and so on. " My daughter will never forget that this
is the gift of the best and most affectionate of mothers." He
gives to each of his grandsons named John one thousand acres
of land, and adds:

" If at the time of my death either of my sons should have
no son named John, then I give the land to any son he may
have named Thomas in token of my love for my father and

veneration for his memory. If there shall be no son, named John or Thomas, then I give the land to the eldest sons, and if no sons to the daughters."

" I had heretofore appointed my sons and son-in-law as executors of my last will. In the apprehension that the appointments of so many executors may produce some confusion in the management of my affairs, I have changed my purpose and have determined to select one of my own sons who may be sufficiently active to attend completely to the business. I therefore appoint my son, James Keith Marshall, to be my sole executor, directing that no surety shall be required from him, and allowing him $1000 for his pains. I hereby revoke all former and other wills and declare this to be my last will, written in my hand, on two sheets of paper, this ninth day of April, one thousand eight hundred and thirty-two.— J. MARSHALL."

Among other possessions Judge Marshall owned a number of slaves. His body-servant, and perhaps his favorite slave, was disposed of in one of the codicils of the will as follows:

" It is my wish to emancipate my faithful servant, Robin, and I direct his emancipation if he chuses to conform to the laws on that subject requiring that he should leave the state, or if permission can be obtained for his continuing to reside in it. In the event of his going to Liberia, I give him one hundred dollars; if he does not go thither I give him fifty dollars. Should it be impracticable to liberaye him consistently with law and his own inclination, I desire that he may chuse his master among my sons, or if he prefer my daughter, he may be held for her and her family as is the other property bequeathed in trust for her, and that he may always be treated as a faithful, meritorious servant.— J. MARSHALL."

CHIEF JUSTICE MARSHALL'S EULOGY UPON HIS WIFE

" Recently while in attendance at a Sunday-School convention at Washington, Mason County, in this state, I was invited, with several others, to dine with the family of the Hon. Martin P. Marshall, a resident of the village.

" Mr. Marshall is one of the most gifted and cultivated men of the State. He was at one time somewhat prominent in public affairs. He is now advanced in years, however, and is living the life of a retired private citizen.

" He is a nephew of the Hon. John Marshall, deceased, formerly Chief Justice of the United States, and was in the earlier years of his life a member of the Chief Justice's family.

" In conversation in regard to his uncle he spoke in terms of the warmest admiration of his character. Daily intercourse with him had taught him to revere and love him. He dwelt particularly upon the simplicity and beauty of his private life. He was a model of what a husband should be to the wife of his bosom in respect to the love which he should cherish for her, the tenderness with which he should watch over her and nurse her in failing health, and the fondness with which he should think of her when death has taken her from his arms.

" Rising in the midst of his remarks, our host invited another gentleman and myself, who were listening to him, into his private apartment, and there opening a drawer, he took out and read to us a paper written by the Chief Justice on the first anniversary of his wife's death, in memory of his love for her, and of the excellences of her life and character.

" I asked him if the paper had ever been published. He said that it had not; that he kept it sacred as a private legacy, and had never obtained his own consent to let it be given to the public. I said to him that I thought it ought to be published, as I believed that it would be read with interest and profit by all into whose hands it would come. Just then we were called to dinner.

" Afterward the conversation in regard to the paper was renewed, and before I left the house, Mr. Marshall yielded his consent to have it published, and handed it to me for that purpose.

" A copy of it is herewith inclosed, with the belief that its publication will increase the respect which the people of this country already feel for the memory of its author, and at the same time enhance their appreciation of the domestic virtues which were so beautifully and admirably illustrated in the life of the great Chief Justice.   D. S.

" Kentucky, August 20, 1881."

The following letter was sent to me by the Rev. D. Stevenson, with a copy of the eulogy which was published in the year 1882 in *Harper's,* Vol. LXV, pp. 771–773.

December 25, 1832.

This day of joy and festivity to the whole Christian world is to my sad heart the anniversary of the keenest affliction which humanity can sustain. While all around is gladness, my mind dwells on the silent tomb, and cherishes the remembrance of the beloved object it contains.

On the 25th of December it was the will of Heaven to take to itself the companion who had sweetened the choicest part of my life, had rendered toil a pleasure, had partaken of all my feelings, and was enthroned in the inmost recess of my heart.

Never can I cease to feel the loss, and to deplore it. Grief for her is too sacred ever to be profound on this day, which shall be during my existence devoted to her memory.

On the 3d of January, 1783, I was united by the holiest bonds to the woman I adored. From the hour of our union to that of our separation I never ceased to thank Heaven for this its best gift. Not a moment passed in which I did not consider her as a blessing from which the chief happiness of my life was derived.

This never-dying sentiment, originating in love, was cherished by a long and close observation of as amiable and estimable qualities as ever adorned the female bosom.

To a person which in youth was very attractive, to manners uncommonly pleasing, she added a fine understanding, and the sweetest temper which can accompany a just and modest sense of what was due to herself.

I saw her first the week she attained the age of fourteen, and was greatly pleased with her.

Girls then came into company much earlier than at present. As my attentions, though without any avowed purpose, nor so open and direct as to alarm, soon became ardent and assiduous, her heart received an impression which could never be effaced. Having felt no prior attachment, she became at sixteen a most devoted wife. All my faults — and they were too many — could never weaken this sentiment. It formed a part of her existence. Her judgment was so sound and so safe that I have often relied upon it in situations of some perplexity. I do not remember ever to have regretted the adoption of her opinion. I have sometimes regretted its rejection.

From native timidity she was opposed to everything adventurous, yet few females possessed more real firmness.

That timidity so influenced her manners that I could rarely prevail on her to display in company the talents I knew her to possess. They were reserved for her husband and her select friends. Though serious as well as gentle in her deportment, she possessed a good deal of chaste, delicate, and playful wit, and if she permitted herself to indulge this talent, told her little story with grace, and could mimic very successfully the peculiarities of the person who was its subject.

She had a fine taste for belle-lettre reading, which was judiciously applied in the selection of pieces she admired.

This quality, by improving her talents for conversation, contributed not inconsiderably to make her a most desirable and agreeable companion. It beguiled many of those winter evenings during which her protracted ill health and her feeble nervous system confined us entirely to each other. I can never cease to look back on them with deep interest and regret. Time has not diminished, and will not diminish, this interest and this regret.

In all the relations of life she was a model with those to whom it was given can not imitate too closely. As the wife, the mother, the mistress of a family, and the friend, her life furnished an example of those who could observe intimately which will not be forgotten. She felt deeply the distress of others, and indulged the feeling liberally on objects she believed to be meritorious.

She was educated with a profound reverence for religion, which she preserved to her last moment. This sentiment among her earliest and deepest impressions gave character to her whole life. Hers was the religion taught by the Saviour of man. She was cheerful, mild, benevolent, serious, humane, intent, on self-improvement and the improvement of those who looked to her for precept or example. She was a firm believer in the faith inculcated by the Church in which she was bred, but her soft and gentle temper was incapable of adopting the gloomy and austere dogmas which some of its professors have sought to ingraft on it.

I have lost her, and with her I have lost the solace of my life. Yet she remains still the companion of my retired hours,

still occupies my inmost bosom.   When alone and unemployed,
my mind unceasingly recurs to her.

More than a thousand times since the 25th of December,
1831, have I repeated to myself the beautiful lines written by
Burgoyne under a similar affliction, substituting Mary for
Anna:

> "Encompassed in an angel's frame
> An angel's virtues lay:
> How soon did Heaven assert its claim,
> And take its own way!

> "My Mary's worth, my Mary's charms,
> Can never more return.
> What now shall fill these widowed arms?
> Ah me! my Mary's urn —
> Ah me! ah me! my Mary's urn."

MARSHALL ON PUBLIC LANDS

Mr. Marshall, from the Committee to whom was referred
the consideration of the expediency of accepting from the
State of Connecticut a cession of jurisdiction of the territory
west of Pennsylvania, commonly called the Western Reserve of
Connecticut, with directions to report by bill, or otherwise,
made the following report:

That, in the year 1606, on the 10th of April, James I,
King of England, on the application of Sir Thomas Gates and
others, for a license to settle a colony in that part of America
called Virginia, not possessed by any Christian prince or
people, between the thirty-fourth and forty-fifth degrees of
north latitude, granted them a charter.   In order to facilitate the settlement of the country, and at the request of the
adventurers, he divided it into two colonies.   To the first
colony, consisting of citizens of London, he granted, "That
they might begin their first plantation and habitation at any
place on the said coast of Virginia or America, where they
shall think fit and convenient, between the said four-and-
thirty and one-and-forty degrees of the said latitude; and
they shall have all lands, &c, from the said first seat of their
plantation and habitation, by the space of fifty miles, of English statute measure, all along the said coast of Virginia and
America, towards the west and southwest, as the coast lieth,
with all the islands, within one hundred miles, directly over

and against the same seacoast; and also all the lands, &c, from said place of their first plantation and habitation, for the space of fifty like English miles, all along the said coast of Virginia and America, towards the east and northeast, or towards the north, as the coast lieth, with all the islands, within one hundred miles, directly over and against the said seacoast; and also all the lands, &c, from the same fifty miles every way on the seacoast, directly into the main land, by the space of one hundred like English miles: and that no other subjects should be allowed to settle on the back of them, towards the main land, without written license from the council of the colony."

To the second colony, consisting of Thomas Hanham and others, of the town of Plymouth, King James granted the tract between the thirty-eighth and forty-fifth degrees of north latitude, under the same description as the aforesaid grant was made to the first colony. To these grants a consideration was annexed, that a plantation should not be made within one hundred miles of a prior plantation.

By the same charter, the King agreed that he would give and grant, by letters patent, to such persons, their heirs, and assigns, as the council of each colony, or the most part of them, should nominate or assign, all the lands, tenements, and hereditaments, which should be within the precincts limited for each colony, to be holden of him, his heirs and successors as for the manor of East Greenwich, in the county of Kent, in free and common soccage only, and not in capite. And that such letters patent should be sufficient assurance from the patentees, so distributed and divided amongst the undertakers for the plantations of the several colonies, and such as should make their plantations in either of the said several colonies in such manner and form, and for such estates, as shall be ordered, and set down by the council of said colony, or the most part of them, respectively, within which the same lands, tenements, or hereditaments, shall lie or be: although express mention of the true yearly value or certainty of the premises, or any of them, or of any other gifts or grants, by the King, or any of his progenitors, or predecessors, to the guarantees was not made, or any statute, &c, to the contrary notwithstanding.

On the 23d of May, 1609, King James, on the application of the first colony for a further enlargement and explanation of the first grant, gave them a second charter, in which they were incorporated by the name of " The Treasurer and Company of Adventurers and Planters of the city of London, for the first colony of Virginia."

In this charter the King grants to them all the lands, &c, in that part of America called Virginia, from the point of land called Cape or Point Comfort, all along the seacoast, to the northward, two hundred miles; and from the said Point of Cape Comfort, all along the seacoast, to the southward, two hundred miles; and all that space and circuit of land, lying from the seacoast of the precinct aforesaid up into the main land throughout, from sea to sea, west and northwest; and also all the islands within one hundred miles along the coast of both seas of the precinct aforesaid.

On the 12th of March, 1611–12, on the representation that there were several islands without the foregoing grant, and contiguous to the coast of Virginia, and on the request of the said first colony, for an enlargement of the former letters patent, as well as for more ample extent of their limits and territories in to the seas adjoining to and upon the coast of Virginia, as for the better government of the said colony, King James granted them another charter. After reciting the description of the second grant, he then proceeds to give, grant, and confirm, to the Treasurer and Company of Adventurers and Planters of the city of London for the first colony of Virginia, and their heirs, &c. " all and singular those islands, whatsoever, situate and being in any part of the ocean, seas, bordering on the coast of our said first colony in Virginia, and being within three hundred leagues of any of the parts heretofore granted to the said Treasurer and Company in said former letters patent as aforesaid, and being within the one-and-fortieth and thirtieth degrees of northerly latitude, with all the lands, &c. both within the said tract of land on the main, and also within the said islands and seas adjoining, &c. Provided, always, That the said islands, or any premises herein mentioned, or by these presents intended, or meant to be conveyed, be not actually possessed or inhabited by any other Christian Prince or State; nor be within the bounds, limits, or territories, of the northern colony, heretofore by us granted, to be planted by divers of our loving subjects in the north part of Virginia.

On the 15th day of July, 1624, James I. granted a commission for the government of Virginia, in which it is alleged that the charters to the Treasurer and Company of Adventurers and Planters of the city of London, for the first colony of Virginia, had been avoided upon a quo warranto brought, and a legal and judicial proceeding therein by due course of law.

On the 20th day of August, 1624, James granted another commission for the government of Virginia, in which it is alleged "Whereupon we, entering into mature and deliberate consideration of the premises, did, by the advice of our Lords of the Privy Council, resolve, by altering the charters of the said company, as to the point of government, wherein the same might be found defective, to settle such a course as might best secure the safety of the people there, and cause the said plantation to flourish; and, yet, with the preservation of the interests of every planter and adventurer, so far north as their present interests shall not prejudice the public plantations; but because the said Treasurer and Company did not submit their charters to be reformed, our proceedings therein were stayed for a time, until, upon quo warranto brought, and a legal and judicial proceeding therein, by due course of law, the said charters were, and now are, and stand avoided."

On the 13th of May, 1625, Charles I. by his proclamation, after alleging that the letters patent, to the colony of Virginia, had been questioned in a legal course, and thereupon judicially repealed, and judged to be void, declares that the government of the colony of Virginia, shall immediately depend on himself, and not be committed to any company or corporation.

From this time Virginia was considered to be a royal Government, and it appears that the Kings of England, from time to time, granted commissions for the government of the same.

The right of making grants of land was vested in and solely exercised by the Crown.

The Colonies of Maryland, North and South Carolina,

Georgia, and part of Pennsylvania, were erected by the Crown, within the chartered limits of the first colony of Virginia.

When the King of France had dominions in North America, the land in question was included in the province of Louisiana, but no part of it was actually settled by any of his subjects. After the conquest of the French possessions in North America by Great Britain, this tract was ceded to the King of Great Britain, by the treaty of Paris, in 1763.

In the year 1774, the Parliament of Great Britain passed an act, declaring and enacting " That all the territories, islands, and countries, in North America, belonging to the Crown of Great Britain, bounded on the south by a line from the bay of Chaluers, along the high lands which divide the rivers that empty themselves into the river St. Lawrence, from those that fall into the sea, to a point in forty-five degrees of north latitude on the eastern bank of the river Connecticut, keeping the same latitude directly west, through the lake Champlain, until in the same latitude it meets the river St. Lawrence; from thence, up the eastern branch of said river to the lake Ontario; thence through the lake Ontario and the river commonly called Niagara; and thence, along by the eastern and southwestern bank of lake Erie, following the bank until the same shall be intersected by the northern boundary, granted by the charter of the province of Pennsylvania, in case the same shall so be intersected; and from thence, along the said northern and western boundaries of said province, until the said western boundary strike the Ohio. But in case the said bank of the said lake shall not be found to be so intersected, then, following the said bank, until it shall arrive at the point of the said bank, which shall be nearest to the northwestern angle of the said province of Pennsylvania! and thence by a right line to the said northwestern angle of said province; and thence, along the western boundary of said province, until it shall strike the river Ohio, and along the bank of the said river, westward, to the banks of the Mississippi; and northward to the southern boundary of the territory granted to the Merchants, adventurers of England, trading to Hudson's Bay; and, also, all such territories, islands, and countries, which have, since the 10th of February, 1763, been made part of the government of Newfoundland, be, and they are hereby, during His Majesty's pleasure, annexed to and made part and parcel of the province of Quebec, as created and established by the said royal proclamation of the 7th of October, 1763.

" Provided, always, That nothing herein contained relative to the boundary of the province of Quebec shall in anywise affect the boundaries of any other colony.

" Provided, always, and be it enacted, That nothing in this act contained shall extend, or be construed to extend, to make void, or to vary, or alter any right, title, or possession derived under any grant, conveyance, or otherwise howsoever of, or to any lands within the said province or provinces thereto adjoining; but that the same shall be in force and have effect as if this act had never been made."

In the year 1620, on the 3d of November, King James gave a charter to the second colony of Virginia: after reciting the grants made to the first colony of Virginia, and stating an application from the second colony for a further enlargement of priviledges, he proceeded to declare " that the tract of land, in America, between the fortieth and forty-eighth degrees of north latitude, from sea to sea, should be called New England; and for the planting and governing the same, he incorporated a council at Plymouth, in the county of Devon, and granted to them and their successors," all that part of America, lying and being in breadth, from forty degrees of northerly latitude, from the equinoctial line, to forty-eight degrees of said northerly latitude inclusively, and in length of, and within all the said breadth aforesaid, throughout all the main lands from sea to sea, together with all the firm lands, &c. upon the main, within the said islands and seas adjoining. Provided, the said islands, or any of the premises before mentioned, and intended by said charter to be granted, be not actually possessed or inhabited by any Christian Prince or State, nor be within the bounds, limits, or territories of the Southern colony, granted to be planted in the south part.   King James, by said charter, commanded and authorized said council at Plymouth, or their successors, or the major part of them to distribute and assign such portions of land to adventurers, &c. as they should think proper.

In the year 1628, 4th March, the council of Plymouth, pursuant to the authority vested in them by their charter, granted to Sir Henry Roswell, and others, a tract of land called Massachusetts: and King Charles I. on the 4th of March, 1629, confirmed the sale, and granted them a charter.   After reciting the description of the grant to the council of Plymouth, and their grant to Sir Henry Roswell, and others, he grants and confirms to them, "all that part of New England in America, which lies and extends between a great river there commonly called Morromack river, alias Merrimack river, and a certain other river there called Charles river, being in the bottoms of a certain bay, there called Massachusetts, alias Mattachusetts, alias Massactusetts bay; and also all and singular those lands and hereditaments whatsoever, lying within the space of three English miles, on the south part of the said river, called Charles river, or of any or every part thereof; and also all and singular, the lands and hereditaments whatsoever, lying and being within the space of three English miles to the southward of the southernmost parts of the said bay, called Massachusetts, alias Mattachusetts, alias Massachusetts bay; and also all those lands and hereditaments whatsoever, which lie and be, within the space of three English miles to the northward of said river, called Morromack, alias Merrimack; or to the northward of any and every part thereof; and all lands and hereditaments whatsoever, lying within the limits aforesaid, north and south, in latitude and in breadth, and in length and longitude of, and within all the breadth aforesaid, throughout the mainlands there, from the Atlantic and Western sea and ocean on the east part to the South sea on the west part, with a proviso not to extend to lands possessed by a Christian Prince, or within the limits of the southern colony."

In the year 1631, on the 19th of March, the Earl of Warwick granted to Lord Say and Seal, and others, all that part of New England in America which lies and extends itself from a river there called Narraganset river, the space of forty leagues, upon a straight line near the sea shore, towards the southwest, west and by south or west as the coast lieth towards Virginia, accounting three English miles to the league, and also all and singular the lands and hereditaments whatsoever, lying and being within the lands aforesaid, north and south, in latitude and breadth, and in length and longitude of, and within all the breadth aforesaid, throughout the main lands there, from the Western ocean to the South sea, &c. and also all the islands, lying in America, aforesaid in said seas, or either of them, on the western or eastern coasts, &c. The territory aforesaid having been in the year preceding by the council of Plymouth granted to said Earl of Warwick.

In 1635, the 7th of June, the council of Plymouth, after having made sundry other grants, surrendered their charter to the Crown.

In the year 1635, Lord Say and Seal, and other associates, appointed John Winthrop their governor and agent, to enter upon and take possession of their territory, which he accordingly did, and began a settlement near the mouth of Connecticut river. About the same time, a number of English colonists emigrated from the Massachusetts to Connecticut river, and after having found themselves to be without the patent of that colony, formed into a political association by the name of the Colony of Connecticut, and purchased of Lord Say and Seal, and others, their grant from the Earl of Warwick, made in 1631; and in 1661 petitioned King Charles the II. setting forth their colonization, their adoption of a voluntary form of Government, their grant from Lord Say and Seal, and others, and their acquisition by purchase and conquest, and praying him to give them a charter of Government, agreeably to the system they had adopted with power equal to those conferred on Massachusetts, or the lords and gentlemen whose jurisdiction right they had purchased, and to confirm the grant or patent which they had obtained as aforesaid of the assigns of the Plymouth council, according to the tenor of a draft or instrument, which they say was ready to be tendered at his gracious order.

King Charles II. referring to the facts stated in the petition aforesaid, granted a charter, dated the 23d of April 1662, in which he constituted and declared John Winthrop and others his associates, a body corporate and politic, by the name of the Governor and Company of the English Colony of Connecticut in New England in America, with privileges and powers of government, and granted and confirmed to the said Governor and company and their successors all that part of his dominions in New England in America, bounded on the east by Narraganset river, commonly called Narraganset bay, where the said river falls into the sea; and on the north by the line of Massachusetts plantation, and on the south by the sea, and in longitude as the line of Massachusetts colony, running from east to west, that is to say, from the said Narraganset bay on the east, to the

South sea, on the west, with the islands thereto adjoining; (which is the present charter of Connecticut.)

On the 23d of April, 1664, King Charles addressed a letter to the Governor and Company of Connecticut, in which, among other things, he speaks of having renewed their charter.

On the 12th of March, 1664, Charles II. granted to James, Duke of York, " all that part of the main land in New England, beginning at a certain place called and known by the name of St. Croix, next adjoining to New Scotland in America, and from thence extending along the sea coast, unto a place called Pennique, or Pennequid, and so up the river thereof unto the furthermost head of the same, as it tendeth northward, and extending from thence unto the river Kennebequie, and upwards by the shortest course to the river called Canada, northward; and also all that island or islands, called by the several name or names of Mattawacks, or Long Island, situate, lying, and being towards the west of Cape Cod and the Narragansets, abutting on the main lands, between the two rivers there called and known by the names of Connecticut, and Hudson's river, together also with the said river called Hudson's river, and all the lands from the west side of Connecticut river to the east side of Delaware bay, and all the several islands, &c.

As the charter to the Duke of York covered part of the lands included in the charter of Connecticut, and as a part of the country had been settled by christian nations prior to the Charter of Connecticut, for which an exception had been made in the charter to the council of Plymouth, though not in that to Connecticut; a dispute arose between the Duke of York and the people of Connecticut, respecting the bounds of their respective grants. King Charles II. having appointed Richard Nichols, and others, commissioners to visit the New England colonies, with power to hear and determine all complaints and appeals, and proceed in all things for providing for and settling the peace of said country.

On the 13th of October, 1664, the General Assembly of the colony of Connecticut appointed agents to wait on said commissioners, which appointment was expressed in the following terms, to wit: Mr. Allen, &c. are desired to accompany the Governor to New York to congratulate His Majesty's honorable commissioners, and if an opportunity offers itself, that they can issue the bounds between the Duke's patent and ours (so as in their judgment may be for the satisfaction of the court) they are empowered to attend to the same, &c. Said commissioners undertook the settlement of said bounds, and on the 30th of November, 1664, determined as follows:

" By virtue of His Majesty's commission, we have heard the difference about the bounds of the patent granted to the Duke of York, and the colony of Connecticut, and having considered the same, &c. we do declare, and order, the southern bound of His Majesty's colony is the sea, and that Long Island is to be under the government of His Royal Highness the Duke of York, as is expressed by plain words in said charters respectively. And also by virtue of His Majesty's commission, and by consent of both the Governors and gentlemen above named, we do also order and declare that the creek or river which is called Monoromock, which is reputed to be about twelve miles to the east of Westchester and a line to be drawn from the east point or side where the fresh water falls into the salt, at high-water mark, north northwest to the line of the Massachusetts, be the western bound of said colony of Connecticut, and all plantations lying westward of that creek and line so drawn shall be under His Royal Highness's government; and all plantations lying eastward of that creek and line to be under the government of Connecticut."

To this the commissioners from Connecticut subscribed in the following manner, viz:

" We the underwritten, on behalf of the colony of Connecticut, have assented unto the determination of His Majesty's commissioners in relation to the bounds and limits of His Royal Highness the Duke's patent and the patent of Connecticut."

This was a settlement of boundary between the interfering charter of Connecticut and that of the Duke of York, as it respected the eastern extent of the latter.

New York being, in June 1673, recovered by the Dutch, and their Government revived, was, in 1674, ceded on a treaty of peace. The Duke obtained a renewal of his patent, and claimed a re-settlement of the same, which was finally effected in 1733, when Biram river, the present line, was established.

Charles the second, on the 4th day of March 1681, granted to William Penn, the first proprietary and Governor of Pennsylvania, all that tract or part of land in America, with the islands therein contained, as the same is bounded, on the east by the Delaware river, from twelve miles distance, northward of Newcastle town, unto the three-and-fortieth degree of northern latitude, if said river doth extend so far northward; but if the said river shall not extend so far northward, then, by the said river so far as it doth extend, and from the head of the said river, the eastern bounds are to be determined by a meridian line, to be drawn from the head of said river, unto the said forty-third degree; the said land to extend westward five degrees in longitude, to be computed from the said eastern bounds; and the said lands to be bounded on the north by the beginning of the three-and-fortieth degree of northern latitude; and on the south by a circle drawn at twelve miles distance from Newcastle, northward and westward, unto the beginning of the fortieth degree of northern latitude; and then by a straight line, westward, to the limits of longitude above mentioned.

On the 27th of November, 1779, the Legislature of Pennsylvania vested the estate of the proprietaries in the Commonwealth.

The charter of Pennsylvania comprehended a part of the land included in the charter of Connecticut, viz: between the forty-first and forty-second degrees of north latitude, in consequence of which a dispute arose respecting the right of soil and jurisdiction.

This dispute came to a final decision before a court of commissioners appointed pursuant to the articles of confederation, on the 30th day of December, 1782, when it was determined that the State of Connecticut had no right to the lands included in the charter of Pennsylvania; and that the State of Pennsylvania had the right of jurisdiction and preemption.

The State of Connecticut acquiesced in the decision aforesaid, respecting the lands claimed by Pennsylvania, and the court of commissioners having final jurisdiction, the claim of Connecticut respecting both soil and jurisdiction is conclusively settled. But Connecticut did not abandon her claim to lands west of Pennsylvania, and at a General Assembly, holden at New Haven on the second Thursday of October, 1783, the following act was passed, viz. "Whereas this

State has the undoubted and exclusive right of jurisdiction and pre-emption to all the lands lying west of the western limits of the State of Pennsylvania, and east of the river Mississippi, and extending throughout from the latitude 41° to latitude 42° and 2′ north, by virtue of the charter granted by King Charles the Second to the late colony, now State of Connecticut, bearing date the 23d day of April, A.D. 1662, which claim and title to make known, for the information of all, to the end that they may conform themselves thereto.

" Resolved, That his excellency the Governor be desired to issue his proclamation, declaring and asserting the right of this State to all the lands within the limits aforesaid; and strictly forbidding all persons to enter or settle thereon, without special license and authority first obtained from the General Assembly of this State."

Pursuant to this resolution, Governor Trumbull issued a proclamation, bearing date the 15th day of November, 1783, making known the determination of the State to maintain their claim to said territory, and forbidding all persons to enter thereon, or settle within the limits of the same.

On the 29th of April, 1784, Congress adopted the following resolutions:

Congress, by their resolution of September 6th, 1780, having thought it advisable to press upon the States having claims to the Western country a liberal surrender of a portion of their territorial claims; by that of the 10th of October in the same year, having fixed conditions to which the Union should be bound on receiving such cessions; and having again proposed the same subject to those States in their address of April the 18th, 1783, wherein, stating the national debt, and expressing their reliance for its discharge, on the prospect of vacant territory in aid of other resources, they, for that purpose as well as to obviate disagreeable controversies and confusions, included in the same recommendations a renewal of those of September 6th, and of October the 10th, 1780, which several recommendations have not yet been fully complied with.

Resolved, That the same subject be again presented to the said States; that they be urged to consider, that the war being now brought to a happy termination, by the personal services of our soldiers, the supplies of property by our citizens, and loans of money from them as well as foreigners; these several creditors have a right to expect that funds will be provided, on which they may rely for indemnification; that Congress still consider vacant territory as an important resource; and that, therefore, said States be earnestly pressed by immediate and liberal cessions to forward these necessary ends, and to promote the harmony of the Union.

The State of Connecticut, prior to the decree of Trenton, offered to make a cession of Western territory, but under such restrictions that Congress refused to accept the same. In consequence of the above recommendation of Congress, the Legislature of Connecticut resumed the consideration of a cession of their Western territory: and, at a General Assembly of the State, on the second Thursday of May, 1786, passed the following act:

" Be it enacted by the Governor, Council, and Representatives, in general court assembled, and by the authority of the same, That the delegates of this State, or any two of them, who shall be attending the Congress of the United States, be, and they are hereby directed, authorized, and fully empowered, in the name and behalf of this State, to make, execute, and deliver, under their hands and seals an ample deed of release and cession of all the right, title, interest, jurisdiction, and claim of the State of Connecticut, to certain Western lands, beginning at the completion of the forty-first degree of north latitude, one hundred and twenty miles west of the western boundary line of the Commonwealth of Pennsylvania, as now claimed by said Commonwealth; and from thence by a line to be drawn north parallel to, and one hundred and twenty miles west of the said west line of Pennsylvania, and to continue north until it comes to 42° and 2' north latitude: whereby all the right, title, interest, jurisdiction, and claim of the State of Connecticut to the lands lying west of the said line, to be drawn, as aforementioned, one hundred and twenty miles west of the western boundary line of the Commonwealth of Pennsylvania, as now claimed by said Commonwealth, shall be included, released, and ceded to the United States in Congress assembled, for the common use and benefit of said States, Connecticut inclusive."

On the 26th of May, 1786, Congress resolved, " that Congress, in behalf of the United States, are ready to accept all the right, title, interest, jurisdiction, and claim of the State of Connecticut to certain western lands, beginning at the cempletion of the forty-first degree of north latitude, one hundred and twenty miles west of the western boundary line of the Commonwealth of Pennsylvania, as now claimed by said Commonwealth; and from thence, by a line to be drawn north parallel to, and one hundred and twenty miles west of the said west line of Pennsylvania, and to continue north until it comes to forty-two degrees two minutes north latitude, whenever the delegates of Connecticut shall be furnished with full powers, and shall execute a deed for that purpose."

On the 14th of September, 1786, the delegates from Connecticut executed a deed of cession agreeably to the above resolution, and it was resolved "that Congress accept the said deed of cession, and that the same be recorded and enrolled among the acts of the United States in Congress assembled."

The cession from Connecticut was accepted by Congress in the same manner and form as the cessions from Virginia, New York, and Massachusetts.

The Legislature of Connecticut, on the second Thursday of October, 1786, passed an act directing the survey of that part of their western territory not ceded to Congress, lying west of Pennsylvania, and east of the river Cayahoga, to which the Indian right had been extinguished; and by the same act, opened a land office for the sale thereof. Under this act, a part of said tract was sold.

The Legislature of Connecticut, in 1792, granted five hundred thousand acres of said territory, being the west part thereof, to certain citizens of the State, as a compensation for property burned and destroyed in the towns of New London, New Haven, Fairfield, and Norwalk, by the British troops in the war between the United States of America and Great Britain. Many transfers of parts of this land have been made for valuable considerations.

In May 1795, the Legislature of Connecticut passed a resolve in the words following:

" Resolved by the Assembly, That a committee be appointed to receive any proposals that may be made by any person or persons, whether inhabitants of the United States, or others, for the purchase of the lands belonging to this State lying west of the west line of Pennsylvania, as claimed by said State. And the said committee are hereby fully authorized and empowered, in the name and behalf of this State, to negotiate with any such person or persons, on the subject of any such proposals, and also to form and complete any contract or contracts for the sale of the said lands, and to make and execute, under their hands and seals, to the purchaser or purchasers, a deed or deeds duly authenticated, quitting, in behalf of this State, all right, title, and interest, juridical and territorial, in and to said lands to him or them, and to his and their heirs forever.

" That before the executing of such deed or deeds, the purchaser or purchasers shall give their personal note or bond, payable to the Treasurer of this State, for the purchase money, carrying an interest of six per centum per annum, payable annually, to commence from the date thereof, or from some future period, not exceeding two years from the date, as circumstances, in the opinion of the committee, may require, and as may be agreed on between them and the said purchaser or purchasers, with good and sufficient sureties, inhabitants of this State; or with a sufficient deposit of bank stock, or other stock of the United States, or the particular States; which note or bond shall be taken, payable at a period not more remote than five years from the date, or if by annual installments, so that the last installment be made payable within ten years from the date, either in specie, or six per cent., three per cent., or deferred stock of the United States, at the discretion of the committee.

" That if the said committee shall find that it will be most beneficial to the State or its citizens, to form several contracts for the sale of the said lands, they shall not consumate any of the said contracts apart by themselves, while the others lie in a train of negotiations only; but all the contracts, which, taken together, shall comprise the whole of the quantity of the said lands, shall be consumated together, and the purchasers shall hold their respective parts, or proportions, as tenants in common of the whole tract, or territory, and not in severalty.

" That the said committee, in whatever manner they shall find it best to sell the said lands, shall, in no case, be at liberty to sell the whole quantity for a principal sum less than one million of dollars in specie, with interest at six per cent. per annum from the time of such sale."

The Legislature, at the same time, appointed a committee to sell said lands, who advertised the same in various newspapers in the United States, and particularly in the Gazette of the United States, published in Philadelphia.

Said committee sold said lands to sundry citizens of Connecticut, and of other States, for the sum of one million two hundred thousand dollars; and on the 9th day of September, 1795, executed to the several purchasers, deeds quitting to them and their heirs forever, all right, title, and interest juridical and territorial of the State of Connecticut, to lands belonging to said State, lying west of the west line of Pennsylvania, as claimed by said State.

The Legislature of Connecticut have appropriated the money arising on the sale of said lands, for the support of schools, and have pledged the annual interest as a perpetual fund for that purpose. The proprietors have paid the principal part of two years' interest to the State, making about the sum of one hundred thousand dollars.

The purchasers have surveyed into townships of five miles square, the whole of said tract lying east of the river Cayahoga, and to which the Indian right has been extinguished; they have made divisions thereof according to their respective proportions; commenced settlements in thirty-five of said townships; and there are actually settled therein about one thousand inhabitants. A number of mills have been built, and roads cut in various directions through said territory, to the extent of about seven hundred miles; numerous sales and transfers of the lands have been made, and the proprietors, in addition to the payments of interest aforesaid, have already expended about the sum of eighty thousand dollars.

While the State of Connecticut was making a disposition of said territory, the following acts took place in the Government of the United States.

In the report of the Secretary of State, respecting the quantity and situation of the lands not claimed by the Indians, nor granted to, nor claimed by any of the citizens of the United States within the territory ceded to the United States by the State of North Carolina, and within the territory of the United States northwest of the river Ohio, are the following clauses:

Under the head of lands reserved by States in their deeds of cession, it is said, " the tract of country presents itself from the completion of the forty-first degree to forty-second degree two minutes of North latitude, and extending to the Pennsylvania line before mentioned, one hundred and twenty miles westward, not mentioned in the deed of Connecticut, while all the country westward thereof was mentioned to be ceded; about two and a half millions of acres of this may, perhaps, be without the Indian lines before mentioned."

In the act of Congress passed May 18th, 1796, entitled " An act providing for the sale of the lands of the United States northwest of the river Ohio, and above the mouth of the Kentucky river," is the following section:

Sec. 4. Be it further enacted, That whenever seven ranges of townships shall have been surveyed below the Great Miami, or between the Scioto river and the Ohio company's purchase, or between the southern boundary of the Connecticut claims, and the ranges already laid off, beginning upon the Ohio river, and extending westwardly; and the plats thereof made and transmitted, in conformity to the provisions of this act, the said section of the six hundred and forty acres (excluding those hereby reserved) shall be offered for sale at public vendue, under the direction of the Governor, or Secretary of the Western Territory, and the Surveyor General; such of them as lie below the Great Miami, shall be sold at Cincinnati; those of them that lie between the Scioto and the Ohio Company's purchase, at Pittsburg; and those between the Connecticut claim and seven ranges at Pittsburg, &c."

On the 21st of January, 1799, Mr. Read, from a committee to whom was referred a bill to accept a cession from Connecticut of the Western Reserve, made a report to the Senate, which was as follows:

At a meeting of commissioners from sundry of the then colonies at Albany, on Tuesday, the 9th of July, it was, among other things, agreed and resolved, as follows:

That His Majesty's title to the northern continent of America appears to be founded on the discovery thereof first made, and the possession thereof first taken in 1497, under a commission from Henry VII. of England, to Sebastian Cabot. That the French have possessed themselves of several parts of this continent, which, by treaties, have been ceded and confirmed to them.

That the right of the English to the whole seacoast from Georgia on the south, to the river St. Lawrence on the north, excepting the island of Cape Breton, and the islands in the Bay of St. Lawrence, remains indisputable.

That all the lands or countries westward from the Atlantic Ocean to the South Sea, between 48 and 34° north latitude, was expressly included in the grant of King Charles I. to divers of his subjects, so long since as the year 1606, and afterwards confirmed in 1620, and under this grant the colony of Virginia claims extent as far west as the South Sea; and the ancient colonies of the Massachusetts Bay and Connecticut were by their respective charters made to extend to the said South Sea; and so that not only the right of the seacoast, but to all the inland countries from sea to sea, has, at all times, been asserted by the Crown of England.

In 1754, some settlements were made from Connecticut on lands on the Susquehanna, about Wyoming, within the chartered limits of Pennsylvania, and also within the chartered limits claimed by Connecticut, which produced a letter from the Governor of Connecticut to the Governor of Pennsylvania, of which the following is an extract:

" WINDSOR, March 13, 1754.

" There being now no unimpropriated lands with us, some of our inhabitants, hearing of this land at Susquehanna, and that it was north of the grant made to Mr. Penn and that to Virginia, are upon a design of making a purchase from the Indians, and hope to obtain a grant of it from the Crown. But Mr. Armstrong informs me that this land is certainly within Mr. Penn's grant. If so, I don't suppose our people had any purpose to quarrel with Pennsylvania. Indeed, I don't know the mind of every private man, but I never heard our leading men express themselves so inclined."

On the same day, Lieutenant Governor Fitch wrote from Hartford a letter on the same subject, of which the following is an extract:

" I do well approve of the notice you take of the attempt some of the people of this colony are making, and the concern you manifest for the general peace, &c. I know nothing of any thing done by the Government to countenance such a procedure as you intimate, and, I conclude, is going on among some of our people. I shall, in all proper ways, use my interest to prevent every thing that may tend to prejudice the general good of these governments, and am inclined to believe that this wild scheme of our people will come to nothing, though I can't certainly say."

At a General Assembly for Connecticut, holden in May, 1755, the Susquehanna Company, as were styled those who were seating lands on that river west of New York, and within the boundaries claimed by Pennsylvania and Connecticut, presented a petition praying the assent of the Legislature to a petition to His Majesty for a new colony within the chartered limits of Connecticut, and describing the lands lying west of New York; whereupon, the Assembly of Connecticut, after reciting the said petition, came to the following resolution:

Resolved, by this Assembly, That they are of opinion that the peaceably and orderly erecting and carrying on some new and well regulated colony or plantation on the lands above mentioned would tend to fix and secure said Indian nations in allegiance to His Majesty and friendship with his subjects; and accordingly hereby manifest their ready acquiescence therein, if it should be His Majesty's royal pleasure to grant said land to said petitioners, and thereon erect and settle a new colony, in such form and under such regulations as might be consistent with his royal wisdom; and also take leave humbly to recommend the said petitioners to his royal favor in the premises.

On the 31st of August, 1779, an agreement was concluded between commissioners duly appointed for that purpose by the States of Virginia and Pennsylvania, respectively, whereby it was agreed " That the line commonly called Mason's and Dixon's line be extended due west five degrees of longitude to be computed from the river Delaware, for the southern boundary of Pennsylvania; and that a meridian drawn from the western extremity thereof to the northern limits of the said States, respectively, be the western boundary of Pennsylvania forever; " which agreement was ratified and finally confirmed by the Legislature of Pennsylvania, by resolution bearing date the 3d day of September, 1780, and by the State of Virginia on the ―― day of 178 ― See Journal of Pennsylvania Assembly, vol. 1 page 519.

On the 6th day of June, 1788, Congress directed the geographer of the United States to ascertain the boundary line between the United States and the States of New York and Massachusetts, agreeably to the deeds of cession of the said States, and also directed that the meridian line between lake Erie and the State of Pennsylvania being run, the land lying west of said line, and between the State of Pennsylvania and lake Erie, should be surveyed, and return thereof made to the Board of Treasury, who were authorized to make sale thereof.

The said land having been sold, in conformity with the above mentioned resolution, to the State of Pennsylvania, Congress, on the 3d day of September, 1788, passed a resolution relinquishing and transferring all the right, title, and claim, of the United States to the government and jurisdiction of the said tract of land, to the State of Pennsylvania forever.

As the purchasers of the land commonly called the Connecticut Reserve hold their title under the State of Connecticut, they cannot submit to the Government established by the United States in the Northwestern territory, without endangering their titles, and the jurisdiction of Connecticut could not be extended over them without much inconvenience. Finding themselves in this situation, they have applied to the Legislature of Connecticut to cede the jurisdiction of the said territory of the United States. In pursuance of such application, the Legislature of Connecticut, in the month of October, 1797, passed an act authorizing the Senators of the said State in Congress to execute a deed of release in behalf of said State to the United States of the jurisdiction of said territory.

The committee are of opinion that the cession of jurisdiction offered by the State of Connecticut ought to be accepted by the United States, on the terms and conditions specified in the bill which accompanies this report.[1]

[1] The above letter is printed in "The American State Papers," Class VIII, Public Lands, Vol. I. Washington: Published by Gales and Seaton, 1832.

CHAPTER V

THE SPEECHES OF JOHN MARSHALL

JOHN MARSHALL was not a great speechmaker; in his time there were many great orators such as Patrick Henry, Daniel Webster, and many others, but he did not speak unless he was almost pressed to do so. However, when he did speak it was with great eloquence, as all records of the Conventions at which he spoke testify, and his speech on the death of Washington shows that he was filled with a great emotion that he was capable of expressing.

In one of Marshall's letters you will notice that he said he never wished to appear in print if he could help it. It seems that the same rule might have been his in regard to oratory,— that he never wished to be heard on the public platform if he could in some manner avoid it.

Webster and Henry never missed an opportunity to air their views, and no doubt this is the case with every man who has the oratorical habit, and who can find an appreciative audience. But Marshall's method was different; he believed in doing his work in a silent way, and in this way he accomplished a great deal, to the discomfiture of those who were opposed to him.

SPEECH OF THE HONORABLE JOHN MARSHALL,

Delivered in the House of Representatives of the United States, on the Resolutions of the Honorable Edward Livingston, relative to Thomas Nash, *alias* Jonathan Robbins

The case is that Thomas Nash, having committed a murder on board a British frigate, navigating the high seas under a commission from his Britannic Majesty, had sought an asylum within the United States, and on this case his delivery was demanded by the minister of the King of Great Britain.

Mr. Marshall said: —Believing as he did most seriously, that in a government constituted like that of the United States, much of the public happiness depended, not only on its being rightly administered, but on the measures of administration being rightly understood: on rescuing public opinion from those numerous prejudices with which so many causes might combine to surround it: he could not but have been highly gratified with the very eloquent, and what was still more valuable, the very able, and very correct argument, which had been delivered by the gentleman from Delaware [Mr. Bayard] against the resolutions now under consideration. He had not expected that the effect of this argument would have been universal, but he had cherished the hope, and in this he had not been disappointed, that it would be very extensive. He did not flatter himself with being able to shed much new light on the subject; but as the argument in opposition to the resolutions has been assailed, with considerable ability, by gentlemen of great talents, he trusted the house would not think the time misapplied which would be devoted to the reestablishment of the principles contained in that argument, and to the refutation of those advanced in opposition to it. In endeavoring to do this, he should notice the observation in support of the resolutions, not in the precise order in which they were made, but as they applied to the different points he deemed it necessary to maintain, in order to demonstrate that the conduct of the executive of the United States could not justly be charged with the errors imputed to it by the resolutions.

His first proposition, he said, was, that the case of Thomas Nash, as stated to the President, was completely within the twenty-seventh article of the treaty of amity, commerce, and navigation, entered into between the United States of America and Great Britain.

He read the article, and then observed: The casus foederis of this article occurs, when a person, having committed murder or forgery within the jurisdiction of one of the contracting parties, and having sought asylum in the country of the other, is charged with the crime, and his delivery demanded, on such proof of his guilt as, according to the laws of the place where he shall be found, would justify his apprehension and commitment for trial, if the offense had there been committed.

The case stated is, that Thomas Nash, having committed a murder on board a British frigate, navigating the high seas under a commission from His Britannic Majesty, had sought an asylum within the United States, and on this case his delivery was demanded by the Minister of the King of Great Britain.

It is manifest that the case stated, if supported by proof, is within the letter of the article, provided a murder committed in a British frigate, on the high seas, be committed within the jurisdiction of that nation.

That such a murder is within their jurisdiction, has been fully shown by the gentleman from Delaware. The principle is, that the jurisdiction of a nation extends to the whole of its territory, and to its own citizens in every part of the world. The laws of a nation are rightfully obligatory on its own citizens in every situation, where those laws are really extended to them. This principle is founded on the nature of civil union. It is supported everywhere by public opinion, and is recognized by writers on the law of nations. Rutherforth, in his second volume, p. 180, says: "The jurisdiction which a civil society has over the persons of its members, affects them immediately, whether they are within its territories or not."

This general principle is especially true, and is particularly recognized with respect to the fleets of a nation on the high seas. To punish offenses committed in its fleet, is the practice of every nation in the universe; and consequently the opinion of the world is, that a fleet at sea is within the jurisdiction of the nation to which it belongs. Rutherforth Vol. II, p. 491, says: "There can be no doubt about the jurisdiction of a nation over the persons which compose its fleets, when they are out at sea, whether they are sailing upon it, or are stationed in any particular part of it."

The gentleman from Pennsylvania [Mr. Gallatin], though he has not directly controverted this doctrine, has sought to weaken it by observing that the jurisdiction of a nation at sea could not be complete even in its own vessels; and in support of this position, he urged the admitted practice of submitting to search for contraband; a practice not tolerated on land, within the territory of a neutral power. The rule is as stated, but is founded on a principle which does not affect the jurisdiction of a nation over its citizens or subjects in its ships. The principle is, that in the sea itself no nation has any jurisdiction. All may equally exercise their rights, and consequently the right of a belligerent power to prevent aid being given to his enemy, is not restrained by any superior right of a neutral in the place.   But if this argument possessed any force, it would not apply to national ships of war, since the usage of nations does not permit them to be searched.

According to the practice of the world, then, and the opinions of writers on the law of nations, the murder committed on board a British frigate, navigating the high seas, was a murder committed within the jurisdiction of the British nation.

Although such a murder is plainly within the letter of the article, it has been contended not to be within its just construction; because, at sea, all nations have a common jurisdiction, and the article correctly construed, will not embrace a case of concurrent jurisdiction.

It is deemed unnecessary to controvert this construction, because the proposition, that the United States had no jurisdiction over the murder committed by Thomas Nash, is believed to be completely demonstrable.

It is not true that all nations have jurisdiction over all offenses committed at sea.   On the contrary, no nation has any jurisdiction at sea, but over its own citizens or vessels, or offenses against itself.   This principle is laid down in 2 Ruth. 488, 491.

The American government has, on a very solemn occasion, avowed the same principle.   The first minister of the French republic asserted and exercised powers of so extraordinary a nature as unavoidably to produce a controversy with the United States.   The situation in which the government then found itself was such as necessarily to occasion a very serious and mature consideration of the opinions it should adopt. Of consequence, the opinions then declared deserve great respect.   In the case alluded to, Mr. Genet had asserted the right of fitting out privateers in the American ports, and of manning them with American citizens, in order to cruise against nations with whom America was at peace.   In reasoning against this extravagant claim, the then Secretary of State, in his letter of the 17th of June, 1793, says: " For our citizens, then, to commit murders and depredations on the members of nations at peace with us, or to combine to do it, appeared to the executive and to those whom they consulted, as much against the laws of the land as to murder or rob, or combine to murder or rob, its own citizens; and as much to require punishment, if done within their limits, where they have a territorial jurisdiction, or on the high seas, where they have a personal jurisdiction, that is to say, one which reaches their own citizens only; this being an appropriate part of each nation, on an element where all have a common jurisdiction."

The well considered opinion, then, of the American government on this subject is, that the jurisdiction of a nation at sea is " personal," reaching its " own citizens only," and that this is " the appropriate part of each nation " on that element.

This is precisely the opinion maintained by the opposers of the resolutions. If the jurisdiction of America at sea be personal, reaching its own citizens only; if this be its appropriate part, then the jurisdiction of the nation cannot extend to a murder committed by a British sailor, on board a British frigate navigating the high seas, under a commission from His Britannic Majesty.

As a further illustration of the principle contended for, suppose a contract made at sea, and a suit instituted for the recovery of money which might be due thereon. By the laws of what nation would the contract be governed? The principle is general, that a personal contract follows the person, but is governed by the law of the place where it is formed. By what law, then, would such a contract be governed? If all nations had jurisdiction over the place, then the laws of all nations would equally influence the contract; but certainly no man will hesitate to admit that such a contract ought to be decided according to the laws of that nation to which the vessel or contracting parties might belong.

Suppose a duel attended with death, in the fleet of a foreign nation, or in any vessel which returned safe to port; could it be pretended that any government on earth, other than that to which the fleet or vessel belonged, had jurisdiction in the case; or that the offender could be tried by the laws or tribunals of any other nation whatever?

Suppose a private theft by one mariner from another, and the vessel to perform its voyage and return in safety, would it be contended that all nations have equal cognizance of the crime, and are equally authorized to punish it?

If there be this common jurisdiction at sea, why not punish desertion from one belligerent power to another, or correspondence with the enemy, or any other crime which may be perpetrated? A common jurisdiction over all offenses at sea, in whatever vessel committed, would involve the power of punishing the offenses which have been stated. Yet all gentlemen will disclaim this power. It follows, then, that no such common jurisdiction exists.

In truth, the right of every nation to punish is limited, in its nature, to offenses against the nation inflicting the punishment. This principle is believed to be universally true.

It comprehends every possible violation of its laws on its own territory, and it extends to violations committed elsewhere by persons it has a right to bind. It extends also to general piracy.

A pirate, under the law of nations, is an enemy of the human race. Being the enemy of all, he is liable to be punished by all. Any act which denotes this universal hostility is an act of piracy. Not only an actual robbery therefore, but cruising on the high seas without a commission, and with intent to rob, is piracy. This is an offense against all and every nation, and is therefore alike punishable by all. But an offense which in its nature affects only a particular nation, is only punishable by that nation.

It is by confounding general piracy with piracy by statute, that indistinct ideas have been produced, respecting the power to punish offenses committed on the high seas.

A statute may make any offense piracy, committed within the jurisdiction of the nation passing the statute, and such offense will be punishable by that nation. But piracy under the law of nations, which alone is punishable by all nations, can only consist in an act which is an offense against all. No particular nation can increase or diminish the list of offenses thus punishable.

It had been observed by his colleague (Mr. Nicholas), for the purpose of showing that the distinction taken on this subject by the gentleman from Delaware (Mr. Bayard) was inaccurate, that any vessel robbed on the high seas could be the property only of a single nation, and being only an offense against that nation, could be, on the principle taken by the opposers of the resolutions, no offense against the law of nations; but in this his colleague had not accurately considered the principle. As a man, who turns out to rob on the highway, and forces from a stranger his purse with a pistol at his bosom, is not the particular enemy of that stranger; but alike the enemy of every man who carries a purse, so those who, without a commission, rob on the high seas, manifest a temper hostile to all nations, and therefore become the enemies of all. The same inducements which occasion the robbery of one vessel, exist to occasion the robbery of others, and therefore the single offense is an offense against the whole community of nations, manifests a temper hostile to all, is the commencement of an attack on all, and is consequently, of right, punishable by all.

His colleague had also contended, that all the offenses at sea, punishable by the British statutes, from which the act of Congress was in a great degree copied, were piracies at common law, or by the law of nations, and as murder is among these, consequently murder was an act of piracy by the law of nations, and therefore punishable by every nation. In support of this position, he had cited 1 Hawk., P. C., 267, 271; 3 Inst., 112, and 1 Woodeson, 140.

The amount of these cases is, that no new offense is made piracy by the statutes; but that a different tribunal is created for their trial, which is guided by a different rule from that which governed previous to those statutes. Therefore, on an indictment for piracy, it is still necessary to prove an offense which was piracy before the statutes. He drew from these authorities a very different conclusion from that which had been drawn by his colleague. To show the correctness of his conclusion, it was necessary to observe, that the statute did not, indeed, change the nature of piracy, since it only transferred the trial of the crime to a different tribunal, where different rules of decision prevailed; but having done this, other crimes committed on the high seas, which were not piracy, were made punishable by the same tribunal; but certainly this municipal regulation could not be considered as proving that those offenses were, before, piracy by the law of nations. Mr. Nicholas insisted that the law was not correctly stated; whereupon Mr. Marshall called for 3 Inst. and read the Statute.

" All treasons, felonies, robberies, murders, and confederacies, committed in or upon the seas, &c., shall be inquired, tried, heard, determined, and judged in such shires, &c., in like form and condition as if any such offense had been committed on the land, &c.

" And such as shall be convicted, &c., shall have and suffer such pains of death, &c., as if they had been attainted of any treason, felony, robbery, or other of the said offenses done upon the land."

This statute, it is certain, does not change the nature of piracy; but all treasons, felonies, robberies, murders and confederacies committed in or upon the sea, are not declared to have been, nor are they, piracies. If a man be indicted as a pirate, the offense must be shown to have been piracy before the statute; but if he be indicted for treason, felony, robbery, murder, or confederacy committed at sea, whether such offense was or was not a piracy, he shall be punished in like manner as if he had committed the same offense on land. The passage cited from 1 Woodeson, 140, is a full authority to this point. Having stated that offenses committed at sea were formerly triable before the Lord High Admiral, according to the course of the Roman civil law, Woodeson says, " but by the statute 27H. VIII., ch. 4, and 28H. VIII., ch. 15, all treasons, felonies, piracies, and other crimes committed on the sea, or where the admiral has jurisdiction, shall be tried in the realm as if done on land. But the statutes referred to affect only the manner of the trial so far as respects piracy. The nature of the offense is not changed. Whether a charge amounts to a piracy or not, must still depend on the law of nations, except where, in the case of British subjects, express acts of Parliament have declared that the crimes therein specified shall be adjudged piracy, or shall be liable to the same mode of trial and degree of punishment."

This passage proves not only that all offenses at sea are not piracies by the law of nations, but also that all indictments for piracy must depend on the law of nations, " except where, in the case of British subjects, express acts of Parliament " have changed the law. Why do not these " express acts of Parliament " change the law as to others than " British subjects? " The words are general; " all treasons, felonies," &c. Why are they confined in construction to British subjects? The answer is a plain one. The jurisdiction of the nation is confined to its territory and to its subjects.

The gentleman from Pennsylvania [Mr. Gallatin] abandons, and very properly abandons, this untenable ground. He admits that no nation has a right to punish offenses against another nation, and that the United States can only punish offenses against their own laws, and the law of nations. He admits, too, that if there had only been a mutiny (and consequently if there had only been a murder) on board the Hermoine, that the American courts could have taken no cognizance of the crime. Yet mutiny is punishable as piracy by the law of both nations. That gentleman contends that the act committed by Nash was piracy according to the law of nations. He supports his position by insisting that the offense may be constituted by the commission of a single act; that unauthorized robbery on the high seas is this act, and that the crew having seized the vessel, and being out of the protection of any nation, were pirates.

It is true that the offense may be completed by a single act; but it depends on the nature of that act. If it be such as manifests general hostility against the world — an intention to rob generally — then it is piracy; but if it be merely a mutiny and murder in a vessel, for the purpose of delivering it up to the enemy, it seems to be an offense against a single nation, and not to be piracy. The sole object of the crew might be to go over to the enemy, or to free themselves from the tyranny experienced on board a ship of war, and not to rob generally.

But should it even be true that running away with the vessel to deliver her up to an enemy was an act of general piracy, punishable by all nations, yet the mutiny and murder was a distinct offense. Had the attempt to seize the vessel failed after the commission of the murder, then, according to the argument of the gentleman from Pennsylvania, the American courts could have taken no cognizance of the crime. Whatever, then, might have been the law respecting the piracy, of the murder there was no jurisdiction. For the murder, not the piracy, Nash was delivered up. Murder, and not piracy, is comprehended in the twenty-seventh article of the treaty between the two nations. Had he been tried then, and acquitted on an indictment for the piracy, he must still have been delivered up for the murder, of which the court could have no jurisdiction. It is certain that an acquittal of the piracy would not have discharged the murder; and, therefore, in the so much relied on trials at Trenton, a separate indictment for murder was foled after an indictment for piracy. Since, then, if acquitted for piracy, he must have been delivered to the British government on the charge of murder, the President of the United

States might, very properly, without prosecuting for the piracy, direct him to be delivered up on the murder.

All the gentlemen who have spoken in support of the resolutions, have contended that the case of Thomas Nash is within the purview of the act of Congress which relates to this subject, and is by that act made punishable in the American courts. This is, that the act of Congress designed to punish crimes committed on board a British frigate.

Nothing can be more completely demonstrable than the untruth of this proposition.

It has already been shown that the legislative jurisdiction of a nation extends only to its own territory, and to its own citizens, wherever they may be. Any general expression in a legislative act must, necessarily, be restrained to objects within the jurisdiction of the legislature passing the act. Of consequence, an act of Congress can only be construed to apply to the territory of the United States comprehending every person within it, and to the citizens of the United States.

But independent of this undeniable truth, the act itself affords complete testimony of its intention and extent. (See Laws of the U. S., Vol I., p. 10.)

The title is, "An act for the punishment of certain crimes against the United States." Not against Britain, France, or the world, but singly "against the United States."

The first section relates to treason, and its objects are, "any person or persons owing allegiance to the United States." This description comprehends only the citizens of the United States, and such others as may be on its territory or in its service.

The second section relates to misprision of treason, and declares, without limitation, that any person or persons, having knowledge of any treason, and not communicating the same, shall be guilty of that crime. Here, then, is an instance of that limited description of persons in one section, and of that general description in another, which has been relied on to support the construction contended for by the friends of the resolutions. But will it be pretended that a person can commit misprision of treason, who cannot commit treason itself? That he would be punishable for concealing a treason, who could not be punished for plotting it? Or can it be supposed that the act designed to punish an Englishman or a Frenchman, who, residing in his own country, should have knowledge of treasons against the United States, and should not cross the Atlantic to reveal them?

The same observations apply to the sixth section, which makes " any person or persons " guilty of misprision of felony, who having knowledge of murder or other offenses enumerated in that section, should conceal them. It is impossible to apply this to a foreigner, in a foreign land, or to any person not owing allegiance to the United States.

The eighth section, which is supposed to comprehend the case, after declaring that if any person or persons shall commit murder on the high seas, he shall be punishable with death, proceeds to say, that if any captain or mariner shall piratically run away with a ship or vessel, or yield her up voluntarily to a pirate, or if any seaman shall lay violent hands on his commander, to prevent his fighting, or shall make a revolt in the ship, every such offender shall be adjudged a pirate and a felon.

The persons who are the objects of this section of the act are all described in general terms, which might embrace the subjects of all nations. But is it to be supposed, that if, in an engagement between an English and a French ship of war, the crew of the one or the other should lay violent hands on the captain, and force him to strike, that this would be an offense against the act of Congress, punishable in the courts of the United States? On this extended construction of the general terms of the section, not only the crew of one of the foreign vessels forcing their captain to surrender to another, would incur the penalties of the act, but if, in the late action between the gallant Truxton and a French frigate, the crew of that frigate had compelled the captain to surrender while he was unwilling to do so, they would have been indictable as felons in the courts of the United States. But surely the act of Congress admits of no such extravagant construction.

His colleagues, Mr. Marshall said, had cited and particularly relied on the ninth section of the act. That section declares, that if a citizen shall commit any of the enumerated piracies, or any act of hostility on the high seas against the United States, under color of a commission from any foreign prince or state, he shall be adjudged a pirate, felon, and robber, and shall suffer death.

This section is only a positive extension of the act to a case which might otherwise have escaped punishment. It takes away the protection of a foreign commission from an American citizen, who on the high seas robs his countrymen. This is no exception from any preceding part of the law, because there is no part which relates to the conduct of vessels commissioned by a foreign power; it only proves that, in the opinion of the legislature, the penalties of the act could not, without this express provision, have been incurred by a citizen holding a foreign commission.

It is then most certain that the act of Congress does not comprehend the case of a murder committed on board a foreign ship of war.

The gentleman from New York has cited 2 Woodeson, 428, to show that the courts of England extend their jurisdiction to piracies committed by the subjects of foreign nations.

This has not been doubted. The case from Woodeson is a case of robberies committed on the high seas by a vessel without authority. There are ordinary acts of piracy, which, as has been already stated, being offenses against all nations, are punishable by all. The case from 2 Woodeson, and the note cited from the same book, by the gentleman from Delaware, are strong authorities against the doctrines contended for by the friends of the resolutions.

It has also been contended, that the question of jurisdiction was decided at Trenton, by receiving indictments against persons there arraigned for the same offense, and by retaining them for trial after the return of the habeas corpus.

Every person in the slightest degree acquainted with judicial proceedings, knows that an indictment is no evidence of jurisdiction; and that in criminal cases, the question of jurisdiction will seldom be made but by arrest of judgment after conviction.

The proceedings after the return of the habeas corpus only prove that the case was not such a case as to induce the judge immediately to decide against his jurisdiction. The question was not free from doubt, and therefore might very properly be postponed until its decision should become necessary.

It has been argued by the gentleman from New York that the form of indictment is, itself, evidence of a power in the court to try the case. Every word of that indictment, said the gentleman, gives the lie to a denial of the jurisdiction of the court.

It would be assuming a very extraordinary principle indeed, to say that the words inserted in an indictment for the express purpose of assuming the jurisdiction of a court should be admitted to prove that jurisdiction. The question certainly depended on the nature of the fact, and not on the description of the fact. But as an indictment must necessarily contain formal words in order to be supported, and as forms often denote what a case must substantially be to authorize a court to take cognizance of it, some words in the indictments, at Trenton, ought to be noticed. The indictments charge the persons to have been within the peace, and the murder to have been committed against the peace, of the United States. These are necessary averments, and, to give the court jurisdiction, the fact ought to have accorded with them. But who will say the crew of a British frigate on the high seas are within the peace of the United States, or a murder committed on board such a frigate against the peace of any other than the British government.

It is then demonstrated, that the murder with which Thomas Nash was charged was not committed within the jurisdiction of the United States, and, consequently, that the case stated was completely within the letter and the spirit of the twenty-seventh article of the treaty between the two nations. If the necessary evidence was produced, he ought to have been delivered up to justice. It was an act to which the American nation was bound by a most solemn contract. To have tried him for the murder would have been mere mockery. To have condemned and executed him, the court having no jurisdiction, would have been murder; to have acquitted and discharged him, would have been a breach of faith and a violation of national duty.

But it has been contended, that although Thomas Nash ought to have been delivered up to the British minister, on the requisition made by him in the name of his government, yet the interference of the President was improper.

This, Mr. Marshall said, led to his second proposition, which was,

That the case was a case for executive and not judicial decision. He admitted implicitly the division of powers stated by the gentleman from New York, and that it was the duty of each department to resist the encroachments of the others.

This being established, the inquiry was, to what department was the power in question allotted?

The gentleman from New York had relied on the second section of the third article of the constitution, which enumerates the cases to which the judicial power of the United States extends, as expressly including that now under consideration. Before he examined that section, it would not be improper to notice a very material misstatement of it made in the resolutions offered by the gentleman from New York. By the constitution, the judicial power of the United States is extended to all cases in law and equity, arising under the constitution, laws and treaties of the United States; but the resolutions declare the judicial power to extend to all questions arising under the constitution, treaties and laws of the United States. The difference between the constitution and the resolutions was material and apparent. A case in law or equity was a term well understood, and of limited signification. It was a controversy between parties which had taken a shape for judicial decision. If the judicial power extended to every question under the constitution, it would involve almost every subject proper for legislative discussion and decision; if to every question under the laws and treaties of the United States, it would involve almost every subject on which the executive could act. The division of power which the gentleman had stated, could exist no longer, and the other departments would be swallowed up by the judiciary. But it was apparent that the resolutions had essentially misrepresented the constitution. He did not charge the gentleman from New York with intentional misrepresentation; he would not attribute to him such an artifice in any case, much less in a case where detection was so easy and so certain. Yet this substantial departure from the constitution, in resolutions affecting substantially to unite it, was not less worthy of remark for being unintentional. It manifested the course of reasoning by which the gentleman had himself been misled, and his judgment betrayed into the opinions those resolutions expressed.

By extending the judicial power to all cases in law and equity, the constitution had never been understood to confer on that department any political power whatever. To come within this description, a question must assume a legal form for forensic litigation and judicial decision. There must be parties to come into court, who can be reached by its process, and bound by its power; whose rights admit of ultimate decision by a tribunal to which they are bound to submit.

A case in law or equity proper for judicial decisions may arise under a treaty, where the rights of individuals acquired or secured by a treaty are to be asserted or defended in court. As under the fourth or sixth article of the treaty of peace with Great Britain, or under those articles of our late treaties with France, Prussia, and other nations, which secure to the subjects of those nations their property within the United States; or, as would be an article which, instead of stipulating to deliver up an offender, should stipulate his punishment, provided the case was punishable by the laws and in the courts of the United States. But the judicial power cannot extend to political compacts; as, the establishment of the boundary line between the American and British dominions; the case of the late guarantee in our treaty with France, or the case of the delivery of a murderer under the twenty-seventh article of our present treaty with Britain.

The gentleman from New York has asked, triumphantly asked, what power exists in our high courts to deliver up an individual to a foreign government? Permit me, said Mr. Marshall, but not triumphantly, to retort the question — By what authority can any court render such a judgment? What power does a court possess to seize any individual, and determine that he shall be adjudged by a forign tribunal? Surely our courts possess no such power, yet they must possess it, if this article of the treaty is to be executed by the courts.

Gentlemen have cited and relied on that clause in the constitution which enables Congress to define and punish piracies and felonies committed on the high seas, and offenses against the law of nations, together with the act of Congress declaring the punishment of those offenses, as transferring the whole subject to the courts. But that clause can never be construed to make to the government a grant of power, which the people making it did not themselves possess. It has already been shown that the people of the United States have no jurisdiction over offenses committed on board a foreign ship against a foreign nation. Of consequence, in framing a government for themselves, they cannot have passed this jurisdiction to that government.   The law, therefore, cannot act upon the case. But this clause of the constitution cannot be considered, and need not be considered, as affecting acts which are piracy under the law of nations.   As the judicial power of the United States extends to all cases of admiralty and marine jurisdiction, and piracy under the law of nations is of admiralty and maritime jurisdiction, punishable by every nation, the judicial power of the United States, of course extends to it.   On this principle the courts of admiralty under the confederation took cognizance of piracy, although there was no express power in Congress to define and punish the offense.

But the extension of the judicial power of the United States to all cases of admiralty and maritime jurisdiction must necessarily be understood with some limitation.   All cases of admiralty and maritime jurisdiction which, from their nature, are triable in the United States, are submitted to the jurisdiction of the courts of the United States.   There are cases of piracy by the law of nations, and cases within the legislative jurisdiction of the nation.   The people of America possessed no other power over the subject, and could, consequently, transfer no other to their courts; and it has already been proved, that a murder committed on board a foreign ship of war is not comprehended within this description.

The consular convention with France has also been relied on, as proving the act of delivering up an individual to a foreign power, to be in its nature judicial, and not executive.

The ninth article of that convention authorizes the consuls and vice-consuls of either nation to cause to be arrested all deserters from their vessels, " for which purpose the said consuls and vice-consuls shall address themselves to the courts, judges, and officers competent."

This article of the convention does not, like the twenty-seventh article of the treaty with Britain, stipulate a national act, to be performed on the demand of a nation; it only authorizes a foreign minister to cause an act to be done, and prescribes the course he is to pursue.   The contract itself is, that the act shall be performed by the agency of the foreign consul, through the medium of the courts; but this affords no evidence that a contract of a very different nature is to be performed in the same manner.

It is said that the then President of the United States declared the incompetency of the courts, judges, and officers, to
execute this contract, without an act of the legislature.   But
the then President made no such declaration.   He has said that
some legislative provision is requisite to carry the stipulations
of the convention into full effect.   This, however, is by no
means declaring the incompetency of a department to perform
an act stipulated by treaty, until the legislative authority shall
direct its performance.

It has been contended, that the conduct of the executive on
former occasions, similar to this in principle, has been such as
to evince an opinion, even in that department, that the case in
question is proper for the decision of the courts.

The fact adduced to support this argument, is the determination of the late President on the case of prizes made within the
jurisdiction of the United States, or by privateers fitted out in
their ports.   The nation was bound to deliver up those prizes,
in like manner as the nation is now bound to deliver up an individual demanded under the twenty-seventh article of the
treaty with Britain.   The duty was the same, and devolved on
the same department.

In quoting the decision of the executive on that case, the
gentleman from New York has taken occasion to bestow a high
encomium on the late President, and to consider his conduct as
furnishing an example worthy the imitation of his successor.

It must be the cause of much delight to the real friends of
that great man, to those who supported his administration while
in office from a conviction of its wisdom and its virtue, to hear
the unqualified praise which is now bestowed on it by those who
had been supposed to possess different opinions.   If the
measure now under consideration shall be found, on examination, to be the same in principle with that which has been cited
by its opponents as a fit precedent for it, then may the friends of
the gentleman now in office indulge the hope, that when he, like
his predecessor, shall be no more, his conduct, too, may be
quoted as an example for the government of his successors.

The evidence relied to prove the opinion of the then executive
on the case, consists of two letters from the Secretary of
State — the one of the 29th of June, 1793, to Mr. Genet, and
the other of the 16th of August, 1793, to Mr. Morris.

In the letter to Mr. Genet, the Secretary says, that the claimant having filed his libel against the ship William in the Court of Admiralty, there was no power which could take the vessel out of court until it had decided against its own jurisdiction; that having so decided, the complaint is lodged with the executive, and he asks for evidence to enable that department to consider and decide finally on the subject.

It will be difficult to find in this letter an executive opinion, that the case was not a case for executive decision. The contrary is clearly avowed. It is true, that when an individual claiming the property as his, had asserted that claim in court, the executive acknowledges in itself a want of power to dismiss or decide upon the claim thus pending in court. But this argues no opinion of a want of power in itself to decide upon the case, if, instead of being carried before a court as an individual claim, it is brought before the executive as a national demand. A private suit instituted by an individual, asserting his claim to property, can only be controlled by that individual. The executive can give no direction concerning it. But a public prosecution, carried on in the name of the United States, can without impropriety be dismissed at the will of the government. The opinion, therefore, given in this letter is unquestionably correct; but it is certainly misunderstood, when it is considered as being an opinion that the question was not in its nature a question for executive decision.

In the letter to Mr. Morris, the secretary asserts the principle, that vessels taken within our jurisdiction ought to be restored, but says it is yet unsettled whether the act of restoration is to be performed by the executive or judicial department.

The principle, then, according to this letter, is not submitted to the courts — whether a vessel captured within a given distance of the American coast was or was not captured within the jurisdiction of the United States, was a question not to be determined by the courts, but by the executive. The doubt expressed is, not what tribunal shall settle the principle, but what tribunal shall settle the fact. In this respect a doubt might exist in the case of prizes, which could not exist in the case of a man. Individuals on each side claimed the property, and therefore their rights could not be brought into court, and there contested as a case in law or equity. The demand of a man made by a nation stands on different principles.

Having noticed the particular letters cited by the gentleman from New York, permit me now, said Mr. Marshall, to ask the attention of the house to the whole course of executive conduct on this interesting subject.

It is first mentioned, in a letter from the Secretary of State to Mr. Genet, of the 25th of June, 1793. In that letter, the secretary states a consultation between himself and the secretaries of the treasury and war (the President being absent), in which (so well were they assured of the President's way of thinking in those cases) it was determined, that the vessel should be detained in the custody of the consuls in the ports, "until the government of the United States shall be able to inquire into, and decide on the fact."

In his letter of the 12th of July, 1793, the secretary writes, the President has determined to refer the questions concerning prizes " to persons learned in the laws." And he requests that certain vessels enumerated in the letter should not depart " until this ultimate determination shall be made known."

In his letter of the 7th of August, 1793, the secretary informs Mr. Genet, that the President considers the United States as bound " to effectuate the restoration of, or to make compensation for, prizes which shall have been made of any of the parties at war with France, subsequent to the 5th day of June last, by privateers fitted out of our ports." That it is consequently expected that Mr. Genet will cause restitution of such prizes to be made and that the United States will cause restitution to be made " of all such prizes as shall be hereafter brought within their ports by any of the said privateers."

In his letter of the 10th of November, 1793, the secretary informs Mr. Genet, that, for the purpose of obtaining testimony to ascertain the fact of capture within the jurisdiction of the United States, the governors of the several states were requested, on receiving any such claim, immediately to notify thereof the attorneys of their several districts, whose duty it would be to give notice " to the principle agent of both parties, and also to the consuls of the nations interested, and to recommend to them to appoint by mutual consent arbiters to decide whether the capture was made within the jurisdiction of the United States, as stated in my letter of the 8th instant, according to whose award the governor may proceed to deliver the vessel to the one or the other party." " If either party refuse to name arbiters, then the attorney is to take depositions on notice, which he is to transmit for the information and decision of the President." "This prompt procedure is the more to be insisted on, as it will enable the President, by an immediate delivery of the vessel and cargo to the party having title, to prevent the injuries consequent on long delay."

In his letter of the 22d of November, 1793, the secretary repeats in substance, his letters of the 12th of July and 7th of August, and says, that the determination to deliver up certain vessels, involved the brig Jane, of Dublin, the brig Lovely Lass, and the brig Prince William Henry. He concludes with saying, "I have it in charge to inquire of you, sir, whether these three brigs have been given up according to the determination of the President, and if they have not, to repeat the requisition that they may be given up to their former owners."

Ultimately it was settled that the fact should be investigated in the courts, but the decision was regulated by the principles established by the executive department.

The decision, then, on the case of vessels captured within the American jurisdiction, by privateers fitted out of the American ports, which the gentleman from New York has cited with such merited approbation; and which he has declared to stand on the same principles with those which ought to have governed in the case of Thomas Nash; which deserves the more respect, because the government of the United States was then so circumstanced as to assure us, that no opinion was lightly taken up, and no resolution formed but on mature consideration. This decision, quoted as a precedent, and pronounced to be right, is found, on fair and full examination, to be precisely and unequivocally the same with that which was made in the case under consideration. It is a full authority to show, that, in the opinion always held by the American government, a case like that of Thomas Nash is a case for executive, and not judicial decision.

The clause in the constitution, which declares, that "the trial of all crimes, except in cases of impeachment, shall be by jury," has also been relied on as operating on the case, and transferring the decision on a demand for the delivery of an individual from the executive to the judicial department.

But certainly this clause in the constitution of the United States cannot be thought obligatory on, and for the benefit of, the whole world. It is not designed to secure the rights of the people of Europe and Asia, or to direct and control proceedings against criminals throughout the universe. It can then be assigned only to guide proceedings of our own courts, and to prescribe the mode of punishing offenses committed against the government of the United States, and to which the jurisdiction of the nation may rightfully extend.

It has already been shown, that the courts of the United States were incapable of trying the crime for which Thomas Nash was delivered up to justice; the question to be determined was, not how his crime should be tried and punished, but whether he should be delivered up to a foreign tribunal which was alone capable of trying and punishing him. A provision for the trial of crimes in the courts of the United States, is clearly not a provision for the performance of a national compact for the surrender to a foreign government of an offender against that government.

The clause of the constitution declaring that the trial of all crimes shall be by jury, has never even been construed to extend to the trial of crimes committed in the land and naval forces of the United States. Had such a construction prevailed, it would most probably have prostrated the constitution itself, with the liberties and the independence of the nation, before the first disciplined invader who should approach our shores. Necessity would have imperiously demanded the review and amendment of so unwise a provision. If, then, this clause does not extend to offenses committed in the fleets and armies of the United States, how can it be construed to extend to offenses committed in the fleets and armies of Britain or of France, or of the Ottoman or Russian empires?

The same argument applies to the observations on the seventh article of the amendments to the constitution. That article relates only to trials in the courts of the United States, and not to the performance of a contract for the delivery of a murder not triable in those courts.

In this part of the argument, the gentleman from New York has presented a dilemma of a very wonderful structure indeed. He says that the offense of Thomas Nash was either a crime or not a crime. If it was a crime, the constitutional mode of punishment ought to have been observed. If it was not a crime, he ought not have been delivered up to a foreign government, where his punishment was inevitable.

It had escaped the observation of that gentleman, that if the murder committed by Thomas Nash was a crime, yet it was not a crime provided for by the constitution, or triable in the courts of the United States; and that if it was not a crime, yet it is the precise case in which his surrender was stipulated by treaty. Of this extraordinary dilemma, then, the gentleman from New York is, himself, perfectly at liberty to retain either form. The gentleman is incorrect in every part of his statement. Murder on board a British frigate is not a crime created by treaty. It would have been a crime of precisely the same magnitude, had the treaty never been formed. It is not punished by sending the offender out of the United States. The experience of this unfortunate criminal, who was hung and gibbeted, evinced to him that the punishment of his crime was of a much more serious nature than the mere banishment from the United States.

The gentleman from Pennsylvania and the gentleman from Virginia have both contended, that this was a case proper for the decision of the courts, because points of law occurred, and points of law must have been decided in its determination.

The points of law which must have been decided are stated by the gentleman from Pennsylvania to be, first, a question whether the offense was committed within the British jurisdiction; and, secondly, whether the crime charged was comprehended within the treaty.

It is true, sir, these points of law must have occurred, and must have been decided but it by no means follows that they could only have been decided in court. A variety of legal questions must present themselves in the performance of every part of executive duty, but these questions are not therefore to be decided in a court. Whether a patent for land shall issue or not is always a question of law, but not a question which must necessarily be carried into court. The gentleman from Pennsylvania seems to have permitted himself to have been misled by the misrepresentation of the constitution made in the resolutions of the gentleman from New York; and, in consequence of being so misled, his observations have the appearance of endeavoring to fit the constitution to his arguments, instead of adapting his arguments to the constitution.

When the gentleman has proved that these are questions of law, and that they must been decided by the President, he has not advanced a single step toward proving that they were improper for executive decision. The questions whether vessels captured within three miles of the American coast, or by privateers fitted out in American ports, were legally captured or not, and whether the American government was bound to restore them, if in its power, were questions of law, but they were questions of political law, proper to be decided, and they were decided by the executive, and not by the courts.

The casus foederis of the guaranty was a question of law, but no man would have hazarded the opinion that such a question must be carried into court, and can only be there decided. So the casus foederis under the twenty-seventh article of the treaty with Britain is a question of law, but of political law. The question to be decided is, whether the particular case proposed be one in which the nation has bound itself to act, and this is a question depending on principles never submitted to courts.

If a murder shall be committed within the United States, and the murderer should seek an asylum in Britain, the question whether the casus foederis of the twenty-seventh article had occurred, so that his delivery ought to be demanded, would be a question of law, but no man would say it was a question which ought to be decided in the courts.

When, therefore, the gentleman from Pennsylvania has established, that in delivering up Thomas Nash, points of law were decided by the President he has established a position which in no degree whatever aids his argument.

The case was in its nature a national demand made upon the nation. The parties were the two nations. They cannot come into court to litigate their claims, nor can a court decide on them. Of consequence, the demand is not a case for judicial cognizance.

The President is the sole organ of the nation in its external relations, and its sole representative with foreign nations. Of consequence, the demand of a foreign nation can only be made on him. He possesses the whole executive power. He holds and directs the force of the nation. Of consequence, any act to be performed by the force of the nation is to be performed through him. He is charged to execute the laws. A treaty is declared to be a law. He must then execute a treaty, where he, and he alone, possesses the means of executing it.

The treaty, which is a law, enjoins the performance of a particular object. The person who is to perform this object is marked out by the constitution, since the person is named who conducts the foreign intercourse, and is to take care that the laws be faithfully executed. The means by which it is to be performed — the force of the nation — are in the hands of this person. Ought not this person to perform the object, although the particular mode of using the means has not been prescribed? Congress unquestionably may prescribe the mode; and Congress may devolve on others the whole execution of the contract, but till this be done, it seems the duty of the executive department to execute the contract by any means it possesses.

The gentleman from Pennsylvania contends that, although this should be properly an executive duty, yet it cannot be performed until Congress shall direct the mode of performance. He says, that although the jurisdiction of the courts is extended by the constitution to all cases of admiralty and maritime jurisdiction, yet if the courts had been created without any express assignment of jurisdiction, they could not have taken cognizance of causes expressly allotted to them by the constitution. The executive, he says, can, no more than courts, supply a legislative omission.

It is not admitted that in the case stated, courts could not have taken jurisdiction. The contrary is believed to be the correct opinion. And although the executive cannot supply a total legislative omission, yet it is not admitted or believed that there is such a total omission in this case.

The treaty, stipulating that a murderer shall be delivered up to justice, is as obligatory as an act of Congress making the same declaration. If, then, there was an act of Congress in the words of the treaty, declaring that a person who had committed a murder within the jurisdiction of Britain, and sought an asylum within the territory of the United States, should be delivered up by the United States, on demand of His Britannic Majesty, and such evidence of his criminality as would have justified his commitment for trial, had the offense been here committed; could the President, who is bound to execute the laws, have justified a refusal to deliver up the criminal, by saying that the legislature had totally omitted to provide for the case?

The executive is not only the constitutional department, but seems to be the proper department to which the power in question may most wisely and most safely be confided.

The department which is entrusted with the whole foreign intercourse of the nation, with the negotiation of all its treaties, with the power of demanding a reciprocal performance of the article, which is accountable to the nation for the violation of its engagements with foreign nations, and for the consequences resulting from such violations, seems the proper department to be entrusted with the execution of a national contract like that under consideration.

If at any time policy may temper the strict execution of the contract, where may that political discretion be placed so safely as in the department whose duty it is to understand precisely the state of the political intercourse and connection between the United States and foreign nations, to understand the manner in which the particular stipulation is explained and performed by foreign nations, and to understand completely the state of the Union?

This department, too, independent of judicial aid, which may, perhaps, in some instances be called in, is furnished with a great law-officer, whose duty it is to understand and to advise when the casus foederis occurs. And if the President should be caused to be arrested under the treaty an individual who was so circumstanced as not to be properly the object of such an arrest, he may perhaps bring the question of the legality of his arrest before a judge by a writ of habeas corpus.

It is then demonstrated, that according to the practice, and according to the principles of the American government, the question whether the nation has or has not bound itself to deliver up any individual, charged with having committed murder or forgery within the jurisdiction of Britain, is a question, the power to decide which rests alone with the executive department.

It remains to enquire, whether in exercising this power, and in performing the duty it enjoins, the President has committed an unauthorized and dangerous interference with judicial decisions.

That Thomas Nash was committed originally at the instance of the British consul at Charleston, not for trial in the American courts, but for the purpose of being delivered up to justice in conformity with the treaty between the two nations, has been already so ably argued by the gentleman from Delaware, that nothing further can be added to that point. He would, therefore, Mr. Marshall said, consider the case as if Nash, instead of having been committed for the purposes of the treaty, had been committed for trial. Admitting even this to be the fact, conclusions which have been drawn from it were by no means warranted.

Gentlemen had considered it as an offense against judicial authority, and a violation of judicial rights, to withdraw from their sentence a criminal against whom a prosecution had been commenced. They had treated the subject as if it was the privilege of courts to condemn to death the guilty wretch arraigned at their bar, and that to intercept the judgment was to violate the privilege. Nothing can be more incorrect than this view of the case. It is not the privilege, it is the sad duty of courts to administer criminal judgment. It is a duty to be performed at the demand of the nation, and with which the nation has a right to dispense. If the judgment of death is to be pronounced, it must be at the prosecution of the nation, and the nation may at will stop that prosecution. In this respect the President expresses constitutionally the will of the nation, and may rightfully, as was done in the case at Trenton, enter a nolle prosequi, or direct that the criminal be prosecuted no further. This is no interference with judicial decisions, nor any invasion of the province of a court. It is the exercise of an indubitable and a constitutional power. Had the President directed the judge at Charleston to decide for or against his own jurisdiction, to condemn or acquit the prisoner, this would have been a dangerous interference with judicial decisions, and ought to have been resisted. But no such direction has been given, nor any such decision been required. If the President determined that Thomas Nash ought to have been delivered up to the British government for a murder committed on board a British frigate, provided evidence of the fact was adduced, it was a question which duty obliged him to determine, and which he determined rightly. If in consequence of this determination he arrested the proceedings of a court on a national prosecution, he had a right to arrest and to stop them, and the exercise of this right was a necessary consequence of the determination of the principal question. In conforming to this decision, the court has left open the question of its jurisdiction. Should another prosecution of the same sort be commenced, which should not be suspended but continued by the executive, the case of Thomas Nash would not bind as a precedent against the jurisdiction of the court. If it should even prove that in the opinion of the executive, a murder committed on board a foreign fleet was not within the jurisdiction of the court, it would prove nothing more; and though this opinion might rightfully induce the executive to exercise its power over the prosecution, yet if the prosecution was continued, it would have no influence with the court, in deciding on its jurisdiction.

Taking the fact, then, even to be as the gentleman in support of the resolutions would state it, the fact cannot avail them.

It is to be remembered, too, that in the case stated to the President, the judge himself appears to have considered it as proper for executive decision, and to have wished that decision. The President and judge seem to have entertain'd on this subject the same opinion; and in consequence of the opinion of the judge, the application was made to the President.

It has then been demonstrated:

1st.   The case of Thomas Nash, as stated to the President, was completely within the twenty-seventh article of the treaty between the United States of America and Great Britain.

2d.   That this question was proper for executive and not for judicial decision; and

3d.   That in deciding it, the President is not chargeable with an interference with judicial decisions.

After trespassing so long, Mr. Marshall said, on the patience of the house, in arguing what had appeared to him to be the material points growing out of the resolutions, he regretted the necessity of detaining them still longer for the purpose of noticing an observation, which appeared not to be considered by the gentleman who made it as belonging to the argument.

The subject introduced by this observation, however, was so calculated to interest the public feelings, that he must be excused for stating his opinion on it.

The gentleman from Pennsylvania had said, that an impressed American seaman, who should commit homicide for the purpose of liberating himself from the vessel in which he was confined, ought not to be given up as a murderer. In this, Mr. Marshall said, he concurred entirely with that gentleman. He believed the opinion to be unquestionably correct, as were the reasons that gentleman had given in support of it. He had never heard any American avow a contrary sentiment, nor did he believe a contrary sentiment could find a place in the bosom of any American. He could not pretend, and did not pretend, to know the opinion of the executive on the subject, because he had never heard the opinions of that department; but he felt the most perfect conviction, founded on the general conduct of the government, that it could never surrender an impressed American to the nation, which, in making the impressment, had committed a national injury.

This belief was in no degree shaken by the conduct of the executive in this particular case.

In his own mind, it was a sufficient defense of the President from an imputation of this kind, that the fact of Thomas Nash being an impressed American was obviously not contemplated by him in the decision he made on the principles of the case. Consequently, if a new circumstance occurred, which would essentially change the case decided by the President, the judge ought not to have acted under the decision, but the new circumstance ought to have been stated. Satisfactory as this defense might appear, he should not resort to it, because to some it might seem a subterfuge. He defended the conduct of the President on other and still stronger ground.

The President had decided that murder committed on board a British frigate on the high seas was within the jurisdiction of that nation, and consequently within the twenty-seventh article of its treaty with the United States. He therefore directed Thomas Nash to be delivered to the British minister, if satisfactory evidence of the murder should be adduced. The sufficiency of the evidence was submitted entirely to the judge. If Thomas Nash had committed a murder, the decision was, that he should be surrendered to the British minister; but if he had not committed a murder, he was not to be surrendered.

Had Thomas Nash been an impressed American, the homicide on board the Hermoine would, most certainly, not have been a murder.

The act of impressing an American is an act of lawless

violence. The confinement on board a vessel is a continuation of that violence, and an additional outrage. Death committed within the United States, in resisting such violence, would not have been murder, and the person giving the wound could not have been treated as a murderer. Thomas Nash was only to have been delivered up to justice on such evidence as, had the fact been committed within the United States, would have been sufficient to have induced his committment and trial for murder. Of consequence, the decision of the President was so expressed as to exclude the case of an impressed American liberating himself by homicide.

He concluded with observing, that he had already too long availed himself of the indulgence of the house to venture further on that indulgence, by recapitulating, or reinforcing, the arguments which had already been urged.

SPEECH OF JOHN MARSHALL OPPOSING PATRICK HENRY
Delivered in the Virginia Convention, June 10, 1788, urging the ratification of the new Constitution

Mr. Chairman: I conceive that the object of the discussion now before us is, whether democracy or despotism be most eligible. I am sure that those who framed the system submitted to our investigation, and those who now support it intend the establishment and security of the former. The supporters of the Constitution claim the title of being firm friends of the liberty and rights of mankind. They say that they consider it as the best means of protecting liberty. We, sir, idolize democracy. Those who oppose it have bestowed eulogiums on monarchy. We prefer this system to any monarchy, because we are convinced that it has a greater tendency to secure our liberty and promote our happiness. We admire it, because we think it a well regulated democracy: it is recommended to the good people of this country; they are, through us, to declare whether it be such a plan of government as will establish and secure their freedom.

Permit me to attend to what the honorable gentleman, Mr. Henry, has said. He has expatiated on the necessity of a due attention to certain maxims — to certain fundamental principles, from which a free people ought never to depart. I concur with him in the propriety of the observance of such maxims. They are necessary in any government, but more essential to a democracy than to any other. What are the favorite maxims of democracy? A strict observance of justice and public faith, and a steady adherence to virtue. These, sir, are the principles of a good government. No mischief, no misfortune, ought to deter us from a strict observance of justice and public faith. Would to heaven that these principles had been observed under the present government! Had this been the case, the friends of liberty would not be so willing now to part with it. Can we boast that our government is founded on these maxims? Can we pretend to the enjoyment of political freedom or security, when we are told that a man has been, by an act of Assembly, struck out of existence without a trial by jury, without examination, without being confronted with his accusers and witnesses, without the benefits of the law of the land? Where is our safety, when we are told that this act was justifiable, because the person was not a Socrates? What has become of the worthy member's maxims? Is this one of them? Shall it be a maxim that a man shall be deprived of his life without the benefit of law? Shall such a deprivation of life be justified by answering that the man's life was not taken secundum artem, because he was a bad man? Shall it be a maxim that government ought not to be empowered to protect virtue?

The honorable member, after attempting to vindicate that tyrannical legislative act to which I have been alluding, proceeded to take a view of the dangers to which this country is exposed. He told us that the principal danger arose from a government which, if adopted, would give away the Mississippi. I intended to proceed regularly, by attending to the clause under debate; but I must reply to some observations which were dwelt upon to make impression on our minds unfavorable to the plan upon the table. Have we no navigation in, or do we derive no benefit from the Mississippi? How shall we retain it? By retaining that weak government which has hitherto kept it from us? Is it thus that we shall secure that navigation? Give the government the power of retaining it, and then we may hope to derive actual advantages from it. Till we do this, we cannot expect that a government which hitherto has not been able to protect it, will have the power to do it hereafter. Have we attended too long to consider whether this government would be able to protect us?

Shall we wait for further proofs of its inefficacy? If on mature consideration the Constitution will be found to be perfectly right on the subject of treaties, and containing no danger of losing that navigation, will he still object? Will he object because eight states are unwilling to part with it? This is no good ground of objection.

He then stated the necessity and probability of obtaining amendments. This we ought to postpone until we come to that clause, and make up our minds whether there be anything unsafe in this system. He conceived it impossible to obtain amendments after adopting it. If he was right, does not his own argument prove that in his own conception, previous amendments cannot be had? For, sir, if subsequent amendments cannot be obtained, shall we get amendments before we ratify? The reasons against the latter do not apply against the former. There are in this state, and in every state in the Union, many who are decided enemies of the Union. Reflect on the probable conduct of such men. What will they do? They will bring amendments which are local in their nature, and which they know will not be accepted. What security have we that other states will not do the same? We are told that many in the states were violently opposed to it. They are more mindful of local interests. They will never propose such amendments as they think would be obtained. Disunion will be their object. This will be attained by the proposal of unreasonable amendments. This, sir, though a strong cause, is not the only one that will militate against previous amendments. Look at the comparative temper of this country now and when the late Federal convention met. We had no idea then of any particular system. The formation of the most perfect plan was our object and wish. It was imagined that the states would accede to, and be pleased with, the proposition that would be made them. Consider the violence of opinions, the prejudices and animosities which have been since imbibed. Will not these operate greatly against mutual concessions, or a friendly concurrence? This will, however, be taken up more properly at another time. He says we wish to have a strong, energetic, powerful government. We contend for a well-regulated democracy. He insinuates that the power of the government has been enlarged by the convention, and that we may apprehend it will be enlarged by others. The convention did not, in fact, assume any power.

They have proposed for our consideration a scheme of government which they thought advisable. We are not bound to adopt it if we disapprove of it. Had not every individual in this community a right to tender that scheme which he thought most conducive to the welfare of his country? Have not several gentlemen already demonstrated that the convention did not exceed their powers? But the Congress have the power of making bad laws it seems. The Senate, with the President, he informs us, may make a treaty which shall be disadvantageous to us; and that, if they be not good men, it will not be a good constitution. I shall ask the worthy member only, if the people at large, and they alone, ought to make laws and treaties. Has any man this in contemplation? You cannot exercise the powers of government personally yourselves. You must trust to agents. If so, will you dispute giving them the power of acting for you, from an existing possibility that they may abuse it? As long as it is impossible for you to transact your business in person, if you repose no confidence in delegates, because there is a possibility of their abusing it, you can have no government; for the power of doing good is inseparable from that of doing some evil.

We may derive from Holland lessons very beneficial to ourselves. Happy that country which can avail itself of the misfortunes of others — which can gain knowledge from that source without fatal experience! What has produced the late disturbances in that country? The want of such a government as is on your table, and having in some measure such a one as you are about to part with. The want of proper powers in the government, the consequent deranged and relaxed administration, the violence of contending parties, and inviting foreign powers to interpose in their disputes, have subjected them to all the mischiefs which have interrupted their harmony. I cannot express my astonishment at his high-colored eulogium on such a government. Can anything be more dissimilar than the relation between the British government and the colonies, and the relation between Congress and the states? We were not represented in Parliament. Here we are represented. Arguments which prove the impropriety of being taxed by Britain do not hold against the exercise of taxation by Congress.

Let me pay attention to the observation of the gentleman who was last up, that the power of taxation ought not to be given to Congress. This subject requires the undivided attention of this House. This power I think essentially necessary; for without it there will be no efficiency in the government. We have had a sufficient demonstration of the vanity of depending on requisitions. How, then, can the general government exist without this power? The possibility of its being abused is urged as an argument against its expediency. To very little purpose did Virginia discover the defects in the old system; to little purpose, indeed, did she propose improvements; and to no purpose is this plan constructed for the promotion of our happiness, if we refuse it now, because it is possible that it may be abused. The confederation has nominal powers, but no means to carry them into effect. If a system of government were devised by more than human intelligence, it would not be effectual if the means were not adequate to the power. All delegated powers are liable to be abused. Arguments drawn from this source go in direct opposition to the government, and in recommendation of anarchy. The friends of the Constitution are as tenacious of liberty as its enemies. They wish to give no power that will endanger it. They wish to give the government powers to secure and protect it. Our inquiry here must be whether the power of taxation be necessary to perform the objects of the Constitution, and whether it be safe, and as well guarded as human wisdom can do it. What are the objects of the national government? To protect the United States, and to promote the general welfare. Protection, in time of war, is one of its principal objects. Until mankind shall cease to have ambition and avarice, wars will arise.

The prosperity and happiness of the people depend on the performance of these great and important duties of the general government. Can these duties be performed by one state? Can one state protect us and promote our happiness? The honorable gentleman who has gone before me, Governor Randolph, has shown that Virginia cannot do these things. How, then, can they be done? By the national government only. Shall we refuse to give it power to do them? We are answered, that the powers may be abused; that, though the Congress may promote our happiness, yet they may prostitute their powers to destroy our liberties. This goes to the destruction of all confidence in agents. Would you believe that men who had merited your highest confidence would deceive you? Would you trust them again after one deception? Why then hesitate to trust the general government? The object of our inquiry is, Is the power necessary, and is it guarded? There must be men and money to protect us. How are armies to be raised? Must we not have money for that purpose? But the honorable gentleman says that we need not be afraid of war. Look at history, which has been so often quoted. Look at the great volume of human nature. They will foretell you that a defenseless country cannot be secure. The nature of man forbids us to conclude that we are in no danger from war. The passions of men stimulate them to avail themselves of the weakness of others. The powers of Europe are jealous of us. It is our interest to watch their conduct, and guard against them. They must be pleased with our disunion. If we invite them by our weakness to attack us, will they not do it? If we add debility to our present situation, a partition of America may take place.

It is, then, necessary to give the government that power, in time of peace, which the necessity of war will render indispensable, or else we shall be attacked unprepared. The experience of the world, a knowledge of human nature, and our own particular experience will confirm this truth. When danger shall come upon us, may we not do what we were on the point of doing once already — that is, appoint a dictator? Were those who are now friends to this Constitution less active in the defense of liberty on that trying occasion than those who oppose it? When foreign dangers come, may not the fear of immediate destruction, by foreign enemies, impel us to take a most dangerous step? Where, then, will be our safety? We may now regulate and frame a plan that will enable us to repel attacks, and render a recurrence to dangerous expedients unnecessary. If we be prepared to defend ourselves, there will be little inducement to attack us. But if we defer giving the necessary power to the general government till the moment of danger arrives, we shall give it then, and with an unsparing hand. America, like other nations, may be exposed to war. The propriety of giving this power will be proved by the history of the world, and particularly of modern republics. I defy you to produce a single instance where requisitions on several individual states composing a confederacy have been honestly complied with. Did gentlemen expect to see such punctuality complied with in America? If they did, our own experience shows the contrary.

We are told that the Confederation carried us through the war. Had not the enthusiasm of liberty inspired us with unanimity, that system would never have carried us through it. It would have been much sooner terminated had that government been possessed of due energy. The inability of Congress, and the failure of states to comply with the constitutional requisitions, rendered our resistance less efficient than it might have been. The weakness of that government caused troops to be against us which ought to have been on our side, and prevented all resources of the community from being called at once into action. The extreme readiness of the people to make their utmost exertions to ward off solely the pressing danger, supplied the place of requisitions. When they came solely to be depended on, their inutility was fully discovered. A bare sense of duty, or a regard to propriety, is too feeble to induce men to comply with obligations. We deceive ourselves if we expect any efficacy from these. If requisitions will not avail, the government must have the sinews of war some other way. Requisitions cannot be effectual. They will be productive of delay, and will ultimately be inefficient. By direct taxation, the necessities of the government will be supplied in a peacable manner, without irritating the minds of the people. But requisitions cannot be rendered efficient without a civil war — without great expense of money, and the blood of our citizens. Are there any other means? Yes, that Congress shall apportion the respective quotas previously, and if not complied with by the states, that then this dreaded power shall be exercised. The operation of this has been described by the gentleman who opened the debate. He cannot be answered. This great objection to that system remains unanswered. Is there no other argument which ought to have weight with us on this subject? Delay is a strong and pointed objection to it.

We are told by the gentleman who spoke last, that direct

taxation is unnecessary, because we are not involved in war. This admits the propriety of recurring to direct taxation if we were engaged in war. It has not been proved that we have no dangers to apprehend on this point. What will be the consequence of the system proposed by the worthy gentleman? Suppose the states should refuse?

The worthy gentleman who is so pointedly opposed to the Constitution proposes remonstrances. Is it a time for Congress to remonstrate or compel a compliance with requisitions, when the whole wisdom of the Union and the power of Congress are opposed to a foreign enemy? Another alternative is, that if the states shall appropriate certain funds for the use of Congress, Congress shall not lay direct taxes. Suppose the funds appropriated by the states for the use of Congress should be inadequate; it will not be determined whether they be insufficient till after the time at which the quota ought to have been paid; and then, after so long a delay, the means of procuring money, which ought to have been employed in the first instance, must be recurred to. May they not be amused by such ineffectual and temporizing alternatives from year to year, until America shall be enslaved? The failure in one state will authorize a failure in another. The calculation in some states that others will fail will produce general failures. This will also be attended with all the expenses which we are anxious to avoid. What are the advantages to induce us to embrace this system? If they mean that requisitions should be complied with, it will be the same as if Congress had the power of direct taxation. The same amount will be paid by the people.

It is objected that Congress will not know how to lay taxes, so as to be easy and convenient for the people at large. Let us pay strict attention to this objection. If it appears to be totally without foundation, the necessity of levying direct taxes will obviate what the gentleman says; nor will there be any color for refusing to grant the power.

The objects of direct taxes are well understood; they are but few; what are they? Lands, slaves, stock of all kinds, and a few other articles of domestic property. Can you believe that ten men, selected from all parts of the state, chosen because they know the situation of the people, will be unable to determine so as to make the tax equal on, and convenient for, the people at large? Does any man believe that they would lay the tax without the aid of other information besides their own knowledge, when they know that the very object for which they are elected is to lay the taxes in a judicious and convenient manner? If they wish to retain the affections of the people at large, will they not inform themselves of every circumstance that can throw light on the subject? Have they but one source of information? Besides their own experience — their knowledge of what will suit their constituents — they will have the benefit of the knowledge and experience of the state legislature. They will see in what manner the legislature of Virginia collects its taxes. Will they be unable to follow their example? The gentlemen who shall be delegated to Congress will have every source of information that the legislatures of the states can have, and can lay the taxes as equally on the people, and with as little oppression as they can. If, then, it be admitted that they can understand how to lay them equally and conveniently, are we to admit that they will not do it, but that in violation of every principle that ought to govern men, they will lay them so as to oppress us? What benefit will they have by it? Will it be promotive of their reelection? Will it be by wantonly imposing hardships and difficulties on the people at large, that they will promote their own interest, and secure their reelections? To me it appears incontrovertible that they will settle them in such a manner as to be easy for the people. Is the system so organized as to make taxation dangerous? I shall not go to the various checks of the government, but examine whether the immediate representation of the people be well constructed. I conceive its organization to be sufficiently satisfactory to the warmest friend of freedom. No tax can be laid without the consent of the House of Representatives. If there be no impropriety in the mode of electing the representatives, can any danger be apprehended? They are elected by those who can elect representatives in the state legislature. How can the votes of the electors be influenced? By nothing but the character and conduct of the man they vote for. What object can influence them when about choosing him? They have nothing to direct them in the choice but their own good. Have you not as pointed and strong a security as you can possibly have? It is a mode that secures an impossibility of being corrupted.

If they are to be chosen for their wisdom, virtue, and integrity, what inducement have they to infringe on our freedom? We are told that they may abuse their power. Are there strong motives to prompt them to abuse it? Will not such abuse militate against their own interests? Will not they and their friends feel the effects of iniquitous measures? Does the representative remain in office for life? Does he transmit his title to his son? Is he secured from the burden imposed on the community? To procure their reelection, it will be necessary for them to confer with the people at large, and convince them that the taxes laid are for their good. If I am able to judge on the subject, the power of taxation now before us is wisely conceded, and the representatives are wisely elected.

The honorable gentleman said that a government should ever depend on the affections of the people. It must be so. It is the best support it can have. This government merits the confidence of the people, and I make no doubt, will have it. Then he informed us again of the disposition of Spain with respect to the Mississippi, and the conduct of the government with regard to it. To the debility of the Confederation alone may justly be imputed every cause of complaint on this subject. Whenever gentlemen will bring forward their objections, I trust we can prove that no danger to the navigation of that river can arise from the adoption of this Constitution. I beg those gentlemen who may be affected by it, to suspend their judgment till they hear it discussed. Will, says he, the adoption of this Constitution pay our debts? It will compel the states to pay their quotas. Without this, Virginia will be unable to pay. Unless all the states pay, she cannot. Though the states will not coin money (as we are told) yet this government will bring forth and proportion all the strength of the Union. That economy and industry are essential to our happiness, will be denied by no man. But the present government will not add to our industry. It takes away the incitements to industry, by rendering property insecure and unprotected. It is the paper on your table that will promote and encourage industry. New Hampshire and Rhode Island have rejected it, he tells us. New Hampshire, if my information be right, will certainly adopt it. The report spread in this country, of which I have heard, is, that the representatives of that state having, on meeting, found they were instructed to vote against it, returned to their constitutents without determining the question, to convince them of their being mistaken, and of the propriety of adopting it.

The extent of the country is urged as another objection, as being too great for a republican government. This objection has been handed from author to author, and has been certainly misunderstood and misapplied. To what does it owe its source? To observations and criticisms on governments, where representation did not exist. As to the legislative power, was it ever supposed inadequate to any extent? Extent of country may render it difficult to execute the laws, but not to legislate. Extent of country does not extend the power. What will be sufficiently energetic and operative in a small territory, will be feeble when extended over a wide-extended country. The gentleman tells us there are no checks in this plan. What has become of his enthusiastic eulogium on the American spirit? We should find a check and control, when oppressed, from that source. In this country, there is no exclusive personal stock of interest. The interest of the community is blended and inseparably connected with that aid of the individual. When he promotes his own, he promotes that of the community. When we consult the common good, we consult our own. When he desires such checks as these, he will find them abundantly here. They are the best of checks. What has become of his eulogium on the Virginia Constitution? Do the checks in this plan appear less excellent than those of the Constitution of Virginia? If the checks in the Constitution be compared to the checks in the Virginia Constitution, he will find the best security in the former.

The temple of liberty was complete, said he, when the people of England said to their king, that he was their servant. What are we to learn from this? Shall we embrace such a system as that? Is not liberty secure with us, where the people hold all powers in their own hands, and delegate them cautiously, for short periods, to their servants, who are accountable for the smallest mal-administration? Where is the nation that can boast greater security than we do? We want only a system like the paper before you, to strengthen and perpetuate this security.

The honorable gentleman has asked if there be any safety

or freedom, when we give away the sword and the purse. Shall the people at large hold the sword and the purse without the interposition of their representatives? Can the whole aggregate community act personally? I apprehend that every gentleman will see the impossibility of this. Must they, then, not trust them to others? To whom are they to trust them but to their representatives, who are accountable for their conduct? He represents secrecy as unnecessary, and produces the British government as a proof of its inutility. Is there no secrecy there? When deliberating on the propriety of declaring war, or on military arrangements, do they deliberate in the open fields? No, sir. The British government affords secrecy when necessary, and so ought every government. In this plan, secrecy is only used when it would be fatal and pernicious to publish the schemes of government. We are threatened with the loss of our liberties by the possible abuse of power, notwithstanding the maxim, that those who give may take away. It is the people that give power, and can take it back. What shall restrain them? They are the masters who give it, and for whom their servants hold it.

He then argues against the system, because it does not resemble the British government in this — that the same power that declares war has not the means of carrying it on. Are the people of England more secure, if the Commons have no voice in declaring war? or are we less secure by having the Senate joined with the President? It is an absurdity, says the worthy member, that the same man should obey two masters — that the same collector should gather taxes for the general government and the state legislature. Are they not both the servants of the people? Are not Congress and the state legislatures the agents of the people, and are they not to consult the good of the people? May not this be effected by giving the same officer the collection of both taxes? He tells you that it is an absurdity to adopt before you amend. Is the object of your adoption to mend solely? The objects of your adoption are union, safety against foreign enemies, and protection against faction — against what has been the destruction of all republics. These impel you to its adoption. If you adopt it, what shall restrain you from amending it, if, in trying it, amendments shall be found necessary? The government is not supported by force, but depends on our free will. When experience shall show us any inconveniences, we can then correct it. But until we have experience on the subject, amendments, as well as the Constitution itself, are to try. Let us try it, and keep our hands free to change it when necessary. If it be necessary to change government, let us change that government which has been found to be defective. The difficulty we find in amending the Confederation will not be found in amending this Constitution. Any amendments, in the system before you, will not go to a radical change; a plain way is pointed out for the purpose. All will be interested to change it, and therefore all exert themselves in getting the change. There is such a diversity of sentiment in human minds, that it is impossible we shall ever concur in one system till we try it. The power given to the general government over the time, place, and manner of election, is also strongly objected to. When we come to that clause we can prove it is highly necessary, and not dangerous.

The worthy member has concluded his observations by many eulogiums on the British constitution. It matters not to us whether it be a wise one or not. I think that, for America at least, the government on your table is very much superior to it. I ask you if your House of Representatives would be better than it is, if a hundredth part of the people were to elect a majority of them. If your Senators were for life, would they be more agreeable to you? If your President were not accountable to you for his conduct,— if it were a constitutional maxim, that he could do no wrong,— would you be safer than you are now? If you can answer, Yes, to these questions, then adopt the British constitution. If not, then, good as that government may be, this is better. The worthy gentleman who was last up, said the confederacies of ancient and modern times were not similar to ours, and that consequently reasons which applied against them could not be urged against it. Do they not hold out one lesson very useful to us? However unlike in other respects, they resemble it in its total inefficacy. They warn us to shun their calamities, and place in our government those necessary powers, the want of which destroyed them. I hope we shall avail ourselves of their misfortunes, without experiencing them. There was something peculiar in one observation he made. He said that those who governed the cantons of Switzerland were purchased by foreign powers, which was the cause of their uneasiness and trouble.

How does this apply to us? If we adopt such a government as theirs, will it not be subject to the same inconvenience? Will not the same cause produce the same effect? What shall protect us from it? What is our security? He then proceeded to say that the causes of war are removed from us; that we are separated by the sea from the powers of Europe, and need not be alarmed. Sir, the sea makes them neighbors to us. Though an immense ocean divides us, we may speedily see them with us. What dangers may we not apprehend to our commerce? Does not our naval weakness invite an attack on our commerce? May not the Algerines seize our vessels? Cannot they, and every other predatory or maritime nation, pillage our ships and destroy our commerce, without subjecting themselves to any inconvenience? He would, he said, give the general government all necessary powers. If anything be necessary, it must be so to call forth the strength of the Union when we may be attacked, or when the general purposes of America require it. The worthy gentleman then proceeded to show, that our present exigencies are greater than they will ever be again.

Who can penetrate into futurity? How can any man pretend to say that our future exigencies will be less than our present? The exigencies of nations have been generally commensurate to their resources. It would be the utmost impolicy to trust to a mere possibility of not being attacked, or obliged to exert the strength of the community. He then spoke of a selection of particular objects by Congress, which he says must necessarily be oppressive; that Congress, for instance, might select taxes, and that all but landholders would escape. Cannot Congress regulate the taxes so as to be equal on all parts of the community? Where is the absurdity of having thirteen revenues? Will they clash with, or injure, each other? If not, why cannot Congress make thirteen distinct laws, and impose the taxes on the general objects of taxation in each state, so that all persons of the society shall pay equally, as they ought?

He then told you that your Continental government will call forth the virtue and talents of America. This being the case, will they encroach on the power of the state governments? Will our most virtuous and able citizens wantonly attempt to destroy the liberty of the people? Will the most virtuous act the most wickedly? I differ in opinion from the worthy gentleman. I think the virtue and talents of the members of the general government will tend to the security, instead of the destruction, of our liberty. I think that the power of direct taxation is essential to the existence of the general government, and that it is safe to grant it. If this power be not necessary, and as safe from abuse as any delegated power can possibly be, then I say that the plan before you is unnecessary; for it imports not what system we have, unless it have the power of protecting us in time of peace and war.

SPEECH OF JOHN MARSHALL
Delivered in the Virginia Convention, June 28, 1788. The 1st and 2d sections of the 3d Article of the Constitution being under consideration

Mr. Chairman: This part of the plan before us is a great improvement on that system from which we are now departing. Here are tribunals appointed for the decision of controversies which were before either not at all, or improperly, provided for. That many benefits will result from this to the members of the collective society, every one confesses. Unless its organization be defective, and so constructed as to injure, instead of accommodating, the convenience of the people, it merits our approbation. After such a candid and fair discussion by those gentlemen who support it,— after the very able manner in which they have investigated and examined it,— I conceived it would be no longer considered as so very defective, and that those who opposed it would be convinced of the impropriety of some of their objections. But I perceive they still continue the same opposition. Gentlemen have gone on an idea that the federal courts will not determine the causes which may come before them with the same fairness and impartiality with which other courts decide. What are the reasons of this supposition? Do they draw them from the manner in which the judges are chosen, or the tenure of their office? What is it that makes us trust our judges? Their independence in office, and manner of appointment. Are not the judges of the federal chosen with as much wisdom as the judges of the state governments? Are they not equally, if not more independent? If so, shall we not conclude that they will decide with equal impartiality and candor? If there be as much wisdom and knowledge in the United States as in a particular state, shall we conclude that the wisdom and knowledge will not be equally exercised in the selection of judges?

The principle on which they object to the federal jurisdiction seems, to me, to be founded on a belief that there will not be a fair trial had in those courts. If this committee will consider it fully, they will find it has no foundation, and that we are as secure there as any where else. What mischief results from some causes being tried there? Is there not the utmost reason to conclude that judges, wisely appointed, and independent in their office, will never countenance any unfair trial? What are the subjects of its jurisdiction? Let us examine them with an expectation that causes will be as candidly tried there as elsewhere, and then determine. The objection which was made by the honorable member who was first up yesterday [Mr. Mason] has been so fully refuted that it is not worth while to notice it. He objected to Congress' having power to create a number of inferior courts, according to the necessity of public circumstances. I had an apprehension that those gentlemen who placed no confidence in Congress would object that there might be no inferior courts. I own that I thought those gentlemen would think there would be no inferior courts, as it depended on the will of Congress, but that we should be dragged to the centre of the Union. But I did not conceive that the power of increasing the number of courts could be objected to by any gentleman, as it would remove the inconvenience of being dragged to the centre of the United States. I own that the power of creating a number of courts is, in my estimation, so far from being a defect, that it seems necessary to the perfection of this system. After having objected to the number and mode, he objected to the subject matter of their cognizance. [Here Mr. Marshall read the 2d section.]

These, sir, are the points of federal jurisdiction to which he objects, with few exceptions. Let us examine each of them with a supposition that the same partiality will be observed there as in other courts, and then see if any mischief will result from them. With respect to its cognizance in all cases arising under the Constitution and the laws of the United States, he says that, the laws of the United States being paramount to the laws of the particular states, there is no case but what this will extend to. Has the government of the United States power to make laws on every subject? Does he understand it so? Can they make laws affecting the mode of transferring property, or contracts, or claims, between citizens of the same state? Can they go beyond the delegated powers? If they were to make a law not warranted by any of the powers enumerated, it would be considered by the judges as an infringement of the Constitution which they are to guard. They would not consider such a law as coming under their jurisdiction. They would declare it void. It will annihilate the state courts, says the honorable gentleman. Does not every gentleman here know that the causes in our courts are more numerous than they can decide, according to their present construction? Look at the dockets. You will find them crowded with suits, which the life of man will not see determined. If some of these suits be carried to other courts, will it be wrong? They will still have business enough.

Then there is no danger that particular subjects, small in proportion, being taken out of the jurisdiction of the state judiciaries, will render them useless and of no effect. Does the gentleman think that the state courts will have no cognizance of cases not mentioned here? Are there any words in this Constitution which exclude the courts of the states from those cases which they now possess? Does the gentleman imagine this to be the case? Will any gentleman believe it? Are not controversies respecting lands claimed under the grants of different states the only controversies between citizens of the same state which the federal judiciary can take cognizance of? The case is so clear, that to prove it would be a useless waste of time. The state courts will not lose the jurisdiction of the causes they now decide. They have a concurrence of jurisdiction with the federal courts in those cases in which the latter have cognizance.

How disgraceful is it that the state courts cannot be trusted! says the honorable gentleman. What is the language of the Constitution? Does it take away their jurisdiction? Is it not necessary that the federal courts should have cognizance of cases arising under the Constitution, and the laws, of the

United States? What is the service or purpose of a judiciary, but to execute the laws in a peacable, orderly manner, without shedding blood, or creating a contest, or availing yourselves of force? If this be the case, where can its jurisdiction be more necessary than here?

To what quarter will you look for protection from an infringement on the Constitution, if you will not give the power to the judiciary? There is no other body that can afford such a protection. But the honorable member objects to it, because he says that the officers of the government will be screened from merited punishment by the federal judiciary. The federal sheriff, says he, will go into a poor man's house and beat him, or abuse his family, and the federal court will protect him. Does any gentleman believe this? Is it necessary that the officers will commit a trespass on the property or persons of those with whom they are to transact business? Will such great insults on the people of this country be allowable? Were a law made to authorize them, it would be void. The injured man would trust to a tribunal in his neighborhood. To such a tribunal he would apply for redress, and get it. There is no reason to fear that he would not meet that justice there which his country will be ever willing to maintain. But, on appeal, says the honorable gentleman, what chance is there to obtain justice? This is founded on an idea that they will not be impartial. There is no clause in the Constitution which bars the individual member injured from applying to the state courts to give him redress. He says that there is no instance of appeals as to fact in common-law cases. The contrary is well known to you, Mr. Chairman, to be the case in this commonwealth. With respect to mills, roads, and other cases, appeals lie from the inferior to the superior court, as to fact as well as law. Is it a clear case, that there can be no case in common law in which an appeal as to fact might be proper and necessary? Can you not conceive a case where it would be productive of advantages to the people at large to submit to that tribunal the final determination, involving facts as well as law? Suppose it should be deemed for the convenience of the citizens that those things which concerned foreign ministers should be tried in the inferior courts; if justice could be done, the decision would satisfy all. But if an appeal in matters of facts could not be carried to the superior court, then it would result that such cases could not be tried before the inferior courts, for fear of injurious and partial decisions.

But, sir, where is the necessity of discriminating between the three cases of chancery, admiralty, and common law? Why not leave it to Congress? Will it enlarge their powers? Is it necessary for them wantonly to infringe your rights? Have you any thing to apprehend, when they can in no case abuse their power without rendering themselves hateful to the people at large? When this is the case, something may be left to the legislature freely chosen by ourselves, from among ourselves, who are to share the burdens imposed upon the community, and who can be changed at our pleasure. Where power may be trusted, and there is no motive to abuse it, it seems to me to be as well to leave it undetermined as to fix it in the Constitution.

With respect to disputes between a state and the citizens of another state, its jurisdiction has been decried with unusual vehemence. I hope that no gentleman will think that a state will be called at the bar of the federal court. Is there no such case at present? Are there not many cases in which the legislature of Virginia is a party, and yet the state is not sued? Is it not rational to suppose that the sovereign power should be dragged before a court. The intent is, to enable states to recover claims of individuals residing in other states. I contend this construction is warranted by the words. But, say they, there will be partiality in it if a state cannot be defendant — if an individual cannot proceed to obtain judgment against a state, though he may be sued by a state. It is necessary to be so, and cannot be avoided. I see a difficulty in making a state defendant, which does not prevent its being plaintiff. If this be only what cannot be avoided, why object to the system on that account? If an individual has a just claim against any particular state, is it to be presumed that, on application to its legislature, he will not obtain satisfaction? But how could a state recover any claim from a citizen of another state, without the establishment of these tribunals?

The honorable member objects to suits being instituted in the federal courts, by the citizens of one state, against the citizens of another state. Were I to contend that this was necessary in all cases, and that the government without it would be defective, I should not use my own judgment. But are not the objections to it carried too far? Though it may not in general be absolutely necessary, a case may happen, as has been observed, in which a citizen of one state ought to be able to recur to this tribunal, to recover a claim from the citizen of another state. What is the evil which this can produce? Will he get more than justice there? The independence of the judge forbids it. What has he to get? Justice. Shall we object to this, because the citizens of another state can obtain justice without applying to our state courts? It may be necessary with respect to the laws and regulations of commerce, which Congress may make. It may be necessary in cases of debt, and some other controversies. In claims for land, it is not necessary, but it is not dangerous. In the court of which state will it be instituted? said the honorable gentleman. It will be instituted in the court of the state where the defendant resides, where the law can come at him, and nowhere else. By the laws of which state will it be determined? said he. By the laws of the state where the contract was made. According to those laws, and those only, can it be decided. Is this a novelty? No; it is a principle in the jurisprudence of this commonwealth. If a man contracted a debt in the East Indies, and it was sued for here, the decision must be consonant to the laws of that country. Suppose a contract made in Maryland, where the annual interest is at six per centum, and a suit instituted for it in Virginia; what interest would be given now, without any federal aid? The interest of Maryland most certainly; and if the contract had been made in Virginia, and suit brought in Maryland, the interest of Virginia must be given, without doubt. It is now to be governed by the laws of that state where the contract was made. The laws which governed the contract at its formation govern it in its decision. To preserve the peace of the Union only, its jurisdiction in this case ought to be recurred to. Let us consider that, when the citizens of one state carry on trade in another state, much must be due to the one from the other, as is the case between North Carolina and Virginia. Would not the refusal of justice to our citizens, from the courts of North Carolina, produce disputes between the states? Would the federal judiciary swerve from their duty in order to give partial and unjust decisions?

The objection respecting the assignment of a bond to a

citizen of another state has been fully answered. But suppose it were to be tried, as he says; what would be given more than was actually due in the case mentioned? It is possible in our courts, as they now stand, to obtain a judgment for more than justice. But the court of chancery grants relief. Would it not be so in the federal court? Would not depositions be taken to prove the payments, and if proved, would not the decision of the court be accordingly?

He objects, in the next place, to its jurisdiction in controversies between a state and a foreign state. Suppose, says he, in such a suit, a foreign state is cast; will she be bound by the decision? If a foreign state brought a suit against the commonwealth of Virginia, would she not be barred from the claim if the federal judiciary thought it unjust? The previous consent of the parties is necessary; and, as the federal judiciary will decide, each party will aquiesce. It will be the means of preventing disputes with foreign nations. On an attentive consideration of these points, I trust every part will appear satisfactory to the committee.

The exclusion of trial by jury, in this case, he urged to prostrate our rights. Does the word court only mean the judges? Does not the determination of a jury necessarily lead to the judgment of the court? Is there any thing here which gives the judges exclusive jurisdiction of matters of fact? What is the object of a jury trial? To inform the court of the facts. When a court has cognizance of facts, does it not follow that they can make inquiry by a jury? It is impossible to be otherwise. I hope that in this country, where impartiality is so much admired, the laws will direct facts to be ascertained by a jury. But, says the honorable gentleman, the juries in the ten miles square will be mere tools of parties, with which he would not trust his person or property; which, he says, he would rather leave to the court. Because the government may have a district of ten miles square, will no man stay there but the tools and officers of the government? Will nobody else be found there? Is it so in any other part of the world, where a government has legislative power? Are there none but officers, and tools of the government of Virginia, in Richmond? Will there not be independent merchants, and respectable gentlemen of fortune, within the ten miles square? Will there not be worthy farmers and mechan-

ics? Will not a good jury be found there, as well as anywhere else? Will the officers of the government become
improper to be on a jury? What is it to the government
whether this man or that man succeeds? It is all one thing.
Does the Constitution say that juries shall consist of officers,
or that the Supreme Court shall be held in the ten miles square?
It was acknowledged, by the honorable member, that it was
secure in England. What makes it secure there? Is it their
constitution? What part of their constitution is there that the
Parliament cannot change? As the preservation of this
right is in the hands of Parliament, and it has ever been held
sacred by them, will the government of America be less honest
than that of Great Britain? Here a restriction is to be found.
The jury is not to be brought out of the state. There is no
such restriction in that government; for the laws of Parliament decide every thing respecting it. Yet gentlemen tell us
that there is safety there, and nothing here but danger. It
seems to me that the laws of the United States will generally
secure trials by a jury of the vicinage, or in such manner as
will be most safe and convenient for the people.

But it seems that the right of challenging the jurors is not
secured in this Constitution. Is this done by our own Constitution, or by any provision of the English government? Is
it done by their Magna Charta, or bill of rights? This privilege is founded on their laws. If so, why should it be objected to the American Constitution that it is not inserted in
it? If we are secure in Virginia without mentioning it in our
Constitution, why should not this security be found in the
federal court?

The honorable gentleman said much about the quitrents
in the Northern Neck. I will refer it to the honorable gentleman himself. Has he not acknowledged that there was no
complete title? Was he not satisfied that the right of the
legal representative of the proprietor did not exist at the
time he mentioned? If so, it cannot exist now. I will leave
it to those gentlemen who come from that quarter. I trust
they will not be intimidated, on this account, in voting on this
question. A law passed in 1782, which secures this. He says
that many poor men may be harassed and injured by the representatives of Lord Fairfax. If he has no right, this cannot
be done. If he has this right, and comes to Virginia, what

laws will his claims be determined by? By those of this state. By what tribunals will they be determined? By our state courts. Would not the poor man, who was oppressed by an unjust prosecution, be abundantly protected and satisfied by the temper of his neighbors, and would he not find ample justice? What reason has the honorable member to apprehend partiality or injustice? He supposes that, if the judges be judges of both the federal and state courts, they will incline in favor of one government. If such contests should arise, who could more properly decide them than those who are to swear to do justice? If we can expect a fair decision any where, may we not expect justice to be done by the judges of both the federal and state governments? But, says the honorable member, laws may be executed tyrannically. Where is the independency of your judges? If a law be exercised tyrannically in Virginia, to what can you trust? To your judiciary. What security have you for justice? Their independence. Will it not be so in the federal court?

Gentlemen ask, What is meant by law cases, and if they be not distinct from facts? Is there no law arising on cases of equity and admiralty? Look at the acts of Assembly. Have you not many cases where law and fact are blended? Does not the jurisdiction in point of law as well as fact, find itself completely satisfied in law and fact? The honorable gentleman says that no law of Congress can make any exception to the federal appellate jurisdiction of facts as well as law. He has frequently spoken of technical terms, and the meaning of them. What is the meaning of the term exception? Does it not mean an alteration and diminution? Congress is empowered to make exceptions to the appellate jurisdiction, as to law and fact, of the Supreme Court. These exceptions certainly go as far as the legislature may think proper for the interest and liberty of the people. Who can understand this word, exception, to extend to one case as well as the other? I am persuaded that a reconsideration of this case will convince the gentleman that he was mistaken. This may go to the cure of the mischief apprehended. Gentlemen must be satisfied that this power will not be so much abused as they have said.

The honorable member says that he derives no consolation from the wisdom and integrity of the legislature, because we call them to rectify defects which it is our duty to remove. We ought well to weigh the good and evil before we determine. We ought to be well convinced that the evil will be really produced before we decide against it. If we be convinced that the good greatly preponderates, though there be small defects in it, shall we give up that which is really good, when we can remove the little mischief it may contain, in the plain, easy method pointed out in the system itself?

I was astonished when I heard the honorable gentleman say that he wished the trial by jury to be struck out entirely. Is there no justice to be expected by a jury of our fellow citizens? Will any man prefer to be tried by a court, when the jury is to be of his countrymen, and probably of his vicinage? We have reason to believe the regulations with respect to juries will be such as shall be satisfactory. Because it does not contain all, does it contain nothing? But I conceive that this committee will see there is safety in the case, and that there is no mischief to be apprehended.

He states a case, that a man may be carried from a federal to an anti-federal corner (and vice versa) where men are ready to destroy him. Is this probable? Is it presumable that they will make a law to punish men who are of different opinions in politics from themselves? Is it presumable that they will do it in one single case, unless it be such a case as must satisfy the people at large? The good opinion of the people at large must be consulted by their representatives; otherwise, mischiefs would be produced which would shake the government to its foundation. As it is late, I shall not mention all the gentleman's argument, but some parts of it are so glaring that I cannot pass them over in silence. He says that the establishment of these tribunals, and more particularly in their jurisdiction of controversies between citizens of these states and foreign citizens and subjects, is like a retrospective law. Is there no difference between a tribunal which shall give justice and effect to an existing right, and creating a right that did not exist before? The debt or claim is created by the individual. He has bound himself to comply with it. Does the creation of a new court amount to a retrospective law?

We are satisfied with the provision made in this country on the subject of trial by jury. Does our Constitution direct trials to be by jury? It is required in our bill of rights, which is not a part of the Constitution. Does any security arise from hence? Have you a jury when a judgment is obtained on replevin bond, or by default? Have you a jury when a motion is made for the commonwealth against an individual; or when a motion is made by one joint obligor against another, to recover sums paid as security? Our courts decide in all these cases, without the intervention of a jury; yet they are all civil cases. The bill of rights is merely recommendatory. Were it otherwise, the consequence would be that many laws which are found convenient would be unconstitutional. What does the government before you say? Does it exclude the legislature from giving a trial by jury in civil cases? If it does not forbid its exclusion, it is on the same footing on which your state government stands now. The legislature of Virginia does not give a trial by jury where it is not necessary, but gives it wherever it is thought expedient. The federal legislature will do so too, as it is formed on the same principles.

The honorable gentleman says that unjust claims will be made, and the defendant had better pay them than go to the Supreme Court. Can you suppose such a disposition in one of your citizens, as that, to oppose another man, he will incur great expenses? What will he gain by an unjust demand? Does a claim establish a right? He must bring his witnesses to prove his claim. If he does not bring his witnesses, the expenses must fall upon him. Will he go on a calculation that the defendant will not defend it, or cannot produce a witness? Will he incur a great deal of expense, from a dependence on such a chance? Those who know human nature, black as it is, must know that mankind are too well attached to their interest to run such a risk. I conceive that this power is absolutely necessary, and not dangerous; that, should it be attended by little inconveniences, they will be altered, and that they can have no interest in not altering them. Is there any real danger? When I compare it to the exercise of the same power in the government of Virginia, I am persuaded there is not. The federal government has no other motive, and has every reason for doing right which the members of our state legislatures have. Will a man on the eastern shore be sent to be tried in Kentucky, or a man from Kentucky be brought to the eastern shore to have his trial? A government, by doing this, would destroy itself. I am convinced the trial by jury will be regulated in the manner most advantageous to the community.

SPEECH OF JOHN MARSHALL ON THE DEATH OF WASHINGTON
Delivered December 18, 1799, in National House of Representatives

MR. SPEAKER:

The melancholy event which was yesterday announced with doubt, has been rendered but too certain. Our Washington is no more! The Hero, the Sage, and the Patriot of America — the man on whom, in times of danger, every eye was turned, and all hopes were placed — lives now only in his own great actions, and in the hearts of an affectionate and afflicted people.

If, Sir, it had not been usual openly to testify respect for the memory of those whom Heaven had selected as its instruments for dispensing good to men, yet such has been the uncommon worth, and such the extraordinary incidents which have marked the life of him whose loss we all deplore, that the whole American nation, impelled by the same feelings, would call with one voice for a public manifestation of that sorrow which is so deep and so universal.

More than any other individual, and as much as to any one individual was possible, has he contributed to found this, our wide-spreading empire, and to give the Western world its independence and freedom. Having effected the great object for which he was placed at the head of our armies, we have seen him converting the sword into the ploughshare, and voluntarily sinking the soldier in the citizen.

Having been twice unanimously chosen the Chief Magistrate of a free people, we see him, at a time when his re-election, with the universal, could not have been doubted, affording to the world a rare instance of moderation, by withdrawing from his high station to the peaceful walks of private life.

However the public confidence may change, and the public affections fluctuate with respect to others, yet, with respect to him, they have in war and in peace, in public and private life, been as steady as his own firm mind, and as constant as his own exalted virtues.

Let us then, Mr. Speaker, pay the last tribute of respect

and affection to our departed friend — let the Grand Council of the nation display those sentiments which the nation feels.

For this purpose, I hold in my hand some resolutions, which I will take the liberty to offer to the House.

The rumor that Washington had died reached Philadelphia the day before the above speech was made,— December 17. On that day Marshall, " in a voice that bespoke the anguish of his mind and with a countenance expressive of the deepest regret," rose, and after stating the calamity that had probably befallen the country, moved an adjournment of the House. The next day, with " suppressed voice and deep emotion," he made the above speech.   When we recall how solicitous Washington was that Marshall should become a member of Congress, and how gratified he was at his election, we cannot but be struck with the circumstance that it was among the first of Marshall's duties to announce the death of the illustrious Washington.

The resolutions that Marshall mentioned were those drafted by General Lee, the last of which described Washington as " first in war, first in peace, and first in the hearts of his countrymen."

CHAPTER VI

QUOTATIONS made from the decisions of Chief Justice Marshall show precisely what his political and economic doctrines were.

THE PREAMBLE AND FORMATION OF THE CONSTITUTION OF U. S.

In Barron v. Mayor,[1] Chief Justice Marshall gives his views on the formation of the Constitution as follows:

"The Constitution of the United States was ordained and established by the people of the United States, for themselves, for their own government, and not for the government of the individual States. The people of the United States framed such a government for the United States as they supposed best adapted to their situation and best calculated to promote their interests." In the case of M'Culloch v. Maryland[2] Chief Justice Marshall says: "The Convention which framed the Constitution was indeed, elected by the State legislatures. But the instrument, when it came from their hands, was a mere proposal, without obligation or pretentions to it. It was reported to the then existing Congress of the United States, with a request that it might ' be submitted to a Convention of Delegates, chosen in each State by the people thereof, under the recommendation of its legislatures, for their assent and ratification.' This mode of proceeding was adopted; and by the Convention, by Congress, and by the State Legislatures, the instrument was submitted to the people. They acted upon it in the only manner in which they can act safely, effectively, and wisely, on such a subject, by assembling in Convention. It is true, they assembled in their several States,— and where else should they have assembled? No political dreamer was

[1] 7 Peters, 247.
[2] 4 Wheaton, 403.

ever wild enough to think of breaking down the lines which separate the States, and of compounding the American people into one common mass of consequence; when they act, they act in their States. But the measures they adopt do not, on that account, cease to be the measures of the people themselves, or become the measures of the State governments.

" From these conventions the Constitution derives its whole authority. The government proceeds directly from the people; is 'ordained and established' in the name of the people; and is declared to be ordained ' in order to form a more perfect union, establish justice, ensure domestic tranquillity, and secure the blessings of liberty to them selves and to their posterity.' The assent of the States, in their sovereign capacity is implied in calling the Convention, and thus submitting that instrument to the people. But the people were at perfect liberty to accept or reject it; and their act was final. It required not the affirmance, and could not be negatived, by the State governments. The constitution as thus adopted was of complete obligation, and bound the State sovereignties.

" It has been said, that the people had already surrendered all their powers to the State sovereignties, and had nothing more to give. But, surely, the question whether they may resume and modify the powers granted to government does not remain to be settled in this country. Much more might the legitimacy of the general government be doubted had it been created by the States. The powers delegated to the State sovereignties are to be exercised by themselves and not by a distinct and independent sovereignty created by themselves. For the formation of a league, such as was the confederation, the State sovereignties were certainly competent. But when, ' in order to form a more perfect union,' it was deemed necessary to change this alliance into an effective government, possessing great and sovereign powers, and acting directly on the people, the necessity of referring it to the people, and of deriving its powers directly from them, was felt and acknowledged by all."

INDEPENDENCE OF JUDICIARY

At the Virginia Constitutional Convention, John Marshall said:

" The judicial department comes home in its effects to every man's fireside; it passes on his property, his reputation, his life, his all.   Is it not to the last degree important that he should be rendered perfectly and completely independent, with nothing to control him but God and his conscience?   I have always thought from my earliest youth till now, that the greatest scourge an angry Heaven ever inflicted upon an ungrateful and a sinning people was an ignorant, a corrupt, or a dependent judiciary."

SUITS AGAINST STATES

At the Virginia Convention [3] called to ratify the Constitution John Marshall said:

" With respect to disputes between a State and the citizens of another State, its jurisdiction has been decried with unusual vehemence.   I hope that no gentleman will think that A State will be called at the bar of a federal court. . . . It is not rational to suppose that the sovereign power should be dragged before a court.   The intent is to enable States to recover claims of individuals residing in other States. . . . But, say they, there will be partiality in it if a State cannot be defendant — if an individual cannot proceed to obtain judgment against a State, though he may be sued by a State.   It is necessary to be so, and cannot be avoided.   I see a difficulty in making a State defendant which does not prevent its being plaintiff."

IMPLIED POWERS

In the case of United States v. Harris [4] we read that " Proper respect for a co-ordinate branch of the government requires the courts of the United States to give effect to the presumption that Congress will pass no act not within its constitutional power.   This presumption should prevail unless the lack of constitutional authority to pass an act in question is clearly demonstrated.   While conceding this, it must, nevertheless, be stated that the government of the United States is one of delegated, limited and enumerated powers.   Therefore every valid act of Congress must find in the Constitution some warrant for its passage."

[3] 3 " Elliot's Debates," 2d edition, 555.
[4] 106 U. S., 635

There is nothing to be found in the Constitution which excludes the exercise of incidental or implied powers. In McCulloch v. Maryland [5] Chief Justice Marshall said, " If the end be legitimate and within the scope of the Constitution, all the means which are appropriate, which are plainly adapted to that end, and which are not prohibited, may be constitutionally employed to carry it into effect."

DIRECT TAXES

Scores of eminent men expressed their views on this subject, but it seems no one pretended to explain fully what the expression, " Direct Taxes," as used in the Constitution, meant. John Marshall who was a member of the Constitutional Convention expressed his views more clearly on the matter than any other man. He says:

" The objects of direct taxes are well understood; they are but few; what are they? Lands, slaves, stock of all kinds, and a few other articles of domestic property."

POWER OF THE STATES TO DESTROY THE GOVERNMENT

In regard to the power of the States, Chief Justice Marshall, in the case of Cohens v. Virginia, gives the following opinion:

" The States can put an end to the Government by refusing to act. They have only not to elect Senators, and it expires without a struggle." [6]

TAX ON INCOME FROM BONDS

In Weston v. Charleston,[7] Chief Justice Marshall said: " The right to tax the contract to any extent, when made, must operate upon the power to borrow before it is exercised, and have a sensible influence on the contract. The extent of this influence depends on the will of a distinct government. To any extent, however inconsiderable, it is a burthen on the operations of government. It may be carried to an extent which shall arrest them entirely. . . . The tax on government stock is thought by this court to be a tax on the contract, a tax on the

[5] 4 Wheaton, 421.
[6] Wheaton, 391.
[7] 2 Peters, 449, 468.

power to borrow money to the credit of the United States, and consequently to be repugnant to the Constitution."

TAXING UNITED STATES BANK

The basic principles upon which the doctrine of Federal taxation rests were laid down by Chief Justice Marshall in a few early decisions on this subject.   These early cases decided by the Supreme Court have controlled very many of the later cases that have come up on this subject, for the principles there established had great weight.   The first great case of this kind was that of McCulloch v. Maryland,[8] which arose in the following manner:

In 1816, an act was passed by Congress, " To incorporate the subscribers of the Bank of the United States."   The bank was subsequently established in Philadelphia, and a branch thereof was also established in Baltimore.   In the 1818 A. D., the General Assembly of Maryland passed an act " To impose a tax on all banks, or branches thereof in the State of Maryland not chartered by the Legislature of that State."   In passing this act Maryland laid a heavy tax on the circulating notes of the branch bank of the United States which was located in the city of Baltimore.   The bank naturally having refused payment of the taxes, suit was brought to recover them and the action of course was sustained in all the courts of Maryland. The case was taken to the Supreme Court of the United States thereupon, where the best legal talent of the land argued on the case.   Chief Justice Marshall rendered the opinion of the Court which is one of the most comprehensive and profound he ever delivered.

In this case there were involved two great questions, of which the first was the power of Congress to charter a bank. After a most thorough exposition of the authority of Congress under the implied powers of the Constitution it was held that Congress had the power to incorporate a bank on the ground that it was one of the necessary agencies to carry out the purposes of the Government.   The second question was this, could the legislature of Maryland pass a law taxing the branch of a bank located within that State without violating the Federal Constitution?   This part of the decision is the one most vital,

[8] 4 Wheaton, 316.

and began by saying: " That the power of taxation is one of vital importance; that it is retained by the States; that it is not abridged by the grant of a similar power to the government of the Union; that it is to be concurrently exercised by the two governments; are truths which have never been denied. . . .

" The sovereignty of a State extends to everything which exists by its own authority, or is introduced by its permission; but does it extend to those means which are employed by Congress to carry into execution power conferred on that body by the people of the United States? We think it demonstrable that it does not. Those powers are not given by the people of a single State. They are given by the people of the United States, to a government whose laws, made in pursuance of the Constitution, are declared to be supreme. Consequently, the people of a single State can not confer a sovereignty which will extend over them. If we measure the power of taxation residing in a State, by the extent of sovereignty which the people of a single State possess, and can confer on its government, we have an intelligible standard applicable to every case to which the power may be applied. We have a principle which leaves the power of taxing the people and property of a State unimpaired; which leaves to a State the command of all its resources, and which places beyond its reach, all those powers which are conferred by the people of the United States on the government of the Union, and all those means which are given for the purpose of carrying those powers into execution. We have a principle which is safe for the States, and safe for the Union. We are relieved, as we ought to be, from clashing sovereignty; from interfering powers; from a repugnancy between a right in one government to pull down what there is an acknowledged right in another to build up; from the incompatibility of a right in one government to destroy what there is a right in another to preserve. We are not driven to the perplexing inquiry, so unfit for the judicial department, what degree of taxation is the legitimate use, and what degree may amount to the abuse of the power. The attempt to use it on the means employed by the government of the Union, in pursuance of the Constitution, is itself an abuse, because it is the usurpation of a power which the people of a single State can not give. We find, then, on just theory, a total failure of this original right to tax the means employed by the government of the Union, for the execution of its powers.   The right never existed, and the question whether it has been surrendered, can not arise.

" That the power to tax involves the power to destroy; that the power to destroy may defeat and render useless the power to create; that there is a plain repugnance, in conferring on one government a power to control the constitutional measures of another, which other, with respect to those very measures, is declared to be supreme over that which exerts the control, are propositions not to be denied. . . .

" If we apply the principle for which the State of Maryland contends, to the Constitution generally, we shall find it capable of changing totally the character of that instrument.   We shall find it capable of arresting all the measures of the government, and of prostrating it at the foot of the States.   The American people have declared their Constitution, and the laws made in pursuance thereof, to be supreme; but this principle would transfer the supremacy, in fact, to the States.

" If the States may tax one instrument, employed by the government in the execution of its powers, they may tax any and every other instrument.   They may tax the mail; they may tax the mint; they may tax patent rights; they may tax the papers of the custom house; they may tax judicial process; they may tax all the means employed by the government, to an excess which would defeat all the ends of government.   This was not intended by the American people.   They did not design to make their government dependent on the States."

The court reached the conclusion that the States have no power, by taxation or otherwise, to retard, impede, burden, or in any way control the operations of the constitutional laws enacted by Congress to carry into execution the powers vested in the general government.   The court also held: (1), That the States were not deprived of resources which they originally possessed.   (2), That they could lay a tax upon the real property of the bank, in common with other real property within the State.   (3), They could also impose a tax on the interest which the citizens of Maryland might hold in the bank, in common with other property of the same description throughout the State.   The pivotal question decided in this branch of the case was, that a State has no power to tax an agency of the general government, for, said Marshall, " the power to tax involves the power to destroy," an expression which has since become a classic in constitutional literature. This opinion established the constitutional principle that the Government of the United States is supreme in power, and independent of the States, in all matters relating to its existence, and that the agencies necessary for its perpetuity are beyond State control, or the power of State taxation. Coming as it did at an early date in our history, from a court having a thorough, and much personal knowledge concerning the formation and adoption of the Constitution, and of the hopes, purposes, and intentions of its framers, this opinion lifted the authority of the general government from the uncertainty which had surrounded it before this, and placed it upon the solid bed-rock of the Constitution. Here the strength and supremacy of the Federal Government began, for this was the first great judicial and constitutional sign-board, leading the way for the progress of the Republic. The great national benefit and influence have never been surpassed by any decision of any court.

A short time later, in the case of Osborn v. The United States Bank,[9] a similar question was considered, the General Assembly of Ohio having passed an act very similar to that of Maryland in regard to the taxation of a branch of the United States Bank. In this case Marshall also delivered the opinion, and in it the opinion in McCulloch v. Maryland, on the subject of the taxation of a government agency by a State, was reviewed and affirmed, the court expressly holding that a State law imposing a tax on one of the branches of a bank of the United States is unconstitutional.

Just five years after the decision in Osborn v. United States bank, another very important question came up before the Supreme Court in the case of Weston v. The City Council of Charleston,[10] which also grew out of the establishment of the United States Bank, and again Justice Marshall delivered the opinion of the majority of the court, for two justices dissented. The case came to the Supreme Court from the State of South Carolina, where the City Council of Charleston had passed an ordinance under which the stock of the United States Bank was made subject to taxation. The owners of the stock obtained a prohibition against levying tax in the lower court of the State, but this was reversed by the higher court and the case conse-

[9] 9 Wheaton, 738.
[10] 2 Peters, 449.

quently went to the Supreme Court of the United States. The main question was, could stock of the United States Bank, held by an individual, be taxed under authority of the State? In the course of his opinion Marshall said:

" If the right to impose the tax exists, it is a right which in its nature acknowledges no limits. It may be carried to any extent within the jurisdiction of the State or corporation which imposes it, which the will of each State and corporation may prescribe. A power which is given by the whole American people for their common good, which is to be exercised at the most critical periods, for the most important purposes, on the free exercise of which the interests certainly, perhaps the liberty of the whole may depend, may be burdened, impeded, if not arrested, by any of the organized parts of the confederacy. In a society formed like ours, with one supreme government for national purposes, and numerous State governments for other purposes, in many respects independent, and in the un-controlled exercise of many important powers, occasional inter-ferences ought not to surprise us. The power of taxation is one of the most essential to a State, and one of the most extensive in its operation. The attempt to maintain a rule which shall limit its exercise, is undoubtedly among the most delicate and difficult duties which can devolve on those whose province it is to expound the supreme law of the land in its application to the cases of individuals. This duty has more than once devolved on this court. In the per-formance of it, we have considered it as a necessary conse-quence, from the supremacy of the government of the whole, that its action, in the exercise of its legitimate powers, should be free and unembarassed by any conflicting powers in the possession of its parts ; that the powers of a State can not right-fully be so exercised as to impede and obstruct the free course of those measures which the government of the States united may rightfully adopt."

" It is not the want of original power in an independent sovereign State, to prohibit loans to a foreign government, which restrains the legislature from direct opposition to those made by the United States. The restraint is imposed by our Constitution. The American people have conferred the power of borrowing money on their government, and, by making that government supreme, have shielded its action, in the exercise of this power, from the action of the local governments. The grant of the power is incompatible with a restraining or controlling power, and the declaration of supremacy is a declaration that no such restraining or controlling power shall be exercised. The right to tax the contract to any extent, when made, must operate upon the power to borrow before it is exercised, and have a sensible influence on the contract. The extent of this influence depends on the will of a distinct government. To any extent, however inconsiderable, it is a burden on the operations of government. It may be carried to an extent which shall arrest them entirely."

The court's conclusion was that a tax on Government stock is a tax on the contract, on the power to borrow money on the credit of the United States, and, therefore, repugnant to the Constitution.

We know that the power to levy taxes and collect them is inherent in every sovereignty and it is doubtful if it was necessary that the Constitution of the United States should have expressly conferred this power upon Congress. It would have had it independent of any Constitutional authority.

POWER OF CONGRESS TO CHARTER BANKS

In his report on the establishment of a National Bank, Mr. Hamilton clearly demonstrated that the power existed in Congress to establish any agency necessary for carrying on the Government. Chief Justice Marshall crystallized this doctrine into law in his opinion which he delivered in the significant case of McCulloch v. Maryland,[11] in which he said:

"Among the enumerated powers, we do not find that of establishing a bank or creating a corporation. But there is no phrase in the instrument which like the Articles of Confederation, excludes incidental or implied powers; and which requires that everything granted shall be expressly and minutely described. Even the 10th amendment which was framed for the purpose of quieting excessive jealousies which had been excited, omits the word 'expressly,' and declares only that the powers 'not delegated to the United States, nor prohibited to the States, are reserved to the States or to the people,' thus leaving the question, whether the particular power

[11] 9 Wheaton, 406.

which may become the subject of contest has been delegated to the one government, or prohibited to the other, to depend on a fair construction of the whole instrument. The men who drew and adopted this amendment had experienced the embarassments resulting from the insertion of this word in the Articles of Confederation, and probably omitted it to avoid those embarassments."

Again (p. 421.) : " If we look to the origin of corporations, to the manner in which they have been framed in that government from which we have derived most of our legal principles and ideas, or to the uses to which they have been applied, we find no reason to suppose that a constitution, omitting, and wisely omitting, to enumerate all the means for carrying into execution the great powers vested in government, ought to have specified this.   Had it been intended to grant this power as one which should be distinct and independent, to be exercised in any case whatever, it would have found a place among the enumerated powers of the government.   But being considered merely as a means, to be employed only for the purpose of carrying into execution the given powers, there could be no motive for particularly mentioning it."

ORIGINAL PACKAGES

Judson, in his " Interstate Commerce," [12] says that the " original package rule " was first announced in 1827 in Marshall's opinion in Brown v. Maryland [13] which was a case where a statute passed by the Legislature of Maryland require importers of foreign articles by the bale or package and persons selling such articles in that way, to obtain a license to do so, which statute was declared unconstitutional by Chief Justice Marshall, who in discussing the question, admitted the difficulty of laying down any fixed rule on the subject as to when the statute applied to imported articles.   He said :

" It is sufficient for the present to say, generally, that when the importer has so acted upon the thing imported, that it has become incorporated and mixed up with the mass of property in the country, it has, perhaps, lost its distinctive character as an import, and has become subject to the taxing power of the State ; but while remaining the property of the importer in his

[12] Judson on " Interstate Commerce," sec. 16.
[13] 12 Wheaton, 441-442.

warehouse in the original form or package in which it was imported, a tax upon it is too plainly a duty on imports to escape the prohibition in the Constitution." [14]   Hence the doctrine of original packages.   There is no statutory definition of the term original package and the courts have not given any fixed definition to the term, but as each case arose have declared whether the article involved was or was not an original package.   In May v. New Orleans,[15] it was held,[16] that where goods were imported from foreign countries and were put up for sale in packages and a number of such packages were enclosed in boxes or cases for purposes of transportation, the box or case in which the packages were shipped and not the packages themselves constituted the original package.   In this case 4 of the justices dissented from the judgment of the court.

Mr. Justice Brown in delivering the opinion of the Court in Austin v. Tennessee [17] referred to Brown v. Maryland, the decision of Chief Justice Marshall, as the source of the doctrine of original packages, intimated that it was doubtful whether the decision would have been the same if the original package in that case had been small instead of large in size, for at that time it was customary to import goods from foreign countries in very large packages.   Mr. Justice Brown in this case said : [18]

" It is safe to assume that it did not occur to the Chief Justice [19] that, by a skillful alteration of the size of the packages, the decision might be used to force upon a reluctant people the use of articles denounced as noxious by the legislatures of the several States."   In Cook v. Marshall,[20] Mr. Justice Brown referred to Chief Justice Marshall, and summed up the doctrine as follows:

" The term ' original package ' is not defined by any statute, and is simply a convenient form of expression adopted by Chief Justice Marshall in Brown v. Maryland, to indicate that a license tax could not be exacted of an importer of goods from a foreign country who disposes of such goods in the form in

[14] 12 Wheaton, 441-2.
[15] 178 U. S., 496.
[16] 508, 509.
[17] 179 U. S., 343.
[18] 179 U. S., 351.
[19] Marshall.
[20] 196 U. S., 270.

which they were imported.   It is not denied that in the
changed and changing conditions of commerce between the
States, packages in which shipments may be made from one
State to another may be smaller than those ' bales, hogsheads,
barrels or tierces,' to which the term was originally applied by
Chief Justice Marshall, but whatever the form or size employed
there must be a recognition of the fact that the transaction is a
bona fide one, and that the usual methods of interstate shipment
have not been departed from for the purpose of evading the
police laws of the States."   It is held by the best authorities,
" that an original package is a package delivered by the importer to the carrier at the initial place of shipment, in the
exact condition in which it was shipped." [21]

STATE INSPECTION LAWS

Chief Justice Marshall in the case of Gibbons v. Ogden,[22]
said :   " The object of inspection laws is to improve the quality
of articles produced by the labor of a country; to fit them for
exportation; or it may be, for domestic use.   They act upon the
subject before it becomes an article of foreign commerce, or of
commerce among the States, and prepare it for that purpose.
They form a portion of that immense mass of legislation,
which embraces everything within the territory of a State, not
surrendered to a general government, all which can be most
advantageously exercised by the States themselves.   Inspection
laws, quarantine laws, health laws of every description, as well
as laws for regulating the internal commerce of a State, and
those which respect turnpike roads, ferries, etc., are component
parts of this mass.

" No direct general power over these objects is granted to
Congress, and consequently, they remain subject to State legislation.   If the legislative power of the Union can reach them,
it must be for national purposes; it must be where the power is
expressly given for a special purpose, or is clearly incidental
to some power which is expressly given.   It is obvious that the
Government of the Union, in the exercise of its express powers,
that, for example, of regulating commerce with foreign nations
and among the States, may use means that may also be employed by a State, in the exercise of its acknowledged powers;

[21] 27 Court of Claims, 278, 282.
[22] Pp. 12-13.

that, for example, of regulating commerce within the State. If Congress license vessels to sail from one port to another in the same State, the act is supposed to be, necessarily, incidental to the power expressly granted to Congress, and implies no claim of a direct power to regulate the purely internal commerce of a State, or to act directly on its system of police. So if a State, in passing laws on subjects acknowledged to be within its control, and with a view to those subjects, shall adopt a measure of the same character with one which Congress may adopt, it does not derive its authority from the particular power which has been granted, but from some other which remains within the State, and may be executed by the same means. All experience shows that the same measures, or measures scarcely distinguishable from each other, may flow from distinct powers; but this does not prove that the powers themselves are identical. Although the means used in their execution may sometimes approach each other so nearly as to be confounded, there are other situations in which they are sufficiently distinct to establish their individuality." [23]

QUARANTINE LAWS

Congress recognized as early as 1799, that the States may pass laws which relate to quarantine and the general preservation of health. At that time acts were passed which authorized the President to direct the revenue officers to aid in the execution of these laws.[24] In Gibbons v. Ogden,[25] Chief Justice Marshall said, The acts of Congress passed in 1796 and 1799, empowering and directing the officers of the General Government to conform to, and assist in the execution of quarantine and health laws of a State proceed, it is said, upon the idea that these laws are constitutional. It is undoubtedly true, that they do proceed upon that idea; and the constitutionality of such laws has never, so far as we are informed, been denied. They are treated as quarantine and health laws, and are so denominated in the acts of Congress and are considered as flowing from the acknowledged powers of the States, to provide for the health of the citizens.[26]

[23] 9 Wheaton, 1.
[24] 1 U. S. Statutes at Large, 474.
[25] P. 205.
[26] 9 Wheaton, 204.

The States can pass quarantine laws for the protection of health and may require the payment of small fees to discharge the expense of such examinations as the States think is necessary.[27]

NATURALIZATION

Chief Justice Marshall in speaking of the rights of a naturalized citizen, in Osborn v. United States Bank [28] says:

" He becomes a member of the society, possessing all the rights of a native citizen, and standing, in the view of the Constitution, on the footing of a native. The Constitution does not authorize Congress to enlarge or abridge those rights. The simple power of the National legislature is, to prescribe a uniform rule of naturalization, and the exercise of this power, exhausts it, so far as respects the individual." [29]   The above is erroneous.   We know that a naturalized citizen does not " possess all the rights of a native citizen " and the Constitution does not put a naturalized citizen on the " footing of a native."   There are certain privileges which belong to a native citizen, prescribed by the Constitution, which can not be conferred on a naturalized citizen and they are among the most esteemed privileges which a native citizen has, among them is the right of eligibility to the presidency.   A naturalized citizen cannot be President, or Vice-President.[30]   Neither can a naturalized citizen be a member of Congress until he has resided in this country a specified length of time.   A little farther on Chief Justice Marshall says in speaking of a naturalized citizen: " He is distinguishable in nothing from a native citizen, except so far as the Constitution makes the distinction.   The law makes none." [31]

HABEAS CORPUS

The privilege of the writ shall not be suspended.

There has been much controversy and great difference of opinion among jurists and law writers because the Constitution fails to say who shall have the power to suspend the

[27] 118 U. S., 455.
[28] 9 Wheaton, 739.
[29] P. 827.
[30] Const., art. 11, sec. 4.
[31] 9 Wheaton, 828.

writ of habeas corpus. In the early case of Bollman v. Swartout,[32] Chief Justice Marshall said:

"If at any time the public safety require the suspension of the writ of habeas corpus, it is for the legislature to say so. That question depends on political considerations, of which the legislature is to decide."

Some say that Marshall's opinion on this subject was obiter dictum, because the question was not necessarily or fairly before the court.

BILLS OF ATTAINDER

In Fletcher v. Peck,[33] Chief Justice Marshall said:

"A bill of attainder may affect the life of an individual, or may confiscate his property, or may do both."

"A bill of attainder is a legislative act which inflicts punishment without a judicial trial. If the punishment be less than death, the act is termed a bill of pains and penalties. Within the meaning of the Constitution, bills of attainder include bills of pains and penalties. In these cases the legislative body, in addition to its legitimate functions, exercises the powers and office of judge; it assumes, in the language of the text books, judicial magistracy; it pronounces upon the guilt of the party, without any of the forms or safeguards of trial; it determines the sufficiency of the proofs produced, whether conformable to the rules of evidence or otherwise; and it fixes the degree of punishment in accordance with its own notions of the enormity of the offense. The bills are generally directed against individuals by name, but they may be directed against a whole class." [34]

BILLS OF CREDIT OF STATES

The evils which produced the prohibitory clause in the Constitution of the United States, was the practice of the States in making bills of credit, and in some instances appraised property, "a legal tender." [35] This clause of the Constitution first came before the Supreme Court of the United States in Craig v. Missouri, the facts in this case were as follows:

[32] 4 Cranch, 101.
[33] 6 Cranch, 138.
[34] Cummings v. State of Mo., 4 Wallace, 323.
[35] Madison's Writings, Vol. 4, 160.

On the 27th of June, 1821, the legislature of Missouri, authorized the State to issue certificates of indebtedness in the following form: "This certificate shall be receivable at the treasury, or any of the loan offices of the State of Missouri, in the discharge of taxes or debts due the State, for the sum of $—— with interest for the same, at the rate of two per centum per annum from this date, the —— day of —— 182—." The question was, whether these certificates were bills of credit. It was held by the majority of the court that they were, and consequently the State of Missouri could not issue them. In delivering the opinion of the majority Chief Justice Marshall said:

"What is a bill of credit? What did the Constitution mean to forbid? In its enlarged, and perhaps literal sense, the term, ' bill of credit,' may comprehend any instrument by which a State engages to pay money at a future day, thus including a certificate given for money borrowed. But the language of the Constitution itself, and the mischief to be prevented, which we know from the history of our country, equally limit the interpretation of the terms. The word ' emit,' is never employed in describing those contracts by which a State binds itself to pay money at a future day, for services actually received, or for money borrowed for present use; nor are instruments executed for such purposes, in common language, denominated ' bills of credit.' To ' emit bills of credit ' conveys to the mind the idea of issuing paper intended to circulate through the community for its ordinary purposes as money, which paper is redeemable at a future day. This is the sense in which the terms have been always understood.

"At a very early period of our colonial history, the attempt to supply the want of the precious metals by a paper medium, was made to a considerable extent; and the bills emitted for this purpose have been frequently denominated bills of credit. During the war of our Revolution, we were driven to this expedient; and necessity compelled us to use it to a most fearful extent. The term has acquired an appropriate meaning; and ' bills of credit ' signify a paper medium, intended to circulate between individuals, and between government and individuals, for the ordinary purposes of society. Such a medium has been always liable to considerable fluctuation. Its value is continually changing; and these changes, often great and sudden, expose individuals to immense loss, are the sources of ruinous speculations, and destroy all confidence between man and man. To cut up this mischief by the roots, a mischief which was felt through the United States, and which deeply affected the interest and prosperity of all, the people declared in their Constitution that no State should emit bills of credit. If the prohibition means anything, if the words are not empty sounds, it must comprehend the emission of any paper medium by a State government for the purpose of common circulation." [36]

OBLIGATION OF CONTRACTS

No State shall pass a law impairing the obligation of contracts.—This was the conclusion Chief Justice Marshall came to in the first great case on this subject, the case of Fletcher v. Peck, [37] which was decided in 1809, twenty years after the establishment of the Government. The case arose as follows:

Under an act passed by the legislature of Georgia in 1795, a tract of land was sold to the Georgia Co., which was composed of individuals. Peck conveyed a part of this land to Fletcher, and in his deed Peck covenanted that the State of Georgia had lawful possession of the land when the act was passed and had a good right to sell it. The nature of the action was for a breach of covenant, in that the letters patent were void because the legislative act was passed through corrupt influences. Then, on the 13th of February, 1796, the legislature passed another act declaring the former act null and void. Thus, the principal question was, whether the legislature could repeal the first act and rescind the sale which had occurred under it, the purchasers being innocent of any defect of title.

Chief Justice Marshall delivered the opinion of the court, and held, that where a legislature of a State grants land in fee, a subsequent legislature cannot repeal the grant if an innocent purchaser has acquired title without knowledge of the infirmity. The grant made by the State amounted to a contract within the Constitution and the subsequent grant made in pursuance of that contract was an executed contract

[36] 4 Peters, 425.
[37] 6 Cranch, 87, 135.

and the State could not pass a law impairing its obligation. Also that contracts made by a State were as much within the prohibition of the Constitution against the impairment of the obligation of a contract as contracts made by an individual. Consequently it was held that, bona fide purchasers having acquired a fee under the act of 1795, the State of Georgia was prohibited from enacting a law which would impair the validity of the grant, and that the prohibition applied to both executory and executed contracts. In 11 Peters, 420, Justice McLean said: " If it were not for the opinion in Fletcher v. Peck, I would think the prohibition as to contracts applied only to executory contracts."

Chief Justice Marshall again delivered the opinion of the court in the next case on this subject which was that of New Jersey v. Wilson, decided in 1812. The legislature of New Jersey passed an act providing that certain lands which the State contemplated purchasing for the use of the Delaware Indians should be exempt from taxation. The lands were accordingly purchased for the Indians and conveyed to them in trust, and thereupon the Indians released their claim to the original lands. The Indians continued to occupy the lands upon which they had moved until 1803, when they were sold to settlers by act of the Legislature, subsequently the Legislature repealed the act of 1758, which exempted the lands from taxation. Chief Justice Marshall held that the original act of the legislature of New Jersey, passed in consideration that the Indians would release their title to the lands, which act declared that the new lands which should be purchased for the Indians should be exempt from taxation, amounted to a contract, and that any subsequent act of the legislature which repealed the original act violated that clause of the Constitution of the United States which prohibits a State from impairing the obligation of a contract.[38]

Chief Justice Marshall again delivered the opinion of the Court in the next case which touched this subject, the famous case of Sturges v. Crowninshield.[39] Here the court held, that an act of the legislature of New York violated this clause of the Constitution. The facts in the case are as follows: Suit was brought against the maker of two promissory notes.

[38] 7 Cranch, 164, 167.
[39] 4 Wheaton 122.

The defendant pleaded as his defense, that he was discharged
from the payment of the notes " under an act for the benefit
of insolvent debtors and their creditors passed by the legislature of New York, in 1811." To this there was a general
demurrer filed. Marshall admitted that a State might pass
a bankrupt law before Congress exercised its power to do so
provided such State law did not impair the obligation of a
contract. The notes sued upon had been executed before the
law was passed and Marshall in his opinion, expressly limited
the decision to the case actually before the court. It was
held that the act of the legislature of New York, so far as
it attempted to discharge the maker of the notes from paying
them, was contrary to the Constitution of the United States,
because it impaired the obligation of contracts.

DEFINITION OF CONTRACT

In the famous case of Dartmouth College v. Woodward,[40]
decided in 1819, the most elaborate exposition in regard to
contract was made. Chief Justice Marshall in his opinion
said, that Dartmouth College was a private and not a public
corporation, and later in his decision, in regard to contracts
said:

" The term ' contract,' as used in this clause of the Constitution, must be understood as intended to guard against a
power of at least doubtful utility, the abuse of which had
been extensively felt; and to restrain the legislature in future
from violating the right to property. That anterior to the formation of the Constitution, a course of legislation had prevailed in many, if not in all, of the States, which weakened
the confidence of man in man, and embarrassed all transactions
between individuals by dispensing with a faithful performance
of engagements. To correct this mischief, by restraining the
power which produced it, the State legislatures were forbidden
' to pass any law impairing the obligation of contracts.' The
contracts referred to were contracts respecting property, under
which some individual could claim a right to something beneficial to himself; and that since the clause in the Constitution
must, in construction, receive some limitation, it may be confined, and ought to be confined, to cases of this description;

[40] 4 Wheaton, 518.

to cases within the mischief it was intended to remedy." Then he proceeded to state that it was not " the purpose of the framers of the Constitution to restrain the States in regulating their civil institutions adopted for internal government, and that the instrument they have given us is not to be so construed may be admitted."

This decision established the important principle, that where a contract had been entered into and the rights of the parties under it had become fixed, a State could not, by legislative enactment, pass a law which would impair those rights.

OBLIGATION OF CONTRACTS DEFINED

Chief Justice Marshall created the first judicial construction of the term obligation of contracts. This was given in Sturges v. Crowninshield,[41] in which he said:

" It would seem difficult to substitute words which are more intelligible, or less liable to misconstruction, than those which are to be explained. A contract is an agreement in which a party undertakes to do, or not to do, a particular thing. The law binds him to perform his undertaking, and this is, of course, the obligation of his contract."

Thus, here we have Marshall's definition of what the Constitution means when it speaks of the obligation of a contract. It is the power or force in the law, which binds or compels one to complete his agreement.

DELEGATION OF POWERS OF PRESIDENT

Chief Justice Marshall delivered the opinion in the case of Marbury v. Madison,[42] and in commenting upon the power of the President said:

" By the Constitution of the United States, the President is invested with certain important political powers, in the exercise of which he is to use his own discretion, and is accountable only to his country in his political character, and to his own conscience. To aid him in the performance of these duties, he is authorized to appoint certain officers, who act by his authority and in conformity with his orders.

" In such cases their acts are his acts; and whatever opinion

[41] 4 Wheaton, 122.
[42] 1 Cranch.

may be entertained of the manner in which executive discretion may be used, still there exists, and can exist, no power to control that discretion. . . . The application of this remark will be perceived by adverting to the act of Congress for establishing the department of foreign affairs. This officer, as his duties were prescribed by that act, is to conform precisely to the will of the President. He is the mere organ by whom that will is communicated. The acts of such an officer, as an officer, can never be examinable by the courts.

"But when the legislature proceeds to impose on that officer other duties, when he is directed peremptorily to perform certain acts, when the rights of individuals are independent on the performance of those acts: — he is so far the officer of the law; is amenable to the laws for his conduct and cannot at his discretion sport away the vested rights of others.

"The conclusion from this reasoning is, that where the heads of departments are the political or confidential agents of the executive, merely to execute the will of the President, or rather to act in cases in which the executive possesses a constitutional or legal discretion, nothing can be more perfectly clear than that their acts are only politically examinable. But where a specific duty is assigned by law, and individual rights depend upon the performance of that duty, it seems equally clear that the individual who considers himself injured has a right to resort to the laws of his country for a remedy." [43]

CHIEF JUSTICE MARSHALL ISSUES SUBPŒNA FOR PRESIDENT JEFFERSON IN BURR TRIAL

How far, if at all, is the President subject to the process of the courts in civil or criminal actions? There has been great diversity of opinion among lawyers and constitutional writers for more than a century on this question. The chief authority in favor of the view that the President is subject to the process of a court is the decision of Chief Justice Marshall, upon application for a subpœna duces tecum directed to President Jefferson in the Burr trial. Here Marshall issued an order for a subpœna duces tecum requiring Jefferson to appear and produce at the trial certain papers, which it was believed he possessed. Chief Justice Marshall said:

[43] 1 Cranch, 165, 166.

" That the President of the United States may be subpœnaed and examined as a witness and required to produce any paper in his possession, is not controverted.   The President, although subject to the general rules which apply to others, may have sufficient motives for declining to produce a particular paper, and those motives may be such as to restrain the court from enforcing its production.   The guard furnished to this high officer to protect him from being harassed by vexatious and unnecessary subpœnas is to be looked for in the conduct of the court after these subpœnas have been issued, not in any circumstances which is to precede their being issued. . . . The court can perceive no objection to a subpœna duces tecum to any person whatever provided the case be such as to justify the process." [44]   Marshall also said:

" In no case of this kind would a court be required to proceed against the President as an ordinary individual.   The objections to such a course are so strong and so obvious that all must acknowledge them." [45]

EXTENT OF JUDICIAL POWERS

What is meant by extending the judicial power to all cases? What is a case in this connection and when does it arise? Chief Justice Marshall said:

" It enables the judicial department to receive jurisdiction to the full extent of the Constitution, laws, and treaties of the United States, when any question respecting them shall assume such a form that the judicial power is capable of acting on it. That power is capable of acting only when the subject is submitted to it by a party who asserts his rights in the form transcribed by law.   It then becomes a case." [46]

WHAT IS A CASE?

" A case in law or equity consists of the right of one party as well as of the other, and may truly be said to arise under the Constitution or a law of the United States, whenever its correct decision depends on the construction of either." [47]

The words case and cause are synonymous in legal nomen-

[44] " Burr's Trial," Vol. I, 182.
[45] " Burr's Trial," Vol. II. 536.
[46] Osborn v. U. S. Bank, 9 Wheaton, 738, 819.
[47] Cohens v. Virginia, 6 Wheaton, 379.

clature and either one means a proceeding in court, a suit or action.[48]

MARSHALL ON CASES AFFECTING AMBASSADORS

On this subject Chief Justice Marshall said:

" If a suit be brought against a foreign minister, the Supreme Court alone has original jurisdiction, and this is shown on the record. But, suppose a suit to be brought which affects the interest of a foreign minister, or by which the person of his secretary, or of his servant, is arrested. The minister does not, by the mere arrest of his secretary, or his servant, become a party to this suit, but the actual defendant pleads to the jurisdiction of the court, and asserts his privilege. If the suit affects a foreign minister, it must be dismissed, not because he is a party to it, but because it affects him. The language of the Constitution in the two cases is different. This court can take cognizance of all cases ' affecting ' foreign ministers; and, therefore, jurisdiction does not depend on the party named in the record. But this language changes when the enumeration proceeds to the States. Why this change? The answer is obvious. In the case of foreign ministers, it was intended, for reasons which all comprehend, to give the national courts jurisdiction over all cases by which they were in any manner affected. In the case of States, whose immediate or remote interests were mixed up with a multitude of cases, and who might be affected in an almost infinite variety of ways, it was intended to give jurisdiction in those cases only to which they were actual parties." [49]

ORIGINAL JURISDICTION OF THE SUPREME COURT

Original jurisdiction means that parties who are authorized to do so may bring an action in the Supreme Court without first having brought it in one of the inferior courts. This clause of the Constitution names those who may do this. They are: 1, ambassadors, 2, other public ministers, 3, consuls, 4, a State. This limits the original jurisdiction of the Supreme Court to a very narrow field. On the subject of original jurisdiction, Chief Justice Marshall said:

[48] Blyen v. U. S., 13 Wallace, 581-595.
[49] 9 Wheaton, 854.

" The original jurisdiction of the Supreme Court, in cases where a State is a party, refers to those cases in which, according to the grant of power made in the preceding clause, jurisdiction might be exercised in consequence of the character of the party, and an original suit might be instituted in any of the Federal courts; not to those cases in which an original suit might not be instituted in a Federal court. Of the last description is every case between a State and its citizens, and perhaps every case in which a State is enforcing its penal laws. In such cases, therefore, the Supreme Court cannot take original jurisdiction. In every other case, that is, in every case to which the judicial power extends, and in which original jurisdiction is not expressly given, that judicial power shall be exercised in the appellate, and only in the appellate form." [50]

TREASON — LEVYING WAR

In Bowlman's case,[51] in 1807 Chief Justice Marshall in regard to treason said: " to constitute treason war must be actually levied against the United States. However flagitious may be the crime of conspiring to subvert by force the government of our country, such conspiracy is not treason. The first must be brought into open action by the assemblage of men for a purpose treasonable in itself, or the fact of levying war cannot have been committed. . . . It is not the intention of the court to say that no individual can be guilty of this crime who has not appeared in arms against his country. On the contrary, if war be actually levied, that is, if a body of men be actually assembled for the purpose of effecting by force a treasonable purpose, all those who perform any part, however minute, or however remote from the scene of action, and who are actually leagued in the general conspiracy, are to be considered as traitors. But there must be an actual assembling of men for the treasonable purpose, to constitute a levying of war."

The opinion of Chief Justice Marshall in the Burr Trial covers the whole doctrine of treason. The courts have never gone beyond it in discussing the general subject. Marshall at the trial of Aaron Burr said, in referring to this language, according to the opinion it is not enough to be leagued

[50] 6 Wheaton 398, 399.
[51] 4 Cranch, 75, 125.

in the conspiracy and that war be levied, but it is also necessary to perform a part; that part is the act of levying war. That part, it is true, may be minute, it may not be the actual appearance in arms, and it may be remote from the scene of action, that is, from the place where the arms are assembled, but it must be a part, and that part must be performed by a person who is leagued in the conspiracy. This part, however minute or remote, constitutes the overt act, of which alone the person who performs it can be convicted.[52]

POWER OF THE COURTS TO ANNUL LAWS

Upon this question John Marshall gave his views at the Virginia Convention, and made his position very clear. He said:

" If the United States were to make a law not warranted by any of the powers enumerated it would be considered by the judges as an infringement of the Constitution which they are to guard. They would not consider such a law as coming under their jurisdiction. They would declare it void. To what quarter will you look for protection from an infringement on the Constitution, if you will not give the power to the Judiciary? There is no other body that can afford such protection.

AS COUNSEL IN WARE v. HILTON MARSHALL DENIES THE POWER TO ANNUL LAWS

In the argument of Marshall in the case of Ware v. Hilton [53] we see that he challenged the power of the court to pass upon the validity of legislation. He said:

" The legislative authority of any country can only be restrained by its own municipal constitution; this is a principle that springs from the very nature of society; and the judicial authority can have no right to question the validity of a law, unless such a jurisdiction is expressly given by the Constitution. It is not necessary to enquire, how the judicial authority should act, if the legislature were evidently to violate any of the laws of God; but property is the creature of civil society, and subject, in all respects, to the disposition and control of civil institutions."

[52] " Burr's Trial," Vol. II, 438, 439.
[53] 3 Dallas, 211.

AS CHIEF JUSTICE, MARSHALL MAINTAINS THE POWER TO ANNUL LAWS

As a member of the Virginia Convention,[54] Marshall held that the judiciary could declare certain laws void, as counsel in Ware v. Hilton [55] his argument was at variance with what he said at the Convention, but as Chief Justice he returned to his original position and expounded the same views he held at the Convention. In his opinion in Marbury v. Madison [56] Chief Justice Marshall said:

" It is emphatically the province and duty of the judicial department to say what the law is. Those who apply the rule to particular cases must of necessity expound and interpret that rule. If two laws conflict with each other, the courts must decide on the operation of each. So, if a law be in opposition to the Constitution; if both the law and the Constitution applied to a particular case, so that the court must either decide that case conformably to the law, disregarding the Constitution; or conformably to the Constitution, disregarding the law; the court must determine which of these conflicting rules governs the case. This is of the very essence of judicial duty."

In Martin v. Hunter [57] Justice Story in his opinion held the same, and that doctrine has been adhered to ever since. Several years later in Cohens v. Virginia,[58] Marshall said:

" The constitution and laws of a State, so far as they are repugnant to the Constitution and laws of the United States, are absolutely void. In a government so constituted, is it unreasonable that the judicial power should be competent to give efficacy to the constitutional laws of the legislature? That department can decide on the validity of the constitution or law of a State, if it be repugnant to the Constitution or to a law of the United States. Is it unreasonable that it should also be empowered to decide on the judgment of a State tribunal enforcing such unconstitutional law? Is it so very unreasonable as to furnish a justification for controlling the words of the Constitution? We think it is not. We think that in a

[54] Eliot, 3, 553.
[55] 3 Dallas, 211.
[56] 1 Cranch, 147.
[57] 1 Wheaton, 264, 304, 344.
[58] 6 Wheaton, 414, 415.

government acknowledgedly supreme, with respects to objects of vital interest to the nation, there is nothing inconsistent with sound reason, nothing incompatible with the nature of government, in making all its departments supreme, so far as respects those objects, and so far as is necessary to their attainment. The propriety of intrusting the construction of the Constitution, and laws made in pursuance thereof, to the judiciary of the Union, has not, we believe, as yet, been drawn into question."

THE GOVERNMENT OF TERRITORIES

The power to acquire territory is inherent in every sovereignty, and the acquisition may be made by treaty, purchase, discovery, or conquest. The most usual mode is by treaty. When territory is acquired by the United States, Congress can form it into a district or subdivision which is inferior to a territory, and in time it can be formed into a territory with a legislature elected by the citizens who are qualified to vote and who reside in such territory. The leading officials are appointed by the President. Much light is given to this subject by Chief Justice Marshall in the case of the American Insurance Company v. Canter,[59] he said:

" Perhaps the power of governing a territory belonging to the United States, which has not, by becoming a State, acquired the means of self-government, may result necessarily from the facts that it is not within the jurisdiction of any particular State, and is within the power and jurisdiction of the United States. The right to govern may be the inevitable consequence of the right to acquire territory. Whichever may be the source whence the power is derived, the possession of it is unquestioned."

AMENDMENTS TO THE CONSTITUTION

In Fletcher v. Peck,[60] Chief Justice Marshall said:
" The principle is asserted, that one legislature is competent to repeal any act which a former legislature was competent to pass; and that one legislature cannot abridge the powers of a succeeding legislature. The correctness of this principle, so

[59] 1 Peters, 541.
[60] 6 Cranch, 87.

far as respects general legislation, can never be controverted. But if an act be done under a law a succeeding legislature cannot undo it. The past cannot be recalled by the most absolute power."

RELIGIOUS TESTS

Commenting upon the provision " But no religious Test shall ever be required as a Qualification to any Office or public Trust under the United States;" Chief Justice Marshall, in M'Culloch v. Maryland,[61] said:

" The powers vested in Congress may certainly be carried into execution, without prescribing an oath of office. The power to exact this security for the faithful performance is not given, nor is it indispensably necessary. The different departments may be established; taxes may be imposed and collected; armies and navies may be raised and maintained; and money may be borrowed, without requiring an oath of office. It might be argued, with as much plausibility as other incidental powers have been assailed, that the Convention was not unmindful of this subject. The oath which might be exacted — that of fidelity to the Constitution — is prescribed, and no other can be required. Yet, he would be charged with insanity who should contend, that the Legislature might not superadd to the oath directed by the Constitution such other oath of office as its wisdom might suggest."

THE ADOPTION OF THE FIRST TEN AMENDMENTS

In regard to the adoption of the first ten amendments John Marshall gives the following account of the situation, in his " Life of Washington," [62] he says:

" In the course of this session was also brought forward a proposition, made by Mr. Madison, for recommending to the consideration and adoption of the States, several new articles to be added to the Constitution.

" Many of those objections to it which had been urged with all the vehemence of conviction, and which in the opinion of some of its advocates, were entitled to serious consideration, were believed by the most intelligent to exist only in imagina-

[61] 4 Wheaton, 316, 416.
[62] Vol. 5, 207-210.

tion, and to derive their sole support from an erroneous construction of the instrument. Others were upon points on which the objectors might be gratified without injury to the system. To conciliate the affections of their brethren to the government, was an object greatly desired by its friends. Disposed to respect what they deemed the errors of their opponents, where that respect could be manifested without a sacrifice of essential principles, they were anxious to annex to the Constitution those explanations and barriers against the possible encroachments of rulers on the liberties of the people which had been loudly demanded, however unfounded, in their judgments, might be the fears by which those demands were suggested. These dispositions were perhaps, in some measure, stimulated to exertion by motives of the soundest policy. The formidable minorities in several of the conventions, which in the legislatures of some powerful States had become majorities, and the refusal of two States to complete the union, were admonitions not to be disregarded, of the necessity of removing jealousies however misplaced, which operated on so large a portion of society. Among the most zealous friends of the Constitution therefore, were found some of the first and warmest advocates for amendments.

" To meet the various ideas expressed by the several conventions; to select from the mass of alterations which they had proposed those which might be adopted without stripping the government of its necessary powers; to condense them into a form and compass which would be acceptable to persons disposed to indulge the caprice, and to adopt the language of their particular States; were labours not easily to be accomplished. But the greatest difficulty to be surmounted was, the disposition to make those alterations which would enfeeble and materially injure the future operations of the government. At length, twelve articles in addition to and amendment of the Constitution were assented to by two-thirds of both Houses of Congress, and proposed to the legislatures of the several States. Although the necessity of these amendments had been urged by the enemies of the Constitution and denied by its friends, they encountered scarcely any other opposition in the State legislatures, than was given by the leaders of the Anti-Federal party. Admitting the articles to be good in themselves, and to be required by the occasion, it was contended that they were not sufficient for the security of liberty; and the apprehension was avowed that their adoption would quiet the fears of the people, and check the pursuit of those radical alterations which would afford a safe and adequate protection to their rights. Viewing many of those alterations which were required as subversive of the fundamentals of the government, and sincerely desirous of smoothing the way to a reunion of political sentiment by yielding in part to objections which had been pronounced important, the Federalists, almost universally, exerted their utmost powers in support of the particular amendments which had been recommended. They were at length ratified by the legislatures of three-fourths of the States, and probably contributed in some degree, to diminish the jealousies which had been imbibed against the Federal Constitution."

An amendment becomes part of the Constitution when it is ratified by the last State necessary to complete the three-fourths of the States required by the Constitution.

THE FIRST TEN AMENDMENTS AS A BILL OF RIGHTS. THE INTENTIONS OF THE FRAMERS

These amendments are limitations upon the powers of the Federal Government, and were intended as a bill of rights. Twenty years after the first ten amendments were adopted, Chief Justice Marshall, in the case of Fletcher v. Peck,[63] said: " The Constitution of the United States contains what may be deemed a Bill of Rights for the people of each State." Whether or not the amendments were meant to be limitations on the States or on the General government was settled by the United States Supreme Court in 1833, in the case of Barron v. Mayor of Baltimore,[64] when Chief Justice Marshall, after referring to the adoption of the amendments, said:

" They contained no expression indicating an intention to apply them to the State governments, and this court cannot so apply them." . . .

" Had the people of the several States, or any of them, required changes in their constitutions; had they required additional safeguards to liberty from the apprehended encroach-

[63] 6 Cranch, 138.
[64] 7 Peters, 143, 247, 249.

ments of their particular governments; the remedy was in their own hands, and would have been applied by themselves. A convention would have been assembled by the discontented States, and the required improvement would have been made by itself. The unwieldy and cumbrous machinery of procuring a recommendation from two-thirds of Congress, and the assent of three-fourths of their sister States, could never have occurred to any human being as a mode of doing that which might be effected by the State itself. Had the framers of these amendments intended them to be limitations on the powers of the State governments, they would have imitated the framers of the original Constitution, and have expressed that intention. Had Congress engaged in the extraordinary occupation of improving the Constitutions of the several States by affording the people additional protection from the exercise of power by their own government in matters which concerned themselves alone, they would have declared this purpose in plain and intelligible language."

" But it is universally understood, it is a part of the history of the day, that the great revolution which established the Constitution of the United States, was not effected without immense opposition. Serious fears were extensively entertained that those powers which the patriot statesmen, who then watched over the interests of our country, deemed essential to union, and to the attainment of those invaluable objects for which union was sought, might be exercised in a manner dangerous to liberty. In almost every convention by which the Constitution was adopted, amendments to guard against the abuse of power were recommended. These amendments demanded security against the apprehended encroachments of the general government — not against those of the local governments."

" These amendments contain no expression indicating an intention to apply them to the State governments."

THE ELEVENTH AMENDMENT, ITS SCOPE

Chief Justice Marshall, in Cohens v. Virginia,[65] of this amendment said:

" That its motive was not to maintain the sovereignty of a

[65] 6 Wheaton, 264, 406, 407.

State from the degradation supposed to attend a compulsory appearance before the tribunals of the nation, may be inferred from the terms of the amendment. It does not comprehend controversies between two or more States, or between a State and a foreign State. The jurisdiction of the court still extends to these cases; and in these a State may still be sued. We must ascribe the amendment, then, to some other cause than the dignity of a State. There is no difficulty in finding this cause. Those who were inhibited from commencing a suit against a State, or from prosecuting one which might be commenced before the adoption of the amendment, were persons who might probably be its creditors. There was not much reason to fear that foreign or sister States would be creditors to any considerable amount, and there was reason to retain the jurisdiction of a court in those cases, because it might be essential to the preservation of peace. The amendment, therefore, extended to suits commenced or prosecuted by individuals, but not to those brought by States.

" The first impression made on the mind by this amendment is, that it was intended for those cases, and for those only, in which some demand against a State is made by an individual in the courts of the Union. If we consider the causes to which it is to be traced, we are conducted to the same conclusion. A general interest might well be felt in leaving to a State the full power of consulting its convenience in the adjustment of its debts, or of other claims upon it, but no interest could be felt in so changing the relations between the whole and its parts, as to strip the government of the means of protecting, by the instrumentality of its courts, the Constitution and laws from active violation. The amendment means the judicial power is not to extend to any suit in law or equity, commenced or prosecuted against one of the United States, by citizens of another State."

A STATE AS A PARTY TO A SUIT. WHEN IT IS A PARTY

In Osborn v. Bank of the United States [66] Chief Justice Marshall said:

" It may, we think, be laid down as a rule which admits of no exception, that, in all cases where jurisdiction depends on

[66] 9 Wheaton, 738, 57.

the party, it is the party named in the record. Consequently, the 11th amendment, which restrains the jurisdiction granted by the Constitution over suits against States, is, of necessity, limited to those suits in which a State is the party on the record. The amendment has its full effect, if the Constitution be construed as it would have been construed had the jurisdiction of the court never been extended to suits brought against a State by the citizens of another State or by aliens." [67]

THE IMPLIED POWERS OF CONGRESS

In the case of McCulloch v. Maryland,[68] Chief Justice Marshall said:

" The sound construction of the Constitution must allow to the national legislature that discretion, with respect to the means by which the powers it confers are to be carried into execution, which will enable that body to perform the high duties assigned to it, in the manner most beneficial to the people. Let the end be legitimate, let it be within the scope of the Constitution, and all means which are appropriate, which are plainly adapted to that end, which are not prohibited, but consist with the letter and spirit of the Constitution, are constitutional."

MARBURY v. MADISON

This was the first great decision of Chief Justice Marshall. It is one of the base-stones of his reputation. Before this, he delivered five opinions, one involving a claim to salvage turning upon an alleged recapture, in which he undertook to review elaborately our relations towards France in 1799, and declared that they were those of a partial war (see Talbot v. Seeman, 1 Cr. 1 (1801)); one relating to the proper method of appropriating waste lands in Kentucky (Wilson v. Mason, 1 Cranch 45 (1801)); one in which he upheld the treaty obligations of the nation, even though such a course might involve an interference with private rights vested under a decree of condemnation in an inferior court (U. S. v. Schooner Peggy, 1 Cranch

---

[67] The decisions are not harmonious and the earlier judgments or opinions have been modified or overruled in regard to the question, " When is a State a party to a suit? "— " Watson on the Constitution," Vol. II, p. 1543.

[68] 4 Wheaton, 316, 421.

103) ; and two involving mere matters of practice, (Resler v. Shehee, 1 Cranch, 111) the latter turning upon considerations of the law relating to executions (Turner v. Fendall, 1 Cranch 117).

The next case was that of Marbury v. Madison (1 Cranch, 137. 1803). The facts of this case were as follows: — In the December term, 1801, Chas. Lee, late Attorney General of the United States, moved for a rule to show cause why a mandamus should not issue addressed to Madison, then Secretary of State, commanding him to deliver a commission to Marbury, whom President Adams, before the expiration of his term,[69] had nominated as a Justice of the Peace for the District of Columbia. The nomination had been confirmed by the Senate. A commission had been filled out, and signed by the President of the United States, and also sealed with the seal of the United States, but it had not been delivered when Thomas Jefferson took the reins of government, as President of the United States. Jefferson countermanded the issue of the commission on the ground that the appointment was incomplete and void on account of the fact, that the commission had remained undelivered. The application made to the Supreme Court was for the exercise of its original jurisdiction under the terms of the Judiciary Act, and the main question undoubt-

[69] " President Adams at length decided to have a cabinet he could control. He asked Pickering to resign. Timothy said he was poor and needed the money, therefore he could not resign. Adams doubtless remembered son-in-law Smith, whom Pickering had opposed on the score of his poverty, and he dismissed Timothy summarily. McHenry, Secretary of War, he also forced to resign. To fill these vacancies, John Marshall was appointed Sec. of State and Samuel Dexter Sec, of War. . . . Mr. Jefferson said that the Federalists, routed at the polls, retreated into the judiciary. This is true. Mr. Adams and his party knew where their haven, their fortress was, and they ran into it. Posts were hurriedly filled with stalwart partizans. Pres. Adams kept on filling up the offices with Federalists till nine o'clock of the last night of his term. The whole administration was made a deep, solid, political color. No Republican spot, stripe, or trimming appeared anywhere to relieve the dull monotony of Federalism.

" John Marshall, already Sec. of State, was given an additional office. He was appointed Chief Justice, a place from which he was to fulminate rank Federalism with authoritative voice for more than a generation.

" The time being short and the object worthy, Mr. Adams continued to sign commissions, and John Marshall, by candle-light, continued to countersign. At midnight, so the story goes, Levi Lincoln stepped into the room, drew Jefferson's watch upon the industrious Marshall, and made him stop." (Watson's " Life of Jefferson," p. 379.)

edly was whether such a writ could issue from the Supreme Court under the gift of a jurisdiction by Congress in direct violation of the terms of the Constitution in distributing original and appellate authority. That delivery was not essential to the validity of letters patent, and that the right of the plaintiff to his office was complete, and hence he was entitled to a remedy, was held by the court. Congress could not give original jurisdiction to the Supreme Court, in cases not sanctioned by the Constitution, so the application must be refused.

The fact that it was the first authoritative announcement by the Supreme Court that it had the right as well as the power to declare null and void an Act of Congress in violation of the Constitution, gave this case wide attention and great importance. This case has established principles which have never been controverted. The ministerial and executive officers of the government all over the country, are by this case subjected to the control of the courts in regard to the execution of a major part of their duties.

The letters of Jefferson show, and the general attitude of both men, Jefferson and Marshall, makes it plain that Marbury and Madison, were the John Doe and Richard Roe of the ejectment; the real issue was between John Marshall and Thomas Jefferson. The opinion of Marshall was regarded by Jefferson as a defiance. He looked at nearly all of Marshall's opinions as being hostile acts.[70]

In this case the decision of the Court turned on the point that Supreme Court had no power to issue a writ of mandamus directing the delivery of the commission. As the Constitution gave to the Court no original jurisdiction in such a case, and the Judiciary Act, in so far as it attempted to increase the jurisdiction, conflicted with the Constitution, and therefore was void. Thus we see that the actual decision was against Marbury. The opinion as a whole infuriated the Jeffersonians to a great degree, and as one writer on the subject says: " It cannot be denied that such an opinion was highly calculated to inflame the Jeffersonians, who contended that Congress, not the Supreme Court of Federalists, had the right to decide the constitutionality of its laws." [71] The decision as a whole

[70] Letter of Thomas Jefferson to Thomas Ritchie, December 25, 1820. "Jefferson's Works," Vol. VII, p. 192.
[71] " The Constitutional Decisions of Marshall," Vol. I, p. 5.

enraged Jefferson and the Republicans and indirectly caused the impeachment of Pickering and a violent attack on the Judiciary which finally culminated in the unsuccessful attempt to impeach Justice Chase. This great decision does not contain a single hint of this intense partisan quarrel that was at the time underlying the case. In the opening words of the case, Chief Justice Marshall said: "The peculiar delicacy of this case, the novelty of some of its circumstances, and the real difficulty attending the points which occur in it, require a complete exposition of the principles on which the opinion to be given by the Court is founded." And later in the decision he says: "The intimate political relation subsisting between the President of the United States and the heads of Departments necessarily renders any legal investigation of the acts of one of those high officers peculiarly irksome, as well as delicate; and excites some hesitation with respect to the propriety of entering into such investigation. Impressions are often received without much reflection or examinations, and it is not wonderful, that in such a case as this the assertion by an individual, of his legal claims in a court of justice, to which claims it is the duty of the court to attend, should at first view be considered by some as an attempt to intrude into the cabinet, and to intermeddle with the prerogatives of the executive." Thus we see from the temper of the opinion that there is much to be read between the lines. The Federalists went to pieces, and Jefferson, his most hated and bitterest political enemy, came into power.

Chief Justice Marshall delivered the opinion of the Court on the 24th of February, 1803.

OPINION OF THE COURT.

At the last term, on the affidavits then read and filed with the clerk, a rule was granted in this case, requiring the secretary of state to show cause why a mandamus should not issue, directing him to deliver to William Marbury his commission as a justice of the peace for the county of Washington, in the district of Columbia.

No cause has been shown, and the present motion is for a mandamus. The peculiar delicacy of this case, the novelty of some of its circumstances, and the real difficulty attending the points which occur in it, require a complete exposition of the principles on which the opinion to be given by the court is founded.

These principles have been, on the side of the applicant, very ably argued at the bar. In rendering the opinion of the court there will be some departure in form, though not in substance, from the points stated in that argument.

In the order in which the court has viewed this subject, the following questions have been considered and decided: —

1st. Has the applicant a right to the commission he demands?

2d. If he has a right, and that right has been violated, do the laws of his country afford him a remedy?

3d. If they do afford him a remedy, is it a mandamus issuing from this court?

The first object of inquiry is,—

1st. Has the applicant a right to the commission he demands?

His right originates in an act of Congress, passed in February, 1801, concerning the district of Columbia.

After dividing the district into two counties, the eleventh section of this law enacts, "that there shall be appointed, in and for each of the said counties, such number of discreet persons to be justices of the peace as the president of the United States shall, from time to time, think expedient, to continue in office for five years.

It appears from the affidavits, that in compliance with this law, a commission for William Marbury, as a justice of the peace for the county of Washington, was signed by John Adams, then president of the United States; after which the seal of the United States was affixed to it; but the commission has never reached the person for whom it was made out.

In order to determine whether he was entitled to this commission, it becomes necessary to inquire whether he has been appointed to the office. For if he has been appointed, the law continues him in office for five years, and he is entitled to the possession of those evidences of office, which, being completed, became his property.

The second section of the second article of the constitution declares that "the president shall nominate, and, by and with the advice and consent of the senate, shall appoint ambassadors, other public ministers, and consuls, and all other officers of the United States whose appointments are not otherwise provided for."

The third section declares that " he shall commission all the officers of the United States."

An act of congress directs the secretary of state to keep the seal of the United States, " to make out and record, and affix the said seal to, all civil commissions to officers of the United States, to be appointed by the president, by and with the consent of the Senate, or by the president alone; provided, that the said seal shall not be affixed to any commission before the same shall have been signed by the president of the United States."

These are the clauses of the constitution and laws of the United States which affect this part of the case.   They seem to contemplate three distinct operations:

1st.   The nomination.   This is the sole act of the president, and is completely voluntary.

2d.   The appointment.   This is also the act of the president, and is also a voluntary act, though it can only be performed by and with the advice and consent of the senate.

3d.   The commission.   To grant a commission to a person appointed might, perhaps, be deemed a duty enjoined by the constitution.   " He shall," says that instrument, " commission all the officers of the United States."

The acts of appointing to office, and commissioning the person appointed, can scarcely be considered as one and the same; since the power to perform them is given in two separate and distinct sections of the constitution.   The distinction between the appointment and the commission will be rendered more apparent by adverting to that provision, in the second section of the second article of the constitution, which authorizes congress " to vest by law the appointment of such inferior officers as they think proper in the president alone, in the courts of law, or in the heads of departments; " thus contemplating cases where the law may direct the president to commission an officer appointed by the courts, or by the heads of departments.   In such a case, to issue a commission would be apparently a duty distinct from the appointment, the performance of which, perhaps, could not legally be refused.

Although that clause of the constitution, which requires the president to commission all the officers of the United States, may never have been applied to officers appointed otherwise than by himself, yet it would be difficult to deny the legislative power to apply it to such cases. Of consequence, the constitutional distinction between the appointment to an office and the commission of an officer who has been appointed remains the same as if in practice, the president had commissioned officers appointed by an authority other than his own.

It follows, too, from the existence of this distinction, that, if an appointment was to be evidenced by any public act other than the commission, the performance of such public act would create the officer; and, if he was not removable at the will of the president, would either give him a right to his commission, or enable him to perform the duties without it.

These observations are premised solely for the purpose of rendering more intelligible those which apply more directly to the particular case under consideration.

This is an appointment made by the president, by and with the advice and consent of the senate, and is evidenced by no act but the commission itself. In such a case, therefore, the commission and the appointment seem inseparable; it being almost impossible to show an appointment otherwise than by proving the existence of a commission. Still, the commission is not necessarily the appointment, though conclusive evidence of it.

But at what stage does it amount to this conclusive evidence?

The answer to this question seems an obvious one. The appointment, being the sole act of the president, must be completely evidenced when it is shown that he has done everything to be performed by him.

Should the commission, instead of being evidence of an appointment, even be considered as constituting the appointment itself,— still, it would be made when the last act to be done by the president was performed, or, at furthest, when the commission was complete.

The last act to be done by the president is the signature of the commission. He has then acted on the advice and consent of the senate to his own nomination. The time for deliberation has then passed. He has decided. His judgment, on the advice and consent of the senate concurring with his nomination, has been made, and the officer is appointed. This appointment is evidenced by an open, unequivocal act; and being the last act required from the person making it, necessarily excludes the idea of its being, so far as respects the appointment, an inchoate and incomplete transaction.

Some point of time must be taken when the power of the executive over an officer not removable at his will must cease. That point of time must be when the constitutional power of appointment has been exercised.   And this power has been exercised when the last act required from the person possessing the power has been performed.   This last act is the signature of the commission.   This idea seems to have prevailed with the legislature when the act passed converting the department of foreign affairs into the department of state.   By that act it is enacted, that the secretary of state shall keep the seal of the United States, " and shall make out and record, and shall affix the said seal to, all civil commissions to officers of the United States to be appointed by the president; " " provided, that the said seal shall not be affixed to any commission before the same shall have been signed by the president of the United States; nor to any other instrument or act without the special warrant of the president therefor."

The signature is a warrant for affixing the great seal to the commission; and the great seal is only to be affixed to an instrument which is complete.   It attests, by an act supposed to be of public notoriety, the verity of the presidential signature.

It is never to be affixed till the commission is signed, because the signature, which gives force and effect to the commission, is conclusive evidence that the appointment is made.

The commission being signed, the subsequent duty of the secretary of state is prescribed by law, and not to be guided by the will of the president.   He is to affix the seal of the United States to the commission, and is to record it.

This is not a proceeding which may be varied, if the judgment of the executive shall suggest one more eligible; but is a precise course accurately marked out by law, and is to be strictly pursued.   It is the duty of the secretary of state to conform to the law; and in this he is an officer of the United States, bound to obey the laws.   He acts, in this respect, as has been very properly stated at the bar, under the authority of law, and not by the instructions of the president.   It is a ministerial act which the law enjoins on a particular officer for a particular purpose.

If it should be supposed that the solemnity of affixing the seal is necessary not only to the validity of the commission, but even to the completion of an appointment, still, when the seal is affixed the appointment is made and the commission is valid. No other solemnity is required by law; no other act is to be performed on the part of the government. All that the executive can do to invest the person with his office is done; and unless the appointment be then made, the executive cannot make one without the coöperation of others.

After searching anxiously for the principles on which a contrary opinion may be supported, none have been found which appear of sufficient force to maintain the opposite doctrine.

Such as the imagination of the court could suggest have been very deliberately examined, and after allowing them all the weight which it appears possible to give them, they do not shake the opinion which has been formed.

In considering this question, it has been conjectured that the commission may have been assimilated to a deed, to the validity of which delivery is essential.

This idea is founded on the supposition that the commission is not merely evidence of an appointment, but is itself the actual appointment; a supposition by no means unquestionable. But for the purpose of examining this objection fairly, let it be conceded that the principle claimed for its support is established.

The appointment being, under the constitution, to be made by the president personally, the delivery of the deed of appointment, if necessary to its completion, must be made by the president also. It is not necessary that the delivery should be made personally to the grantee of the office; it never is so made. The law would seem to contemplate that it should be made to the secretary of state, since it directs the secretary to affix the seal to the commission after it shall have been signed by the president. If then, the act of delivery be necessary to give validity to the commission, it has been delivered when executed and given to the secretary for the purpose of being sealed, recorded, and transmitted to the party.

But in all cases of letters patent certain solemnities are required by law, which solemnities are the evidences of the validity of the instrument. A formal delivery to the person is not among them. In cases of commissions, the sign manual of the president, and the seal of the United States, are those solemnities. This objection, therefore, does not touch the case.

It has also occurred as possible, and barely possible, that the transmission of the commission, and the acceptance thereof, might be deemed necessary to complete the right of the plaintiff.

The transmission of the commission is a practice directed by convenience, but not by law. It cannot, therefore, be necessary to constitute the appointment, which must precede it, and which is the mere act of the president. If the executive required that every person appointed to an office should himself take means to procure his commission, the appointment would not be the less valid on that account. The appointment is the sole act of the president; the transmission of the commission is the sole act of the officer to whom that duty is assigned, and may be accelerated or retarded by circumstances which can have no influence on the appointment. A commission is transmitted to a person already appointed; not to a person to be appointed or not, as the letter enclosing the commission should happen to get into the post-office and reach him in safety, or to miscarry.

It may have some tendency to elucidate this point, to inquire whether the possession of the original commission be indispensably necessary to authorize a person, appointed to any office, to perform the duties of that office. If it was necessary, then a loss of commission would lose the office. Not only negligence, but accident or fraud, fire or theft, might deprive an individual of his office. In such a case, I presume, it could not be doubted but that a copy from the record of the office of the secretary of state would be, to every intent and purpose, equal to the original. The act of congress has expressly made it so. To give that copy validity, it would not be necessary to prove that the original had been transmitted and afterwards lost. The copy would be complete evidence that the original had existed, and that the appointment had been made, but not that the original had been transmitted. If, indeed, it should appear that the original had been mislaid in the office of state, that circumstance would not affect the operation of the copy. When all the requisites have been performed which authorize a recording officer to record any instrument whatever, and the order for that purpose has been given, the instrument is, in law, considered as recorded, although the manual labor of inserting it in a book kept for that purpose may not have been performed.

In the case of commissions, the law orders the secretary of state to record them. When, therefore, they are signed and sealed, the order for their being recorded is given; and whether inserted in the book or not, they are, in law, recorded.

A copy of this record is declared equal to the original, and the fees to be paid by a person requiring a copy are ascertained by law. Can a keeper of a public record erase therefrom a commission which has been recorded? Or can he refuse a copy thereof to a person demanding it on the terms prescribed by law?

Such a copy would, equally with the original, authorize the justice of the peace to proceed in the performance of his duty, because it would, equally with the original, attest his appointment.

If the transmission of a commission be not considered as necessary to give validity to an appointment, still less is its acceptance. The appointment is the sole act of the president; the acceptance is the sole act of the officer, and is, in plain common sense, posterior to the appointment. As he may resign, so may he refuse to accept; but neither the one nor the other is capable of rendering the appointment a nonentity.

That this is the understanding of the government is apparent from the whole tenor of its conduct.

A commission bears date, and the salary of the officer commences, from his appointment; not from the transmission or acceptance of his commission. When a person appointed to any office refuses to accept that office, the successor is nominated in the place of the person who has declined to accept, and not in place of the person who had been previously in office, and had created the original.

It is, therefore, decidedly the opinion of the court, that, when a commission has been signed by the president, the appointment is made; and that the commission is complete when the seal of the United States has been affixed to it by the secretary of state.

When an officer is removable at the will of the executive, the circumstance which completes his appointment is of no concern; because the act is at any time revocable; and the commission may be arrested, if still in the office. But when the officer is not removable at the will of the executive, the appointment is not revocable, and cannot be annulled. It has conferred legal rights which can not be resumed.

The discretion of the executive is to be exercised until the appointment has been made. But having once made the appointment, his power over the office is terminated in all cases where by law the officer is not removable by him. The right to the office is then in the person appointed, and he has the absolute, unconditional power of accepting or rejecting it.

Mr. Marbury, then, since his commission was signed by the president, and sealed by the secretary of state, was appointed; and as the law creating the office gave the officer a right to hold for five years, independent of the executive, the appointment was not revocable, but vested in the officer legal rights, which are protected by the laws of his country.

To withhold his commission, therefore, is an act deemed by the court not warranted by law, but violative of a vested legal right.

This brings us to the second inquiry; which is,—

2d. If he has a right, and that right has been violated, do the laws of his country afford him a remedy?

The very essence of civil liberty certainly consists in the right of every individual to claim the protection of the laws whenever he receives an injury. One of the first duties of government is to afford that protection. In Great Britain the King himself is sued in the respectful form of a petition, and he never fails to comply with the judgment of his court.

In the third volume of his Commentaries, page 23, Blackstone states two cases in which a remedy is afforded by mere operation of law.

" In all other cases," he says, " it is a general and indisputable rule, that, where there is a legal right, there is also a legal remedy by suit, or action at law, whenever that right is invaded."

And afterwards, page 109 of the same volume, he says, " I am next to consider such injuries as are cognizable by the courts of the common law. And herein I shall for the present only remark that all possible injuries whatsoever, that did not fall within the exclusive cognizance of either the ecclesiastical, military, or maritime tribunals, are, for that very reason, within the cognizance of the common-law courts of justice; for it is a settled and invariable principle in the laws of England that every right when withheld must have a remedy, and every injury its proper redress."

The government of the United States has been emphatically termed a government of laws, and not of men. It will certainly cease to deserve this high appellation, if the laws furnish no remedy for the violation of a vested legal right.

If this obloquy is to be cast on the jurisprudence of our country, it must arise from the peculiar character of the case.

It behooves us, then, to inquire whether there be in its composition any ingredient which shall exempt it from legal investigation, or exclude the injured party from legal redress. In pursuing this inquiry, the first question which presents itself is, whether this can be arranged with that class of cases which come under the description of damnum absque injuria, a loss without an injury.

This description of cases never has been considered, and it is believed never can be considered, as comprehending offices of trust, of honor, or of profit. The office of justice of peace in the District of Columbia is such an office; it is therefore worthy of the attention and guardianship of the laws. It has received that attention and guardianship. It has been created by special act of congress, and has been secured, so far as the laws can give security, to the person appointed to fill it, for five years. It is not, then, on account of the worthlessness of the thing pursued, that the injured party can be alleged to be without remedy.

Is it in the nature of the transaction? Is the act of delivering or withholding a commission to be considered as a mere political act, belonging to the executive department alone, for the performance of which entire confidence is placed by our constitution in the supreme executive; and for any misconduct respecting which, the injured individual has no remedy?

That there may be such cases is not to be questioned; but

that every act of duty, to be performed in any of the great departments of government, constitute such a case, is not to be admitted.

By the act concerning invalids, passed in June, 1794, vol. 3, p. 112, the Secretary of War is ordered to place on the pension list all persons whose names are contained in a report previously made by him to congress. If he should refuse to do so, would the wounded veteran be without remedy? Is it to be contended that where the law in precise term, directs the performance of an act, in which an individual is interested, the law is incapable of securing obedience to its mandate? Is it on account of the character of the person against whom the complaint is made? Is it to be contended that the heads of departments are not amenable to the laws of their country?

Whatever the practice on particular occasions may be, the theory of this principle will certainly never be maintained. No act of the legislature confers so extraordinary a privilege, nor can it derive countenance from the doctrines of the common law. After stating that personal injury from the king to a subject is presumed to be impossible, Blackstone, vol. 3, p. 255, says, " but injuries to the rights of property can scarcely be committed by the crown without the intervention of its officers; for whom the law, in matters of right, entertains no respect or delicacy: but furnishes various methods of detecting the errors and misconduct of those agents, by whom the king has been deceived and induced to do a temporary injustice."

By the act passed in 1796, authorizing the sale of the lands above the mouth of Kentucky river (vol. 3, p. 299), the purchaser, on paying his purchase money, becomes completely entitled to the property purchased; and on producing to the Secretary of State the receipt of the treasurer upon a certificate required by the law, the President of the United States is authorized to grant him a patent. It is further enacted that all patents shall be countersigned by the Secretary of State, and recorded in his office. If the Secretary of State should choose to withhold this patent; or, the patent being lost, should refuse a copy of it; can it be imagined that the law furnishes to the injured person no remedy?

It is not believed that any person whatever would attempt to maintain such a proposition.

It follows, then, that the question, whether the legality of an act of the head of a department be examinable in a court of justice or not, must always depend on the nature of that act.

If some acts be examinable, and others not, there must be some rule of law to guide the court in the exercise of its jurisdiction.

In some instances there may be difficulty in applying the rule to particular cases; but there cannot, it is believed, be much difficulty in laying down the rule.

By the constitution of the United States, the President is invested with certain important political powers, in the exercise of which he is to use his own discretion, and is accountable only to his country in his political character and to his own conscience. To aid him in the performance of these duties, he is authorized to appoint certain officers, who act by his authority, and in conformity with his orders.

In such cases, their acts are his acts; and whatever opinion may be entertained of the manner in which executive discretion may be used, still there exists, and can exist, no power to control that discretion. The subjects are political. They respect the nation, not individual rights, and being intrusted to the executive, the decision of the executive is conclusive. The application of this remark will be perceived by adverting to the act of congress for establishing the department of foreign affairs. This officer, as his duties were prescribed by that act, is to conform precisely to the will of the President. He is the mere organ by whom that will is communicated. The acts of such an officer, as an officer, can never be examinable by the courts.

But when the legislature proceeds to impose on that officer other duties; when he is directed peremptorily to perform certain acts; when the rights of individuals are dependent on the performance of those acts; he is so far the officer of the law; is amenable to the laws for his conduct; and cannot at his discretion sport away the vested rights of others.

The conclusion from this reasoning is, that where the heads of departments are the political or confidential agents of the executive, merely to execute the will of the President, or rather to act in cases in which the executive possesses a constitutional or legal discretion, nothing can be more perfectly

clear then that their acts are only politically examinable.   But
where a specific duty is assigned by law, and individual rights
depend upon the performance of that duty, it seems equally
clear that the individual who considers himself injured,
has a right to resort to the laws of his country for a remedy.

If this be the rule, let us inquire how it applies to the case
under the consideration of the court.

The power of nominating to the senate, and the power of
appointing the person nominated, are political powers, to be
exercised by the President according to his own discretion.
When he has made an appointment, he has exercised his whole
power, and his discretion has been completely applied to the
case.   If, by law, the officer be removable at the will of the
President, then a new appointment may be immediately made,
and the rights of the officer are terminated.   But as a fact
which has existed cannot be made never to have existed, the
appointment cannot be annihilated; and consequently, if the
officer is by law not removable at the will of the President,
the rights he has acquired are protected by the law, and are
not resumable by the President.   They can not be extinguished
by executive authority, and he has the privilege of asserting
them in like manner as if they had been derived from any
other source.

The question whether a right has vested or not, is, in its
nature, judicial, and must be tried by the judicial authority.
If, for example, Mr. Marbury had taken the oaths of a magistrate, and proceeded to act as one, in consequence of
which a suit had been instituted against him, in which his
defense had depended on his being a magistrate, the validity
of his appointment must have been determined by judicial
authority.

So, if he conceives that, by virtue of his appointment, he
has a legal right either to the commission which has been made
out for him, or to a copy of that commission, it is equally a
question examinable in a court, and the decision of the court
upon it must depend on the opinion entertained of his appointment.

That question has been discussed, and the opinion is, that the
latest point of time which can be taken as that at which the
appointment was complete, and evidenced, was when, after the

signature of the President, the seal of the United States was affixed to the commission.

It is, then, the opinion of the Court.

1st. That by signing the commission of Mr. Marbury, the President of the United States appointed him a justice of the peace for the county of Washington, in the District of Columbia; and that the seal of the United States, affixed thereto by the Secretary of State, is conclusive testimony of the verity of the signature, and of the completion of the appointment; and that the appointment conferred on him a legal right to the office for the space of five years.

2d. That, having this legal title to the office, he has a consequent right to the commission; a refusal to deliver which is a plain violation of that right, for which the laws of his country afford him a remedy.

It remains to be inquired whether,

3d. He is entitled to the remedy for which he applies. This depends on,

1st. The nature of the writ applied for; and,

2d. The power of this court.

1st. The nature of the writ.

Blackstone, in the 3d volume of his Commentaries, page 110, defines a mandamus to be "a command issuing in the king's name from the court of king's bench, and directed to any person, corporation, or inferior court of judicature within the king's dominions, requiring them to do some particular thing therein specified, which appertains to their office and duty, and which the court of king's bench has previously determined, or at least supposes, to be consonant to right and justice."

Lord Mansfield, in 3 Burrow, 1266, in the case of The King v. Baker et al., states, with much precision and explicitness, the cases in which this writ may be used.

"Whenever," says that very able judge, "there is a right to execute an office, perform a service, or exercise a franchise, (more especially if it be in a matter of public concern, or attended with profit,) and a person is kept out of possession, or dispossessed of such right, and has no other specific legal remedy, this court ought to assist by mandamus, upon reasons of justice, as the writ expresses, and upon reasons of public policy, to preserve peace, order and good government." In the same case he says, "this writ ought to be used upon all occasions where the law has established no specific remedy, and where in justice and good government there ought to be one."

In addition to the authorities now particularly cited, many others were relied on at the bar, which show how far the practice has conformed to the general doctrines that have been just quoted.

This writ, if awarded, would be directed to an officer of government, and its mandate to him would be, to use the words of Blackstone, " to do a particular thing therein specified, which appertains to his office and duty, and which the court has previously determined, or at least supposes, to be consonant to right and justice." Or, in the words of Lord Mansfield, the applicant, in this case, has a right to execute an office of public concern, and is kept out of possession of that right.

These circumstances certainly concur in this case.

Still, to render the mandamus a proper remedy, the officer to whom it is to be directed, must be one to whom, on legal principles, such writ may be directed; and the person applying for it must be without any other specific and legal remedy.

1st. With respect to the officer to whom it would be directed. The intimate political relation subsisting between the President of the United States and the heads of departments, necessarily renders any legal investigation of the acts of one of those high officers peculiarly irksome, as well as delicate; and excites some hesitation with respect to the propriety of entering into such investigation. Impressions are often received without much reflection or examination, and it is not wonderful that in such a case as this the assertion, by an individual, of his legal claims in a court of justice, to which claims it is the duty of that court to attend, should at first view be considered by some, as an attempt to intrude into the cabinet, and to intermeddle with the prerogatives of the executive.

It is scarcely necessary for the court to disclaim all pretensions of such jurisdiction. An extravagance, so absurd and excessive, could not have been entertained for a moment. The province of the court is, solely, to decide on the rights of individuals, not to inquire how the executive, or executive officers, perform duties in which they have a discretion. Questions in their nature political, or which are, by the constitution and laws, submitted to the executive, can never be made in this court.

But, if this be not such a question; if, so far from being an intrusion into the secrets of the cabinet, it respects a paper which, according to law, is upon record, and to a copy of which the law gives a right, on the payment of ten cents; if it be no intermeddling with a subject over which the executive can be considered as having exercised any control; what is there in the exalted station of the officer, which shall bar a citizen from asserting, in a court of justice, his legal rights, or shall forbid a court to listen to the claim, or to issue a mandamus directing the performance of a duty, not depending on executive discretion, but on particular acts of congress, and the general principles of law?

If one of the heads of departments commits any illegal act, under colour of his office, by which an individual sustains an injury, it cannot be pretended that his office alone exempts him from being sued in the ordinary mode of proceeding, and being compelled to obey the judgment of the law. How, then, can his office exempt him from this particular mode of deciding on the legality of his conduct, if the case be such a case as would, were any other individual the party complained of, authorize the process?

It is not by the office of the person to whom the writ is directed, but the nature of the thing to be done, that the propriety or impropriety of issuing a mandamus is to be determined. Where the head of a department acts in a case, in which executive discretion is to be exercised; in which he is the mere organ of executive will; it is again repeated, that any application to a court to control, in any respect, his conduct would be rejected without hesitation.

But where he is directed by law to do a certain act affecting the absolute rights of individuals, in the performance of which he is not placed under the particular direction of the President, and the performance of which the President cannot lawfully forbid, and therefore is never presumed to have forbidden; as for example, to record a commission, or a patent for land, which has received all the legal solemnities; or to give a copy of such record; in such cases, it is not perceived on what ground the courts of the country are further excused from the duty of giving judgment that right be done to an

injured individual, than if the same services were to be performed by a person not the head of a department.

This opinion seems not now, for the first time, to be taken
up in this country.

It must be well recollected that in 1792, an act passed directing the Secretary of War to place on the pension list such
disabled officers and soldiers as should be reported to him,
by the circuit courts, which act, so far as the duty was imposed
on the courts, was deemed unconstitutional; but some of the
judges thinking that the law might be executed by them in the
character of commissioners, proceeded to act, and to report in
that character.

This law being deemed unconstitutional at the circuits was
repealed, and a different system was established; but the question whether those persons who had been reported by the
judges, as commissioners, were entitled, in consequence of that
report, to be placed on the pension list, was a legal question,
properly determinable in the courts, although the act of placing
such pensions on the list was to be performed by the head
of a department.

That this question might be properly settled, congress passed
an act in February, 1793, making it the duty of the Secretary
of War, in conjunction with the attorney general, to take such
measures as might be necessary to obtain an adjudication of
the Supreme Court of the United States on the validity of any
such rights, claimed under the act aforesaid.

After the passage of this act, a mandamus was moved for,
to be directed to the Secretary of War, commanding him to
place on the pension list, a person stating himself to be on the
report of the judges.

There is, therefore, much reason to believe, that this mode
of trying the legal right of the complainant was deemed by the
head of a department, and by the highest law officer of the
United States, the most proper which could be selected for
the purpose.

When the subject was brought before the court, the decision was, not that a mandamus would not lie to the head of
a department directing him to perform an act, enjoined by law,
in the performance of which an individual had a vested interest; but that a mandamus ought not to issue in that case;

the decision necessarily to be made of the report of the commissioners did not confer on the applicant a legal right.

The judgment, in that case, is understood to have decided the merits of all claims of that description; and the persons, on the report of the commissioners, found it necessary to pursue the mode prescribed by the law subsequent to that which had been deemed unconstitutional, in order to place themselves on the pension list.

The doctrine, therefore, now advanced, is by no means a novel one.

It is true that the mandamus, now moved for, is not for the performance of an act expressly enjoined by the statute.

It is to deliver a commission; on which subject the acts of congress are silent. This difference is not considered as affecting the case. It has already been stated that the applicant has, to that commission a vested legal right, of which the executive cannot deprive him. He has been appointed to an office, from which he is not removable at the will of the executive; and being so appointed, he has a right to the commission which the secretary has received from the President for his use. The act of congress does not indeed order the Secretary of State to send it to him, but it is placed in his hands for the person entitled to it; and cannot be more lawfully withheld by him than by any other person.

It was at first doubted whether the action of detinue was not a specific legal remedy for the commission which has been withheld from Mr. Marbury; in which case a mandamus would be improper. But this doubt has yielded to the consideration that the judgment in detinue is for the thing itself, or its value. The value of a public office not to be sold is incapable of being ascertained; and the applicant has a right to the office itself, or to nothing. He will obtain the office by obtaining the commission, or a copy of it from the record.

This, then, is a plain case for a mandamus, either to deliver the commission, or a copy of it from the record; and it only remains to be inquired,

Whether it can issue from this court.

The act to establish the judicial courts of the United States authorizes the Supreme Court " to issue writs of mandamus in cases warranted by the principles and usages of law, to any courts appointed, or persons holding office, under the authority of the United States."

The Secretary of State, being a person holding an office under the authority of the United States, is precisely within the letter of the description, and if this court is not authorized to issue a writ of mandamus to such an officer, it must be because the law is unconstitutional, and therefore absolutely incapable of conferring the authority, and assigning the duties which its words purport to confer and assign.

The constitution vests the whole judicial power of the United States in one Supreme Court, and such inferior courts as congress shall, from time to time, ordain and establish. This power is expressly extended to all cases arising under the laws of the United States; and, consequently, in some form, may be exercised over the present case; because the right claimed is given by a law of the United States.

In the distribution of this power it is declared that "the Supreme Court shall have original jurisdiction in all cases affecting ambassadors, other public ministers and consuls, and those in which a state shall be a party. In all other cases, the Supreme Court shall have appellate jurisdiction."

It has been insisted, at the bar, that as the original grant of jurisdiction, to the Supreme and inferior courts, is general, and the clause, assigning original jurisdiction to the Supreme Court, contains no negative or restrictive words, the power remains to the legislature, to assign original jurisdiction to that court in other cases than those specified in the article which has been recited; provided those cases belong to the judicial power of the United States.

If it had been intended to leave it in the discretion of the legislature to apportion the judicial power between the supreme and inferior courts according to the will of that body, it would certainly have been useless to have proceeded further than to have defined the judicial power, and the tribunals in which it should be invested. The subsequent part of the section is mere surplusage, is entirely without meaning, if such is to be the construction. If congress remains at liberty to give this court appellate jurisdiction, where the constitution has declared their jurisdiction shall be original; and original jurisdiction where the constitution has declared it shall be appellate, the distribution of jurisdiction, made in the constitution, is form without substance.

Affirmative words are often, in their operation, negative of other objects than those affirmed; and in this case, a negative or exclusive sense must be given to them, or they have no operation at all.

It cannot be presumed that any clause in the constitution is intended to be without effect; and, therefore, such a construction is inadmissible, unless the words require it.

If the solicitude of the convention, respecting our peace with foreign powers, induced a provision that the Supreme Court should take original jurisdiction in cases which might be supposed to affect them; yet the clause would have proceeded no further than to provide for such cases, if no further restriction on the powers of congress had been intended. That they should have appellate jurisdiction in all other cases, with such exceptions as congress might make, is no restriction; unless the words be deemed exclusive of original jurisdiction.

When an instrument organizing fundamentally a judicial system divides it into one supreme, and so many inferior courts as the legislature may ordain and establish; then enumerates its powers, and proceeds so far to distribute them, as to define the jurisdiction of the Supreme Court by declaring the cases in which it shall take original jurisdiction, and that in others it shall take appellate jurisdiction; the plain import of the words seems to be, that in one class of cases its jurisdiction is original, and not appellate; in the other it is appellate, and not original.   If any other construction would render the clause inoperative, that is an additional reason for rejecting such other construction, and for adhering to their obvious meaning.

To enable this court then, to issue a mandamus, it must be shown to be an exercise of appellate jurisdiction, or to be necessary to enable them to exercise appellate jurisdiction.

It has been stated at the bar that the appellate jurisdiction may be exercised in a variety of forms, and that if it be the will of the legislature that a mandamus should be used for that purpose, that will must be obeyed.   This is true, yet the jurisdiction must be appellate, not original.

It is the essential criterion of appellate jurisdiction, that it revises and corrects the proceedings in a cause already instituted, and does not create that cause. Although, therefore, a mandamus may be directed to courts, yet to issue such a writ to an officer for the delivery of a paper, is in effect the same as to sustain an original action for that paper, and, therefore, seems not to belong to appellate, but to original jurisdiction. Neither is it necessary in such a case as this, to enable the court to exercise its appellate jurisdiction.

The authority, therefore, given to the Supreme Court, by the act establishing the judicial courts of the United States, to issue writs of mandamus to public officers, appears not to be warranted by the constitution; and it becomes necessary to inquire whether a jurisdiction so conferred can be exercised.

The question, whether an act, repugnant to the constitution, can become the law of the land, is a question deeply interesting to the United States; but happily, not of an intricacy proportioned to its interest. It seems only necessary to recognize certain principles, supposed to have been long and well established, to decide it.

That the people have an original right, to establish for their future government, such principles, as, in their opinion, shall most conduce to their own happiness is the basis on which the whole American fabric has been erected. The exercise of this original right is a very great exertion; nor can it, nor ought it, to be frequently repeated. The principles, therefore, so established, are deemed fundamental. And as the authority from which they proceed is supreme, and can seldom act, they are designed to be permanent.

This original and supreme will organizes the government, and assigns to different departments their respective powers. It may either stop here, or establish certain limits not to be transcended by those departments.

The government of the United States is of the latter description. The powers of the legislature are defined and limited; and that those limits may not be mistaken, or forgotten, the constitution is written. To what purpose are powers limited, and to what purpose is that limitation committed to writing, if these limits may, at any time, be passed by those intended to be restrained? The distinction between a government with limited and unlimited powers is abolished, if those limits do not confine the persons on whom they are imposed, and if acts prohibited and acts allowed, are of equal obligation.   It is a proposition too plain to be contested, that the constitution controls any legislative act repugnant to it; or, that the legislature may alter the constitution by an ordinary act.

Between these alternatives there is no middle ground.   The constitution is either a superior paramount law, unchangeable by ordinary means, or it is on a level with ordinary legislative acts, and, like other acts, is alterable when the legislature shall please to alter it.

If the former part of the alternative be true, then a legislative act contrary to the constitution is not law: if the latter part be true, then written constitutions are absurd attempts, on the part of the people, to limit a power in its own nature illimitable.

Certainly all those who have framed written constitutions contemplate them as forming the fundamental and paramount law of the nation, and, consequently, the theory of every such government must be, that an act of the legislature, repugnant to the constitution, is void.

This theory is essentially attached to a written constitution, and, is consequently, to be considered by this court, as one of the fundamental principles of our society.   It is not therefore to be lost sight of in the further consideration of this subject.

If an act of the legislature, repugnant to the constitution, is void, does it, notwithstanding its invalidity, bind the courts, and oblige them to give it effect?   Or, in other words, though it be not law, does it constitute a rule as operative as if it was a law?   This would be to overthrow in fact what was established in theory; and would seem, at first view, an absurdity too gross to be insisted on.   It shall, however, receive a more attentive consideration.

It is emphatically the province and duty of the judicial department to say what the law is.   Those who apply the rule to particular cases, must of necessity expound and interpret that rule.   If two laws conflict with each other, the courts must decide on the operation of each.

So if a law be in opposition to the constitution; if both the law and the constitution apply to a particular case, so that the court must either decide that case conformably to the law, disregarding the constitution; or conformably to the constitution, disregarding the law; the court must determine which of these conflicting rules governs the case. This is of the very essence of judicial duty.

If, then, the courts are to regard the constitution, and the constitution is superior to any ordinary act of the legislature, the constitution and not such ordinary act, must govern the case to which they both apply.

Those, then, who controvert the principle that the constitution is to be considered, in court, as a paramount law, are reduced to the necessity of maintaining that courts must close their eyes on the constitution, and see only the law.

This doctrine would subvert the very foundation of all written constitutions. It would declare that an act which, according to the principles and theory of our government, is entirely void, is yet, in practice, completely obligatory. It would declare that if the legislature shall do what is expressly forbidden, such act, notwithstanding the express prohibition, is in reality effectual. It would be giving to the legislature a practical and real omnipotence, with the same breath which professes to restrict their powers within narrow limits. It is prescribing limits, and declaring that those limits may be passed at pleasure.

That it thus reduces to nothing what we have deemed the greatest improvement on political institutions, a written constitution, would of itself be sufficient in America, where written constitutions have been viewed with so much reverence, for rejecting the construction. But the peculiar expressions of the constitution of the United States furnish additional arguments in favour of its rejection.

The judicial power of the United States is extended to all cases arising under the constitution.

Could it be the intention of those who gave this power, to say that in using it the constitution should not be looked into? That a case arising under the constitution should be decided without examining the instrument under which it arises?

This is too extravagant to be maintained.

In some cases, then, the constitution must be looked into by the judges. And if they can open it at all, what part of it are they forbidden to read or to obey?

There are many other parts of the constitution which serve to illustrate this subject.

It is declared that " no tax or duty shall be laid on articles exported from any state." Suppose a duty on the export of cotton, of tobacco, or of flour; and a suit instituted to recover it. Ought judgment to be rendered in such a case? ought the judges to close their eyes on the constitution, and only see the law?

The constitution declares " that no bill of attainder or ex post facto law shall be passed."

If, however, such a bill should be passed, and a person should be prosecuted under it; must the court condemn to death those victims whom the constitution endeavours to preserve?

" No person," says the constitution, " shall be convicted of treason unless on the testimony of two witnesses to the same overt act, or on confession in open court."

Here the language of the constitution is addressed especially to the courts. It prescribes, directly for them, a rule of evidence not to be departed from. If the legislature should change that rule, and declare one witness, or a confession out of court, sufficient for conviction, must the constitutional principle yield to the legislative act?

From these, and many other selections which might be made, it is apparent, that the framers of the constitution contemplated that instrument as a rule for the government of the courts, as well as of the legislature.

Why otherwise does it direct the judges to take an oath to support it? This oath certainly applies in an especial manner, to their conduct in their official character. How immoral to impose it on them, if they were to be used as the instruments, and the knowing instruments, for violating what they swear to support.

The oath of office, too, imposed by the legislature, is completely demonstrative of the legislative opinion on this subject. It is in these words: " I do solemnly swear that I will administer justice without respect to persons, and do equal right to the poor and to the rich; and that I will faithfully and impartially discharge all the duties incumbent on me as, according to the best of my abilities and understanding, agreeably to the constitution and laws of the United States."

Why does a judge swear to discharge his duties agreeably
to the constitution of the United States, if that constitution
forms no rule for his government? if it is closed upon him,
and cannot be inspected by him?

If such be the real state of things, this is worse than solemn
mockery.   To prescribe, or to take this oath, becomes equally
a crime.

It is also not entirely unworthy of observation, that in declaring what shall be the supreme law of the land, the constitution itself is first mentioned; and not the laws of the United
States generally, but those only which shall be made in pursuance of the constitution, have that rank.

Thus, the particular phraseology of the constitution of the
United States confirms and strengthens the principle, supposed
to be essential to all written constitutions, that a law repugnant
to the constitution is void; and that courts, as well as other
departments, are bound by that instrument.

The rule must be discharged.[72]

MARSHALL'S DECISION IN GIBBONS V. OGDEN

The judicial construction of the commerce clause begins
in 1824 with Chief Justice Marshall's opinion in Gibbons v.
Ogden, wherein a grant of land the State of New York for
the exclusive right to navigate the waters of New York with
boats propelled by fire or steam was held void as repugnant
to the commerce clause of the Constitution, so far as the act
prohibited vessels licensed by the laws of the United States
for carrying on the coast trade from navigating the said waters
by fire or steam.

The broad and comprehensive construction of the term
" commerce " in this opinion is the basis of all subsequent
decisions construing the commerce clause, and is the recognized source of authority.   Commerce is more than traffic;
it includes intercourse.   The power to regulate is the power
to prescribe the rules by which commerce is to be governed.
This power like all others vested in Congress is complete in
itself, and may be exercised to its utmost extent, and acknowledges no limitations other than as prescribed in the Constitution.   The Court said that the powers over commerce with for-

[72] Cranch, sec. 154-180 inclusive.

eign nations and among the various states is vested in Congress as absolutely as it would be in a single government having in its Constitution the same restrictions on the exercise of the power as is found in the Constitution of the United States. The power comprehended navigation within the limits of every State so far as navigation may in any manner connected with commerce with foreign nations or among the several states, or with the Indian Tribes, and therefore it passed beyond the jurisdictional line of New York and included the public waters of the State which were connected with foreign or interstate commerce.

In this opinion we find that the most important and far reaching declaration was that of the supremacy of the Federal power, so that in any case of conflict the act of Congress was supreme, and state laws must yield thereto, though enacted in the exercise of powers which are not controverted. In the Passenger Cases [73] the rule declared in this case was applied in holding invalid certain State statutes imposing taxes upon alien passengers. It was said that included navigation and intercourse and the transportation of passengers.

The Court said in the Pensacola Telegraph Company case [74] that since the case of Gibbons v. Ogden it had never been doubted that commercial intercourse was an element which comes within the power of regulation by Congress, and that the power thus granted was not confined to the instrumentalities of commerce known or in use when the Constitution was adopted, but kept pace with the progress of the country, adapting themselves to the new developments of time and circumstances. In the language of the Court: " They extend from the horse with its rider to the stage coach, from the sailing vessel to the steamboat, from the coach and steamboat to the railroad, and from the railroad to the telegraph, as these new agencies are successively brought into use to meet the demands of increasing population and wealth. They were intended for the government of the business to which they relate at all times and under all circumstances." In a late case it was said [75] that the commerce which Congress could regulate

[73] 7 Howard 283 (1849), 12 L.Ed. 702.
[74] 96 U. S. 1 (1877), 24 L.Ed. 708, 711. Construing act of July 24, 1866, as a prohibition of all State monopolies in interstate telegraph business.
[75] W. U. Tel. Co. v. Pendleton, 122 U. S. 347 (1887), 30 L.Ed. 1187.

included not only the interchange and transportation of com-
modities or visible and tangible things, but the carriage of
persons and the transmission by telegraph of ideas, orders
and intelligence. Importation into one state from another
is the indispensable element and the test of interstate commerce; and every negotiation, contract, trade and dealing between citizens of different States which contemplates and uses
such importation, whether it be of goods, persons or information, is a transaction of interstate commerce [76] which commerce therefore includes not only communication by telephone
between points in different States,[77] but also communication
through a correspondence school, where the intercourse and
communication relates to matters of regular and continuous
business and the conduct of such business, therefore, through
local agencies is exempt from state control or interference.[78]

COMMERCE POWERS

Definition: — The opinion in the case of Gibbon v. Ogden [79]
was delivered by Chief Justice Marshall and is regarded as
one of his greatest judicial utterances, the path before him
being untrodden by any Federal decision save his own in the
Brig Wilson case. The opinion which Marshall delivered,
and in which no authority was cited was so able, so profound
and masterful that it announced the principle which all future
decisions have followed. In this great decision, the chief
justice among other things said:
" As men whose intentions require no concealment, generally
employ the words which most directly and aptly express the
ideas they intend to convey, the enlightened patriots who

[76] From opinion of Sanborn, J., in Butler Brothers Shoe Co. v. United
States Rubber Co., 156 Federal, 1, C. C. A. 8th Cir., quoted by the Supreme Court, in International Text-book Co. v. Pigg, 217 U. S. 91 (1910).
[77] Richmond v. Southern Bell Tel. Co., 174 U. S. 761. U. S. v. West-
man, 182 Fed. 1017 (Ore. 1910). The White Slave Traffic Act was sustained as within the commerce power of Congress. It was also sustained
by the District Court, E. D. of Texas, 187 Fed. 992 (1911), holding that
the transportation of persons was commerce and that Congress, under its
power of regulation as per Lottery Cases, could prohibit a class of commerce in the interest of Public Morals.
[78] International Text-book Co. v. Pigg. 217 U. S. 91, where it was
held that a corporation working under a system of credits through a list of
attorneys of different states was held liable to a state license tax.
[79] 9 Wheaton, 1.

framed our Constitution, and the people who adopted it, must be understood to have employed words in their natural sense, and to have intended what they have said.   If, from the imperfection of human language, there should be serious doubts respecting the extent of any given power, it is a well settled rule, that the objects for which it was given, especially when those objects are expressed in the instrument itself, should have great influence in the construction.   We know of no reason for excluding this rule from the present case.   The grant does not convey power which might be beneficial to the grantor, if retained by himself, or which can enure solely to the benefit of the grantee; but is an investment of power for the general advantage, in the hands of agents selected for that purpose; which power can never be exercised by the people themselves, but must be placed in the hands of agents, or lie dormant.   We know of no rule for construing the extent of such powers, other than is given by the language of the instrument which confers them, taken in connection with the purposes for which they were conferred.

" Commerce, undoubtedly, is traffic, but it is something more; it is intercourse.   It describes the commercial intercourse between nations, and parts of nations, in all its branches, and is regulated by prescribing rules for carrying on that intercourse.

" If commerce does not include navigation, the government of the Union has no direct power over that subject, and can make no law prescribing what shall constitute American vessels, or requiring that they shall be navigated by American seamen.   Yet this power has been exercised from the commencement of the government, has been exercised with the consent of all, and has been understood by all to be a commercial regulation.   All America understands, and has uniformly understood, the word ' commerce,' to comprehend navigation. It was so understood, and must have been so understood when the Constitution was framed.   The power over commerce, including navigation, was one of the primary objects for which the people of America adopted their government, and must have been contemplated in forming it.   The convention must have used the word in that sense, because all have understood it in that sense; and the attempt to restrict it comes too late. . . .

"The word used in the Constitution, then, comprehends, and has always been understood to comprehend, navigation; and a power to regulate navigation is as expressly granted as if that term had been added to the word 'commerce.'"

After defining the term "commerce," as used in the Constitution, and having decided that it embraced navigation, Marshall then proceeded to consider the question: "To what commerce does this power extend?" He said: "The Constitution informs us, to commerce with foreign nations and among the several States, and with the Indian tribes."

Later in the decision he continued: "It has, we believe, been universally admitted, that these words comprehend every species of commercial intercourse between the United States and foreign nations. No sort of trade can be carried on between this country and any other, to which this power does not extend. . . . Commerce, as the word is used in the Constitution, is a unit, every part of which is indicated by the term."

He next came to the subject of commerce between the States. He said: "The subject to which the power is next applied is to commerce 'among the several States.' The word 'among' means intermingled with. A thing which is among others is intermingled with them. Commerce among the States, can not stop at the external boundary line of each State, but may be introduced into the interior." In order to distinguish what may be called State commerce from the broader expression of commerce among the States, and to establish the rule for the discrimination in such cases, Marshall said: "It is not intended to say that these words comprehend that commerce which is completely internal, which is carried on between man and man in a State, or between different parts of the same State, and which does not extend to, or affect other States. Such a power would be inconvenient, and is certainly unnecessary.

"Comprehensive as the word 'among' is, it may very properly be restricted to that commerce which concerns more States than one. The phrase is not one which would probably have been selected to indicate the completely interior traffic of a State, because it is not an apt phrase for that purpose; and the enumeration of the particular classes of commerce to which the power was to be extended, would not have been made, had the intention been to extend the power to every description. The enumeration presupposes something not enumerated; and that something, if we regard the language, or the subject of the sentence, must be the exclusively internal commerce of a State. The genius and character of the whole government seem to be, that its action is to be applied to all the external concerns of the nation, and to those internal concerns, which affect the States generally; but not to those which are completely within a particular State, which do not affect other States, and with which it is not necessary to interfere, for the purpose of executing some of the general powers of the government. The completely internal commerce of a State, then, may be considered as reserved for the State itself.

" But in regulating commerce with foreign nations, the power of Congress does not stop at the jurisdictional lines of the several States. It would be a very useless power, if it could not pass those lines. The commerce of the United States with foreign nations, is that of the whole United States. Every district has a right to participate in it. The deep streams which penetrate our country in every direction, pass through the interior of almost every State in the Union, and furnish the means of exercising this right. If Congress has the power to regulate it, that power must be exercised whenever the subject exists. If it exists within the States, if a foreign voyage may commence or terminate at a port within a State.

" This principle is, if possible, still more clear, when applied to commerce ' among the several States.' They either join each other in which case they are separated by a mathematical line, or they are remote from each other, in which case other States lie between them. What is commerce ' among ' them; and how is it to be conducted? Can a trading expedition between two adjoining States commence and terminate outside of each? And if the trading intercourse be between two States remote from each other, must it not commence in one, terminate in the other, and probably pass through a third? Commerce among the States, must, of necessity, be commerce within the States. In the regulation of trade with the Indian Tribes, the action of the law, especially when the Constitution was made, was chiefly within a State. The power of Congress, then, whatever it may be, must be exercised within the territorial jurisdiction of the several States. . . .

" We are now arrived at the inquiry — what is this power? It is the power to regulate; that is, to prescribe the rule by which commerce is to be governed.   This power, like all others vested in Congress, is complete in itself, may be exercised to its utmost extent, and acknowledges no limitations, other than are prescribed in the Constitution. . . . The power of Congress, then, comprehends navigation within the limits of every State in the Union, so far as that navigation may be, in any manner, connected with ' commerce with foreign nations, or among the several States, or with the Indian Tribes.'   It may, of consequence, pass the jurisdictional line of New York, and act upon the very waters to which the prohibition now under consideration applies."

By analyzing this great opinion we see that Marshall defined with masterful genius the important term and words in this clause, and settled many questions arising out of their consideration, and made them all so clear that no mistake could be made in the meaning of his language.

(1). He defined commerce, and said it was traffic and intercourse, and that it described commercial intercourse between nations, and parts thereof.

(2). Said that the language of this clause shows that commerce includes navigation.

(3). Decided that every species of commercial intercourse between the United States and foreign nations is comprehended; that no sort of trade can be carried on between this and other countries to which this power does not extend; that commerce as used in the Constitution, is a unit, every part of which is indicated by the term.

(4). Defined the word " among " as meaning " intermingled with."   Made it quite plain that it was restricted to that commerce which concerned more States than one.

(5). Commerce that is completely internal not comprehended in this clause, and concerns only the State where carried on.

(6). In regulating commerce with foreign nations the power of Congress does not stop at State lines, because it is that of the whole United States.

(7). Commerce among the States must be commerce with

the states necessarily, and the power of Congress must be exercised within the territorial jurisdiction of the States.

(8). In regard to " what is this power of Congress? " he said, it is the power to regulate, the power to prescribe the rule by which commerce shall be governed. That it is vested in Congress, is complete in itself, and may be exercised to its utmost extent, for it has no limitations beyond those found in the Constitution.

Every definition of commerce which has been given by the courts since this decision, reflects the definition given by Chief Justice Marshall.

In regard to power of Congress over commerce among the States, Marshall says: [80]

" In regulating commerce with foreign nations, the power of Congress does not stop at the jurisdictional lines of the several States. It would be a very useless power if it could not pass those lines. The commerce of the United States with foreign nations, is that of the whole United States. If Congress has the power to regulate it, that power must be exercised whenever the subject exists, and this principle, if possible, is still more clear when applied to commerce ' among the States.' "

This important case which is so often discussed is given a place here for several reasons. One of them being to show what the method of the Expounder of the Constitution was like, and the thorough manner of attacking the various details. Many think that this opinion is overlauded, and that it lays down too barely and didactically, with too small a basis of argument and history, the American doctrine of Constitutional law.

[80] Gibbons v. Ogden, 9 Wheaton, 195.

CHAPTER VII

THE DEATH OF CHIEF JUSTICE MARSHALL

CHIEF JUSTICE MARSHALL died July 6, 1835, at the age of eighty, having seen during his lifetime the firm establishment of nearly all the fundamental doctrines of American Constitional and International Law as applied by the courts of the country.

The bulk of this work was done by Chief Justice Marshall himself.   As I have mentioned elsewhere in this volume, there were but five cases of any importance before the Supreme Court of the United States prior to 1801, when John Marshall was made Chief Justice.   How great was his share of the work may be judged by the following figures.   Between 1801 and 1835 there were 62 decisions of a Constitutional nature, in 36 of which Marshall wrote the opinion.   Of a total of 1,215 cases during that period, in 94 no opinions were filed, in 15 the decision was "by the court," and of the remaining 1,106 cases Marshall delivered the opinion in 519.

During the same period of time there were 196 cases involving questions of International Law, or in some way affecting international relations.   In 80 of these the opinion was delivered by Marshall; in 37, by Story; in 28, by Johnson; in one each by Baldwin, Cushing, and Duvall; and in 8 the opinion was given "by the court." [1]

No doubt the members of the legal profession at that time looked forward to the appointment of Judge Joseph Story as Marshall's successor.   But, as Jackson's phrase put it, " the school of Story and Kent " could expect no favors at the hands of the President, for their political constitutional views differed too widely.   Story wrote: " Whoever suceeds Marshall will have a most painful and discouraging duty.   He will follow a man who cannot be equalled, and all the public will see or think they see the difference. . . . I take it for granted that all of us who are on the bench are hors de combat."

[1] Address by John Bassett Moore before the Delaware State Bar Association, February 5th, 1901.

John Quincy Adams, in his diary of July 10, 1835, says: " John Marshall died at Philadelphia last Monday. He was one of the most eminent men that this country has ever produced — a Federalist of the Washington School. The Associate Judges from the time of his appointment have generally been taken from the Democratic or Jeffersonian party. Not one of them, excepting Story, has been a man of great ability. Several of them have been men of strong prejudices, warm passions, and contracted minds; one of them occasionally insane. Marshall, by the ascendancy of his genius, by the amenity of his deportment, and by the imperturbable command of his temper, has given a permanent and systematic character to the decisions of the Court, and settled many great constitutional questions favorably to the continuance of the Union. Marshall has cemented the Union which the crafty and quixotic democracy of Jefferson had a perpetual tendency to dissolve. Jefferson hated and dreaded him. It is much to be feared that a successor will be appointed of a very different character. The President of the United States now in office, has already appointed three Judges of the Supreme Court; with the next appointment he will have constituted the Chief Justice and a majority of the Court. He has not yet made one good appointment. His Chief Justice will be no better than the rest."

Six months after Chief Justice Marshall's death Roger B. Taney, of Maryland, was appointed by President Jackson. As Charles Warren in " The History of the American Bar " says, " This was a surprise to most of the Bar." Chief Justice Taney's decisions showed a decided reaction from the centralizing views of Chief Justice Marshall. This was first seen in three cases in 1837, in each of which a State Statute alleged to be in violation of the Federal Constitution was upheld.

BIBLIOGRAPHY

ANECDOTES of John Marshall. In *World's Work*, Vol. I, Feb. 1901, pp. 394-395.

BARRE, W. L. John Marshall. In his "Lives of Illustrious Men of America," pp. 426-452. Cincinnati, 1859. 8°.

BINNEY, HORACE. An eulogy on the life and character of John Marshall, Chief Justice of the Supreme Court of the United States. Philadelphia: J. Crissy & G. Goodman, 1835. 70 pp. 8°.

BINNEY, HORACE. Same. In Waldie, A. Select Circulating Library, Vol. 6, pp. 327-335. Philadelphia, 1835. 4°.

BINNEY, HORACE. Binney's eulogy on Chief Justice Marshall. In "American Jurist," Vol. 14, Oct., 1835, pp. 462-465.

BLACK, JOHN C. John Marshall. In Illinois State Bar Association. Proceedings, Vol. 20, pt. 2, July 14-15, 1896, pp. 25-45.

BLACK, JOHN C. John Marshall. In *Albany Law Journal*. Vol. 54, July 25, 1896, pp. 55-62.

BRADLEY, JOSEPH P. Saint Mémin's Portrait of Marshall. In *Century Magazine*, Vol. 38, Sept., 1889, pp. 778-781.

BROOKS, ELBRIDGE S. The Story of John Marshall, of Richmond, called "The great Chief Justice." In his "Historic Americans," pp. 161-174. New York, 1899. 8°.

BROWNE, IRVING. John Marshall. In his "Short Studies of Great Lawyers," pp. 201-217. Albany, N. Y., 1878.

BRYANT, JAMES R. M. Eulogium on Chief Justice Marshall, delivered in the Unitarian church, Washington city, on the 24th of September, 1835, at the request of the Union literary society. Washington: Printed by Jacob Gideon, Jr., 1835. 16 pp.

BARNES, WILLIAM HORATIO. "The Supreme Court of the United States: a series of Biographies." With an introduction, by Samuel F. Miller. Washington, D. C.: W. H. Barnes & Co., 1877. (2), 116 pp. Portraits. 4°.

BATEMAN, HORATIO. Biographies of Two Hundred and Fifty Distinguished National Men. 1st ed. New York; John T. Giles & Co., 1871. 12°. P. 50.

CARSON, HAMPTON LAWRENCE. The Supreme Court of the United States: its History, and its Centennial Celebration, Feb. 4, 1890. Prepared under direction of the Judiciary Centennial Committee. Philadelphia: A. R. Keller Co.

1892. 2 vols. Portraits. 4°. Contains biographies of all the chief and associate Justices.

CURTIS, WILLIAM ELEROY. "The Seven Chief Justices of the United States." In *Chautauquan*, Vol. 25, July, 1897, pp. 339-347. John Jay, Oliver Ellsworth, John Marshall, Roger B. Taney, Salmon P. Chase, Morrison R. Waite, and Melville W. Fuller.

CASSODY, JOHN B. John Scott and John Marshall. In *American Law Review*, Vol. 33, Jan.-Feb., 1899, pp. 1-27.

CENTENNIAL anniversary of the elevation of John Marshall to the office of Chief Justice of the Supreme Court of the United States of America. (The) . . . February 4th, 1901. Celebration in the City of Philadelphia under the auspices of the Law Association of Philadelphia. (etc.) Philadelphia: G. H. Buchanan and Co., 1901. 68 pp. Portrait. 8°. Oration by J. T. Mitchell.

CHIEF JUSTICE MARSHALL.
In *American Quarterly Review*, Vol. 18, Dec., 1835, pp. 473-489.
In *Green Bag*, Vol. 3, Dec., 1891, pp. 541-542.
In *National Quarterly Review*, Vol. 33, Sept., 1876, pp. 229-242.
In *New York Review*, Vol. 3, Oct., 1838, pp. 328-361.
In *North American Review*, Vol. 42, Jan., 1836, pp. 217-241. A review of the life of John Marshall, by Joseph Story.

CHIEF JUSTICE MARSHALL'S Public Life and Service. In *North American Review*, Vol. 26, Jan., 1828, pp. 1-40.

COOKE, JOHN ESTEN. Early Days of John Marshall. In *Historical Magazine*, Vol. 3, June, 1859, pp. 165-169.

CRAIGHILL, ROBERT T. John Marshall. In his " The Virginia Peerage," Vol. 1, pp. 231-284. Richmond, 1880. 8°.

DICKINSON, MARQUIS FAYETTE, JR. John Marshall. The tribute of Massachusetts; being the addresses delivered at Boston and Cambridge, February 4th, 1901, in commemoration of the one hundredth anniversary of his elevation to the bench as Chief Justice of the United States. Boston: Little, Brown and Company, 1901. xvii, 120 pp. Portraits. 8°.

DILLON, JOHN FORREST, ed. John Marshall; life, character, and judicial services as portrayed in the centenary and memorial addresses and proceedings throughout the United States on Marshall day, 1901, and in the classic orations of Binney, Story, Phelps, Waite, and Rawle; compiled and edited with an introduction by John F. Dillon. Chicago: Callaghan and Co., 1903, 3 vols. Plates, portraits, facsimiles. 8°.

Dodd, William E.   Chief Justice Marshall and Virginia, 1813-
1821. In *American Historical Review*, Vol. 12, July, 1907,
pp. 776-787.

Finch, Francis Miles.   Chief Justice John Marshall.   Mar-
shall Day Address, Cornell University, Feb. 4th, 1901.
Ithaca, N. Y., 1901.   11 p.   Portrait.   8°.   Reprinted from
Cornell *Alumni News*.

Flanders, Henry.   The Life of John Marshall.   Philadelphia:
T. & J. W. Johnson & Co., 1905.   x, 278 pp.   Portrait.
8°.   Originally issued in the Author's "Lives and Times of
the Chief Justices of the United States."

Fuller, Melville W.   Chief Justice Marshall.   In the *Dial*
(Chicago), Vol. 6, May, 1885, pp. 10-12.   Reprinted in the
Dial, Vol. 9, Oct., 1888, pp. 128-130.

Gray, Horace.   An address on the life, character and influence
of Chief Justice Marshall, delivered at Richmond on the
fourth day of February, 1901, at the request of the State
Bar Association of Virginia and the Bar Association of the
city of Richmond.   Washington, D. C.: Pearson print.
office, 1901.   (2), 49 pp.   8°.   Authorities consulted other
than Supreme Court decisions: pp. 45-47..

Great American Judge, A (John Marshall).   In *Spectator*, Vol.
86; Feb. 9, 1901, pp. 198-199.

Griswold, Rufus Wilmot.   John Marshall.   In his " The Prose
Writers of America," pp. 85-88.   Philadelphia, 1847.   8°.

Griswold, Rufus Wilmot.   Marshall.   In " Homes of American Statesmen," pp. 263-274.   New York, 1858.   8°.

Hardy, Sallie E. Marshall.   Chief Justice Marshall.   In
Magazine of American History, Vol. 12, July, 1884, pp.
62-71.

Hardy, Sallie E. Marshall.   John Marshall, Third Chief Justice of the United States, as son, brother, husband, and
friend.   In *Green Bag*, Vol. 8, Dec., 1896, pp. 479-492.

Hardy, Sallie E. Marshall.   The Will of a Great Lawyer.
How Chief Justice Marshall Devised His Estate.   In *Green
Bag*, Vol. 8, Jan., 1896, pp. 4-6.

Houghton, Walter R.   John Marshall.   In his " Kings of
Fortune," pp. 437-456.   Chicago, 1885.   8°.

John Marshall.   In *Albany Law Journal*, Vol. 13, June 24,
1876, pp. 442-445.   Same in *Washington Law Reporter*,
Vol. 3, July 1, 1876, pp. 156-157; July 8, 1876, pp. 163-164.

John Marshall.   In *American Law Record*, Vol. 5, July, 1876,
pp. 55-59.

John Marshall.   I. Soldier, Lawyer, Statesman, and Man.

II. Judge and Jurist. In *Green Bag*, Vol. 13, April, 1901, pp. 157-195; May, 1901, pp. 213-267.

JOHN MARSHALL Day; centennial proceedings of the Chicago Bar, Feb. 4, 1901; including proceedings before the Supreme Court of Illinois. (Chicago: The Associated committees of Illinois, from the press of Hollister Bros., 1901.) 794 pp. Portrait. Facsimile. 4°.

JONES, FRANCIS R. John Marshall. In *Green Bag*, Vol. 13, Feb., 1901, pp. 53-64.

LEHMANN, FREDERICK W. John Marshall. An address before the Bar Association of Des Moines, Iowa. (Des Moines? 1900?) 46 pp. 8°.

LIBBY, CHARLES FREEMAN. John Marshall; an address delivered at . . . (Bowdoin) college on Feb. 4th, 1901, the centenary of the installation of John Marshall as Chief Justice of the United States. Brunswick, Maine. By the college, 1901. 37 pp. 8°.

LIFE OF JUDGE MARSHALL. In *Port Folio*, Vol. 13, Jan., 1815, pp. 1-6.

LODGE, HENRY CABOT. An address upon Chief Justice Marshall. Delivered at the Auditorium in Chicago on the fourth day of Feb., 1901, at the request of the Bar Associations of the State of Illinois and the city of Chicago. Washington: Pearson printing office, 1901. 30 pp. 8°.

LODGE, HENRY CABOT. John Marshall, Statesman. In *North American Review*, Vol. 172, Feb., 1901, pp. 191-204.

LOSSING, J. BENSON. John Marshall. In his "Eminent Americans," pp. 216-218. New York, 1886. 12°.

McCABE, JAMES D. John Marshall. In his "Great Fortunes," pp. 417-434. Cincinnati and Chicago, 1871. 8°

McCLAIN, EMLIN. Chief Justice Marshall as a Constructive Statesman. Iowa City, Ia.: The State Historical Society, (1903?) 42 pp. 4°. Cover-title. Reprinted from the October, 1903, number of the Iowa *Journal of History and Politics.* "The substance of this paper was delivered as an address before The Grant Club, Des Moines, on Feb. 19, 1903. In the form in which it is here published it was read in full before the Political Science Club, Iowa City, on March 9, 1903."

MACVEAGH, WAYNE. John Marshall. An address delivered upon the invitation of the American Bar Association and a joint committee of Congress, in the Hall of the House of Representatives, Feb. 4, 1901. Washington, D. C.: Judd and Detweiler, printers, 1901, 36 pp. 4°.

MAGRUDER, ALLAN BOWIE. John Marshall. Boston and New York: Houghton, Mifflin and Company, (1885) viii. 290 pp. 12°. (American Statesmen.)

MAGRUDER, ALLAN BOWIE. John Marshall. (Large paper edition.) Boston and New York: Houghton, Mifflin & Co., 1898. viii (6), 296 pp. Plates. Portraits. Facsimile. 8°. (American Statesmen, V. 10.)

MARSHALL, MARIA NEWTON. The Marshall Memorial Tablet. In *Green Bag,* Vol. 14, Aug., 1902, pp. 372-373.

MEANS, D. MAC G. Chief Justice Marshall. In *The Nation,* Vol. 72, Feb., 1901, pp. 104-105.

MOORE, FRANK. John Marshall. In his " American Eloquence," Vol. 2, pp. 1-32. New York, 1862. 4°

MOORE, JOHN BASSETT. John Marshall. Boston: Ginn & Co., 1901. (2), 393-411 pp. 8°. Address delivered before the Delaware Bar, at Wilmington, Feb. 4, 1901. Reprinted from *Political Science Quarterly,* Vol. XVI, No. 3.

MOSES, ADOLPH. How to celebrate John Marshall day, Feb. 4, 1901; pub. by direction of the executive committee of the Illinois Bar Association. (Chicago): Illinois Bar Assoc., (1900). 16 pp. 8°.

MOSES, ADOLPH. " John Marshall Day." Series of letters and endorsements in answer to circular advocating the celebration of " John Marshall Day," Feb. 4, 1901. (n. p.) 1899. 34 pp.

OLNEY, RICHARD. Chief Justice Marshall. In the *Outlook,* Vol. 67, Mar. 9, 1901. pp. 573-576.

OLNEY, WARREN. Chief Justice Marshall. In *American Law Review,* Vol. 34, July-Aug., 1900, pp. 550-561.

P. T. John Marshall. In *American Law Review,* Vol. 1, Apr., 1867, pp. 432-442.

PAULDING, WILLIAM I. A contribution to history (relating to John Marshall). In *Lippincott's Magazine,* Vol. 2, Dec., 1868, pp. 623-626.

PERRY, BENJAMIN F. John Marshall. In his " Biographical Sketches of Eminent American Statesmen," pp. 467-477. Philadelphia, 1887. 8°.

PATTERSON, T. ELLIOTT. History of Three Chief Justices of the United States Supreme Court. In *Law Students' Helper,* Vol. 5. Sept., 1897, pp. 321-323; Oct., 1897, pp. 353-355; Nov., 1897, pp. 383-385. Contents. I. John Marshall. II. Roger Brooke Taney. III. Salmon Portland Chase.

PHELPS, EDWARD J. Annual address. (John Marshall.) In

American Bar Association. Transactions, Vol. 2, pp. 173-192. Philadelphia, 1879. 8°.

PHELPS, EDWARD J. Chief Justice Marshall and the Constitutional Law of His Time. An address before the American Bar Association at Saratoga, August 21, 1879. Philadelphia: E. C. Barkley & Son, 1879. 22 pp. 8°. Also in his "Orations and Essays," edited by J. G. McCullough, pp. 27-53. New York, 1901. 8°.

PROCTOR, L. B. Jefferson's Contempt of Chief Justice Marshall's Opinions. In Albany *Law Journal*, Vol. 44, Oct. 24, 1891, pp. 342-343.

RAWLE, WILLIAM HENRY. Unveiling of the Statue of Chief Justice Marshall, at Washington, May 10, 1884. Oration. Philadelphia: Allen, Lane & Scott's printing house, 1884. 31 pp. 4°.

RHODE ISLAND BAR ASSOCIATION. John Marshall Day: Celebration by the Rhode Island Bar Association and Brown University, Feb. 4, 1901: address by Le Baron Bradford Colt; introductory address by Francis Colwell. (Providence: Rhode Island Printing Co., 1901.) 53 pp. Portrait. 8°.

ROANE, SPENCER. Roane on the National Constitution. Reprints from the Richmond *Chronicle* and Richmond *Enquirer*. In the John P. Branch "Historical Papers," Vol. 2, June, 1905, pp. 47-122. Richmond, 1905, 8°. "No apology is offered for devoting so much space in the Branch papers this year to the life and work of Judge Spencer Roane. Henry Adams and the other historians of the period have but little to say of Roane or of the protest which he constantly made against Chief Justice Marshall, and the files of the Richmond *Enquirer*, which gave so much of the history of Virginia at the time, are easily accessible. John Marshall and the Supreme Court of the United States, as will be seen, were subjects of lively attack." (Introduction.)

RUSSELL, ALFRED. John Marshall. In *American Law Review*, Vol. 35, Jan.-Feb., 1901. pp. 1-7.

STORY, JOSEPH. An address by Mr. Justice Story on Chief Justice Marshall. Delivered in 1852 (1835) at request of the Suffolk (Mass.) Bar. Rochester, N. Y.: The Lawyers' Cooperative Publishing Co., 1900. 60 pp. Portraits. 8°.

SCOTT, HENRY W. John Marshall. In his "Distinguished American Lawyers," pp. 537-544. New York, 1891. 8°.

STORY, JOSEPH. Life of Chief Justice Marshall. In *American
    Law Magazine*, Vol. 1, July, 1843, pp. 243-301.
STORY, JOSEPH. Mr. Justice Story's Eulogy of Chief Justice
    Marshall. In *American Jurist*, Vol. 14, Oct., pp. 448-454.
STORY, JOSEPH. John Marshall, LL.D., Chief Justice of the
    United States. In *Current Comment*, Vol. 1, June 15, 1889,
    pp. 213-224; July 15, 1889, pp. 253-261.
TERHUNE, MARY VIRGINIA H. The Marshall House. In her
    "Some Colonial Homesteads and Their Stories," pp. 84-103.
    New York, 1897. 8°.
THAYER, JAMES BRADLEY. John Marshall; an address delivered
    in Sander's Theatre, Cambridge, before the Law School of
    Harvard University and the Bar Association of the City of
    Boston on Feb. 4, 1901. Cambridge: J. Wilson & Son,
    1901. 48 pp. 4°.
THAYER, JAMES BRADLEY. John Marshall. In *Atlantic
    Monthly*, Vol. 87, Mar., 1901, pp. 328-341.
THAYER, JAMES BRADLEY. John Marshall. Boston & New
    York: Houghton, Mifflin and Co., 1901. (8), 157, (1) pp.
    Portrait. 12°. (Riverside Biographical Series, No. 7.)
THOMAS JEFFERSON's Opinion of John Marshall and His Court.
    In *American Law Review*, Vol. 35, Jan.-Feb., 1901, pp.
    63-77.
UNITED STATES. Congress. Exercises at the ceremony of the
    unveiling of the statue of John Marshall, Chief Justice of
    the United States, in front of the Capitol, Washington, May
    10, 1884. With the address of Chief Justice Waite and
    the Oration of W. H. Rawle. Washington: Government
    printing office, 1884. 92 pp. Frontispiece. 4°.
WAITE, CATHERINE V. John Marshall. In Chicago *Law Times*,
    Vol. 1, Apr., 1887, pp. 109-121.
WAITE, MORRISON REMICK. The Orations of Chief Justice
    Waite and of William Henry Rawle on the Occasion of the
    Unveiling of the Bronze Statue of Chief Justice Marshall
    at Washington, May 10, 1884. Chicago: T. H. Flood &
    Co., 1900. 58 pp. Portrait. 8°.
WILLIAMS, GEORGE HENRY. Address on John Marshall, deliv-
    ered by Hon. Geo. H. Williams before the Legislative As-
    sembly of the State of Oregon, Feb. 4, 1901. Salem, Ore.:
    W. H. Leeds, state printer, 1901. 19 pp. 8°.
WILSON, JOHN R. John Marshall. In *American Law Review*,
    Vol. 22, Sept.-Oct., 1888, pp. 706-730.
WYNNE, JAMES. Chief Justice Marshall. In his "Lives of
    Eminent Literary and Scientific Men of America," pp. 231-
    300. New York, 1850. 12°.

SUPPLEMENTAL

FLANDERS, HENRY. The Lives and Times of the Chief Justices of the United States. New York: James Cockcroft & Co., 1875. 2 Vol. Frontispiece. 8°. Chief Justice Marshall (Life) Vol. 2, pp. 279-550.

FRENCH, BENJAMIN FRANKLIN. Biographia Americana. New York: Published by D. Mallory, 1825. vii. 356 pp. 8°. John Marshall. Page 228.

JONES, ABNER D. The American Portrait Gallery. New York: J. M. Emerson and Co. 1855. Portraits. 8°. Chief Justice Marshall, pp. 97-98.

BEARD, CHARLES A. The Supreme Court and the Constitution. New York: The Macmillan Company, 127 pp. Based on an article published in the *Political Science Quarterly,* March, 1912.

CASSODY, JOHN B. John Scott and John Marshall, or Chief Justice Marshall contrasted with Lord High Chancellor Eldon. In Illinois State Bar Association Proceedings, 1900. Springfield: 1900, pt. 2. pp. 69-100. Also printed in *American Law Review,* Jan.-Feb., 1899, Vol. 33, pp. 1-27.

CENTENNIAL of Chief Justice Marshall. In United States Reporter, New York, 1901. Vol. 180. Appendix, pp. 643-716. "Supreme Court decisions referred to," p. 713. "Authorities consulted other than Supreme Court Decisions," pp. 713-715.

MILLIKEN, JOHN D. The early days of Marshall. In Bar Association of State of Kansas, 1901. Clay Centre, 1901, pp. 86-99.

GROSSCUP, PETER S. (Judge). On John Marshall. In Vol. 19, *National Corp. Rep.,* p. 544.

STORY'S Tribute to Chief Justice Marshall Before His Death. In Vol. 19, *Nat. Corp. Rep.,* p. 471.

JOHN MARSHALL day information. Running numbers of the *National Corporation Reporter.* Commencing 18, *Nat. Corp. Rep.,* p. 713 *et seq.*

CORRESPONDENCE on the subject of indorsing the celebrations of "John Marshall Day" throughout the United States. In Vol. 19, *National Corporation Reporter,* pp. 7, 716, 761, 836, 876, and 908.

WYTHE, GEORGE. Law Teacher of Chief Justice Marshall. In Vol. 20, *National Corporation Reporter,* p. 80.

CHESLEY, J. HARRY. Marshall's Military Honors in War and Peace. A short but interesting article. In Vol. 20, *National Corporation Reporter,* p. 116.

358   BIBLIOGRAPHY

CHESLEY, J. HARRY. The Ancestry of Chief Justice Marshall. In Vol. 20, *National Corporation Reporter,* p. 550. A short article.

BIOGRAPHICAL Notice of John Marshall. In Vol. 30, Federal Cases, pp. 1385-1386.

CHARACTERISTICS of John Marshall, by Randall M. Ewing. In Vol. 3, Tennessee Bar Association Reports, pp. 135.

MARTINEAU, HARRIET. "Retrospect of Western Travel." 1838. A good description of Marshall and his oratory.

MEADE, WILLIAM. "Old Churches, Ministers, and Families of Virginia." 1872. Vol. 2, pp. 216 *et seq.*

MURRAY, CHARLES A. "Travels in North America." 1839. Vol. 1, p. 158.

MYERS, GUSTAVUS. "History of the Supreme Court of the United States." Chicago: C. H. Kerr and Company. 1912. 823 pp.

SWAN, CHARLES H. Quelques décisions récentes de la Cour Suprème des États-Unis en motière de travail. Bruxelles, Office de la Revue (1909) 23 pp. Extrait de la *Revue Economique Internationale,* Novembre, 1909.

WILSON, HENRY H. John Marshall and the Federal Constitution. In Nebraska State Bar Association Proceedings, 1906-1909. Omaha: 1909. pp. 213-230.

MÜLLER, F. W. Die Rechtsprechung der Supreme Court of the United States. Betreffend Art. 1 Absatz 10 der Verfassung der Vereinigten Staaten. Zartschrift für Volkerrecht und Bundesstaaterrecht. 1908. Vol. 3, pp. 25-41. Literatur, p. 41.

HITCHCOCK, HENRY. Constitutional Development in the United States as Influenced by Chief Justice Marshall. Pp. 53-121. Constitutional History. Addresses delivered at the University of Michigan. 1889.

ARTICLES that are more or less valuable and interesting may be found in the following Legal Magazines:

American Jurist, Vol. 22, p. 247.

Virginia Law Register, Vol. 15, p. 807.

Current Comment, Vol. 1, pp, 213, 253. A sketch with portrait. (J. Story.)

Law Student's Helper, Vol. 5, p. 321. Sketch with portrait.

Chicago Law Times, Vol. 1, p. 109.

Chicago Law Times, Vol. 86, p. 175.

Minnesota Law Journal, Vol. 4, p. 104.

Chicago Legal News, Vol. 28, p. 380.

American Law Register, Vol. (N. S.) 33, p. 426.

Albany Law Journal, Vol. 2, p. 126. Address by Professor Parsons.

PERIODICALS mentioned below have articles on Marshall, most of which give some information that is valuable.

American Quarterly Review, Vol. 18, p. 473. December, 1835.

World's Work, Vol. 1, p. 394.

National Quarterly Review, Vol. 33, p. 229. Semtember, 1876.

New York Review, Vol. 3, p. 361, October, 1838.

North American Review, Vol. 26, p. 1.

Historical Magazine, Vol. 3, p. 165.

American Historical Review, Vol. 12, p. 776.

Spectator, Vol. 86, p. 198.

Lippincott's, Vol. 2, p. 623.

Political Science Quarterly, Vol. 16, No. 3.

Atlantic Monthly, Vol. 87, p. 328.

Edinburgh Review, May, 1820, p. 113.

Christian Review, Vol. 1, p. 83.

Edinburgh Review, Vol. for October, 1808.

New England Magazine, new series, Vol. 20, p. 527. Old Series, Vol. 9, p. 151.

North American Review, Vol. 1, p. 331; Vol. 5, p. 115; Vol. 10, p. 89. Vol. 13, p. 79; Vol. 17, pp. 148 and 167; Vol. 18, p. 90; Vol. 19, p. 277 and 287; Vol. 20, pp. 444 and 453; Vol. 21, p. 128; Vol. 22, p. 259.

Reformed Quarterly, Vol. 34, p. 428.

Pearson's Magazine (N. Y.), Chief Justice John Marshall: the father of American Judicial Despotism. By A. L. Benson. Vol. 26, pp. 320-30. S. 11.

American Almanac. 1836. (Boston.) pp. 305-307. Obituary.

Sewanee Review. John Marshall, Southern Federalist. Vol. 9, p. 129.

Longman's Magazine. Voyage of John Marshall. Vol. 37, p. 147.

Book Buyer. John Marshall's Work as Diplomat and Litterateur. By L. Swift. Vol. 20, pp. 364-366. June, 1900.

REPORTS of cases decided by the Hon. John Marshall, in the Circuit Court of the United States for the District of Virginia and North Carolina, from 1802 to 1833, inclusive, edited by John W. Brockenbrough (with a memoir by J. Hopkinson). Philadelphia: 1837. 2v. 8°. (I. McLean Reports., 555.)

SPEECHES in the Constitutional Convention of Virginia. 1789. In Elliot's Debates, Vol. 3, pp. 229, 419, 551.

Writings of John Marshall, late Chief Justice, upon the Federal
Constitution. Boston: 1839, p. 730. 8°. Republished.
Washington, 1890, p. 725.
Benton, Thomas H. Death of Chief Justice Marshall. In
"Thirty Years' View." 1854. Vol. I, p. 681.
Hopkinson, John. "Memoir of John Marshall." In J. W.
Brockenbrough's Reports of Cases Decided by John Mar-
shall. (1837.)
Kennedy, William. "Life of Wirt." Volume I, pp. 161-206.
Potter, Clarkson N. Marshall and Taney. American Bar
Association Report. 1881. p. 175.
Van Santvoord, George. John Marshall. "Sketches of the
Lives of the Chief Justices." 1882. pp. 337-522.
Obituary Proceedings. John Marshall. 1 McLean Reports.
555, 30 Fed. Cas. 1323.
Obituary Proceedings in United States Supreme Court. 10
Peters Reports VII.
Biographical Notice. 30 Federal Cases, 1385.
Senate Report. 544. 1 Sess., 48 Congress.
Wirt, William. "The British Spy." Letter, 99. 178-181.

WRITINGS OF JOHN MARSHALL

The Constitutional Decisions of John Marshall; edited, with an
introductory essay, by Joseph P. Cotton, Jr. New York,
G. P. Putnam's Sons, 1905. 2 vols.
John Marshall, complete constitutional decisions, edited, with
annotations historical, critical, and legal, by John M. Dillon.
Chicago: Callaghan and Co. 1903. xi, (1), 799 pp. Por-
trait. 2 fold. facs. 8.
A history of the colonies planted by the English on the continent
of North America, from their settlement, to the commence-
ment of that war which terminated in their independence.
Philadelphia: A. Small, 1824. xv, (9)-486 pp. 8°.
Originally published as an introduction to the author's "Life
of George Washington."
A letter of Marshall to Jefferson, 1783, by R. G. Thwaites.
(New York? 1905) pp. 815-817. 4°. Cover-title. Re-
printed from the *American Historical Review,* Vol. X, No.
4, 1905.
Letters of John Marshall, Secretary of State, Aug. 23, 1800;
Sept. 20, 1800; Dec. 2, 4, 1800. In American State Papers.
Foreign Relations, Vol. 2, pp. 386-387, 388-389, 486-490.
Washington, 1832. F°.
The Life of George Washington. Compiled under the inspection

of the Hon. Bushrod Washington, from original papers.
Philadelphia: C. P. Wayne, 1804-1807. 5 vols. 8°.
Atlas. 4°. Same. 2d ed., rev. Philadelphia: Crissy &
Markly, 1833. 2 vols. 8°. Atlas. 8°.
Life of George Washington. Written for the use of schools.
Philadelphia, 1838. 12°.
Het leven van George Washington, uit deszelfs oorspronglijke
papieren onder toezigt van Bushrod Washington. Uit het
Engelsch door J. Werninck. Haarlem: A. Loosjes, 1805-
1809. 10 vols. in 6. Plates. Maps. 8°.

SUPPLEMENTAL

MASSACHUSETTS Historical Society, Proceedings. Letters from
John Marshall to Timothy Pickering and Mr. Justice Story.
2d Series, Vol. XIV, pp. 321-360. Boston: 1900, 1901. 8
vols., pp. xx, 502.
SLAUGHTER, WM. B. " Reminiscences of Distinguished Men,"
with an autobiography. Madison, Wisconsin. Published
by the author. Chapter III, John Marshall, pp. 102-124.
Godfrey & Crandall, Printers and Publishers, 1878.
OPINION of the Supreme Court of the United States at January
term, 1832, delivered by Mr. Chief Justice Marshall in the
case of Samuel A. Worcester v. The State of Georgia.
Washington: Printed by Gales and Seaton, 1832.
CALENDAR of Virginia State Papers and other manuscripts.
Some of Marshall's letters, etc., pp. 12, 115-116, 399. Vol.
IX. Richmond, Va.: 1890. Jan. 1, 1799, to Dec. 31, 1807.
Arranged and edited and printed under authority of H. W.
Flourney, Secretary of the Commonwealth and State Libra-
rian.
SAME. Vol. 7, pp. 101-102, 120, 148, 228-229, 234-235, 347, 347-
348, 309, 383-384, 403-404, 446, 309, 451.
SAME. Vol. 6, pp. 546, 547, 581, 600-601.
MARSHALL, JOHN. Message from the President of the United
States, transmitting a report from the Secretary of State
(John Marshall), with sundry documents relative to the
subject of the resolution of the 24th inst. 27 February,
1801. 12 pp. 8°. Same. In American State Papers, For-
eign Relations, Vol. 2, pp. 345-347. Washington, 1832. F°.
Relating to the treaty of amity with Great Britain.
MARSHALL, JOHN. The writings of John Marshall upon the
Federal Constitution. Boston: J. Munroe & Co., 1839. xix,
728 pp. 8°. A collection of Marshall's Constitutional
opinions.

CONGRESSIONAL DOCUMENTS RELATING TO MAR-
SHALL IN FRANCE, AS ENVOY EXTRAORDINARY
AND MINISTER PLENIPOTENTIARY, 1798, IN-
CLUDING THE X. Y. Z. CORRESPONDENCE

INSTRUCTIONS to Charles Cotesworth Pinckney, John Marshall,
and Elbridge Gerry, envoys extraordinary and ministers
plenipotentiary to the French Republic, referred to in the
message of the President of the United States of the third
instant. Philadelphia: Printed by Way and Groff, 1798.
20 pp. 12°.

INSTRUCTIONS to the envoys extraordinary and ministers plenipotentiary from the United States of America to the French
Republic, their letters of credence and full powers, and the
dispatches received from them relative to their mission.
Published by the Secretary of State, in conformity with the
resolution of Congress of the 22d June, 1798. Philadelphia:
Printed by W. Ross (1798). 131 pp. 8°.

FRANCE. Message from the President, communicated to Con-
gress, March 5, 1798. In American State Papers, Foreign
Relations, Vol. 2, pp. 150-151. Washington, 1832. F°.
Transmitting communications from envoys extraordinary.

FRANCE. Message from the President, communicated to Congress, March 19, 1798. In American State Papers, Foreign
Relations, Vol. 2, p. 152. Washington, 1832. F°.

MESSAGE of the President of the United States to both houses
of Congress, April 3d, 1798. (Philadelphia, 1798.) 71 pp.
8°. Same. In American State Papers, Foreign Relations,
Vol. 2, pp. 153-168. Washington, 1832. F°.

MESSAGE of the President of the United States to both houses
of Congress, May 4th, 1798. 72 pp. 8°. Communications
from envoys extraordinary. Same. In American State
Papers, Foreign Relations, Vol. 2, pp. 169-182. Washington, 1832. F°.

MESSAGE from the President of the United States, accompanying the communications from the Envoys extraordinary to
the French Republic, received since the fourth of May last.
5th June, 1798. Philadelphia: Printed by Way & Groff,
(1798). 17 pp. 12°.

MESSAGE from the President of the United States, accompanying a communication, No. 8, from the Envoys extraordinary
to the French Republic. Received at the office of the Secretary of State on Thursday the 14th instant. 18th June,
1798. Philadelphia: Printed by Joseph Gales, (1798).
72 pp. 8°.

MESSAGE from the President of the United States, accompanying a report of the Secretary of State, containing observations on some of the documents, communicated by the President, on the eighteenth instant. 21st January, 1799. Philadelphia: Printed by John Ward Fenno, 1798. (2), 45, (92) pp. 8°.

INDEX

INDEX